AREA STUDIES IN THE GLOBAL AGE

AREA STUDIES
IN THE GLOBAL AGE

COMMUNITY, PLACE, IDENTITY

Edited by Edith W. Clowes and Shelly Jarrett Bromberg

NIU Press / DeKalb

Northern Illinois University Press, DeKalb 60115
© 2016 by Northern Illinois University Press
All rights reserved

25 24 23 22 21 20 19 18 17 16   1 2 3 4 5

978-0-87580-727-0 (paper)
978-1-60909-187-3 (ebook)

Book and cover design by Shaun Allshouse

Library of Congress Cataloging-in-Publication Data
Names: Clowes, Edith W., editor. | Bromberg, Shelly Jarrett., editor.
Title: Area studies in the global age : community, place, identity / edited
   by Edith W. Clowes and Shelly Jarrett Bromberg.
Description: DeKalb, IL : NIU Press, [2015] | Includes bibliographical
   references and index.
Identifiers: LCCN 2015040411 (print) | LCCN 2015044059 (ebook) | ISBN
   9780875807270 (pbk. : alk. paper) | ISBN 9781609091873 (ebook)
Subjects: LCSH: Area studies.
Classification: LCC D16.25 .A727 2015 (print) | LCC D16.25 (ebook) | DDC
   909—dc23
LC record available at http://lccn.loc.gov/2015040411

Contents

Illustrations

Acknowledgments

The idea of this volume began at a conference on "Identity and Community after the Cold War Era," held in August 2011 at the University of Kansas, Lawrence, Kansas. The conference brought together a broad array of scholars from many disciplines to examine the legacy of the Cold War across the globe in the late twentieth and early twenty-first centuries. Our first thanks go to the Department of Education (Title VI), the Department of Defense, and the Office of the Dean of Arts and Science at the University of Kansas, all of which provided funding for the conference.

This collection of essays is the product of exemplary teamwork. We wish to thank our contributors, all of whom were consistently timely and thoughtful in each phase of this process. So too, we are grateful for the patient support of the NIUP team and, specifically, the tireless work of Amy Farranto and Nathan Holmes and their encouragement of this interdisciplinary experiment. Kathleen Thompson, who composed our index, did an outstanding job, which we hope will make this book even more useful than it otherwise might be.

We were also fortunate to have the support of our home institutions, the University of Kansas and Miami University of Ohio, and later in the process the University of Virginia. The time and funding provided enabled us to create a book that we hope will stretch everyone's horizons.

Finally, we wish to thank our families, friends, and colleagues who were generous in their encouragement and understanding throughout these past years. Without their grounding, this work would have been much more difficult.

Preface

Area studies combine the multidisciplinary teaching and research about a particular area of the world with intensive study to attain a high level of proficiency of at least one area language. Our book, *Area Studies in the Global Age: Community, Place, Identity*, offers an introduction to contemporary area studies for students entering graduate programs, as well as scholars and other readers interested in a comparative view of area studies. Since the so-called "turn" of the late 1980s and early 1990s, area studies have become a kind of border zone, under attack from constituent disciplines, both social sciences and humanities, each for different reasons.[1] In many colleges and universities they have yielded in interest to umbrella studies, such as foreign affairs or international relations, which have less rigorous requirements. Although it is difficult to define their actual object of study (because it is diffuse), area studies have proven to be an indispensable component of the academic curriculum, as well as general American knowledge about the world. Area studies serve two main purposes. The first is to train future experts with advanced foreign-language proficiency and strong humanistic and social-scientific knowledge of a world area in its global context. The second purpose is to provide Americans, and the English-speaking world more generally, with rich, multifaceted, well-contextualized analyses and interpretations of the world's communities. Among the foci of area studies are the perceived structures of authority and authenticity in a society, defined at an appropriate geographical scale (whether global, national, regional, or local) and type of formation (whether cultural, social, economic, or political, or a mix of various types).

Area Studies in the Global Age is devoted to examining the interrelation between three constructions central to any human culture—community, place, and identity. It builds on research by scholars from a wide range of disciplines, specializing in diverse parts of the world, including Africa; Central, East, and North Asia; Eastern and East Central Europe; and Latin America. While remaining rigorously true to the realia of our particular research areas, we set forth the clearly distinctive features of the cultures treated here and encourage well-documented commonalities to rise to the surface. Recognizing the claim of our so-called "global" world—which purportedly transcends spatial and cultural boundaries—to have opened the world's borders to trade, communication, and economic opportunity, the analyses presented in each chapter show again and again that particular communities in which people live their lives and the places to which they perceive themselves as belonging are of life-defining importance. Beyond the rituals, narratives, symbols, and human archetypes that define a community, the space to which these elements attach meaning are crucial to a member's self-perception and self-understanding. Through this process of attaching significance, a "space" becomes a "place," and the meaningful place becomes an indispensable emblem for defining and understanding identity.[2]

Despite the increasingly mixed ("hybrid") and "displaced" identities that the world's migrant populations are adopting, belonging to a group and a place—imagined and constructed as those may be—and articulating and enacting an identity, are crucial components for a meaningful life. In short, we bring the following question to this book, which is at once a place-defining and border-crossing experiment: beyond the usual, and very pressing, global material concerns of our time (such as environmental change, availability of water and health care, and abuse of human rights), are there traceable commonalities among the communities and their identities that we treat here? Fully aware that each chapter represents one small piece of colored glass in the hugely complicated mosaic that is the contemporary world, we argue that in these fifteen chapters certain dominant figures do emerge that promote a nuanced picture of identity and community in the early twenty-first century.

In *Area Studies in the Global Age* we have undertaken the challenge of putting into practice the original interdisciplinary mission of US area studies. Area studies are the ideal site for pathbreaking interdisciplinary inquiry; since their founding in the 1940s, they were intended to draw on both social-science and humanistic research methodologies. Our introduction to area studies draws on a variety of approaches and techniques—including conducting interviews and surveys in the field; constructing and coding databases; building typologies; rendering rhetorical, structural, and thematic analyses of print sources from contemporary writing culture; using archival documents; and interpreting fiction and other creatively produced texts. Typically, research produced with the support of area studies funding has tended to pay most attention to policy decisions, economic numbers and trends, powerful social-political groups (elites), and political leaders. With a number of exceptions that do examine leaders, their rhetoric, and their decision-making processes, articulated and enacted at the top of the power structure, the focus of most chapters is on the voices, perceptions, and mentalities of ordinary people not in power, and their articulations of community, their behavioral enactments of a particular identity, and their attachment to a particular place to which they have assigned symbolic meaning. Of crucial importance to all the chapters is the target community's definition of "our place"—and how that place shapes identity.

This book developed following a conference on "Identity and Community after the Cold War Era," held in August 2011 at the University of Kansas in Lawrence, Kansas. Scholars from a broad array of disciplines and area studies programs joined forces to explore and discuss recent developments in local and regional communities and, as the conference call for papers put it, to probe how these developments have affected the "community of all peoples and the formation of new communities across the world." At the conclusion of the conference, several University of Kansas area and international studies directors held a roundtable discussion about the future of our research in these often contested communities, places, and identities. When a group of graduate students approached the organizers to convey their enthusiasm about the "introduction to area studies" that they felt they had received over the previous three days, their excitement confirmed our decision to press forward with a book designed precisely for beginning graduate students, as well as other readers interested in expanding their knowledge.

Central to the conference discussion was the shifting nature of the world after the opening of the Iron Curtain, the coming of NAFTA and other "open border" trade agreements, the end of apartheid, and the opening of other seemingly fixed and closed borders. These themes are the foci of *Area Studies in the Global Age*. One of the points of contention at the conference was the emblem of the Cold War, which was relevant to some world areas but not necessarily to others. The idea of the Cold War implied a specific post–World War II world order with a dominant "imagined geography" of geopolitical power and influence. The Cold War binary pairs opposing "communist vs. capitalist," USSR vs. USA, and East vs. West, were much less important in certain parts of the world than the colonial binary relationship contrasting the North and South. These binaries have generally shattered, though other binaries increasingly plague the world, such as the growing and destabilizing differential between rich and poor. Despite the growth in the 1990s of "big picture" theories, such as rational choice theory, cultural anthropology and various postmodernist theories have underscored the importance of local and regional development in the increasingly complex, postbinary world. It is in these local communities, for example, that various waves of new religious fervor have found a reliable foothold, as well as young people to support new power structures, staff new armies, and enforce new claims on territory. To highlight these perspectives, our group agreed to a simpler title, *Area Studies in the Global Age: Community, Place, and Identity*.

An enduring criticism of area studies concerns the unfocused descriptiveness and lack of interpretive framework of area-specific research. It was curious, though perhaps not entirely surprising, that many conference participants indeed did employ sophisticated framing concepts and often shared concepts, assumptions, and theories. Along with the work of theorists, such as political anthropologist Benedict Anderson, philosopher Etienne Balibar, cultural studies scholar Homi Bhabha, psychologist Julia Kristeva, and historian Pierre Nora, the research of many area-specific specialists can open fresh questions and avenues of research beyond their own area of the world. Thus, two features of *Area Studies in the Global Age* orient students to the uses of various methodologies and concepts. Each chapter contains a description of methodologies employed, consideration of the ways in which material and data were collected, and definitions of guiding critical concepts. An annotated bibliography of useful theory and scholarship found at the back of the book will help beginning researchers formulate their research questions.

Although the topics in this book cut across major areas of the world, analyses are typically local and regional. As different as people may seem in diverse parts of the world, all define themselves through borders. Beyond their strategic importance, borders more than ever have profound meanings for the people who draw them and believe in them, and whom in turn they define. For example, the Mexican-US, the Russian-Ukrainian, the Hungarian-Serbian, and the Iraqi-Turkish borders have never been more important to the governments and regional residents involved. The terrain we inhabit, the meaning we give to that "space" that turns it into meaningful "place," the communities to which we perceive ourselves to belong, and the ways in which we see our communities with respect to others—all shape our "identity." And that identity informs the decisions we make and the ways we carry them out. Place-oriented narratives of self, histories, memories, rituals, traditions—all are the fundamental ground on which social and political communities are built and identity is formed.

Area studies provide a reality check to large-model fashions in political studies and economics, particularly "rational choice theory" and "formal theory." They offer local and regional perspectives on the global crisis of community, as well as a range of topics and disciplinary approaches that make interdisciplinary academic research exciting and productive. Among the authors of this book are cultural, social, and art historians, literary critics, geographers, and international relations experts. All of the authors have professional proficiency in languages other than English—an indispensable tool for understanding the vocabularies of local and regional identity and community, and their relationships to global processes.

Interdisciplinarity is the touchstone of *Area Studies in the Global Age.* Though governmental and private funding agencies alike have paid lip service to interdisciplinarity, area studies research has typically remained in the

bailiwick of the social sciences. To our knowledge this book engages and com-
bines more fully than any other a broad set of methodologies that area studies
scholars need in their toolkits. Some approaches are traditional, which in and
of itself is no reason to exclude them. A qualitative examination of state actors,
their rhetoric, and their formation of state-generated communities, remains a
useful approach (Vanderbush). The study of arts communities as sites of resistance to state censorship and police control likewise echoes Cold War realia,
which, unfortunately, remain in force (Apostol, Callen).

Other approaches are newer to area studies. Several chapters (Bromberg,
Harris, MacGonagle) employ memory studies to address questions concerning writing and rewriting national history. Three chapters (Smiley, Thelen,
Chen/Kennedy) combine quantitative and qualitative methods to address
issues of "mental geography" and the ways in which ordinary people transform terrain or space into meaningful place. In all three chapters a focus on
subjectivities and personal perceptions across a sizable data sample suggests a
useful explanation of the reasons for which a community might either cooperate with or resist central government leadership.

Still other chapters use a combination of traditional intellectual historical
perspectives applied to current public debates; the close, interpretive reading
of literary and visual "texts," which are central to articulating place, community, and identity; and theoretical frameworks new to area studies. A number of chapters employ discourse theory (Clowes, Hanks, Vanderbush) and
human rights theory (Janzen). For many of the chapters, fieldwork involving
both qualitative and quantitative data from interviews with human subjects
was crucial to obtaining new insights into the nature of specific identities and
communities (Greene, Chen/Kennedy, Omelicheva, Smiley, Thelen). The main
chapters are bookended by an introduction that defines area studies and its
main themes in the "post-turn" world and a conclusion that offers an international relations perspective that both supports and challenges area studies
(Zarakol). To help readers discern commonalities in this mosaic, we have
divided the chapters into four thematic parts—rethinking national history, contrasting regional and national identities, challenges to civil society, and legacies
of imperial systems. A brief introduction to each of the book's four parts frames
crucial concepts, highlights common themes, and previews each chapter. Further commonalities emerge in chapters across the book's four parts.

Area Studies in the Global Age offers a productive reinvention of area studies,
now employing social science and humanities tools to attend to the subjectivities and experiences of people in all kinds of communities across the world. It
draws attention away from leaders and the "halls of power" and listens closely
to voices that articulate perceptions and represent groups that either are or

could eventually become mobilized to tip the scales of power. We intend these approaches to challenge the reader to define the broad outlines of place-oriented identity and community in our complex twenty-first-century world.

Notes

1. The word *turn* is taken from the German term *die Wende*, used to describe the end of the Soviet regime and the transition to parliamentary democratic governance in the five states of the former German Democratic Republic, resulting in 1990 in the reunification of all sixteen states as the Federal Republic of Germany.

2. Two crucial conceptual frames for this book come from Clifford Geertz, *The Interpretation of Cultures* (New York: Basic Books, 1973); and Robert Sack, *A Geographical Guide to the Real and the Good* (London: Routledge, 2003).

AREA STUDIES IN THE GLOBAL AGE

Introduction
Area Studies after Several "Turns"

EDITH W. CLOWES AND SHELLY JARRETT BROMBERG

"Not only is the world not flat: in many ways it has been getting less flat. . . . At the last round of trade negotiations, the Uruguay Round, for the poorest countries of the world, it wasn't that they got a small share of the gains—everybody expected that; that's power politics—but they actually wound up worse off than they had been before, it was so unbalanced, so asymmetric."
—Joseph Stiglitz, Carnegie Endowment, 2006[1]

In the light of world events of the early twenty-first century these words by economist Joseph Stiglitz sound mild but still prescient. Embedded in them is the warning that despite the much-heralded promise of the new democratization and globalization of the 1990s, many countries and peoples in the new century were not only not better off but indeed sinking further into poverty and debt. The world of the twenty-first century has seen an effort by United States administrations and the media to minimize the problems lurking behind regime changes in Eurasia, Southeast Asia, the Middle East, and Africa, while at the same time reducing funding to train the specialists who provide government and media with reliable information "on the ground." On one hand, since the mid-1990s various US administrations and members of the press have often promoted a self-congratulatory discourse, asserting the progress of US-led "globalization" and "democratization"—this stance despite the attacks of September 11, 2001, the repeated worldwide economic downturns of the new century, and the rise of brutal, religiously motivated tyrannies. As late as 2004 Thomas Friedman coined the term "flat earth" to express the idea that the world economy expanding across relatively open geographical borders, enabled by fiber-optic technology, the Internet, and social media, would benefit billions of people. These new technologies, developed since the late 1990s, were supposed to be "empowering individuals," allowing a "flat" or at least more level playing field in which everyone has equal opportunity and equal access to material well-being.[2] On the other hand, the 1990s wave of democratization of previously authoritarian states—meaning the transition to more transparent, secular, and representative forms of government—has largely stalled or ebbed. The gap between the world's richest and poorest is wider than ever.[3] The opening of borders and the tremendous power of social media have sometimes produced just the opposite of the intended results; they have allowed previously isolated individuals and groups to mass together and form more virulent communities, including the resurgence of ultra-rightist religious movements and the rise to power of religiously oriented national-isms in Africa and Eurasia. Clearly the "newly liberated" did not always veer toward a Western notion of democracy—communities formed in the wake of repression, war, or trauma can mirror the behavior of their previous oppres-sors. Indeed, Paulo Freire's observation that the oppressed often become the oppressor during struggles of liberation too often holds true.[4] The victims of the new oppressors have been women and other people, who have benefited, or stood to benefit, from new democratic rights and the global expansion of wealth, from secular, inclusive educational systems, religious tolerance, and more open trade policies. Functional slavery, sexual slavery, vast migrations, new political and religious oppression by a new minority in power—all are hallmarks of the world's new disorder.

This superficial celebration of world democracy and the benefits of glo-balization inevitably has resulted in a view that area studies are "parochial," which in turn has contributed to the shrinkage of area studies funding by the government and to the absorption of area studies curricula into inter-national studies in American universities.[5] The result is the weakening and further underfunding of area programs that for decades produced language proficiency and broad cultural, political, and economic training needed to build knowledge about local and regional communities in poorly understood parts of the world. The world saw the impact of inconsistent funding and training, for example, in American adventures in Afghanistan and Iraq at the start of which the US government scrambled to identify well-trained language experts and reliable local and regional information.

Currently general "global studies" or "international studies" programs enjoy popularity among students and administrators alike partly because they typically have few foreign-language and special area requirements and because they save faculty positions. Students tend to read English-language sources, which give them a dangerously skewed view of the world's communities and systems of change. Without the rigorous requirement for foreign-language proficiency, students' understanding of area mentalities and values remains rudimentary. On the other hand, it should be said that proponents of area studies have not done enough to highlight the crucial cross-disciplinary and interdisciplinary nature of their work and the necessity of language learning to a high degree of proficiency. Ultimately, by supporting a more general and less rigorous curriculum for understanding the world, the US government and the academy have wasted a valuable resource developed over many decades.

— — —

Area Studies in the Global Age addresses the issue of parochialism, by juxtaposing an array of mainly nonelite communities across the world. The organization of material is intended to add useful detail, needed for understanding the real local and regional effects of democratizing and globalizing initiatives. Our goal is to introduce new students of area and global studies and related disciplines to the methodologies that produce accurate, real-world information. The communities studied here are dealing with some form of crisis that leads their members to rethink their identity. In some cases, that crisis may have been precipitated, indeed, by the very act of opening borders that globalization wrought.

The approaches to area studies deployed here share some basic assumptions about human nature. We believe that most humans need to have some sort of stable community and place, however imagined, to which they perceive themselves to belong. Lacking those elements and faced with serious economic, political, or other crises and challenges, people are likely to rebel in unforeseen ways that might seem to a US observer not to serve their "best interests." The foreign policy, academic, and finance communities ignore those specifics at their own peril. These assumptions are quite different from the "enlightenment" view informing democratization and globalization that human nature is universally "rational," however that slippery term is defined. People everywhere, so economists' and the international relations community's "rational choice" thinking goes, make decisions in the same consistent or "rational" way, regardless of culture, taste, or belief, by "evaluating costs and benefits and acting so as to maximize their net benefits."[6] The question about what people perceive themselves to need and how they make decisions is certainly more complicated than simply "being consistent" or adhering to Western-inspired notions of what people "ought" to want. For example, by no means is the question of a universal human nature always answered by a model of identity that one scholar has called the American "self-interested individualist prototype."[7] The research presented in *Area Studies in the Global Age* shows that while the struggle for personal betterment defined in terms of civil and human rights might sometimes hold true, other goals often take priority, for example, a strong community, political-cultural ambitions, and a secure place to which "our community" belongs, or, indeed, mere survival under a newly oppressive regime.

Rational choice thinking is still influential in international relations curricula in American universities. It is a real concern that these same simplistic assumptions then spill into US foreign policy, as students become professional specialists, who in turn become employees and later employers in government, business, international development, and the academy. Representatives of international organizations fostering what they hope will be beneficial reform often know too little about local and regional mentalities and systems of value to be effective in promoting positive change. As Mariya Omelicheva suggests in her book, *"Democracy" for Central Asia? Perspectives and Strategies Promoted from Without and Within*, organizations supporting democratic practices often lack cultural awareness, sensitivity, and knowledge of local contexts. The Western democratizers' own experiences typically overshadow the context and background information on the transitional states.[8] *Area Studies in the Global Age* makes the case for a more detailed and ultimately effective view of the world, alert to the subjectivities of ordinary communities, the views and desires of people and groups who are not in power but who hold passionately to a particular identity. In doing so, our book also makes the case for an area studies sensitive to shifting transnational and transcontinental subjectivities.

— — —

The "new approaches" to area studies that we claim here are not necessarily new. Our project is committed to practicing what area studies proponents inside and outside the US government have always touted but have not practiced—a rigorous and self-aware interdisciplinarity, deploying both humanities and social-science techniques and methodologies, to study diverse societies and cultures. Before we define the new area studies further, it will be helpful to summarize a brief history of area studies, how they began and how they have evolved. Instituted in the last years of World War II with support from US government intelligence services, area studies had the goal of collecting information about poorly understood, non-Western parts of the world in order to keep the United States and the "free" world "safe" from communism.[9] Eventually, under Title VI the US Department of Education funded national resource centers at major research universities to spread information to the educated community; foreign language and area studies fellowships (FLAS) to support the study of crucial languages; and Fulbright-Hays grants for specialist research in critically important countries. In the late 1980s and early 1990s, as the Soviet empire unraveled and the Chinese empire turned toward something resembling a capitalist, market economy, that need seemed obviated.

Although colonialism in Africa officially ended in various countries at various times after the end of World War II, giving way to major community and identity shifts, apartheid ended in South Africa at about the same time as the Cold War, thus removing one of the engines for producing communist-oriented resistance communities. In Latin America and elsewhere, the United States' military and political support for anticommunist dictators during the Cold War era was now recast as economic and military backing in the guise of democratizing the region. As Greg Grandin argues, for Latin America after the Cold War, democracy "came to be defined strictly in the astringent terms of personal freedom rather than social security."[10] For many countries, this economic and political autonomy was tied directly to neoliberal policies and forms of democracy that were "now being prescribed as the most effective weapon in the war on terrorism," used to guarantee stability in the region.[11]

With the end of these worldwide threats in the 1990s, area studies seemed less relevant to US policymaking and consequently declined as a curricular and research priority. After their failure to predict the changes of the 1980s and 1990s, many leading academic players in the old area studies—specialists in politics and economics—left the field. Economics departments reduced area studies tenure-track positions at universities across the country and devoted their research and teaching to large-scale modeling.[12] Politics departments often combined area studies and international relations specializations into one faculty position.

Some academics argued that area studies were too closely connected to the Central Intelligence Agency and other intelligence branches of the US government.[13] While some supporters characterize area studies research as "rigorous and detailed knowledge," critics often see it as being too descriptive and narrowly parochial, lacking a theory, a set of definitions of its research questions and objects, and an interpretive framework.[14] Still others criticize area studies practitioners for replicating in their actual research real imbalances of power between the United States and other less wealthy countries.[15] In other words, US researchers were not heeding the voices and opinions of researchers and other actors in other countries and regions. Area studies in its original form, we claim, did not live up to its original definition as an interdisciplinary area of inquiry. While focusing mainly on the social sciences, many critics did urge interdisciplinary approaches, though, we repeat, typically only among the social sciences.[16]

Throughout the 1990s, the Departments of Defense and State recognized the training of foreign area specialists with professional proficiency in what they defined as the "critical" languages of the world as a priority for continued US security. Both departments developed a number of sources of government funding to promote high-level foreign-language learning. In 1991 the Boren Bill created the National Security Education Program (NSEP) to send US students abroad to perfect their foreign language skills. Since the attacks of September 11, 2001, the Department of Defense has supported the development of civilian foreign-area experts. Since 2002 through its Language Flagship Program it has funded centers and scholarships for students at universities throughout the United States to produce language speakers functional at a "superior" level of full professional proficiency. From 2005 to 2015 the US Army used the controversial Human Terrain System (HTS), an organization that hired and imbedded anthropologists in US Army units in battlefield areas, beginning in Iraq and Afghanistan and then expanding to regions of Africa.[17] The purpose of the HTS program was to learn more about the structures of authority and the needs of local communities in order to win civilians to the invaders' side (that is, the US/NATO side), rather than to fight only on the "kinetic" terrain of the battlefield. For the history of area studies the most important aspect of this program was the recognition in the highest halls of US military power that language proficiency and cultural knowledge were central to military efforts. In 2006, the US Department of State created the Critical Languages Program to send students to perfect their language skills in non-central, non-English-speaking parts of the target country. And in 2007 the Department of Defense funded Project GO, meant to support foreign-language learning among ROTC cadets.

In these initiatives, funding for area studies curricula has lagged as funding has increased to develop advanced language curricula and language support programs. The Department of Education's Title VI program has been wildly inconsistent in its support of area studies teaching and research. In 1997 the Ford Foundation helped to renew and rethink area studies through the "Crossing Borders" initiative, which gave middle-sized grants to twenty-five US universities and colleges to develop area studies curricula and to encourage programs to create new networks and partners. Strongly challenged by forces of "globalization"—understood as trade and movement of peoples and resources across relatively open borders—area studies programs had to confront the question, "Are there definable world areas?"[18] Our provisional answer is "yes," with the understanding that borders, though much more porous than they were in the Cold War, are not only not dissolving but are strengthening as large-scale migration and other cross-border crises continue. In many cases borders have only become more complicated and now include boundaries both internal and external to nation-states. Borders do not exactly coincide with geopolitical territories, cultures, and languages as traditionally assumed. *Area Studies in the Global Age* provides a more fragmented and nuanced but

also more pertinent definition of current world areas and the issues confronting them. In a real sense, this book defines specific communities, identity
formations, and constructed places—and the borders that continue to shape
them—while also representing a useful experiment in the spirit of the 1997
Ford Foundation initiative in "crossing borders" and defining commonalities,
in terms of both geographical place and discipline-specific methodologies and
research agendas.

— — —

We define the new area studies as a set of culture- and geography-specific
objects of study that can be investigated with the benefit of multiple disciplinary
and comparative area perspectives that are designed to produce useful, reliable
knowledge about those objects. The practical purpose of area studies is still
to develop specialists with professional-level foreign-language proficiency and
broad-sector knowledge in particular world areas and, as much as possible, also
among world areas. The new area studies strive to achieve the following:

- bring into focus self-perceptions and subjectivities, as well as perceptions of
  what might be called "spatial belonging" of ordinary people in their locally,
  regionally, nationally, and supranationally defined communities;
- reach beyond the traditional area studies objects of study—political actors and
  institutions of state power—to include the actions and perceptions of non-elite
  communities as more than just "reactions" to state directives; and investigate
  grassroots formations of communities, innovations, and vocabularies of identity
  through all sorts of media—religion and the arts, as well as political rhetoric and
  ethnic narratives—all in the context of institutions of authority and power;
- promote inter-area comparison and contrast based on rigorously gathered,
  authentic facts, and resist the move toward global modeling that has little real-
  world explanatory force, while also recognizing and taking advantage of useful
  and important quantitative research approaches favored by political scholars
  and economists;
- respect the view that to ignore subjectivities and complexities of people in particular cultures is risky behavior that leads to continued errors in international
  policy.

The new area studies draw on several methodologies, conjoining where relevant detailed textual interpretation and attention to products of writing
culture and artistic production with larger-database typological analysis and
statistical findings. Traditional humanities are strong for their attention to

subjectivities, close reading and thematic and structural interpretation of cultural texts, and sensitivity to rhetorical registers that can tell us more about "message" than a naïve reading can. Humanities approaches are strengthened through area studies exigencies of relevant context building; awareness of structures of power, authority, and authenticity; and knowledge of historical, social, political, cultural, and economic backgrounds. Of particular usefulness in this book are approaches garnered from postcolonial and postcommunist theory and research on imagined and imaginative geographies, memory studies, discourse analysis, and gender studies.

Social sciences—among them, sociology, politics, and economics—traditionally have been strong in constructing the "big picture," which means numerical, normative generalizations about social, economic, and political formations and attitudes. In contrast, particularly cultural anthropology and human geography have developed strength in detailed, "thick description" of specific communities, their social composition and structure, rituals, narratives, and symbols. Human geography places greater emphasis on the context of the particular place that a community constructs, and its symbolic meanings.[19] Applied to area studies contexts, social science approaches become more attentive to other—perhaps not "normal" or "average" but still significant—subjectivities, their cultural rituals and expressions of identity. In short, the new area studies employ a strong use of qualitative cultural description and interpretation, combined with numerical analysis, and argue that institutions are composed of people with particular views, beliefs, predilections, and ritualized behavior patterns, which are always messy and complex but well worth the study.[20]

"Being interdisciplinary" is more than what has been termed "parallel play" in the same "sandbox."[21] Competent new area studies specialists should be proficient in a number of different methodologies. This book is for graduate students who will become government, business, NGO, and academic specialists of the future; it defines what counts as credible primary sources and data, and it presents approaches to collecting and interpreting several types of materials and data with the goal of promoting productive interdisciplinary thinking. These approaches offer a corrective, too, to international relations, which strive for a big picture, a "transportable generalization," based on studying top-down elite structures and government and economic institutions, a generalization that international relations specialists want to apply anywhere in the world.[22] This research is guided by two questions: how best to study cultural subjectivities, mentality, and closely held systems of value among people who are not elite and live their lives outside of circles of power, though both affected by and affecting policy; and how best to define the concept of successful change. We urge area studies students to focus in part on ordinary people in their self-defined communities and investigate their value systems, mentalities, and actions; and on that basis to build an accurate picture of these perceptions and their interaction with broader decision-making processes.

Area studies have always put strong emphasis on geographical space. Here we give space a somewhat different focus, concentrating on the concept of geocultural "place"—alternatively called "imaginative geography," "imagined geography," or "mental geography"—as an area or space in which a particular community defines its identity and distinguishes itself from other communities who are perceived as not belonging. It is space defined symbolically as that place where "we" belong and through which "we" interpret our history and our hopes for the future, and, importantly, to which "they," the others, do not belong. With this emphasis, area studies interdisciplinarity can offer a discerning view of the effects of large-world trends on particular communities and their identities; the impact of those communities on large-world trends; as well as tracking similarities and contrasts among the world's myriad communities.

— — —

In *Area Studies in the Global Age,* borders emerge as a decisive kind of space, crucial to delineating place, community, and identity. In her conclusion to the book Ayşe Zarakol uses the important psychological-spatial concept of the "liminal" to define nation-states in the early twenty-first century. Many psychologists (Jung), anthropologists (van Gennep, Turner), literary theorists (Bakhtin, Lotman), and cultural studies scholars (Bhabha) have defined the idea of the liminal and, in other words, the idea of threshold or border experience that, broadly speaking, changes one's perspective and defines one's sense of belonging to a community.[23] The ubiquity of the term belies the globalizing view that the world is flat and free of borders. It is precisely the perception of borders and thresholds that challenge existing power and promise resistance, even rebellion. In some cases, such as with political, cultural, or economic avant-gardes, the liminal experience can produce culturally, socially, and politically innovative formations. Zarakol uses the liminal to designate states situated complexly between the Great Powers, particularly the United States, China, and Russia. She has in mind states that do not clearly fit into a traditional imagined geography or a community of shared values, clearly belonging, for example, to geopolitical notions of the East or the West, geo-economic concepts of the North or the South. Repeatedly, the "liminal" and various forms of threshold, or border, experience are foregrounded in *Area Studies in the Global Age.* While our focus remains on community and identity formation with relation to meaningful place, it will become clear that, in contrast to global theory touting the benefits of open borders, defining borders, crossing borders, changing public spheres, and shifting culturally embedded behaviors all belong to this book's bigger theme of the "liminal."

Political scholars have called the notion of "region" (and presumably all other kinds of meaningful "place") a "spatial construct" and a mere metaphor for other economic, political, and social forces at work.[24] In this view, "region" as such is not a cause but a product. In *Area Studies in the Global Age* we view regional, local, as well as national "place" as focal points for identity formation and meaningful human activity—certainly a "spatial construct," but created by communities building meaning in a particular space perceived as "ours." Indeed, it may be the "liminal" that is the guiding metaphor for the new emphasis on border experience in *Area Studies in the Global Age*, now used to understand a world undergoing shifts, displacements, and disorientations as to "who we are" and "where we belong." An infamous prison transformed into a memorial space; a museum with former political inmates as the guides; a rural village being squeezed as an enclave in an amoeba-like, burgeoning city; a shared heroic narrative becoming the object of contention between new states; a security police archive re-created as art object—all are examples of transformational change, open-ended struggles sometimes to change and sometimes to maintain geocultural structures of identity and community.

Beyond demonstrating the variety of approaches and methodologies available to area studies and various strategies for building relevant context, *Area Studies in the Global Age* offers pieces in a mosaic that open to view the world as perceived by mainly non-elite people confronting some sort of crisis or challenge to their identity, who might be building or reinventing community, or are struggling to keep community viable after the borders opened—or, further, may be trying to establish new borders in order to build new community. The communities in our world, as these studies suggest, are reevaluating globalization and democratization—whether surviving the destruction of community, in part, because of changing borders, reworking community memory, rethinking a symbolically significant place, or building community across borders.

Notes

1. Joseph E. Stiglitz and Joanne J. Myers, book presentation and interview on *Making Globalization Work*, Carnegie Council, October 5, 2006, accessed June 27, 2014, https://www.carnegiecouncil.org/studio/multimedia/20061005/5397.html/_res/id=sa_File1/Making_Globalization_Work.pdf.

2. See Thomas Friedman, *The World Is Flat* (New York: Farrar, Straus and Giroux, 2005), 10–11.

3. Stiglitz and Myers, *Making Globalization Work*.

4. See Paulo Freire, *Pedagogy of the Oppressed* (New York: Continuum, 1990), 28–29.

5. For an informative discussion of the "rational choice" craze in politics departments of the 1990s and its effect on area studies, see: Jonathan Cohn, "Irrational Exuberance," *The New Republic* (Oct. 25, 1999), http://www.newrepublic.com/article/politics/78956/political-science-irrational-exuberance, accessed Sept. 12, 2015. For the more functional, "on the ground" concept of "thinking automatically," written by World Bank teams, see: World Bank. 2015. *World Development Report 2015: Mind, Society, and Behavior*. Washington, DC: World Bank. doi: 10.1596/978-1-4648-0342-0. License: Creative Commons Attribution CC BY 3.0 IGO.

6. See, for example, Laurence R. Iannaccone, "Rational Choice: Framework for the Scientific Study of Religion," *Rational Choice Theory and Religion: Summary and Assessment*, ed. L. Young. NY: Routledge, 1997, 27–28.

7. Bruce Cumings, "Boundary Displacement: Area Studies and International Studies During and After the Cold War," *Bulletin of Concerned Asian Scholars* 29, no. 1 (January–March 1997): 23.

8. Mariya Omelicheva, *Democracy in Central Asia: Competing Perspectives and Alternative Strategies* (Lexington: University Press of Kentucky, 2015).

9. Two informative books on US area studies and the history of US Department of Education Title VI support are: David L. Szanton, ed., *The Politics of Knowledge: Area Studies and the Disciplines* (Berkeley: University of California Press, 2004); and David Wiley and Robert Glew, eds., *International and Language Education for a Global Future: Fifty Years of U.S. Title VI and Fulbright-Hays Programs* (East Lansing: Michigan State University Press, 2009). A more feisty history can be found in Bruce Cumings, "Boundary Displacement."

10. Greg Grandin, *The Last Colonial Massacre: Latin America in the Cold War* (Chicago: University of Chicago Press, 2011), xxiii.

11. Ibid.

12. Szanton, *Politics of Knowledge*, 19.

13. Mark Selden, "Asia, Asian Studies, and the National Security State: A Symposium," *Bulletin of Concerned Asian Scholars* 29, no. 1 (January–March 1997): 4.

14. Toby Alice Volkman, "Introduction," *Crossing Borders* (n.p.: Ford Foundation, 1999), xi, accessed June 11, 2014, http://www.pacitaabad.com/PDF/Crossing%20Borders.pdf; Sonia E. Alvarez et al., "Revisioning Latin American Studies," *Cultural Anthropology* 26, no. 2 (2011): 226.

15. Sophia A. McClennan, "Area Studies Beyond Ontology: Notes on Latin American Studies, American Studies, and Inter-American Studies," *A Contra Corriente* 5, no. 1 (Fall 2007): 173; Alvarez et al., "Revisioning," 229.

16. Cumings, "Boundary Displacement," 26; Volkman, *Crossing Borders*, vi; Matthias Basedau and Patrick Köllner, "Area Studies and Comparative Area Studies: A Primer on Recent Debates and Methodological Challenges," *Japan Aktuell* (2007), 25, accessed June 7, 2014, http://www.giga-hamburg.de/sites/default/files/openaccess/japanaktuell/2007_2/giga_jaa_2007_2_basedau_koellner.pdf.

17. Norman Nigh, *CIWAG Case Study on Irregular Warfare and Armed Groups: An Operator's Guide to Human Terrain Teams*, CIWAG case study series 2011–2012, ed. Andrea Dew and Marc Genest (Newport, RI: US Naval War College, Center on Irregular Warfare and Armed Groups, 2012). For a sampling of the extensive controversy on HTS, see Robert Albro, "Anthropology and the Military: AFRICOM, Culture and Future of Human Terrain Analysis," *Anthropology Today* 26, no. 1 (February 2010): 22–24. On the end of the HTS, see: http://www.counterpunch.org/2015/06/29/the-rise-and-fall-of-the-human-terrain-system/.

18. Volkman, *Crossing Borders*, ix.

19. Our overall approach builds on Clifford Geertz's "semiotic" approach to culture and his understanding of the concept of "thick description" in *The Interpretation of Cultures* (New York: Basic Books, 1973). For a brief but useful human-geographical introduction to the issue of borders, see Alexander C. Diener and Joshua Hagen, *Borders: A Very Short Introduction* (New York: Oxford University Press, 2012).

20. Alvarez, "Revisioning," 226, 231.

21. Ibid., 238.

22. Valerie Bunce, "Comparative Democratization: Big and Bounded Generalizations," *Comparative Political Studies* 33 (2000): 708.

23. See, for example, Carl Gustav Jung, *Man and His Symbols* (London: Picador, 1978); Arnold van Gennep, *The Rites of Passage* (1960, rpt. London: Routledge, 2004); Victor Turner, "Betwixt and Between: The Liminal Period in *Rites de Passage*," in *The Proceedings of the American Ethnological Society* (1964), 4–20; Victor Turner, *The Ritual Process: Structure and Anti-Structure* (1969; rpt. Chicago: Aldine, 1995); Mikhail Bakhtin, *Problems of Dostoevsky's Poetics* (Minneapolis: University of Minneapolis Press, 1984); Yuri Lotman, *Universe of the Mind: A Semiotic Theory of Culture* (Bloomington: Indiana University Press, 2001); and Homi Bhabha, *The Location of Culture* (London: Routledge, 1994).

24. Bunce, "Comparative Democratization," 721.

PART I

Reclaiming the National Narrative
Authority and Liminal Identities

Brief Introduction

I n the early twenty-first century, countries across the world are encountering complications following from the jubilant democratizing processes of the late twentieth century. The first part of *Area Studies in the Global Age* treats states and cultures in which those in power claimed to have defeated various forms of authoritarian government and, at least to begin with, enjoyed the trust of a large segment of the population. The four cases considered here are Taiwan, Russia, the Dominican Republic, and South Africa. Each polity has engaged in recasting the historical narrative of its country as a story of national success, and in most cases of popular democratic success. In some cases, however, such as Russia, the link between popular liberation and new parliamentary democratic institutions of governance are tenuous. Most of these examples find themselves on the edge, in a "liminal," borderline position between the forces of an authoritarian past and the aspirations for a "democratic" present and future.

All the cases investigated here deploy the methodologies of "memory studies" to show state and popular efforts to craft a firm national identity out of this porous material.[1] Taiwan's recollection of the past deals with opening to public discussion historical periods often considered shameful, such as the fifty years of Taiwan's submission to Japan. Russia's recasting of history has to do with continued emphasis and memorialization of the Soviet victory in World War II, a bright moment in the totalitarian twentieth century. Dominicans are engaging in a dispute between exiles and those in power in the Dominican Republic over narratives and memorials, either justifying or castigating the dictator Trujillo's murderous treatment of the political opposition. In South Africa those in power appear to be backsliding after their splendid victory over apartheid. In every case, citizenry and state employ a number of tactics to secure their version of national memory—retelling the past whether in history textbooks for the schools or through public monuments.

In each of the following four chapters, borders of various kinds play a crucial role in rethinking national narratives, and in each a different form of liminality emerges. It will be well to remember the original anthropological definitions of the "liminal" with its reference to the transitional period between childhood and adulthood. The liminal marks a border crossing, a time of disorientation and confusion, when rules do not seem to apply in the usual way.

In her chapter Megan Greene presents Taiwan as a country with a complicated past. Taiwan has been a colony, an occupied zone, and a military state, and is currently a democracy with a freely and fairly elected parliamentary government—though now in competition with the People's Republic of China, or Mainland China, for its status as an independent Chinese state. Since the 1990s, increasing freedom of speech has fostered a lively debate about what to emphasize in Taiwan's history and how to express it in Taiwan's museums, parks, and school curriculum—in short, how to craft Taiwanese community and identity. Greene compares views on national identity in two different eras, the Nationalist Party military rule from the 1950s to the 1980s and the later democratically elected government. She focuses on these two periods when the government created (or, in the latter case, sought to create) two quite different national identities with contrasting purposes. In addition to collecting material in libraries and archives, between 2006 and 2008 Greene conducted field interviews and visited parks, museums, and memorials.

Adrienne Harris deals with Russia, a country that, for the second time in the twentieth century, transformed the world, this time when it gave up its empire in 1991. Russia is liminal in many senses, but territorially so because its current borders have been severely diminished compared to the Soviet borders (and before that, the borders of the old tsarist empire)—particularly to the west and the south. In this liminal period of disorientation and slippage back to an authoritarian order, the popular search for national heroes and stories that instill pride motivate Harris's study of the process of retrofitting a World War II hero, the partisan Zoya Kosmodemyanskaya, who was killed by Nazis while on a mission. In the post-Soviet decades she has also been pictured as a Russian Orthodox martyr, a shift that Harris links to a larger trend among some Russians toward a religiously defined form of national identity. Interestingly, in terms of reimagined national "place," the map of European Russia is dotted with memorials to this soldier-saint.

The chapter on Robben Island by Elizabeth MacGonagle treats South Africa's shift from a white-dominated to a post-apartheid, democratically elected system of governance through the lens of the country's most notorious prison. With the end of apartheid in the 1990s, Robben Island shed its former penal function and was renovated as a "place of memory." It has become a museum and, in some sense, a sacred site to commemorate South Africa's worst oppression of its black residents. After the 1990 end of apartheid (which went as far as complete segregation and the rescinding of black South Africans' citizenship) and with free elections in 1994, Robben Island became a "place of memory," a mecca that has helped the African National Congress (ANC) government to heal the borders and divisions created by apartheid and build a multiracial national community. MacGonagle investigates the South African process of creating national myth, finding new problems in the ANC's preference for certain historical facts and foregrounding of certain cult figures, such as Nelson Mandela. A suspect "liminal" piece of this process is the practice of hiring former political prisoners as guides in the museum, a problem that MacGonagle links to the party currently in power, the ANC, and its hopes for retaining power in the future.

Shelly Jarrett Bromberg's chapter on the Mirabal sisters explores the current debate in the Dominican Republic and the Dominican diaspora about how best to inscribe the memory of the anti-Trujillo heroes and movements in twenty-first-century national consciousness. Drawing on a broad range of materials, including press reports, film, literature, and testimonials, as well as museums and physical and virtual Internet memorials, she asks why since the mid-1990s ordinary Dominicans have increasingly challenged the traditional national narrative nurtured by the family and supporters of the dictator Trujillo. Part of the answer, she argues, has to do with geography and borders. Dominicans have sustained the debate by crossing national borders, publishing materials, and establishing webpages that place the narrative outside of physical boundaries. Ultimately, the dispute itself is liminal in its inconclusiveness. No clear voice appears to speak for Dominican identity.

A repeating pattern in all of these chapters (and occasionally others) is the tendency of national identity and community to center around particular historical events and heroes. Identity becomes fixed in spatial focal points, such as parks, museums, and statues, which do more than simply commemorate. They create sacred ground for significant groups among the citizenry, and they make it easier to continue the debate, which can bring a variety of results, both salutary and divisive—to deepen splits within the community, to massage historical fact, now from the point of view of the new government, and, on the positive side, to continue the discussion and to articulate in clear, visible form the facts of a repressed history so that they will not be forgotten.

Notes

1. For a classic discussion of the difficulties in late twentieth-century definitions and uses of the term *identity*, see Rogers Brubaker and Frederick Cooper, "Beyond 'identity'," Theory and Society, 29 (2000), 1-47.

Understanding Taiwan's Colonial Past
Using History to Define Taiwan's 21st-Century Identity

J. MEGAN GREENE

The 1945 return of Taiwan to the government of the Republic of China (ROC), a government and a nation that had not existed when the Qing Dynasty lost Taiwan to Japan following the Sino-Japanese War in 1895, signaled the conclusion of an embarrassing period in China's history, a period during which China had been unable to maintain even tenuous control over its entire territory. The very word *guangfu* (光復) that the Nationalist Party or KMT commonly used to refer to the event indicated that something lost had been recovered, a notion that resonated strongly with the KMT after it later lost control of mainland China and retreated to Taiwan. Rather than dwelling on the loss, however, the KMT preferred to celebrate the recovery of Taiwan and to look forward to its eventual recovery of the Chinese "mainland," and the KMT's treatment of Taiwan's past reflected this preference. Taiwan's colonial past was, from the perspective of the KMT, not a period to celebrate or dwell upon, but instead a shameful period to be erased and forgotten. This process of erasure was most evident in the cultural reconstruction policies that the KMT undertook in Taiwan in the 1950s and 1960s (outlawing the use of the Japanese and Taiwanese languages in schools, for example), but it can also be seen in the various narratives of the past that were presented in KMT-controlled cultural institutions during the long martial law era (1947–1987), when the KMT ruled with a tight fist as a single-party state. During the decade following the end of martial law, numerous efforts were made by scholars, politicians, and victims of the KMT's authoritarian government to recapture forgotten aspects of Taiwan's past, and as a consequence of these activities Taiwan's colonial eras have increasingly been recognized and celebrated since the 1990s, although there remain varied interpretations of that past.

In spite of the KMT's authoritarianism, for much of the martial law era Taiwan was understood by most of the world to be "Free China." Until the 1970s the ROC on Taiwan was recognized by most states and major nongovernment organizations as China, whereas the Communist People's Republic of China (PRC) was seen as a destructive interloper, temporarily occupying most of China's territory and heavily influenced by the imperialist Soviet Union. This view was shared by KMT leaders, who were deeply anticommunist and committed to the West's perspective on the Cold War. The KMT used domestic policy, and in particular domestic cultural policy, to further this idea among the people of Taiwan, though many of them had been born and raised as citizens of the Japanese empire and had little feeling of connection to China. Taiwan served, therefore, as a battleground on which the politics (though not the wars) of the Cold War were played out. Identity was (and remains) at the center of the battle, as Taiwan is one of the few places in the world that continues to be deeply affected by the legacy of the Cold War.

As an open and vocal Taiwan Independence movement[1] grew following the lifting of martial law in 1987, residents of Taiwan increasingly engaged in open debates over Taiwan's identity. Was it a nation or a province, Chinese or not, did either the ROC (the KMT's government) or the PRC truly have a right to govern it? Activists on both sides look for answers to these questions in the historical record, and as a result Taiwan's history has become a highly politicized arena in which the PRC and various political factions in Taiwan all seek to present evidence to support their differing ideas about what Taiwan's identity is and what its political future should be. In other words, since the mid-1990s, in these battles over the appropriate way to tell the story of Taiwan's history, the playing out of contemporary identity politics continues in a place that, owing to the legacy of Cold War politics, is neither a fully recognized independent nation nor a part of the People's Republic of China.

A particularly good example of this tension is the varied treatment in contemporary Taiwan of its colonial experiences, which had under the KMT generally been viewed as a negative feature of a weak past, but which in the early twenty-first century came to be celebrated by many Taiwanese nationalists as a distinctive feature of a rich, multicultural, and uniquely *not* Chinese past. This chapter examines how Taiwan's colonial past has been represented both during the martial law era and in the first decade of the twenty-first century, and how those representations have been used to create community and construct identity. In investigating this topic, this chapter seeks to add to the extensive literature on identity in Taiwan by considering how states employ the past in the construction of a hegemonic national narrative, and by showing that the broader political and economic context in which a state operates can facilitate or limit the efficacy of such efforts.

Early scholarship from the late 1980s and early 1990s on identity in Taiwan tended to focus on ethnicity and social groupings to explain identity as expressed through political divisions. Such scholars as Alan Wachman set up the dominant patterns of analysis by looking at the relationship between people's political position on the question of Taiwan independence and things like birthplace ("mainland" China or Taiwan) and language use (Mandarin or Taiwanese).[2] Analysis of survey data and polls by other political scientists showed that in the late 1980s and early 1990s, those who supported independence were mostly Taiwanese-born and Taiwanese-speaking, and those who believed Taiwan to be Chinese were mostly Chinese-born and Mandarin-speaking.[3] This analysis understood identity to be an expression of a political position (pro- or anti-independence) that stemmed primarily from family background. Further scholarly study has shown, however, that identity is not solely an expression of ethnicity (or subethnicity) and that it does not always manifest itself in clearly defined political categories. This has become increasingly the case as more and more mainlanders and Taiwanese have intermarried and language policies have loosened up. As Taiwan's political arena democratized in the 1990s, identity increasingly became a subject of debate and discussion among the residents of Taiwan, and individuals and political entities alike have found increasingly diverse ways to express and understand their own identities. By the late 1990s scholars such as Leo Ching and A-Chin Hsiau were searching for expressions of identity in literature, film, and other cultural products, and looking across the 1945 divide to find the roots of a uniquely Taiwanese identity in the Japanese colonial period or even earlier.[4] Shifts in regional economic and political conditions and an increasingly complex set of social interactions between Taiwan and China have also played a significant role in shaping identity in contemporary Taiwan, as the work of scholars such as Sara Friedman and William Kirby demonstrates.[5] Within the context of this extensive and ever-growing body of literature on identity in Taiwan, scholars such as Joseph Allen, Stephane Corcuff, and Yeh Wen-hsin have begun to consider how representations and interpretations of the past play a role in the construction of identity in Taiwan.[6] This chapter contributes to that trend in the literature and looks specifically at how Taiwan's national governments have sought to employ history to help Taiwan's citizens construct identity. It looks comparatively at two eras in which two separate governments tried to construct two very different identities that aimed at different ends, and explores how each of these governments manipulated the narrative of Taiwan's colonial past to serve these ends.

Methods and Sources

The sources for this chapter are primarily public representations of the past that can be found in textbooks, museums, and other public spaces. Most but not all of these sources are products of some branch of the ROC government. The Ministry of Education determines curriculum in Taiwan, and until 1997 all textbooks were written and produced by a single government institution, the National Institute for Compilation and Translation. In 1997 textbooks were deregulated, and numerous private publishing companies quickly began to market textbooks offering varying interpretations of the past, though all must conform to a basic set of standards that is outlined by the Ministry of Education. Most parks and museums in Taiwan are also under government control; however, many are controlled not by the national government, but by municipal or county governments that may not, in the post–martial law era, share the political perspective of whichever party happens to control the presidency and the legislature. Some museums are privately owned, and their exhibits may therefore express the perspective of their owners or boards of trustees. Not all exhibits are explicitly politicized, but many, especially those set up by the Ministry of Education, have a clear political subtext. I collected my materials, as most historians do, in libraries and archives, but also through interviews and visits to museums and parks in the summers of 2006 and 2008, though my observations are also informed by over two decades of visits (long and short) to Taiwan and by the abundant scholarship on Taiwan's identity and politics. Many of the 2006 exhibits were temporary, as were the political appointees I interviewed, and so, whereas the discussion of the martial law era makes some sweeping observations about a thirty-year period of time (from the mid-1950s to the late 1980s), the discussion of the first decade of the twenty-first century is based largely on snapshots taken in the summers of 2006 and 2008, and the ongoing conversation about Taiwan's identity has taken numerous twists and turns in the period since then.

Viewing the Past under Martial Law

A survey of education policy and textbooks from the martial law era reveals that the KMT shaped much, though not all, of its cultural policy around an attempt to erase Taiwan's Japanese past and to replace any sense of a Japanese identity among Taiwan's residents with a sense of a Chinese identity instead. Japanese language signage was forbidden, newspapers and other media were presented in Chinese (even if the literate public was not perfectly equipped to read the language), and languages other than Mandarin were banned in schools. In addition, perhaps because of communication failures, or possibly because of discriminatory attitudes, the KMT generally ignored or overlooked Japanese-trained professionals and skilled laborers as it sought to redevelop Taiwan's postwar economy. As a consequence, a whole generation of local experts in agriculture, mining, medicine, and industry were largely shoved out of any sort of leading role in the economy (and many among this class fell victim to the KMT's brutal repression in the wake of the February 28 incident of 1947). In other words, little in the KMT's treatment of their "recovered" citizens suggests that the KMT saw anything worth remembering in Taiwan's colonial experience, though the economic and social modernization that had taken place under Japanese rule did serve as an important foundation upon which the KMT established its own developmental policies. The complexity of this relationship between the KMT and Taiwan's colonial past can be seen in examples such as Taipei's New Park. As Joseph Allen has shown through an examination of the park's history, the KMT erased overtly Japanese monumentation and imagery, and in the 1960s, replaced it with more overtly sino-centric monumentation. In spite of these physical transformations, however, the space continued to be used in essentially the same ways as in the Japanese colonial period, and probably by many of the same people who undoubtedly operated within complex webs of familial, linguistic, cultural, and political networks that shaped their sense of identity.[7]

The KMT did not and could not systematically erase all evidence of the Japanese presence, nor could it subordinate all of Taiwan's particular cultural features to its own attempts to establish cultural hegemony. Its education system, the media, and state-operated institutions of high culture all sought to sinicize Taiwan. But at the same time, the KMT permitted local culture to exist, so that in the 1960s, for example, there was a flourishing Taiwanese-language film industry, the state actually promoted local Taiwanese dramatic arts, the government made very public use of Japanese-constructed buildings (the best example of this is the ROC's presidential palace), and institutions like Japanese-style bathhouses continued to flourish. Although there is ample evidence to suggest that the KMT wished to make Taiwan Chinese, therefore, there is also evidence that it was willing to allow Taiwan to retain some of its particular, regional, and, in certain cases, explicitly Japanese features.

Though not necessarily wishing to cut the Taiwanese off entirely from their cultural past, the KMT was still driven by the imperative of building a loyal citizenry, for which purpose it turned, as it had in the 1930s and 1940s in China, to the education system as a tool. Courses on such subjects as history, civics, and geography, in particular, provided an opportunity for the KMT to shape young people's understanding of who they were and how they were connected to a KMT state that had recently migrated from China. These textbooks constructed a common narrative of China's history that clearly positioned Taiwan within the Chinese orbit, and that made it clear that Taiwan's colonial eras (under the Japanese and the Dutch) were anomalous, rather than defining, moments. If one looks at history textbooks from the early KMT period on Taiwan, one can gain some insight into the standard take on Taiwan's colonial past that the KMT sought to propagate from the 1950s to the 1990s, during which time all students across Taiwan were taught with the same books and in accordance with a carefully constructed curriculum. In general, Taiwan and its history are not well represented in KMT history textbooks of that era, which focus instead on Chinese history. Taiwan, in fact, only comes up briefly at three points in the textbook narrative: the seventeenth century, the late nineteenth century, and 1945 and after, each of which is a moment of transition. At each of these moments, Taiwan is described as being either returned to or taken away from the Chinese, so even though the KMT did not choose to dwell upon the specific features of Taiwan's colonial past, the fact that it had been colonized remained essential to the narrative of Taiwan's history that the KMT wished ROC citizens to understand. The very short narratives in these three sections focus on the taking of Taiwan by or from the Dutch, Chinese, and Japanese, and while the Dutch and Japanese presence is characterized as imperialistic, the Chinese presence (even, in fact, the Manchu[8] presence) is characterized as entirely natural and as having long historical precedent. Moreover, the language used to describe Dutch and Japanese designs on Taiwan is quite negative in tone, whereas the language used to describe the Chinese "recovery" of Taiwan in the late seventeenth century and again in 1945 is quite positive.

The first mention of Taiwan in all editions of high school history textbooks from the martial law era appears in a description of military resistance to the conquering Manchu Qing by the great Ming loyalist Zheng Chenggong, who is celebrated both for his resistance to the Qing, and for liberating Taiwan from Dutch rule and bringing Chinese modes of government and social organization to the island. The texts describe Zheng as a very filial Ming loyalist and a great warrior who used his military skills to oust the Dutch from what had previously been Chinese territory. Following his recovery of Taiwan, he organized a new government, established laws, encouraged agricultural development, and made military preparations to return the Ming to power in China. His legacy in Taiwan, according to the narrative, was his fighting spirit and a tradition of Chinese nationalism.[9] Taiwan comes up here primarily because it is a locus of Chinese nationalist and anti-imperialist activity. There is little question that the textbook writers were eager to demonstrate that there was a tradition of such activity in Taiwan. Nothing at all is said about what Taiwan experienced under the brief period of Dutch rule; the emphasis is on the removal of the Dutch.

Like the high school textbook narratives of the 1950s and 1960s, middle school textbook narratives emphasized the successful return of Taiwan to Chinese/Manchu rule, but did so using more clearly political language. The middle school narrative emphasizes the parallel with the KMT's recovery of Taiwan in 1945 by employing the same vocabulary that the KMT commonly used to describe its acquisition of Taiwan in 1945. Zheng is described as having "recovered" (*guangfu*) Taiwan, which, according to the narrative, had belonged to China during both the Yuan and Ming dynasties.[10]

As in the case of the description of Zheng's retreat to Taiwan, the textbook treatment of Taiwan's 1895 transfer to Japanese control and the subsequent period of Japanese colonial rule focuses not on the features of life under the Japanese or on Japanese economic and social development of Taiwan, but on the spirit of resistance among the people of Taiwan. As the 1954 middle school history text noted, although the Qing government (not Chinese, of course) was willing to give up Taiwan, the people of Taiwan were not cooperative, elected a president, established a Republic of Taiwan, and raised an army to resist Japan. But they lost. From that time, Taiwan was occupied by the Japanese and only returned to China after World War II.[11] This very short narrative highlights resistance and provides no information whatsoever about Japanese colonial rule. The high school textbooks of both 1954 and 1967 are somewhat more detailed in their description of the resistance, and of how it represents an example of Chinese nationalism, but not of what conditions in Taiwan were like under the Japanese. According to the 1954 text, Taiwan became a Japanese colony after China was "victimized" by Japan, but this only "strengthened the traditional nationalistic revolutionary spirit" of "our Taiwan brothers." Mainlanders, too, were calling for the return of Taiwan to China, and this was a particular concern for Chiang Kai-shek from the mid-1920s until the end of World War II.[12]

Notable in these short sections on Taiwan's transitional moments is the absence of any description of Taiwan or the lives and experiences of its people. To the extent that one can learn anything at all of what people in Taiwan were doing under the Japanese, it is not how they were transformed, shaped, or governed by the Japanese, but how they resisted Japanese rule. This resistance, moreover, is described as entirely consistent with and stemming from the emergent Chinese nationalism of the early twentieth century. One possible explanation for this omission is that Taiwan's 1950s textbooks were essentially the same ones that the KMT had used in China. By the late 1960s, however, textbooks had been revised, but even so, the sections on Taiwan were not significantly expanded or developed.

In these narratives, the significant parts of Taiwan's colonial past were (1) that its colonial moments ended in successful sinification; (2) that the Taiwanese resisted; and (3) that in these moments of resistance one can see Taiwan developing an appropriate spirit of Chinese nationalism. These short and underdeveloped textbook treatments represent the standard narrative that students in the martial law era learned in school. This narrative, one that essentially omitted discussion of Taiwan's colonial periods except insofar as they could be used to demonstrate the existence of a Chinese nationalism in Taiwan, was reinforced by other KMT-controlled cultural institutions. Many museums in Taiwan, for example, were built around collections of Chinese materials, many of which (as in the case of the National Palace Museum that opened in 1965) were brought from China to Taiwan by the KMT. The aspects of Taiwan's past that were celebrated with monuments tended to be aspects that appeared in the narratives discussed above. So, for example, there was a monument of Zheng Chenggong in Taipei New Park, and Zheng sites in Tainan were also opened to the public. Taiwan's colonial past was basically buried under KMT rule. Historians were discouraged from studying it except as a sort of hobby, students were not taught about it, and public spaces did not commemorate it.

Representations of Taiwan's Colonial Past and Identity Politics in Twenty-First-Century Taiwan

After martial law was lifted in 1987, scholars, students, political activists, and the general public took great interest in uncovering Taiwan's forgotten history, and particularly in digging out the truth about KMT brutality in the early martial law era. These sorts of truth and reconciliation activities took place primarily under the watchful eye of the opposition Democratic Progressive Party (DPP), the popularity of which was deeply rooted in its open criticism of the KMT's oppressive practices. As Taiwan democratized over the course of the 1990s, and as the authoritarianism of the more recent past was revealed, catalogued, and laid to rest, growing numbers of historians in Taiwan turned to more distant pasts and began to conduct increasingly sophisticated and rich studies of both the Japanese colonial period and Taiwan under the Qing. Though most of this recent scholarship on Taiwan's history is firmly grounded in archival and material culture sources, and is not heavily politicized, political actors, particularly those in the DPP, have remained especially interested in Taiwan's history. The major subtext for this interest has been the desire to demonstrate the various ways in which Taiwan is *not* Chinese. This interest in Taiwan's history became politically evident during DPP leader Chen Shui-bian's presidency from 2000 to 2008. During this period, Taiwan's colonial past was uncovered, explored, and celebrated as part of an extensive exercise in the construction of a Taiwanese national identity. In this climate, even KMT politicians, including President Ma Ying-jeou, have also begun to recognize the importance of remembering all aspects of Taiwan's past, though their political rationale for doing so may not be quite the same as that of DPP politicians. Under the Chen administration's leadership, a new emphasis on Taiwan's colonial past became visible in all sorts of venues, including museums, monuments, and other public spaces, as well as in textbooks, and its appearance was the result of a systematic effort on the part of various government-controlled cultural institutions, including the Ministry of Education, between 2000 and 2008. As was the case under martial law, therefore, textbook narratives were reinforced by public history.

One major difference in the recent period, however, is that although the Ministry of Education has the authority to shape school curricula, it no longer controls textbook production. Textbook production was deregulated in 1999, and since that time textbook producers have had considerable latitude in their interpretation of the standard curriculum, which lays out in skeletal fashion the subject matter that is to be covered, but not the way in which the subjects should be interpreted. This means that although some textbooks interpret material in ways that conform to the intent behind curricular reforms, others do not. Teachers and schools can now choose from among an array of textbooks to teach the required material, and the presentation of the subject matter therefore varies from school to school and classroom to classroom.

In 2006 the DPP implemented a new high school history curriculum that introduced an entire term on Taiwan history at the high school level. The semester-long Taiwan history course was the first of four terms of history that all high school students had to take in Taiwan. It was followed by a single semester of Chinese history, and then a full year of world history. Notable features of this curriculum are that it was the first high school history curriculum to reduce Chinese history to a single semester, expand Taiwan history to an entire semester, and begin the history curriculum with Taiwan.

The Taiwan semester of this new curriculum was divided into four broad periods. The first focused on aboriginal cultures, and the seventeenth century as a multicultural society. The second examined political, social, and economic development under the Qing as well as Taiwan's external relations during that period. The third described Taiwan under Japanese imperialism, focusing on politics, economic and infrastructural development, colonial society and culture, the development of art and literature, the Kominka (assimilation) movement, and World War II. And the final portion of the semester focused on contemporary Taiwan, including segments on martial law, the lifting of martial law, economics, social change, and a globalized Taiwan.[13]

Each of the four sections of this course was designed to place Taiwan into a broad international context, or at least a context that was not solely Chinese, and to reinforce the multicultural dimensions of Taiwan's past. Part one considered Taiwan as having been inhabited by aborigines of Austronesian (rather than Chinese) origin and then made it clear that subsequent migrants to Taiwan included but were not all Chinese. The section on the "multicultural" seventeenth century aimed to show that in addition to aboriginal groups, Taiwan's population included Dutch and Spaniards, as well as Han Chinese.[14] With this framework in place, a student reading part two (on the Qing era) might be more likely to view both Zheng Chenggong and the Qing as colonizing forces comparable to the Dutch. In fact, the phrase "immigrant society" was used in the curricular guidelines to refer to the Han Chinese in Taiwan, most of whom migrated there at some point during the Qing. Even if the reader did not conclude that the Chinese were themselves imperialists, there was still considerable emphasis in this section on the external relations of Taiwan, including the arrival of British imperialists in Danshui in the nineteenth century following its opening as a treaty port. The third part of the Taiwan semester focused entirely on ways in which Taiwan was shaped and influenced by the Japanese, and the fourth part again was shaped in such a way as to suggest the possibility that Taiwan was, in 1945, recolonized by the Chinese (this time the KMT and not the Qing), and also positioned Taiwan in the late twentieth century in a global, rather than Chinese, social and economic frame. There is little question that this curricular structure sought to place Taiwan in the middle of a web of imperialist and globalizing activities, all of which have shaped its history and made it into what it is today. The curriculum guided students to consider the possibility that today's Taiwan is what it is because of this highly globalized, international, and colonial past, and it created the potential for some textbook writers to go so far as to overtly state that Taiwan was colonized not only by the Dutch and Japanese, but also by the Chinese.

Not only does Taiwan's Ministry of Education guide curricular decisions, it also controls a number of prominently located exhibit spaces that it can use, if it so chooses, to reinforce the ideas it promotes in schools. The DPP's Minister of Education, Tu Cheng-sheng, devoted much of the museum space over which he had control in 2006 (when I happened to be looking at these

things) to exhibits on seventeenth-century Taiwan (though Tu had been constructing exhibits on Taiwan's seventeenth century for several years prior to
2006 in his previous role as director of the National Palace Museum).[15] Some
of these exhibits focused on the multiculturalism of the seventeenth century,
and in particular the diversity of foreign influences (Dutch and Chinese) on
Taiwan. There is no reasonable historical basis for claiming that Taiwan ever
really became culturally or even politically Dutch in any meaningful way, but
the impression one gets from these exhibits is that the Dutch influence was at
least as great as that of the Chinese in the seventeenth century, even though
there were many more Chinese than Dutch in Taiwan at the time. There is
little doubt that the political aims of these Ministry of Education–sponsored
exhibits were to identify the Chinese as latecomers to the Taiwan scene, and to
clarify for exhibit viewers that Taiwan has a rich history of diversity and that
China is but one of a number of places that has influenced Taiwan.

Perhaps the best example of this sort of exhibit was "Once upon a Time
in Taiwan: An Educational Exhibit on Daily Life in Taiwan during Dutch
Colonial Rule in the Seventeenth Century," which was showing in the rear
exhibit hall of the Chiang Kai-shek Memorial Hall in the summer of 2006.[16]
The exhibit was put together by the cultural affairs office of the Executive
Yuan, with the assistance of the Dutch chamber of commerce, and its sponsors included a number of Dutch-owned multinational corporations such as
Philips, KLM, and Heineken. Although on the day that I visited the exhibit
there were no school groups in attendance, it seemed to be designed for such
an audience. Its placement in the Chiang Kai-shek memorial, however, virtually guaranteed that at least some foreign visitors would also pass through.
Most of the exhibit was divided into topics such as government, ships, the
marketplace, and school, which offered the possibility of comparison between
the three main cultural groups (Aborigines, Dutch, and Chinese) on the island
in the seventeenth century. To more fully illustrate this point, the exhibit also
included three walk-in "houses" that represented the three major cultures,
and showed differences in lifestyle, architecture, furniture, and so on. The
exhibit presented Taiwan as a truly multicultural society that was shaped by
Aborigines, Dutch, and Chinese, and the structure of the exhibit strongly suggested that their influence on seventeenth-century Taiwan was spread fairly
evenly across the three groups. As the exhibit brochure noted in both Chinese
and English: "Almost four hundred years ago, numerous Chinese and Europeans started trading, building cities and roads in Taiwan. In the end this
would dramatically change the lives of the many different Aborigine tribes,
who lived on the island for thousands of years. During the period of the Dutch
occupation of Taiwan a multi-cultural society developed in the south of the

island, with all its unique and interesting features."[17] Not only was Taiwan (or at least, southern Taiwan) multicultural, according to this narrative, it was unique (and thus distinct from China).

It is not solely in the south that evidence of a multicultural, colonial past can be found, however. In spite of the fact that tourist material uses its Spanish name, the exhibits in Fort Santo Domingo, in Danshui, also commemorate the Dutch era as well as the mid-nineteenth-century treaty port era, both of which contributed to the development of Danshui. The fort, which was built by the Dutch and later renovated by the Qing on a site that had earlier been occupied by the Spanish, became the British consular residence in the 1860s. On the site are two buildings: one the fort, and the other a Victorian addition, the consular residence, both of which were renovated by the Taipei County Government, which, during the Chen Shui-bian era, was DPP-controlled.

A permanent exhibit in the fort centers on the historical development of Danshui and starts visitors off with the following phrase: "The development of Tamsui [Danshui] can be traced back to Europe's grand navigation epoch in the fifteenth century." This places Taiwan squarely and proudly within the European orbit. The exhibit proceeds to note the Chinese origins of the age of grand navigation in the fifteenth-century voyages taken by Zheng He, and to recognize that the area around Danshui had long been a locus of trade and interaction between Chinese and Aborigines. In this narrative, the Chinese are thus clearly placed with the Dutch, Spanish, and English in the category of outsiders who navigated the seas and had colonial designs on Taiwan.[18]

The second building, the British Consular Residence, as part of the celebration of the site's 2004 renovation, dedicated a space to informing the public about the foreign nations that had occupied the fort. So in 2005 the building housed exhibits about Spain, in 2006 about Holland, and in 2007 about Great Britain (Britain had continued to occupy the residence through the Japanese colonial era and until 1972). In the summer of 2006 the exhibit space was being used to house a Rembrandt exhibit consisting mostly of reproductions of his paintings. As the introductory plaque said, "It was a coincidence that the Dutch artist Rembrandt van Rijn, one of the most prestigious painters in the world, finished his most famous painting 'The Nightwatch' in 1642, and during this period the Dutch East-India Company was fast reaching its peak and most powerful position in its colonizing efforts in Formosa. . . . Therefore, Tamsui [Danshui] Historic Sites would like to use this connection between Rembrandt and the VOC in order to join in with the 'Rembrandt 400th birthday' celebration."[19] Though the connection between Rembrandt and Danshui seems rather tenuous, the Taipei County Cultural Office, which managed the site, was clearly looking for ways to both remind visitors of the fleeting

Dutch presence in Taiwan, and also to insert Taiwan into a Dutch sphere in the twenty-first century.

The exhibits described above lacked subtlety. They were designed, for the most part, to reeducate a public that had been taught to think of Taiwan as Chinese, and they were motivated by an overt political agenda. The heavy emphasis on a Dutch past and on Taiwan's long-term engagement with the world through trade, empire, and migration was designed to encourage Taiwanese to understand themselves as products of a multicultural and globalized society of which the Chinese were only a part.

Though these early exhibits took a heavy-handed approach to reeducating people, by 2008 public exhibits were beginning to demonstrate a more nuanced and sophisticated approach to Taiwan's colonial past, one that suggested that the public might already be thinking of Taiwan's past differently. An excellent example of this more subtle approach is the exhibit "The Story of Collection in a Century" put on in the summer of 2008 by the National Taiwan Museum to commemorate its one hundredth anniversary. The Museum, which had originally been established by the Japanese as the Taiwan Viceroy's Office Museum and was later renamed the Taiwan Provincial Museum under KMT rule, has always "served as a vital conduit to raise awareness of Taiwan's natural and cultural history."[20] However, it has done so in a series of very different political contexts. In its most recent guise, as the National Taiwan Museum, a name it was given in 1999, it has taken on a more explicitly political role as the "national" museum of Taiwan.[21] The exhibit provided a history of the museum by describing the collecting activities of the various scientists and scholars who built the collection, which comprised specimens of Taiwan's native flora and fauna as well as cultural relics and everyday items from Taiwan's numerous aboriginal groups. The collectors themselves, each of whom was dedicated to the study of a different dimension of Taiwan's human and physical geography, served as the organizing focus for the exhibit. Displays informed the visitor of the reasoning behind the collection of a given type of object, but also of the pivotal role in each case of a particular collector. Of the twelve collectors highlighted in the exhibit, seven were Japanese, four were Chinese, and only one was Taiwan-born.[22] Through this detailed display structure, the exhibit explicitly acknowledged the role played by Taiwan's Japanese colonizers in cataloguing and mapping the human and natural features of the island. At the same time, it placed Japanese, Chinese, and Taiwanese collectors next to each other in a way that highlighted the multicultural nature of the past century and treated the Japanese imperial period as little more than part of the longer continuum of Taiwan's history, a part that was very important in helping Taiwan to become what it now is.[23]

Conclusion

Owing to the legacies of pre–World War II Japanese imperialism, the Chinese Civil War, and the outbreak of the Cold War, Taiwan has experienced a series of identity crises in the postwar era. First, after its liberation from Japanese colonial rule and its "return" to the control of the government of the Republic of China, it was reconstructed as a Chinese province. After the KMT's full-scale retreat to Taiwan in 1949, the island's identity was recast as "Free China," as Taiwan and some surrounding islands were the only parts of the Republic of China that remained under KMT control. Since the end of martial law in 1987, with the advent of a fully functioning democracy, the island has undergone yet another series of exercises in identity construction that have been driven by the competing political agendas of Taiwan's major political parties, but that have involved much more active participation by Taiwan's citizens than earlier identity reconstruction exercises did. Not only did political actors have a more limited set of tools to manipulate identity construction than had been at the disposal of the authoritarian KMT under martial law, they were operating in a markedly different environment with respect to popular access to knowledge about Taiwan and popular participation in economic and social networks that linked people to China. In this environment, these more recent state-led attempts to impose a hegemonic historical narrative on the population were doomed to be less effective than those of the KMT under martial law.

The narrative that the KMT promoted during the martial law era was marked by an absence of discussion of Taiwan and a heavy emphasis on the history of China. The political environment required that the ROC government maintain a fiction of a strong China with friendly and supportive relations with the West, in particular. Taiwan's (and indeed China's) embarrassing encounters with the West and Japan were not to be discussed more than was absolutely necessary, though appropriately constructed memories of these encounters could be useful in assisting Taiwan's citizens to build a spirit of resistance that would be necessary to defend against the PRC. The KMT was assisted in the dissemination of this narrative by its single-party authoritarian rule under martial law, which gave it strong censorship control over the media, permitted it to dominate school curricula, and gave it considerable power through mechanisms such as state-controlled entrance and civil service examinations to determine who would be in positions of authority in both bureaucratic and educational positions.

By the first decade of the twenty-first century, however, things had changed dramatically, and one could find proud and detailed celebrations of Taiwan's colonial past almost anywhere one looked, suggesting that for at least some Taiwanese, the KMT had merely repressed a sense of identity rooted in the colonial past, rather than entirely replacing it with a new Chinese identity. No longer was the Japanese colonial era viewed as a humiliating moment to be forgotten, and a new interest in the brief Dutch colonial era emerged among historians, museum curators, and others. Bookstores sold reproductions of Japanese-era postcards and coffee-table books about the Japanese colonial era, Japanese colonial sites were renovated and turned into tourist destinations, and museums regularly displayed exhibits about the Dutch colonial era. Even the National Palace Museum, which is very Sino-centric, housed exhibits on topics such as "Ilha Formosa: The Emergence of Taiwan on the World Scene in the Seventeenth Century."[24] To a large extent, these phenomena were driven by a desire among the public to learn more about Taiwan's past. However, as the examples described in this chapter have shown, they were also driven by the political agendas of Taiwan's major political actors. Celebrations of Taiwan's unique historical experiences (different from those of China) and its past engagements with non-Chinese cultures and civilizations were politically useful for a DPP government bent on promoting Taiwanese nationalism, seeking to help young people to develop a distinctively Taiwanese identity, and furthering an independence agenda. In attempting to use the historical narrative to help shape identity, the DPP was merely following in the footsteps of its KMT predecessors. The methods the DPP used were similarly blunt and heavy-handed, though its attempts to construct a new historical narrative in educational venues were in many respects thwarted by the new, open, and broadly participatory political environment as well as by Taiwan's growing connectedness to China through economic and social networks.

Notes

1. The ROC and PRC have been at a virtual political standstill since 1949, and although the ROC government no longer claims to be the rightful government of China (it did through the entire martial law era), the PRC government does maintain the claim that Taiwan is a part of China. As a result, no government or NGO can recognize both the PRC and the ROC as separate states, and the PRC has stated that it will not hesitate to use force if Taiwan should officially declare independence. In other words, although Taiwan has an entirely separate system of government and set of laws from China, and although its residents have all the rights and responsibilities that citizens of any democracy might have, Taiwan is not widely recognized as a nation.

2. Alan Wachman, *Taiwan: National Identity and Democratization* (Armonk, NY: M. E. Sharpe, 1994).

3. See, for example, Hung-mao Tien, ed. *Taiwan's Electoral Politics and Democratic Transition: Riding the Third Wave* (Armonk, NY: M. E. Sharpe, 1996); John Fuh-sheng Hsieh, "Ethnicity, National Identity, and Domestic Politics in Taiwan," *Journal of Asian and African Studies* 40 (2005): 13.

4. Leo Ching, *Becoming "Japanese": Colonial Taiwan and the Politics of Identity Formation* (Berkeley: University of California Press, 2001); A-Chin Hsiau, *Contemporary Taiwanese Cultural Nationalism* (London: Routledge, 2000). See also Faye Yuan Kleeman, *Under an Imperial Sun: Japanese Colonial Literature of Taiwan and the South* (Honolulu: University of Hawaii Press, 2003); Melissa J. Brown, *Is Taiwan Chinese? The Impact of Culture, Power, and Migration on Changing Identities* (Berkeley: University of California Press, 2004); Xiaokun Song, *Between Civic and Ethnic: The Transformation of Taiwanese Nationalist Ideologies (1895–2000)* (Brussels: VUB Press, 2009).

5. Sara L. Friedman, "Mobilizing Gender in Cross-Strait Marriages: Patrilineal Tensions, Care Work Expectations, and a Dependency Model of Marital Immigration," in *Mobile Horizons: Dynamics Across the Taiwan Strait*, ed. Yeh Wen-hsin (Berkeley: Institute of East Asian Studies, 2013); William C. Kirby, "Global Business across the Taiwan Strait: The Case of the Taiwan Semiconductor Manufacturing Company Limited," in *Mobile Horizons*, ed. Yeh Wen-hsin; Stephane Corcuff, "Liminality and Taiwan Tropism in a Post-colonial Context. Schemes of National Identification Among Taiwan's 'Mainlanders' on the Eve of Kuomintang's Return to Power," in *The Politics of Difference in Taiwan*, ed. Tak-wing Ngo and Hong-zen Wang (New York: Routledge, 2011); Stephane Corcuff, "Taiwan's Mainlanders under Chen Shui-buian. A Shift from the Political to the Cultural?" in *Taiwanese Identity in the 21st Century: Domestic, Regional and Global Perspectives*, ed. Gunter Schubert and Jens Damm (London: Routledge, 2011).

6. Joseph R. Allen, *Taipei: City of Displacements* (Seattle: University of Washington Press, 2012); Stephane Corcuff, ed., *Memories of the Future: National Identity Issues and the Search for a New Taiwan* (Armonk, NY: M. E. Sharpe, 2002); Yeh Wen-hsin, "A Quiet Revolution: Oppositional Politics and the Writing of Taiwanese History," in *Mobile Horizons: Dynamics Across the Taiwan Strait*, ed. Yeh Wen-hsin (Berkeley: Institute of East Asian Studies, 2013). See also Mark Harrison, *Legitimacy, Meaning and Knowledge in the Making of Taiwanese Identity* (New York: Palgrave Macmillan, 2006); J. Megan Greene, "History, Identity, and Politics: The First Chen Shui-bian Administration's Efforts to Craft Taiwan's History," in *Presidential Politics in Taiwan: The Administration of Chen Shui-Bian*, ed. Steve Goldstein and Julian Chang (Norwalk, CT: EastBridge, 2008); and "The Historical Narrative and Taiwan Identity: The State Sponsored Historical Enterprise in Taiwan in the 1950s and 60s," *Chinese Historical Review* 13, no. 1 (Spring 2006): 78–91.

7. Allen, *City of Displacements*.

8. China was governed by Manchus, a steppe people from the northwest of China, during the Qing Dynasty (1644–1911). The Manchus wrested power in the 1640s from the Chinese Ming Dynasty.

9. Guoli bianyi guan [NICT], ed., *Guomin xuexiao lishi keben, gaoji di er zhuan* [National History Textbook, Advanced, Volume 2] (Taipei: Taiwan sheng zhengfu jiaoyu ting, 1964), 46. This is a high school textbook.

10. Guoli bianyi guan [NICT], ed., *Lishi, di san zhuan, chuji 3* [History, Volume 3] (Taipei: Taiwan sheng zhengfu jiaoyu ting, 1954), 44. This is a middle school textbook. There is limited evidence to support the assertion that Taiwan was Chinese prior to the 1680s.

11. Ibid., 119.

12. Guoli bianyi guan [NICT], ed., *Lishi, di er zhuan, gaoji 2*, [History, Advanced, Volume 2] (Taipei: Taiwan sheng zhengfu jiaoyu ting, 1954), 321–22.

13. "Putong gaoji zhongxue kecheng zhixing gangyao" [Outline for the Implementation of the Common High School Curriculum] (Taipei: Ministry of Education, June 2005), 39–79.

14. "Han Chinese" refers to Chinese people originating from or residing in mainland China who are not members of an ethnic minority group. Over 90 percent of Chinese in China are Han.

15. The Taiwan room at the National Palace Museum has housed such exhibits (for example, "Ilha Formosa: The Emergence of Taiwan on the World Scene in the Seventeenth Century"), and there have been other such exhibits in the basement of the National Taiwan Museum. This effort to revive and re-narrate the seventeenth century was also apparent in revisions to the history curriculum that occurred during Tu Cheng-sheng's tenure as minister of education (2004–2008).

16. These observations are based on notes from my visit to that exhibit on June 1, 2006, and on the brochure from the exhibit.

17. "Once Upon a Time in Taiwan" brochure, collected June 1, 2006.

18. These observations were made on a visit to the fort on June 20, 2006. Even the sixteenth-century Japanese are mentioned. According to the exhibit, they had designs on Taiwan under Hideyoshi.

19. Exhibition plaque, Rembrandt exhibit, British Consular Residence, Danshui, June 20, 2006.

20. "The Story of Collection in a Century: Special Exhibition of National Taiwan Museum, 5-18-2008 to 11-2-2008," brochure collected at National Taiwan Museum, 2008. This multilingual brochure was published in Chinese, English, and Japanese.

21. As the Taiwan independence movement gained strength in the late 1990s, capturing the support even of the president and leader of the KMT, Lee Teng-hui, names of public buildings, spaces, and institutions increasingly reflected this new understanding of Taiwan as a nation rather than a province of China.

22. Detailed descriptions of the roles of the collectors can be found in the exhibit catalogue, "The Story of Collection in a Century" [Bainian wuyu] (Taipei: Guoli Taiwan Bowuguan, 2008).

23. In fact, one might read the layout of the exhibit as implying that the Chinese, too, were just another imperial conqueror.

24. The National Palace Museum, which is filled with Chinese treasures that the KMT brought with them to Taiwan, is not only a major destination for Taiwanese school groups and families, it is also the one spot that nearly every tourist (especially those from the PRC) makes sure to go to in Taiwan, so exhibits in this venue that promote a uniquely Taiwan identity can play a diplomatic role in addition to helping people from elsewhere to understand Taiwan's unique past and its separate identity.

Patriot or Saint?

The Resurrection of a Soviet Hero and Post-Soviet Identity

ADRIENNE M. HARRIS

or centuries, Russians have struggled to define their collective identity, debated what unites the inhabitants of Russia, and repeatedly reevaluated their Russianness.[1] Between 1917 and 1991, Russians belonged to a larger community, the Soviet Union, and policymakers and propagandists consciously promoted this overarching Soviet identity. When the Soviet Union dissolved on December 25, 1991, Russians found themselves struggling with a complicated identity and, to an extent, an identity vacuum. Who exactly were the Russians and how should they respond? What aspects of their identity would outlast the Soviet state? What parts of the past should they salvage and which should they reject? No longer "Soviet," Russians fiercely debated their identity as a nation, as an "imagined community."[2] The enormity of this identity vacuum should not be underestimated. Homi Bhabha defines a nation as "a system of cultural signification"[3] in which national identity is located in a nation's cultural signs: its narratives, images, monuments, and heroes. In the decades since the collapse of the Soviet Union, Russians have reevaluated, rejected, and embraced the cultural signs and revised the history and myths inherited from the Soviet past.[4] In actuality, this revision began in 1987, before the collapse of the Soviet Union, following Mikhail Gorbachev's implementation of the glasnost and perestroika policies.[5] In many ways, these two policies contributed greatly to the collapse of the Soviet Union. Nevertheless, the dissolution of the USSR resulted in an intensification of debate as citizens struggled to define themselves collectively and to rewrite their national history when their nation no longer existed.

Two decades after this cataclysmic event, one of the most frequently cited, contested, and revered Soviet heroes continues to be Zoya Kosmodemyanskaya. Cultural studies scholar Catriona Kelly demonstrates through her work on Stalinist martyr Pavlik Morozov that an analysis of a myth or cult can shed light on both the circumstances that produced the hero as well as the cultural climate of subsequent decades.[6] Indeed, Zoya's image can be used as a lens through which to view the Soviet period as well as the post-Soviet transition. The purpose of this chapter is to analyze a small piece of the Zoya cult, asking how Zoya has helped define post-Soviet identity in a fractured Russia. Since 1991, disparate groups have begun using her image and narrative to define themselves, emphasizing her Communist, Soviet, Russian, and even Orthodox roots. With growing use of the Internet, these groups find themselves sharing space on forums dedicated to Zoya and other war heroes. Although she was initially a polarizing figure in 1991, she has increasingly functioned as a unifying figure and might yet prove foundational in the construction of a post-Soviet identity in Russia. Etienne Balibar has characterized nationality and religion as "two great competing models of a total institution . . . both which give death a symbolic signification." Zoya remains relevant precisely because she exists at a site of tension between these institutions: the Soviet and Russian nationalities and the Russian Orthodox religion.[7]

In my study of Zoya's role in Soviet and post-Soviet culture,[8] I analyze material in a wide variety of genres: published texts—novels; lyric, narrative, and epic poetry; plays; film scripts; newspaper articles; films; songs; informal interviews—mostly with librarians; card catalogs; public sculptures and art; museums and memorial sites; Internet sites, forums, and blogs; and archival documents—letters, articles, unpublished texts and photographs, and ritualized performances. Archival documents offer a glimpse into official and private responses to Zoya's narrative, the development of propaganda, the initiatives behind monuments, and the performance of commemorative rituals (documented in photographs and on film). I build on work from a wide variety of disciplines: history; literary and cultural studies, including visual cultural studies; anthropology; and gender studies. My background in literary, folklore, and cultural studies leads me to approach these hagiographic and "historical" narratives as constructed texts as I search for common themes and literary tropes that point to Kosmodemyanskaya's idealized characteristics and lead to broader conclusions related to valued traits. From the fields of history and cultural anthropology, I analyze narratives as reflections of collective memory and its evolution. From gender studies, I note gender-specific descriptors and gendered depictions of her body: how pronounced are her breasts? Is she wearing a dress, even though she was executed in pants? These approaches allow me to contextualize and understand the role of World War II heroes, women's images, and collective memory in Soviet and post-Soviet Russia.

The cult of Zoya began in January 1942. In late November 1941, a young woman operating behind enemy lines in the Moscow region was captured in the process of burning down a stable in the village of Petrishchevo. Although gravely tortured and forced to march undressed and barefoot for hours in the

FIGURE 1. School portrait of Zoya Kosmodemyanskaya, courtesy of the Russian State Archive of Socio-Political History.

snow, the woman, who identified herself simply as "Tanya," refused to divulge any information about her mission, and instead, delivered an inspiring speech to the Russian villagers assembled to watch her be hanged on November 29. The body hung in the square a month, and on New Year's Eve, perhaps as a warning, inebriated Nazis stabbed it with bayonets and cut off the left breast before finally submitting the body for burial. After the area's liberation several weeks later, Petr Lidov, a correspondent for the Soviet newspaper *Pravda*, learned of "Tanya's" fate. Lidov published the story in *Pravda* on January 27, 1942, and "Tanya" was identified as an eighteen-year-old Moscow schoolgirl, Zoya Kosmodemyanskaya, a special forces scout serving in the Partisan Unit No. 9903. Lidov's article contained all the hagiographic elements necessary, including Sergei Strunnikov's gruesome photograph of her exhumed body, to ensure Zoya's secular canonization as a Hero of the Soviet Union, and to fix her central position in the pantheon of Soviet saints.

Lidov's article allowed for a multiplicity of interpretations by the Soviet public. He simultaneously celebrated her military contribution, reported her inspiring last words, and relayed minute details about her torture, constructing a woman combatant/beautiful victim narrative. From the early days of Zoya's veneration, artists and writers responded to her story by creating literary and artistic depictions of her that could not be defined by a single femininity; she was at once a brave soldier, a loyal *komsomolka* (a female member

FIGURE 2. Sergei Strunnikov's postmortem photograph, courtesy of the Russian State Archive of Socio-Political History.

of the Communist Youth League), a dutiful daughter, and a pure girl; and as such, soldierly, filial, and maidenly femininities overlapped in her image and narrative. During the war, Zoya motivated her compatriots through two means. Many Soviet citizens were moved to emulate her behavior, proclaiming "We will be like Tanya!" Furthermore, angered by the victimization of such a young and innocent girl, her followers fought and worked harder, hoping to avenge Zoya by means of a Soviet war victory. Unique to Zoya's situation, the Soviet citizenry would retain a lasting image of Zoya's sacrifice and suffering: Strunnikov's accompanying photograph depicted an almost erotic image of the beautiful young woman, with her shirt pulled open, exposing her mutilation, and the rope still attached to her neck. In her cultural analysis of pain, literary critic Elaine Scarry reminds us that we must analyze wounds within their individual cultural contexts, in relation to other cultural signs.[9] Readers likely did not know that the body had been mutilated after death. Regardless, the image would have had a profound impact on a population that, until a generation before, had believed in the sanctity of the whole body upon death, so that it could enter the afterlife intact. Although rape was never mentioned, authors reacted to an assumption of violation by emphasizing Zoya's purity and her honor to acknowledge the violence perpetrated against her body. On a metaphorical level, Zoya's body represented Moscow and Russia (prior to the turning point in World War II—when they were most vulnerable), both grammatically feminine, both deeply tied to the maternal archetype. One can read the mutilation of her body and the desecration of maternal potential symbolized by her breast as mutilation of these greater symbolic feminine bodies. Zoya spontaneously became a national symbol in 1942. David Marsland notes that national symbols "recruit . . . individuals and organizations into national movements" and strengthen their commitment to those movements.[10] Zoya's fellow citizens collectively mourned her and vowed to avenge her by working harder and fighting more fiercely to defeat Nazi Germany. Reflecting upon Zoya's wartime function, conservative journalist Viktor Kozhemiako writes: "'For Zoya!'—this cry was carried through the ranks of defenders of the Motherland in the most difficult moment of the war . . . she appeared as a symbol of our invincibility and a sign of our coming victory."[11]

Recognizing the resonance of Zoya's image and narrative, the Soviet Union quickly began shaping her legacy to suit its purposes. Subsequent monuments and works of literature often engaged with Strunnikov's photograph and Lidov's narrative. From the war to the perestroika era, the Communist Youth League (Komsomol) attempted to control her representations and her role in culture as an ideal young woman. Her image evolved as individuals negotiated her memory for themselves within the context of Soviet propaganda. During the postwar period, Zoya came to function as a type of Soviet saint, further impacting the evolution of her monuments. The Komsomol and educational system introduced youth to Zoya through organized museum visits, presentations, and politically correct readings, and developed her myth. "Myth" should be understood as a specific narrative that aids a community in the construction of an identity, without any comment on the validity of the narrative; Zoya's case shows how multiple communities can adapt a narrative to construct their collective identities. During the Soviet period, Zoya's communities were Russia and the Soviet Union, and her identities were correspondingly politically Soviet and ethnically Russian. Then, as today, various members of these communities employed Zoya's narrative in the promotion of their identities. Zoya's narrative was such a powerful myth that it existed even before the politicized Soviet war cult detailed by historian Nina Tumarkin. During the Brezhnev era, as historian Jonathan Brunstedt has shown, party officials attempted to strengthen a nonethnic, Soviet national identity by embracing the war cult.[12] During the 1960s and 1970s, Zoya's image was folded into this war cult. Monuments to her proliferated and populated the vast expanse of the Soviet Union, from Rybnitsa, Moldova to Magnitogorsk. Even if they were not necessarily aware of the functions of national symbols, journalists writing in the 1960s and 1970s were quite mindful of Zoya's role as a symbol of positive qualities, claiming that she symbolized "purity and heroism," courage, fearlessness, and immortality.[13]

For the most part, Zoya's image was a unifying one. Her monolithic image began to crack, however, during the last years of the Soviet period. In 1991, at the end of glasnost, after challenging almost all of the Soviet "Truths," journalists finally questioned the last two previously untouched themes: the cult of Lenin and the cult of World War II, both saintly in nature.[14] In the process of this investigation, journalists projected the larger debate about the war upon its national symbols. The image of Zoya, a sacred martyr to some, and an extension of totalitarian propaganda for others, splintered in what was left of the fractured Soviet collective memory, and she became a locus of charged debate about the legacy of the Soviet Union and the righteousness of the Soviet war experience. Challenges to her story, and Soviet hagiography as a whole, demonstrated a need to probe even the most revered aspects of Soviet culture. Rumors and questions that had long circulated about Zoya and her *podvig*, or heroic feat, gained validity when they appeared in the press. Questions included: What was Zoya doing when she was killed? How could she have withstood the hours of torture? Was she mentally ill? Schizophrenic or masochistic? Who captured and executed her? Was she the girl executed in Petrishchevo? If not, then who was killed in Petrishchevo? Was anyone killed in Petrishchevo?

As challenges to the narrative removed Zoya from the sacred realm of myth and transformed her into a historical personage, believers were enraged. Political scientist Kathleen Smith explains that "liberals," whom she defines as "an assortment of Russian anticommunists who supported a mixture of market economics and political pluralism,"[15] linked commemoration of the war with Stalinism and demanded critical thinking about the war, relinquishing Soviet mythology as a means of moving forward beyond the Soviet experiment. Meanwhile, conservative communists considered such challenges to be threats to their patriotic heritage.[16] They ardently defended Zoya's narrative by citing canonical texts and reciting the dogma they had known from childhood. They objected to questioning the validity of Zoya's narrative in the first place. When a Komsomol-sponsored criminal investigation in cooperation with the KGB failed to produce earth-shaking results, the debate died down and museum officials and journalists lamented the public ignorance of Zoya altogether. The cult of Zoya slipped into a kind of hibernation as Russians weathered an unstable economy and changing values. Museum visits plummeted. The first ten years after the collapse of the Soviet Union saw a wave of anxiety and an identity vacuum that many attempted to fill.[17] During these first years, interest in religious cults grew dramatically.[18] In 1996, Boris Yeltsin futilely announced a contest for the new Russian idea to give the country direction. Communists continued to promote Soviet achievements, and above all, those related to the Great Patriotic War. Conservative journalists often proclaimed that forgetting war heroes like Zoya was akin to executing them anew,[19] but many, especially members of the younger generation, simply lost interest in Soviet heroes.[20]

Zoya's is an exceptional case. By 1996, visits to her museum had increased, even if they remained a fraction of the Soviet museum visits. Zoya's museum had received funds for both renovations and upkeep,[21] in contrast to other museums, which were repurposed or left to rot. By the end of the decade, it was clear that the Russian nation as a whole was more committed to remembering Zoya rather than most other war heroes. However, the second post-Soviet decade would see a wide variety of commemorations, as disparate groups approached her image by promoting various versions of their fractured past.

Rather than reinstating Yeltsin's search for the Russian idea, in 2000, the fifty-fifth anniversary of victory, Putin turned to World War II in his unifying rhetoric aimed at reviving patriotism and forging a national identity.[22] The capital cities of Moscow and St. Petersburg saw the renewal of Soviet commemorative rituals at sites sacred to the war, and Putin reintegrated "memory lessons" into the education system. During these "memory lessons," students learned about their forebearers' sacrifice during the war.[23] The renewed interest in World War II led to a steady stream of Russian films, documentaries, and miniseries and included a 2005 documentary that retold the Soviet narrative about Zoya.[24] These films have helped to develop patriotic pride and focus attention on the war.

With renewed interest in the war and with the documentary reinforcing the Soviet narrative of Zoya's *podvig*, the 2006 desecration of a Zoya statue in the symbolic city of Volgograd, formerly Stalingrad, prompted public outcry and local government action. The horrified responses corroborated what Michael E. Geisler proposes in his discussion of national symbols, that "the actual *destruction* of an important national monument carries a very different, and often traumatic, emotional charge."[25] The vandalism of her statue showed that the Soviet past *was* still contested, even in hero-cities,[26] but the public outcry that resulted in a 2008 "resurrection" of Zoya united veterans, communists, educators, and others as they restored and updated her image. Volgograd, of all places, is defined by World War II. Approaching the city, one sees the mammoth allegory of the Motherland calling her children to defend her. As in other cities destroyed in World War II, Volgograd's streets bear the names of fallen heroes. What is Volgograd if *not* for its war hero identity?

Victor Fetisov's 2008 restoration of Zoya, a dramatic departure from Soviet depictions, looks nothing like the plaster bust it replaced but is marked by features tied to the Soviet narrative and related mythology. The fabric of Zoya's slip is wrinkled and her bunched-up jacket alludes to sacrifice by emphasizing her left breast, the one cut off after her death. As in previous depictions, the folds of fabric clothe a strong body and her bound hands are clenched in fists. The figure's bare feet recall her martyrdom and her nearly naked, barefoot march in the snow on her last night. By constructing his three-meter statue out of white marble, a more permanent substance than the plaster of the original, Fetisov reflected the late-Soviet themes of Zoya's eternal youth and immortality. The white stone also alludes to the figure's innocence, a core theme from the inception of the myth. One can read Zoya's image as a representation of the Russian land itself and the women who experienced the war. Desecrated during the occupation, she remains the embodiment of purity, strength, and resilience. In contrast to the Motherland allegory, the lack of an elevated podium eliminates the distance between the viewer and the statue, removes Zoya from the overarching Soviet war cult, grounds her to the earth, and resituates her in the present as a concrete example of one who gave her life for her nation.

The statue, dedicated to "young, unconquerable patriots," demonstrates a view of heroism inherited from the Soviet, Communist past. Zoya is strong, determined, pure, self-sacrificing, and patriotic. This patriotism, this love for her country, is what makes her unconquerable. The dedication references the

FIGURE 3. Fetisov's sculpture in Volgograd.

unified collective of young people who put their nation before their individual selves in a way that passers-by, many attending the neighboring high school, might ponder. In his discussion of *lieux de mémoire* or sites of memory, Pierre Nora argues that at these sites, memory asserts itself as commemoration at the historical moment that marks a break from the past or a "sense that memory has been torn. . . . There are *lieux de mémoire*, sites of memory, because there are no longer *milieux de mémoire*, real environments of memory."[27] The Volgograd Zoya might make these passers-by remember not just Zoya, but other lessons from World War II. Through the inscription, the statue sends a message of strength and unity through patriotism and continues the process of turning Zoya's memorial into a national monument that began with the 2006 vandalism. Historian Bill Niven has pointed out that one should avoid reading war memorials as politically neutral sites, as commemorative rituals often involve political interests and can be particularly useful in constructing a collective political identity in the present.[28] Through the desecration of a simple bust erected by pioneers,[29] the vandals reignited the broader debate about the war, its heroes, and its Soviet heritage. Thus, the act transformed Zoya's regional monument into a national monument. The vague nature of the inscription legitimizes the reading of her statue as a monument to all veterans who served in World War II.

Volgograd has proven to be a dynamic site, a site of tensions where Zoya's myth continues to represent the conflict over the Soviet heritage. With respect to the increased attention devoted to and the dynamic treatment of Zoya's legacy, Volgograd is typical; the most interesting, revisionary developments have occurred in peripheral locations rather than in the capital cities. For instance, in Moscow and its environs, the rituals performed at sites tied to Zoya specifically—her execution site and her grave—function as renewed extensions of Soviet commemoration involving students honoring her memory. Many regional cities, like Volgograd, are located in the so-called "red belt," the region in which communist and conservative parties enjoy more popularity than in the capitals. However, in some of these cities, the cult of Zoya transcends the question of whether one should embrace or reject the Communist past and connects her narrative to a deeper past.

A movement originating in Tambov, the capital of the region in which Zoya was born, has taken the metaphorical "resurrection" of Zoya one step further. With the resurgence of the Russian Orthodox Church, Zoya is also being brought into the company of saints. At a 2008 conference marking what would have been her eighty-fifth birthday, a Tambov State University professor proposed the canonization of Zoya as a great martyr in the Orthodox Church, and a group of Tambov residents sent a formal request to Church officials.

FIGURE 4. Manizer's sculpture in St. Petersburg.

The Church defended its refusal to canonize Zoya by pointing out that she had been "a Komsomol member and Stalinist." While the online discussion that follows the article "Kosmodemyanskaya Must Become Saint Zoya"[30] shows that many Russians feel that ecclesiastical canonization is unnecessary or inappropriate, grassroots campaigns to situate Zoya within an Orthodox context have been developing in Tambov for at least a decade.

The roots of Zoya's canonization movement extend much further into the past than the Volgograd resurrection campaign and are specifically East Slavic.[31] Tumarkin has shown how the makers of Soviet propaganda relied upon Orthodox models for the cult of Lenin and later Stalin, demonstrating the compatibility of Orthodox forms with communist meaning. The veneration of saints, ancestors, and relics never entirely died out under Soviet rule. *Podvig* itself is originally an Orthodox concept. Elina Kahla notes that "the concept of *podvig*, connoting an exploit, a feat, or the virtuousness of a person, is organically linked with the concept of vita: the vita is about the exploits of a saint."[32]

Strunnikov's photograph showed a mutilated corpse with a serene, uncorrupted face, which did not go unnoticed by a people owning a long tradition of venerating uncorrupted corpses as saints. Thus Lidov's hagiographic account of Zoya's *podvig* and the accompanying photograph were enough to prompt Russians revising their past through an Orthodox prism to find saintliness in Zoya.[33]

Moreover, beyond simply focusing on Zoya's deeds, some of the most ardent proponents of the movement to canonize Zoya point to her supposedly Orthodox background. In doing so, they utilize a Soviet method of appraising its citizenry: the evaluation of citizens based on their roots—peasant, worker, intelligentsia, priestly, noble, etc. In Zoya's background, one finds a particularly useful bit of information: Bolsheviks executed Zoya's paternal grandfather for being a priest in 1918. He was canonized a saint in 2000. So if Zoya's grandfather had been an enemy of Bolshevism and her family was persecuted for their Orthodox beliefs, then, by extension, Zoya came from an entirely different background from the one Soviet propagandists promoted; in the view of the canonization proponents, she had always been a member of the Orthodox community, albeit secretly. Other advocates have reverted to mysticism to strengthen the connection between Zoya and her saintly grandfather: according to a local rumor, Zoya's grandfather had had an omen of his grandchildren's[34] martyrdom in a vision of two angels descending to the earth.[35]

While the resurrection of Zoya's image in Volgograd strengthens the ties between Zoya and her Soviet heritage, the Orthodox believers' emphasis on her ancestry and the initiative to canonize her as an Orthodox saint reconnect this Soviet martyr to her Orthodox, tsarist past. Their focus on her surname also links Zoya to two foundational early Christian martyrs, Cosmos and Damian, and gives evidence of a push to recast this Soviet woman as the most recent iteration of a millennium-long martyr tradition. By identifying the origins of Zoya's martyrdom in the deep Christian past, the Tambov group presents evidence that potentially undermines communist groups that cast Zoya as primarily a Soviet patriot. Balibar has posited that community rests "on the possibility of *hierarchizing* of all 'belongings,' making them compatible to each other."[36] His assertion might help us to understand why devout Orthodox acknowledge Zoya's wartime self-sacrifice yet focus on a supposed Orthodox connection.

In addition to drafting demands for canonization in letters and articles and on the Internet, proponents of canonization have begun visually connecting Zoya to the Orthodox tradition, creating neo-hagiographical depictions. One artist has painted a neo-icon depicting an infantilized Zoya as an Orthodox martyr.[37] For thirty thousand rubles, or roughly one thousand dollars, one can order a copy of "The Ascension of Zoya" from a St. Petersburg artist.[38] In addition to new visual representations of Zoya as an Orthodox martyr, some of her supporters have begun resituating her Stalinist form within the context of Orthodoxy. For instance, opposite the title page of the most recent book-length publication dedicated to Zoya, *You Remain Alive among the People: A book about Zoya Kosmodemyanskaya*, the editors included a photograph of Matvei Manizer's statue, erected in Tambov in 1947 in front of an Orthodox church.[39] The barrel of her rifle stands parallel to the crosses atop the cupolas. The photographer captured the image so that the statue of Zoya appears to look back toward the church. The church, Zoya, and the trees between them all form one composite picture in which she appears to be an extension of the church. Since the church stands behind the statue, the photograph sends the message that the Orthodox Church played a role in Zoya's formation and, as this is a Stalin-era statue, asserts the Church's role in the war. The photo sends the message that although obscured, the Church was always present and responsible for deeds such as Zoya's. Considering the extent to which Orthodoxy is entrenched in visual symbolism, these visual tactics are not surprising.

Cultural studies scholar Eliot Borenstein points out that in the first years after the collapse, Russians searching for an authentically Russian identity turned to folk heroes and the Romanovs.[40] However, after World War II ceased to be contested, even those who disavowed Communism and the Soviet past could also appropriate the war myth and the Soviet heroes of their youth into their Russian historical narratives, so long as Stalin and Communist baggage are absent or explained away, as in Zoya's neo-iconography and narratives.

As Kathleen Smith argues, "collective remembering has to do with framing the past in ways that attempt to capture the common experience that defines group identity."[41] Zoya's cult reveals a desire to embrace the memory of the war, in spite of knowledge revealed during glasnost, by cleansing the narrative of Stalinism and resituating it within an Orthodox context so that one may employ the myth in the formation of a truly Russian identity. A recent poem, written in 2001 by Vladimir Lesovoi of Nizhnyi Novgorod, does precisely that:

> Pray for Zoya and Sasha,[42]
> For our poor Motherland.
> Virgin Mary, Mother of God,
> Save those who died for just deeds,
> For the land, forests, and fields,
> For youth and for friends
> Even though they were Komsomol members,
> By choosing their own deaths, they were volunteers.
> Pray for Sasha and for Zoya—
> Lying under a mason's star,
> But the Lord received the charity
> For deathly torture, suffering.
> Who, in battle, gave with Eternal Blood,
> Consumed with heavenly love for Russia.
> Put a cross for them on their grave,
> So the Trinity will be strengthened.
> Submit an intention in a temple,
> So that they will not live in shame.
> Nothing will humiliate these moments—
> You know—the children of Cosmos and Damian.
> Simply, I count soldiers among the saints.
> Pray for Zoya and Sasha!
> They will shield our Motherland from harm![43]

So, if you pray for Zoya and her brother, Sasha (Aleksandr), they will protect the Russian homeland—they will intercede as national patrons. Their resituation within an Orthodox context would *strengthen* the Russian nation. Lesovoi also focuses on their martyrdom, for the "eternal blood" shed in battle. Although the Soviets celebrated martyrdom, martyrdom always has occupied a central position in Russian national identity. After all, the first Russian saints, Boris and Gleb, were canonized for peacefully submitting to death. Literary and religious scholar Judith Deutsch Kornblatt has shown that early in the post-Soviet period, many Russians began using Orthodoxy to define themselves,[44] so if "Orthodox" equals "Russian," then Lesovoi rerussifies Zoya and her brother. So too, historian Andrew Jenks has noted a similar approach to Soviet hero, cosmonaut, and martyr Yuri Gagarin. The post-Soviet period has seen numerous attempts to recast Gagarin as a secretly devout Orthodox believer,[45] so the reidentification of Zoya as Orthodox, and thus Russian, conforms to a larger trend toward the rehabilitation of Soviet heroes.

War heroes have proven to be useful in the construction of post-Soviet identity once their images are framed within the appropriate context. As we have seen in Tambov, Manizer's Stalin-era Zoya remains elevated above her compatriots on her pedestal yet marches forward in sync with the Orthodox Church. The recently opened Zoya Kosmodemyanskaya childhood room in the Osinovye Gai Zoia and the Aleksandr Kosmodemyanskye Museum attempt russification through a related means. Curators have situated the hero in a specifically Russian space by draping the room in Russian folk material culture: East Slavic folk textiles adorn the room from ceiling to floor, including a lengthy embroidered towel draped over icons in an icon corner, typical in traditional Russian homes. One wall bears a large portrait depicting an idealized Russian countryside, complete with a stream running through green hills and foregrounded birch trees, the national tree of Russia.[46] The birch tree and folk linens supplant Zoya's political past, replacing her Soviet identity with a Russian identity. The room entrenches the hero in a constructed ethnic Russianness, and it serves as an idealized space—fertile ground for selfless children who love their Motherland.

All of the above-mentioned efforts to cultivate Zoya's memory and incorporate her image into a post-Soviet Russian identity corroborate Edith Clowes's assertion that in post-Soviet identity, the periphery serves as "a place of creative intersections and productive challenges to the self-justifications of the center."[47] The dedication of the new museum in Osinovye Gai, the canonization movement in Tambov, and the resurrection of Zoya in Volgograd all transpired on the periphery. In contrast, Zoya's monuments and museums in the Moscow region have not evolved significantly during the post-Soviet period, in spite of renovation in Petrishchevo and relocation in Moscow. The exhibits remain largely unchanged from the Soviet period. Zoya's memory has proven to be considerably more dynamic outside of the center, beyond the capital cities.

Most strikingly, 2012 saw the dedication of the newest monument to Zoya in Zaporozhye, Ukraine, a primarily Russian-speaking city in Eastern Ukraine. This controversial monument stands next to a controversial Stalin statue in front of the local Communist Party headquarters. In this primarily Russian-speaking part of Ukraine, Zoya's memory transcends the political

border and plays a role among metaphorically displaced people; once Russian-speaking citizens of the Soviet Union, which privileged Russian, they
are now minority citizens of Ukraine. Unlike Fetisov's Volgograd Zoya, the
Zaporozhye Zoya resembles Stalin-era representations and points to a nostalgic longing for the Soviet past. In short, the most recent monument to Zoya
stands on the periphery of a periphery.

What specific role does Zoya serve for those preserving her memory? The
recent appropriation of Zoya's image by various groups shows how post-Soviet
Russians mine the narratives that formed Soviet collective memory. The resurrection of collective interest in Zoya complements the nationalist reappropriation of World War II under Vladimir Putin. Simultaneously, under Putin's
presidency, Russia has seen the most canonizations since the reign of Ivan IV.[48]
Zoya unifies disparate groups, appealing to those who identify with Soviet
myths and those who look to the deeper past for meaning. Perhaps Zoya will
maintain a prominent position in Russia's pantheon of heroes long after the collapse of the Soviet Union precisely because her image and narrative are both so
deeply rooted in overlapping layers of Russian culture, because she transcends
her Soviet origins, and because she sacrificed herself for the Soviet Union's most
celebrated victory, a victory that has only grown in significance under Putin.

In his analysis of post-Soviet cults, Borenstein notes that "rather than being
a distortion of truly Russian values, new religious movements are, if anything,
a distillation of a number of important trends in contemporary Russian culture . . . both the 'cults' in the former USSR and their detractors provide a
vivid snapshot of the Russian postmodern condition."[49] The last decade has
shown that for some, Zoya and the generation she represents have redeemed
the crimes of Stalinism, the regime that produced her, showing that celebrated
heroes of Stalin's time are worthy of veneration.

To answer the question in my title, it seems clear that for most, Zoya is both
a patriot and a saint because she suffered and died a martyr's death for her
nation. She represents a higher truth, an idealized version of Russian, Soviet,
and Orthodox values. Her various advocates celebrate her for her selfless love
for Russia. Her image acts as the antithesis of the figure Sergei Oushakine
identifies as the "New Russian Woman," a post-Soviet projection of unfamil-
iar, self-centered, and debauched tendencies associated with the "New Russia."[50] In contrast, Zoya functions as an idealization of the native selflessness
and morality that the religious associate with the Russian Orthodox Church
and that Communists nostalgic for the Soviet past deem Soviet. Zoya's appeal
to disparate groups during the past decade strongly suggests that Zoya's image
is foundational in the formation of a post-Soviet identity in Russia, an identity
strongly tied to the sacred memory of World War II.

The Fetisov monument, the canonization movement, the Zoya and Aleksandr room in Osinovye-Gai, and the apparition of Zoya before the Communist Party headquarters in Zaporozhye all exemplify what Svetlana Boym has termed "restorative nostalgia." Boym claims that restorative nostalgia "attempts a trans-historical reconstruction of the lost home. . . . Restorative nostalgia does not think of itself as nostalgia, but rather as truth and tradition. . . . Restorative nostalgia protects the absolute truth." She argues that it remains at the "core of recent national and religious revivals."[51] The nostalgic longing has served as fertile ground for Putin's increasingly strong post-Soviet revitalization of the cult of World War II. Zoya stands as a symbol of Soviet and Russian heroism. As the Internet continues to foster communities and connect diverse and geographically dispersed people through forums and blogs,[52] especially those living in the Russian periphery, the various representations of her image will likely continue to converge and evolve into an idealization of a specifically post-Soviet, Russian identity.

Notes

1. Simon Franklin and Emma Widdis, eds., *National Identity in Russian Culture: An Introduction* (Cambridge: Cambridge University Press, 2004), xi.

2. Benedict Anderson, *Imagined Communities: Reflections on the Origin and Spread of Nationalism* (London: Verso, 2006), 6–7.

3. Homi Bhabha, ed., *Nation and Narration* (London: Routledge, 1990), 2.

4. See Kathleen E. Smith, *Mythmaking in the New Russia* (Ithaca, NY: Cornell University Press, 2002); James V. Wertsch, *Voices of Collective Remembering* (Cambridge: Cambridge University Press, 2002).

5. Glasnost was Mikhail Gorbachev's policy of freedom of information and openness, and transparency in the activities of all government institutions in the Soviet Union (1986–1991). Perestroika refers to Gorbachev's political, economic, and social policy of restructuring the Soviet Union (1986–1991).

6. Catriona Kelly, *Comrade Pavlik: The Rise and Fall of a Soviet Boy Hero* (London: Granta, 2006).

7. Etienne Balibar, "Culture and Identity," trans. J. Swenson, in *The Identity in Question*, ed. John Rajchman (New York: Routledge, 1995), 180–81.

8. Balibar has questioned whether there can be such a thing as "Soviet culture" (177). I would argue emphatically that, yes, there was a Soviet culture that transcended the boundaries of Russia, Ukraine, etc., and that a post-Soviet culture exists in the various republics of the former Soviet Union.

9. Elaine Scarry, *The Body in Pain: The Making and Unmaking of the World* (Oxford: Oxford University Press, 1985), 118.

10. David Marsland, "National Symbols," in *Encyclopedia of Nationalism*, ed. Athena S. Leoussi (New Brunswick, NJ: Transaction, 2001), 220.

11. Viktor Kozhemiako, "Smertiiu smert' poprav," *Sovetskaia Rossiia*, accessed February 12, 2005, http://www.sovross.ru/old/2005/17/17_3_1.html.

12. Jonathan Brunstedt, "Building a Pan-Soviet Past: The Soviet War Cult and the Turn Away from Ethnic Particularism," *Soviet and Post-Soviet Review* 38 (2001): 149–71, esp. 167.

13. RGASPI (the Russian State Archive of Socio-Political History), F. M-7, Op. 2, D. 649/16, Ll, 30–31.

14. Nina Tumarkin, *The Living and the Dead: The Rise and Fall of the Cult of World War II in Russia* (New York: Basic Books, 1994), 187–88.

15. Smith, *Mythmaking*, 3.

16. Ibid., 85–86.

17. See Mikhail Yampolsky, "In the Shadow of Monuments: Notes on Iconoclasm and Time," trans. John Kachur, in *Soviet Hieroglyphics: Visual Culture in Late Twentieth-Century Russia*, ed. Nancy Condee (Bloomington: Indiana University Press, 1995), 93–112, esp.109–10; E. Borenstein, "Suspending Disbelief: Cults and Post-Modernism in Post-Soviet Russia," in *Consuming Russia: Popular Culture, Sex, and Society since Gorbachev*, ed. Adele Marie Barker (Durham, NC: Duke University Press, 1999), 437–62.

18. Borenstein, "Suspending Disbelief," 455–56.

19. Viktor Kozhemiako, "Tret'ia kazn': Zoiu i drugikh nashikh geroev opiat' ubivaiut," *Sovetskaia Rossiia*, November 29, 1997, 4.

20. Children's librarian N. V. Naumova claims that when offered two books, one presenting the hero as a Komsomol member or pioneer and one withholding this information, children almost always choose books that do not mention these vestiges of the Soviet period (interview with Naumova, July 23, 2010, at the State Children's Library in Moscow).

21. Kozhemiako, "Tret'ia kazn', 4.

22. Stephen Norris, "Guiding Stars: The Comet-like Rise of the War Film in Putin's Russia: Recent World War II Films and Historical Memories," *Studies in Russian and Soviet Cinema* 1, no. 2 (2007): 165; Lisa A. Kirschenbaum, *The Legacy of the Siege of Leningrad, 1941–1945: Myths, Memories, and Monuments* (Cambridge: Cambridge University Press, 2006), 287; Elizabeth A. Wood, "Performing Memory: Vladimir Putin and the Celebration of World War II in Russia," *Soviet and Post-Soviet Review* 38 (2011): 172–200.

23. Wood describes these "memory lessons" or *uroki pamiati* in Wood, "Performing Memory," 177–78.

24. Vladimir Kharchenko-Kulikovskii, *Zoia Kosmodem'ianskaia: Pravda o podvige (Zoia Kosmodem'ianskaia: The Truth about Her Feat* (Moskva: Studiia Tretii Rim, 2005).

25. Michael E. Geisler, "Introduction: What are National Symbols—and What Do They Do to Us?" in *National Symbols, Fractured Identities: Contesting the National Narrative*, ed. Michael E. Geisler (Middlebury, VT: Middlebury College Press, 2005), xxiii.

26. A "hero-city" is a Soviet honorary title granted to cities for their heroism and resistance to Nazism. All twelve cities are defined, in part, by their role in World War II.

27. Pierre Nora, "Between Memory and History: Les Lieux de Mémoire," *Representations* 26 (Spring 1989): 7.

28. Bill Niven, "War Memorials at the Intersection of Politics, Culture, and Memory," *Journal of War and Culture Studies* 1, no. 1 (2008): 40–41.

29. Pioneers were the communist equivalent of boy and girl scouts.

30. Liudmila Minaeva and Karina Vystavkina, "Kosmodem'ianskaia dolzhna stat' sviatoi Zoei," *Komsomol'skaia Pravda—Voronezh*, accessed September 23, 2008, http://www.kp.ru/daily/24168/380297/.

31. The East Slavic nations are Russia, Ukraine, and Belarus.

32. Elina Kahla, *Life as Exploit: Representations of Twentieth-Century Saintly Women in Russia* (Helsinki: Kikimora, 2007), 46.

33. In her analysis of partisan Liudmila Dediukhina's inclusion in a recent anthology "Realost' sviatosti," Kahla finds that "the representation of one major virtue, such as fighting Nazism, is the most important common denominator in Russian politically oriented neo-hagiography." Ibid., 50.

34. Zoia's brother Aleksandr, sixteen at the time of her execution, enrolled in a military academy and became a tank commander, demonstrating to the nation how one should avenge his sister. He was killed in battle on April 13, 1945, and was posthumously named a Hero of the Soviet Union.

35. Valentina Kuchenkova, "Otets Petr, Zoia, Shura," *Mir Bozhii* 1 (2001), http://vos.1september.ru/articlef.php?ID=200201704.

36. Balibar, "Culture and Identity," 189.

37. *Zoya Kosmodem'ianskaia forum*, accessed May 27, 2010, http://i057.radikal.ru/1003/9b/972681ff437e.jpg.

38. Michael Yudin's art website, accessed March 31, 2011, http://svoboda-hudozhnika.tiu.ru/p136152-voznesenie-zoi-kartina.html.

39. Manizer's statue is the most widely reproduced sculpture of Zoya. In addition to the 1947 Tambov copy, variants of the statue also stand in the Partizanskaia (formerly Izmailovskii Park) metro station in Moscow (1944) and in Victory Park in St. Petersburg (late 1970s). You can see the Tambov version with the church behind it at this site, accessed January 15, 2012, http://russights.ru/post_1315399427.html.

40. Borenstein, "Suspending Disbelief," 455–56.

41. Smith, *Mythmaking*, 5.

42. Zoya's brother, Aleksandr (1925–1945).

43. Vladimir Lesovoi, "Pravda o podvige Zoi i Sashi," *Nash Sovremennik: Literaturno-khudozhestvennyi i obshchestvenno-politicheskii ezhemesiachnyi zhurnal* 11 (2006), accessed December 11, 2011, http://www.nash-sovremennik.ru/p.php?y=2006&n=11&id=3.

44. Judith Deutsch Kornblatt, "'Christianity, Anti-Semitism, Nationalism': Russian Orthodoxy in a Reborn Orthodox Russia," in Barker, *Consuming Russia*, 415. While 82 percent of Russian respondents call themselves Orthodox, only 42 percent of Russians call themselves "believers," so Russians employ Orthodoxy as an identity marker that transcends religion. John Garrard and Carol Garrard, *Russian Orthodoxy Resurgent: Faith and Power in the New Russia* (Princeton, NJ: Princeton University Press, 2008), 245.

45. Andrew Jenks, *Russian History Blog*, accessed November 27, 2011, http://russianhistoryblog.org/2011/11/gagarin-as-christ/.

46. Marina Tursinaia, ed., *My Pobedili: 1941–1945*, accessed August 3, 2012, http://www.1941-1945-2010.ru/zoya1-06-00.htm.

47. Edith W. Clowes, *Russia on the Edge: Imagined Geographies and Post-Soviet Identity* (Ithaca, NY: Cornell University Press, 2011), 171.

48. Kahla, *Life as Exploit*, 60.

49. Borenstein, "Suspending Disbelief," 439.

50. Serguei Oushakine, "The Fatal Splitting: Symbolizing Anxiety in Post-Soviet Russia," *Ethnos Journal of Anthropology* 66, no. 3 (2001): 291–319.

51. Svetlana Boym, *The Future of Nostalgia* (New York: Basic Books, 2001), xviii.

52. Tursinaia, ed., *My Pobedili: 1941–1945*, accessed June 22, 2011, http://molodguard.ru/forum/viewtopic.php?f=15&t=277.

History and Memory in an African Context
A Case Study of Robben Island

ELIZABETH MACGONAGLE

W e all engage in memory work, but history—that is, our understandings and interpretations of it—plays a central role in framing acts of remembering. My interest in Africa's past has led me
to consider the tension between history and memory on the African continent and in the Diaspora. History and memory both matter for identities and
communities. Many scholars have come to view history as a form of social
memory, rather than an unbiased narrative or story.[1] They acknowledge that
collective memory, in turn, is a form of history, for how people remember
helps us to make sense of our past, ground us in the present, and prepare us
for the future.[2] Indeed, the ways in which we remember—and forget—shape
and shift our interpretations of history, of change over time, of disruption and
of continuity.[3] History *is* representation, and cultural memories are deployed to
benefit certain groups over others. "Traditions" turn into honored cultural institutions. The state shapes the identity of the national community by producing
historical narratives. Yet as the identity of the South African nation has changed
so dramatically since the 1990s, so has the notion of community. Groups once
fairly rigid under the segregated society of South African apartheid now cross
boundaries and challenge old orders. Not everything has changed, however, as
history and memory demonstrate in this African context.

National myths emerge from a blend of history and memory, fact and fiction. These myths are often quite inauthentic, but they become authentic and
highly symbolic, often appearing to be "natural." The state promotes a collective memory and attempts to control this very public memory despite its
ambiguous nature.[4] Yet often there are competing narratives that manage to
slowly erode national myths over the long term or swiftly override them in a
flash during political and economic transitions. Moments of transformation,
such as the heady time surrounding South Africa's attainment of full independence in 1994, provide evidence with which to examine how disclosure and
silence (public and private) work to shape social representations of history.

The setting for this examination of identity and community as manifested in national memory is Robben Island, the site of one of South Africa's most notorious prisons. Although the island itself near Cape Town has been used as a prison since the sixteenth century, it is known in the African collective memory as the place that held political prisoners who opposed the apartheid regime during the second half of the twentieth century (from 1961 to 1991).[5] It is the South African Alcatraz, if one were to make an American comparison. Nelson Mandela is the most famous former prisoner, but there are other leaders of the anti-apartheid struggle who endured the harsh conditions of confinement and forced labor in the quarry on Robben Island. They include Walter Sisulu, Ahmed Kathrada, and Jacob Zuma. In a small house on a separate area of the island, the apartheid regime kept Robert Sobukwe in solitary confinement. After the release of all political prisoners, this one island at the southern tip of the country emerged in the 1990s to encompass a national memory in the new South Africa. My focus in this chapter is on the histories and memories that encircle Robben Island, for the politics of remembering that surround the island and its past uses are as fraught with charged memories as the unsuccessful attempts of South Africans over several centuries to escape from confinement there.

Robben Island as a Site of Memory

The island is a significant *site of memory*, a physical space that reflects legacies of racism and oppression, while also marking the eventual triumph of the long liberation struggle against apartheid. The concept of *lieux de mémoire* (sites of memory) emerged from the scholarship of the historian Pierre Nora, who argued that spaces rooted in memory replaced traditional forms of memory. Nora has criticized historians for their heavy focus on social structures and a lack of sympathy "to the countless subjective and local views."[6] Likewise, I argue that attention to realms of memory can reveal multiple, important voices that need to be heard and analyzed. Nora's influential work on sites of memory in France suggests that history is suspicious of memory: "Memory installs remembrance within the sacred; history, always prosaic, releases it again."[7] Nora's work on memory has highlighted some of the assumptions and problems associated with the cultivation of heritage and the making of national or regional pasts. A growing group of scholars from an array of disciplines has enriched the concerns raised by Nora with their contributions over the past decade or so, including a substantial number who focus on Africa.[8] Robben Island, like the former slave forts in West Africa, is a "burdened" site of memory, since the island "graphically and viscerally embodies both the horrors of political repression and the victory of surviving against the odds," as Annie Coombes argues in her work on public memory after apartheid.[9]

Robben Island Museum opened in January 1997, and its website notes that the histories and memories emanating from Robben Island serve as "a poignant reminder to the newly democratic South Africa of the price paid for freedom."[10] The narrative of struggle and resistance lies at the heart of the new South African state, given that the ruling party since 1994, the African National Congress (ANC), labored to end apartheid for decades. But how does the recent wave of tourists and local visitors to the Island, a UNESCO World Heritage Site since 1999, affect the legitimization of the South African state in this postapartheid era? What is the state's relationship with the collective memory surrounding the island, given the deep connections of the African National Congress to this space? Although the political prisoners were released with the fall of apartheid, the prison walls still hold a history of overlapping and competing perspectives. In this chapter I analyze how South Africans and other stakeholders remember and manipulate both history and memory on Robben Island, where the physical remnants of the prison and the surrounding terrain serve as memorials to be interpreted by former prisoners and guards, local South Africans, and foreign tourists.[11] As Harriet Deacon has convincingly argued, the "significance of the island today lies not so much in what actually happened there as in how its history has been interpreted and represented."[12] My investigation of the intersections between history and memory draws on methods that include participant observation from site visits, a consideration of past uses, analysis of the public and official presentation of the island's history, and the reflections of visitors and former prisoners. As Jarrett Bromberg and other authors argue in their respective chapters, museums and memorials are texts themselves that serve as public expressions of identity.

There is a powerful mythology surrounding Robben Island that clouds and shrouds it. Harry Garuba observes, "The island is one of those overtextualised places and sites which become impossible to 'see' or narrate without the conditioning of prior texts and discourses."[13] Robben Island plays a central role in the dominant narrative of the liberation struggle, and former prisoners talk of leaving the island with a "university" degree and becoming men in this gendered and politicized space. The Robben Island Museum website notes that this educational philosophy involved "strategies for a future society based on tolerance, respect and non-racialism [that] were nurtured and implemented by political prisoners. The emphasis on education, debate, and on lifelong learning is a testimony to the fight for justice and education, and is a key to Robben Island's role as a heritage site and its human rights discourse."[14]

According to Deacon, former prisoners brokered this interpretation of the island as "the crucible of change in South Africa."[15] Indeed, Kgalema Motlanthe, one of South Africa's former presidents, reflected in a 1992 interview:

> These were very enriching years in that we were a community of people who ranged from the totally illiterate to people who could very easily have been professors at universities. We shared basically everything, every problem even of a personal nature we discussed with others and a solution would be found. The years out there were the most productive years in one's live [sic], we were able to read, we read all the material that came our way, took an interest in the lives of people even in the remotest corners of this world. To me those years gave meaning to life.[16]

Meaning Is Given to Life and Myth

The discourse surrounding Robben Island suggests, at first glance, that there was one apartheid (of the Afrikaner, or Boer) fought by one adversary (the ANC). But, in fact, there were many apartheids, large and small, that were attacked by a multitude of brave men and women from various groups (that made up the anti-apartheid movement) seeking freedom. Thus, there are "various personal and public memories of the island, memories which are often unequal in scope and power."[17] This reality has led to a contested symbolism surrounding the island and "eddies of debate" that, in the words of Deacon, "are now part of a broader contest over the structure and meaning of the new South Africa and how to interpret its past."[18] Memory pools around Robben Island run deep, for the collective memory of the island is wrapped up in the legitimation of the postapartheid state and the narrative of struggle that defined the African National Congress during the apartheid era.[19]

In South Africa, there is "an active tradition of probing the relationships between memory and history, within the academy, the heritage sector and in public discourse," as Pumla Dineo Gqola notes in her work on slave memory in South Africa.[20] Oral history is supported, promoted, and respected alongside a post-apartheid push to reveal the workings of the apartheid state and its opponents.[21] This feeds into the broader human rights culture of a new nation that has overcome adversity. The Truth and Reconciliation Commission is evidence of this need to expose the histories of lies, trauma, secrets, violence, and repression that long have been hidden just below the surface of South African history.

A bold example of drawing from memory pools in the attempt to engage in memory work related to Robben Island comes through the use of former political prisoners as guides on the island. By employing former inmates of the prison, Robben Island Museum is attempting to "give 'voice'" through narrative, as Harry Garuba argues.[22] And yet there is "not likely" to be "a space for the truly personal experience to emerge in the narratives of the tour guides of Robben Island who had been inmates in the prison," according to Garuba.[23] Rather, the dominant public narrative of the anti-apartheid struggle structures the discourse and overshadows individual agency. The complicated nature of history also interferes with a packaged museum narrative. So despite the paradox noted by Garuba of having former political prisoners as "objects on display" that are also "subjects with a speaking voice," the collective memory of "the struggle" dominates the experience of visitors to the island.[24] Once again, multiple memories and identities of various communities flow into the memory pools that encircle the island. Yet Robben Island is "remembered" by locals and tourists in a certain way through specific scripted experiences.

Garuba himself, a South African academic, has written of his own initial unease about the use of former inmates as tour guides.[25] He questioned the logic of making "the sufferers tell the story of their personal pain all over, again and again, several times a day, to an audience of tourists."[26] He thus explored how individual memories relate to larger questions of memory, subjectivity, and agency.[27] As difficult as it may be to ask former prisoners to interact with tourists, this activity seems more appropriate to me than an earlier situation I encountered in 1999 just as Robben Island was declared a World Heritage Site. During that visit, which was before the construction of the Nelson Mandela gateway, a former prison guard operated a small "gift shop" at the modest ferry terminal on the mainland.[28] He sold postcards and small souvenir items. Although one can see the value of including this white man in the public face of the island's past, there seemed to be no accountability in his current line of work selling trinkets on the waterfront. Here was a defender of the apartheid regime now exploiting his former role for capitalist gain after the closure of the prison and the end of an era. More recently, during a visit in 2012, a woman of color served as my tour guide during the bus trip to several locations on the island. Once we reached the prison, a former political prisoner took over as our guide to provide an "authentic" tour of the structure and to detail the segregated treatment of inmates under the apartheid regime. This guide, Sipho Nkosi, shared some of his personal stories with humor and grace while also providing information about the grueling, inhumane conditions that prisoners endured on the island.

Symbolism and the State

In considering postcolonial memory, specifically memories after the end of apartheid, I am concerned with "the ongoing effects and processing of . . . historical consciousness."[29] Specifically, I question how the state has sought to shape public memory surrounding Robben Island for audiences local and global, domestic and international. One of the first things that may not come to mind when you think of Robben Island is slavery. That is probably because the recent use of the island as a prison for political activists jailed during the apartheid regime is more familiar to the modern world as a cultural marker. Slavery in South African history has only surfaced recently in popular culture, prompting Gqola, among others, to examine the recent visibility of slave memory. Slaves were imprisoned on the island as part of a pattern since the seventeenth century, when Europeans first used Robben Island to banish, isolate, and imprison those who resisted enslavement and other colonizing endeavors.[30] Even though South Africans have actively shaped their own histories in their ties to Robben Island, the site is frozen in a particular period for many people—the time during the imprisonment of Nelson Mandela. This telescoping of the island to its recent use as a maximum-security prison since 1961 allows the island to "escape" from earlier histories as well as more recent developments since Mandela's transfer to Pollsmoor prison on the mainland. The island was used in the eighteenth century to detain "the worst criminals and most dangerous political opponents of the Dutch East India Company."[31] In the nineteenth century, the island housed a hospital for lepers, the insane, and the sick poor, with the last patients removed in 1931.[32]

Attempts to recast the island's symbolic meaning occurred not only in the 1990s, but also earlier in the mid-nineteenth century. At that time, there was a call to reform the island asylum on humanitarian grounds and attempts to promote it as a place of cures rather than banishment.[33] Scholars have documented the contested future of Robben Island over the course of the twentieth century, which included calls to transform the island into a leisure resort, peace center, or nature reserve. Given the island's great political and symbolic value for the anti-apartheid movement, the apartheid regime relocated many imprisoned leaders in 1982 to prisons on the mainland to minimize the significance of the island as a site of resistance.[34] Yet this move neither erased the memory of these resistance leaders among their supporters worldwide, nor diminished the symbolism of Robben Island as a place of injustice controlled by a racist regime. The island remained a rock-hard symbol of oppression.

Even though this symbol of oppression and injustice no longer houses political prisoners, Robben Island has helped to legitimize the post-apartheid state since 1994 by proclaiming that activists-as-survivors have triumphed. These former prisoners moved from behind bars to the front of the nation as prominent leaders and government officials. Some of the most memorable images of Mandela spread throughout the world include his February 1990 walk of freedom (after his release from Victor Verster prison on the mainland) and the casting of his own ballot during the first nonracial democratic elections in 1994. The mere existence of the prison on Robben Island, as a former prison today, evokes the political prisoner–turned-leader narrative of other newly independent African states such as the Congo (with Patrice Lumumba), Kenya (with Jomo Kenyatta), and Ghana (with Kwame Nkrumah). The liberation of prisoners becomes a symbol of national liberation and a signal that these men are prepared (through participating in the "university of the struggle") to lead the nation.[35] Political significance emerges from the personal experiences of former South African prisoners, and some serve as "cultural brokers" who are "redefining public images of the island through the publication of prisoner memoirs and interviews in the press."[36] Robben Island, and Mandela's imprisonment there, has come to represent African resistance and the liberation of South Africa.

There are other cases of governments attempting full control of heritage sites and representations of history associated with them. In neighboring Zimbabwe, the archaeological ruins of Great Zimbabwe, a medieval city, are one example of this, both with their silences and the state's pronouncements of Great Zimbabwe as a place of national liberation.[37] Great Zimbabwe and Robben Island are used "as a means of locating and constructing 'national' memory" through the symbolism of independence, poignantly and ironically, since the island was a prison.[38] When Robben Island became a national monument in 1996, its empty cells stood as "the first monument to the death of apartheid."[39] And even though most South Africans have not visited the island, Robben Island stood out in the public memory as a place to celebrate victory rather than a space to commemorate martyrs.[40] With the country transformed into the "new South Africa," a Rainbow nation, the island was remade to mark the end of apartheid, celebrate the achievement of democracy, and forecast the hopes for South Africa's future. Thus, Robben Island has come to be forward-looking and to symbolize the *future* of South Africa rather than its past.[41] Robben Island played an important and contested role in the shaping of public memory during South Africa's transition to democracy in the 1990s, in part by glossing over personal memories in favor of constructing this forward-looking metanarrative. Conversely, the privately run Museum of Apartheid in Johannesburg may preserve some personal memories as it tries to construct a public memory that does look back in time, despite the fact that scholars have convincingly argued that heritage is actually something new even though it looks old.[42]

What does it mean today to remember on Robben Island, where apartheid is exposed in some of its nakedness? For South Africans and foreign visitors, there are histories and memories of the past that confront issues of morality and race as the island is used to build South Africa's future.[43] Public heritage programs of the Robben Island Museum include school tours, independent camps, and nation-building youth camps that aim to "develop a sense of citizenship in young people based on a culture of human rights and responsibilities."[44] There is also a resource center on the island for researchers and interns. Public outreach included a play staged in 2010 at the Nelson Mandela Gateway on the mainland waterfront.[45] One might argue, as Deacon has, that the island now "houses what is at the heart of the new South Africa."[46] The state, however, uses the island to build a future out of a stock narrative of public memories that erase personal ones. The island diverts attention away from persistent poverty throughout South Africa and unfilled promises of the African National Congress. The closure of the prison on the island and the election of Nelson Mandela in 1994 serve as happy endings to a packaged story that fails to acknowledge the broad scope of continued suffering in South Africa.

The Island and the Shadow of Mandela

What would people think of Robben Island if Mandela had not been imprisoned there for so many years? Mandela is so deeply rooted in South Africa's recent past, so essential to its histories and memories, so enshrined and worshiped, that he is rendered untouchable (and yet so very touchable, as in approachable) by people around the world. From concerts in Europe and YouTube clips, to Nelson Mandela Avenue in New York City, Mandela is an icon, a hero, a statesman, a revered elder, and a family man. His name is also synonymous with Robben Island and the public memory surrounding it. But does this obscure other histories and other prisoners? Perhaps not, since Mandela represents every man, every prisoner. His sheer likability, his natural grace and gravitas, and his respected spirit of resistance allowed him to be the face behind so many unnamed others who suffered the same injustice and fought against the same indignities. Mandela's popularity and connection to the island bring foreign tourists to the Robben Island Museum, where they arguably learn more about South Africa's past than they do on safari. The mainland departure point for a ferry to the island is called the Nelson

Mandela Gateway (opened officially by Mandela on December 1, 2001), and this name says something about Mandela and his connection to the island. Upon arriving at the gateway, you have access to a part of Mandela—to his cellblock on the island, to a view of his most intimate, yet public, space for seventeen years. Mandela's personal becomes public through the viewing of his cell. The connection of the *place* of Robben Island is made through the *person* of Mandela.

In fact, during fieldwork in 2007, one group of tourists that I observed at the Nelson Mandela Gateway considered abandoning their plans to visit the island when they were told that Mandela's cell was closed for renovations. They quite vocally expressed their dismay at this state of affairs and asked the local South African who had announced the news of Mandela's cell closure, "Why didn't you tell us before we bought our tickets?" Although there were several posted signs in the gateway that noted the situation, they prepared to leave the ferry queue and secure a refund for their tickets. The South African who had made the announcement then reminded the crowd that there were other cellblocks to visit that housed additional political prisoners. This information, delivered, and received it seems, as a reproach, prompted them to remain in line to board the ferry and tour the island with Mandela's cell sight unseen. This incident is just one example of how Mandela's ties to the island bind him so tightly to meanings and memories surrounding it. The state, and the tourist, cannot consider history and memory on Robben Island without dealing with Mandela's connections to it and the discourse surrounding South Africa's past.[47]

Memory Work

Robben Island is a physical space, but it is also a key location for situating the nation, as Coombes has argued.[48] The island is a symbol of national transformation and a symbol of the new nation. This significance has "important consequences for national identity" in South Africa.[49] But the prominent symbolism of Robben Island also binds it so closely to Mandela and superimposes a metanarrative of the public (or his private-cum-public) over the personal. Even the former political prisoners who serve as tour guides cannot overcome this staging, for Robben Island is a politically sensitive site that the state has managed to situate into the "official" public memory as a national symbol of a promising future emerging out of a tragic past. The ANC has been careful to avoid any "vulgar commercialism" (in the words of Ahmed Kathrada) that might exploit the popularity of Mandela, and they have successfully prevented a "circus" atmosphere from arising, as Mandela himself feared early on in 1991 when there was talk of turning the island into a resort with a casino.[50] With memory as "a site of struggle for liberation and ideological contestation," history takes a back seat to this drama on Robben Island.[51]

Recent perceptions of the state's role in the past continue to shape how memory and history function on Robben Island. A collective memory has coalesced around the time of the imprisonment of Mandela and other political prisoners. On the one hand, this move toward a "more consensual history" serves to repair the fractured landscape of South African memory.[52] But the ties that bind may also cut; collective histories and identities need to be built on realities rather than myths alone. The twentieth-century view promoted by the ANC is the "short history" in South Africa's historical consciousness, despite the different periods of the island's—and indeed the nation's—deeper history. The prison on Robben Island and the museum at the Nelson Mandela Gateway are official representations of the resistance to apartheid that defines South Africa's recent past. And yet the island and museum serve to solidify the ANC's hold on the *future* more so than its grip on the past. The prolific written and oral histories emanating from South Africa may offer representations of the past, but the memory making that takes place around Robben Island is of a decidedly future-oriented nature.

One hopes that more inclusive histories will develop and compete to transcend history as it stands today.[53] South Africa's public memory, much of it bound up with Robben Island, has shaped a national identity. The many fluid communities within a democratic South Africa, however, have the power to influence the direction of the nation through renegotiation and, in turn, chart their own destinies.

Notes

1. See, for instance, work on an anthropology of memory by Abdelmajid Hannoum, including "Memory at the Surface: Colonial Forgetting and Racial Citizenship in France," in *Cultural Critique* (in press).

2. I am using the term *collective memory* to describe a memory that "emphasizes its social or collective nature" as outlined by Jeffrey K. Olick, Vered Vinitzky-Seroussi, and Daniel Levy in their introduction to *The Collective Memory Reader* (Oxford: Oxford University Press, 2011), 5. My interest in this type of memory follows the work of Halbwachs and others. See, for example, Maurice Halbwachs, *The Collective Memory* (New York: Harper and Row, 1980). For a pertinent discussion of collective and public memories, see the introduction to Ana Lucia Araujo, ed., *Politics of Memory: Making Slavery Visible in the Public Space* (New York: Routledge, 2012).

3. See, for example, Paul Ricoeur, *Memory, History, Forgetting* (Chicago: University of Chicago Press, 2004).

4. See, for example, David W. Blight, "Historians and 'Memory,'" *Common-Place* 2, no. 3 (April 2002), http://www.common-place.org/vol-02/no-03/author/.

5. Portuguese convicts were first imprisoned in about 1525. A chronology is listed on the Robben Island Museum website at www.robben-island.org.za/.

6. John Bodar, "Pierre Nora, National Memory, and Democracy: A Review," *Journal of American History* (December 2000), 953.

7. Pierre Nora, "Between Memory and History: Les Lieux de Mémoire," *Representations* 26 (1989), 9.

8. Two recent examples are João Sarmento, *Fortifications, Post-colonialism and Power: Ruins and Imperial Legacies* (Surrey: Ashgate, 2011), and Katharina Schramm, "The Slaves of Pikworo: Local Histories, Transatlantic Perspectives," *History and Memory* 23, no. 1 (Spring/Summer 2011): 96–130.

9. Annie E. Coombes, *History after Apartheid: Visual Culture and Public Memory in a Democratic South Africa* (Durham, NC: Duke University Press, 2003), 69.

10. Robben Island Museum website.

11. The remaining prison buildings were all built after 1960. Other nineteenth-century buildings from the Victorian village and installations from World War II are also on the island. Harriet Deacon, "Remembering Tragedy, Constructing Modernity: Robben Island as a National Monument," in *Negotiating the Past: The Making of Memory in South Africa*, ed. Sarah Nuttall and Carli Coetzee (Oxford: Oxford University Press, 1998), 164, 169.

12. Deacon, "Remembering Tragedy, Constructing Modernity," 164.

13. Harry Garuba, "A Second Life: Museums, Mimesis, and the Narratives of the Tour Guides of Robben Island," in *Desire Lines: Space, Memory and Identity in the Post-Apartheid City*, ed. Noëleen Murray, Nick Shepherd, and Martin Hall (London: Routledge, 2007),132.

14. Robben Island Museum website.

15. Deacon, "Remembering Tragedy, Constructing Modernity," 173.

16. Kgalema Motlanthe in a July 14, 1992 interview with Padraig O'Malley, collected in *The Heart of Hope: South Africa's Transition from Apartheid to Democracy*, posted at http://www.nelsonmandela.org/omalley/. The interview transcript is available at http://www.nelsonmandela.org/omalley/index.php/site/q/03lv00017/04lv00344/05lv00607/06lv00633.htm. Portions of this same excerpt are also cited in James Myburgh, "Who is Kgalema Motlanthe?" *Politics Web* (September 25, 2008), http://www.politicsweb.co.za/politicsweb/view/politicsweb/en/page71619?oid=104369&sn=Detail.

17. Deacon, "Remembering Tragedy, Constructing Modernity," 161. For one personal memory that was shaped by the resistance movement, see Indres Naidoo, as told to Albie Sachs, *Robben Island: Ten Years as a Political Prisoner in South Africa's Most Notorious Penitentiary* (New York: Vintage, 1982).

18. Deacon, "Remembering Tragedy, Constructing Modernity," 161.

19. The idea of memory pools is from Joyce Carol Oates, "A Widow's Story," *New Yorker*, December 13, 2010, 74–75.

20. Pumla Dineo Gqola, *What Is Slavery to Me? Postcolonial/Slave Memory in Post-apartheid South Africa* (Johannesburg: Wits University Press, 2010), 10.

21. Patrick Harries pointedly notes, however, that this movement favors consensus over division to produce "an ambiguous and sometimes confusing image" related to the operation and impact of apartheid. "From Public History to Private Enterprise: The Politics of Memory in the New South Africa," in *Historical Memory in Africa: Dealing with the Past, Reaching for the Future in an Intercultural Context*, ed. Mamadou Diawara, Bernard Lategan, and Jörn Rüsen (New York: Berghahn, 2010), 126.

22. Garuba, "A Second Life," 129.

23. Ibid., 143.

24. Ibid.

25. Garuba is an Associate Professor at the University of Cape Town.

26. Garuba, "A Second Life," 131–32.

27. Ibid., 132.

28. In July 2012 there was a gift shop on the island's pier and another on the mainland inside the Nelson Mandela Gateway. Items for sale included children's books, t-shirts, and caps celebrating Nelson Mandela International Day (July 18).

29. Gqola, *What Is Slavery to Me?*, 10.

30. Robben Island Museum website.

31. Deacon, "Remembering Tragedy, Constructing Modernity," 162.

32. Ibid.

33. Ibid., 174–75.

34. Ibid., 168.

35. Ibid., 174.

36. Ibid., 163, 165.

37. Joost Fontein has pointed this out in *The Silence of Great Zimbabwe: Contested Landscapes and the Power of Heritage* (New York: UCL, 2006).

38. Coombes, *History after Apartheid*, 93.

39. Deacon, "Remembering Tragedy, Constructing Modernity," 164.

40. Ibid., 164–65.

41. Ibid., 164.

42. Ibid., 177; Garuba, "A Second Life," quoting Kirshenblatt-Gimblett in his epigraph.

43. Robben Island is one of many sites that attempt to confront visitors, at least partially. The apartheid museum in Johannesburg and a number of other sites strive to accomplish this too.

44. Robben Island Museum website. A council appointed by the Minister of Arts and Culture governs the museum.

45. Robben Island Museum website.

46. Deacon, "Remembering Tragedy, Constructing Modernity," 178.

47. For an interesting discussion of Mandela as a tourist attraction and initiatives to erect statues of Mandela in various parts of South Africa, see chapter 10 of Sabine Marschall, *Landscape of Memory: Commemorative Monuments, Memorials and Public Statuary in Post-apartheid South-Africa* (Leiden: Brill, 2010).

48. Coombes, *History After Apartheid*.

49. Deacon, "Remembering Tragedy, Constructing Modernity," 165.

50. Ibid., 170.

51. Ali Khangela Hlongwane, "Commemoration, Memory and Monuments in the Contested Language of Black Liberation: The South African Experience" *Journal of Pan African Studies* 2, no. 4 (June 2008): 135.

52. Patrick Harries, "From Public History to Private Enterprise," 121, 125. This shift echoes a global movement of creating more inclusive histories.

53. I take inspiration for this point from Lucy Campbell's Transcending History Tours, based in Cape Town, https://sites.google.com/site/capeslaveroutetours/.

"Ten Million Trujillos Is All We Are"
Dominican Identity beyond the *Trujillato*

SHELLY JARRETT BROMBERG

n the final pages of the Pulitzer Prize–winning novel *The Brief Wondrous Life of Oscar Wao* (2007), Oscar's sister, Lola, as she is leaving the Dominican Republic for what she expects to be the last time, stoically concludes, "Ten million Trujillos is all we are."[1] This idea that the legacy of dictator Rafael Trujillo persists and continues to shape Dominican identity and the nation is salient. Indeed, throughout the past fifty-one years, the *trujillato*, as his reign was and is called, has been present politically, socially, and culturally. It was Trujillo's right-hand man, Joaquín Balaguer, who would occupy the presidency on three different occasions between 1960 and 1996. And while the Trujillo family asserts they want no part in the country's political activities, their presence on the national stage has been most recently confirmed by the publication of Angelita Trujillo's memoir of her father, *Trujillo mi Padre: En Mis Memorias*, which won the Dominican Republic's "National Literature Award" for 2009.[2] Consisting of over six hundred pages replete with hundreds of photographs of the Trujillo family, this monumental work presents a very different account of Trujillo and his exploits over the course of his thirty-one-year reign.

In sharp contrast to the dominant narratives of previous years, however, in which Trujillo is posited as the father and modernizer of the Dominican Republic, the voices of opposition to this revisionist history are growing in a variety of public and individual forums both on the island and in the United States. What is at stake here is much more than simply competing versions of Dominican history. Rather, for many, the ongoing attempt to rewrite the thirty-one years of the Trujillo dictatorship and the subsequent decades of "Trujillismo without Trujillo" implies the erasure of collective memories and experiences that, for many Dominicans, are key markers of their national and cultural identity. As W. James Booth explains, collective memory relies on a shared "life in common," which binds together the past and the present. When a community is "robbed" of these shared memories, "something that is a part of us, something essential to who we are" is destroyed.[3] What then has changed in Dominican experience to make possible this overt refusal to accept the fictions perpetrated by supporters of Trujillo and the *trujillato*?

For the Dominican Republic one of the most important and salient examples of this struggle for Dominican identity can be found in the ongoing debate surrounding the lives and murder of the Mirabal sisters in November 1960. The legacy of the Mirabal sisters, who are still considered important figures in the anti-Trujillo movement of their day, is in fact a key cultural marker of Dominican identity that has taken on added significance in the years following the end of the Cold War. After three decades of overt and covert US intervention in the Dominican government following Trujillo's assassination in 1961, the "Butterflies," as they were called, emerged as an important example of resistance and resilience that would reawaken lost histories and ignite future ones central to contemporary expressions of Dominican identity and nationhood. Yet their "meaning" in contemporary Dominican nationalism has been complicated by the insistence on the part of many of Trujillo's heirs and followers that Trujillo was not involved in the death of the sisters and that groups such as the Manolo Tavárez foundation and others are guilty of blasphemy and left-wing propaganda.[4] Two interrelated events, which are the focus of this chapter, highlight how the oppositional narratives of the *trujillato*, long suppressed in contemporary Dominican society, become important sites of confrontation that recall the traumatic legacy of dictatorship and renew Dominican identity. First, the 1994 publication of Dominican American Julia Alvarez's novel, *In the Time of the Butterflies*, would raise the level of awareness of the Mirabal sisters in the Dominican Republic, the United States, and the world. Second, the 1996 election of the first post-Balaguerian president, Leonel Fernández, would indirectly and then more openly challenge the dominant *trujillato*, leading to the institutionalization of the anti-Trujillo struggle during the dictatorship, including the role of the Mirabal sisters. This chapter investigates their legacy as a touchstone for Dominican identity in the twenty-first century.

Methodology and Definition of Terms

In this chapter I use a variety of discourses about the Mirabal sisters drawn from films, novels, memoirs, webpages, media accounts, museums, and memorials. I chose these sources because, in varying degree, they are public expressions of experience and identity. How these "texts" impact and are impacted by the place of the Dominican Republic in relation to US foreign policy during and after the Cold War helps to illuminate the island nation's struggle to remember the past and imagine the future, especially in relation to the competing legacies of the Mirabal sisters and Trujillo. Clearly, the veneration of the sisters, especially as mothers and martyrs, fits well within the predominantly masculine discourses of Dominican identity, even in the present. I also agree with Maja Horn when she argues that any study of "dominicanidad" must take these discourses into account in order to counter the oversimplified concepts of homogenized identity promoted by the *trujillato*.[5] Yet even in this traditional reading of their exploits, these women became forces of change that, first, would expose the limits of masculine power and brutality and, second, would provide, at the very least, the beginnings of a more nuanced and contemporaneous recognition of the role of women as leaders and revolutionaries within the Dominican Republic.

Discussions of identity, nation, even community are complex and value-laden. Globalization, transnationalism, and the ever-shifting boundaries of nation-states at the turn of the last century further challenge conventional concepts of place and being. How a state constructs its story through its official discourse also involves the creation and incorporation of identities and communities. National identities are rarely monolithic. Rather, one should understand these national stories not in terms of nation or nationalism but as "nationhood," which can have multiple identities in a globalized world where there is, say, one identity for foreign consumption and another that is "real and authentic" for the citizens of a country.[6] This idea that a nation or a people purposefully projects different identities is especially useful for understanding how Dominicans opposed to the continuation of the *trujillato* negotiated meaning for themselves while, likewise, having to deal with the often overwhelming presence of the US government throughout the Cold War period and beyond. It is through these "several competing belongings," as Etienne Balibar describes them, that Dominicans first challenge and then ultimately overturn the official discourse of post-Trujillo national identity.[7]

Finally, Benedict Anderson's understanding of nations defined as a product of a group's creation of self-prescribed identities, and of borders, languages, and cultures, is an important point of departure for any exploration of contemporary Dominican concepts of nation and collective identity. For Anderson, communities imagine themselves through a variety of expressions, including the creation of monuments and museums, although the official national presentation of this identity may, in fact, deviate from the lived realities of the communities purported to be represented.[8] The creation of monuments, statues, and other commemorative works in public spaces is a way of instituting that event or individual(s) within the collective and/or national consciousness.

The French historian Pierre Nora describes these as *lieux de mémoire* (places of memory), which, "become a symbolic element of the memorial heritage of any community" but also can contain "latent or hidden aspects of national memory and its whole spectrum of sources regardless of their nature."[9] For the Dominican Republic, these physical reminders of the past would serve as contested sites of national identity.

Legacy of the Butterflies

"Butterflies" was the name given to the Mirabal sisters—Patria, Minerva, and María Teresa—by members of el Movimiento del 14 de Junio (the 14th of June Movement). The Mirabal family lived in Ojo del Agua in the Cibao valley, known for its rich agricultural lands. They possessed some land and a dry goods store, which enabled them to live a comfortable, albeit provincial, life. On January 10, 1960, in the home of Patria, the oldest daughter, and her husband Pedro González, the 14th of June Movement was formed. They named the movement in honor of a group of Dominican exiles whose plans to overthrow Trujillo on that day in 1959 went horribly wrong, and who were killed by Trujillo's armed forces. Like their sister Patria, both María Teresa and Minerva married leaders of the 14th of June Movement and both, along with their sister, were active in the organization until their untimely deaths. As with all other individuals or groups who opposed him, Trujillo accused the 14th of June Movement of being infiltrated by exiles and communists.[10] By most accounts, Minerva Mirabal was the leader of the movement, yet her relationship to Trujillo had actually begun years earlier when, as a teenager, she refused Trujillo's advances, a move that resulted in the imprisonment of her father, who would die shortly after his release.[11] For some ten years before her death, Trujillo ostracized, harassed, and attempted to destroy her and her family, first through economic means and, finally, through torture and death.

As the work of the 14th of June Movement grew more intense and open, Trujillo's henchman, Johnny Abbes, arrested Manolo Tavárez Justo (Minerva's husband) and Leandro Guzmán (María Teresa's husband), followed quickly by the arrest of both Minerva and María Teresa in January 1960.[12] While Minerva and María Teresa were released in February, their husbands remained incarcerated, first at the infamous prison "La Victoria" in Santo Domingo. Then, in November 1960, they were moved to a jail near Puerto Plata on the other side of the island. For the women, visiting their husbands required a treacherous journey over the mountains, and their fears of being ambushed were well founded. A few weeks before their death, Trujillo would publicly state that the only two remaining problems for him were the Catholic Church and the Mirabal family.[13] On November 25, 1960, Patria, Minerva, and María Teresa, on their way back from the Puerto Plata prison, were stopped by Trujillo's men, dragged from their car into a sugar cane field, and beaten to death. The sisters' heroism came to "symbolize most dramatically the dangerous, yet strong resistance to Trujillo."[14] The next thirty-plus years would be characterized by the intimidation of the surviving members of the Mirabal family along with a significant portion of the Dominican population. Although Trujillo was dead, many of his supporters, most notably Joaquin Balaguer, held sway over the Dominican government until the 1990s. Any acknowledgment of the sisters' political activism ran counter to the neo-Trujillo regime's attempts to maintain control over the country and its people. In fact, in his account of his brief time as the US ambassador, John Bartlow Martin described the Mirabals as "three pretty young sisters" and acknowledged that their death added to the "mystique" of the 14th of June Movement, which he, and the US government, worried could fall to the communists at any moment in the post-assassination chaos of the country.[15]

The United States' role in delaying and eventually underplaying any investigation into the sisters' deaths, and its continued support for Trujillo, at least initially, was tied to the Dominican Republic's unfortunate geography. The Dominican Republic shares much with both Cuba to the northwest and Puerto Rico to the southeast, including language, history, and US economic and political influence. Trujillo had long understood the geopolitical advantages of this relationship, and as the Cold War heated up, he was one of the United States' staunchest allies against the spread of communism. During the Eisenhower administration, the Dominican Republic permitted the United States to set up a tracking station for its missile program and was rewarded with financial and technical assistance for its own growing air force.[16] The fear of Soviet expansionism in the Caribbean buoyed Trujillo's relationship with the United States because he was able to contain and repress dissent by linking it to possible communist activities.[17] The arrival of Castro as the new leader of Cuba, however, set off a chain of speculation by the Eisenhower and Kennedy administrations concerning the future of the Dominican Republic as well as a fear that continued support for Trujillo could lead to a similar revolt on the island. Even after Trujillo's assassination on June 30, 1961, the United States worked quickly, along with the provisional Dominican government, to contain any and all suggestions of revolution or clandestine groups.[18] Acknowledgment of the role of the Mirabal sisters and members of the 14th of June Movement in attempting to overthrow Trujillo was a potential source of rebellion that neither the United States nor the neo-Trujillo elements in the Dominican Republic would risk. There would be no repeat of Castro-led communism in the Dominican future.

Trujillo's Legacy

By 1960, Rafael Leonidas Trujillo had been in power for thirty years. Trujillo's rise began during the first US occupation of the Dominican Republic from 1916 to 1924. As a young officer, Trujillo quickly moved up through the ranks, and when the Marines departed in 1924, they left Trujillo in charge.[19] By 1927 he was a general, and by 1930 the president. He possessed a nearly preternatural understanding of nation building, which resulted in the refashioning of the country as one large homage to him and his rule. By 1936, Santo Domingo was renamed "Cuidad Trujillo," and the highest mountain in the country became "Pico Trujillo." Trujillo seemed well aware of the benefits of these very public reminders, which became a powerful tool through which his "name and image were conflated with the Dominican nation itself." Trujillo, in fact, was re-creating Dominican national identity. In addition to the ubiquitous photo of "El Jefe" (The Boss) in every Dominican home, by some estimates, at the time of his death there were "eighteen hundred sculptures" of Trujillo throughout the country.[20] Finally, along with massive public works projects and consolidation of the military, he constructed countless monuments, buildings, and structures that would bear his name or that of a family member. This "reconstruction of the Fatherland" would dominate the physical and psychological landscape of the country throughout the *trujillato* and beyond.

He also reimagined the role of his country on the international scene, espe-cially with the advent of the Cold War. Yet as Trujillo's reach began to include the murder of foreigners like the Spanish intellectual Dr. Jesús de Galíndez (1959), whose doctoral thesis was a scathing attack on Trujillo's government, and the failed plot to assassinate the president of Venezuela, Rómulo Betan-court (1960), relations with Washington soured. By 1960, there was growing concern in Washington, the OAS, and the CIA that Trujillo's thirty-year con-trol of the country could end in a repeat of the Cuban crisis. In a February 1961 declassified memorandum for the newly elected president, John F. Kennedy, Arthur Schlesinger summarized Kennedy's options for dealing with Castro and Cuba. Along with suggestions for destabilizing Cuba, Schlesinger sug-gested a third possibility, asking, "Could we not bring down Castro and Trujillo at the same time?"[21] Earlier, in the fall of 1960, the CIA had pro-vided rifles to Dominican rebels, but with the failed Bay of Pigs invasion in April 1961, the agency withdrew support for the assassination, forgetting, apparently, to repossess the rifles.[22] Although the details of the United States' involvement in Trujillo's assassination remain unclear, the role of the Kennedy administration in the country after Trujillo's regime is well documented. The day after Trujillo's assassination in May 1961, Kennedy, returning from Paris, outlined "three possibilities in descending order of preference: a democratic regime, a continuation of the Trujillo regime, or a Castro regime." Kennedy went on to say, "We ought to aim at the first, but really can't renounce the second until we are sure we can avoid the third."[23]

For the next four years, through diplomacy, economic incentives, and ultimately force, the US government would waver between the first two options in hopes of avoiding the third. By April 1965, the ongoing fear of a Castro/Communist takeover of the Dominican Republic culminated in the second US military occupation of the island in the twentieth century. Any remaining hopes that the United States might reach an agreement with Dominicans opposed to Trujillo's legacy were destroyed with the landing of the Marines.[24] Undoubtedly, the Cuban Missile Crisis of October 1962 contributed to the strained relationship between the United States and any Latin American government seen as hostile or unstable. Although the Soviets ultimately withdrew the ships armed with nuclear warheads, the experience had a lasting effect on the people and policies of the United States. The fear of nuclear war and of communism greatly complicated the line between rational concern and a "neurotic form of anxiety" about any and all suggestion of a nuclear conflict.[25] Although, for many Cold War scholars, there was no "second Cuba in the making," the United States' illogical fear of a regional communist takeover led to increasingly belligerent policies toward Latin American governments during the period.[26]

The United States' success at preventing a Castro/Communist revolution in the Dominican Republic, however, was only partial. For many throughout Latin America, Cuba's strategic and political victories over the United States became a source of inspiration. Likewise, the growing discontent on the part of many Latin Americans concerning the overdetermined Cold War ideology fueled a cultural form of resistance shared by young Dominicans who, in the following years, would continue to defy what they saw as the cultural imperialism of the West and of the United States.[27] The US Marines formally withdrew from the Dominican Republic in September 1966, ending seventeen months of occupation. Left behind were over "400 United States officials," working at all levels of the government.[28] While this bureaucratic presence would lessen over time, the United States continued to intervene in the domestic policies of the Dominican Republic, sometimes to support Balaguer or one of his cronies, and other times to admonish him or his associates.

Although not overtly present, the continued involvement of the United States in Dominican politics throughout the Cold War decidedly impacted Dominicans' ability to engage in the "task of mourning" that often accompanies the end of dictatorship when the physical and psychological abuses of the past are made public.[29] Unable to fully interrogate the national story of the *trujillato*, even at the conclusion of the 1980s, life after Trujillo had changed little for most Dominicans. There were few literary works that criticized or even discussed the brutal reign of Trujillo and, in general, the past remained disjointed and inaccessible.[30]

Neil Larsen's description of the dictatorship as a fragmented history recorded in the Dominican imaginary underscores how the wound of the traumatic *trujillato* remained open for many Dominicans long after Trujillo's death. The shadow cast by those thirty-one years was lengthened by the continued political and economic collusion between the US and Dominican governments, which were determined to erase the past through economic incentives, political accommodation and, when all else failed, force and intimidation.[31] In the absence of historical continuity between their shared past and future, many Dominicans experienced a kind of trauma that can lead to an ongoing sense of fear and crisis long after the end of a collective ordeal. Unable to mourn the past or, for that matter, acknowledge the present traumas of shared experience, it is no wonder that for many in the Dominican Republic, life continued to be defined by the fear, anxiety, and despair that often accompany the suppression of a national trauma and leave a community with an alienated and fragmented sense of identity.[32]

Memory, Memorials, and the Mirabal Sisters

The story of the Mirabal sisters and their resistance to Trujillo would be central to a new Dominican national imaginary that would replace the same post–Cold War Castro/Communist rhetoric that had suppressed much of the Dominican peoples' struggles against Trujillo and the neo-Trujillo governments that dominated the country until the 1990s. Their story becomes real and authentic for Dominicans on the island and in the United States.

One important factor of post–Cold War identity in the Dominican Republic was the political and cultural role of its citizens who migrated to the United States. Between 1990 and 2000, there was an 89 percent increase in the number of Dominicans living in the United States.[33] Many of these recent arrivals were joining family members already well established in the United States, especially in the Northeast. Indeed, many Dominicans lived in both countries, and this binational experience would, for better and worse, create a more expansive, complex, and unique sense of Dominican nationhood on the island and in the United States. This continual movement between two countries with distinct cultural and political institutions is clearly similar to Bhabha's "unity of opposites" where the "intersubjective and collective experiences of nationness, community interest, or cultural value are negotiated" between Dominicans and the United States.[34] The Cuban literary scholar Antonio Benitez Rojo sees this kind of ongoing movement as essentially Caribbean and as being best understood not in terms of geography but rather as an ongoing series of negotiations among a variety of experiences and expressions, be they historical, cultural, political, or social.[35] The Dominican literary scholar Silvio Torres-Salliant echoes this more expansive and interrelated understanding of identity in his argument against the use of the term transnational for Dominican identity: "we can no longer see the Dominican Republic and the United States as separate, isolated national domains, but as part and parcel of a single (unevenly developed) sociocultural, economic, and political field."[36] The importance of this *multipersonal* approach toward individual and collective identity is that it allows for a greater range of possibilities for "belonging."[37] This more expansive understanding means, in turn, that "belonging to a *culture* means belonging to a network, to an *intersection* of cultures."[38]

It seems only fitting, then, that the novel of a young Dominican-American author, Julia Alvarez, would be the meeting point between the Dominican past and its future. *In the Time of the Butterflies* (1994), based on the stories of the Mirabal sisters, chronicles the lives of the four sisters from the beginning of Trujillo's dictatorship in 1938 to the murder of three of them in November 1960, as retold by Dedé, the surviving sister. Alvarez's work was not the first to acknowledge the importance of the sisters. In 1969 Pedro Mir, one of the Dominican Republic's most well-known poets, published "Amén de Mariposas" (For the Butterflies), an epic poem that intertwines the fate of the three sisters with the colonial and neocolonial history of the country. Then, in 1976 Ramón Alberto Ferreras published the first narrative about the Mirabal sisters, simply titled *Las Mirabal*.[39] Alvarez acknowledges both of these works in the final page of her novel, explaining that each was "helpful in providing facts and inspiration."[40]

Alvarez's story of her journey to writing the book is, in many respects, a reflection of how the Mirabals' legacy continued to haunt Dominicans both on the island and in the United States. In a 1996 essay, "Chasing the Butterflies," she explains that she was vaguely aware of their story as a child because shortly after she and her family arrived in the United States (a virtually impossible feat in itself), her father came home with an issue of *Time* magazine that detailed the murder of the sisters. Forbidden from looking at it, Alvarez notes that her parents continued to live "as if the SIM (Trujillo's secret police) might show up at our door any minute and haul us away."[41] It was as an adult, however, that Alvarez would return to the Dominican Republic in 1986, rediscover the Mirabal sisters, and decide that "only by making them real, alive, could I make them mean anything to the rest of us."[42] Thus, her choice of using the sisters' covert name in her title is deliberate and serves as an important touchstone for Dominicans in the United States and the Dominican Republic. Although her novel helped to awaken the long-repressed trauma of Trujillo and the heroism of the Butterflies, Alvarez is careful to note in her postscript that her goal was not to add to the myth of the sisters, which, she felt, had left them inaccessible and out of reach "for us, ordinary men and women." Rather, she saw her work as an important contribution to recapturing the heroism of all Dominicans during the dark thirty-one years of Trujillo's rule.[43]

In the years following the publication of the novel, the story of the Mirabal sisters took on added importance in a variety of ways. Between the United States publication of the novel in 1994 and the opening of the Museo de Memorial in 2011, there has been a steady increase in the number of tributes, films, biographies, and social media sites dedicated to the sisters in Spanish and English. Their history can be found in novels ranging from the Nobel Prize–winning author Mario Vargas Llosa's *La fiesta del chivo* (Festival of the Goat)[44] (2000) to more recent examples such as the Pulitzer Prize–winning novelist Junot Díaz's *The Brief Wondrous Life of Oscar Wao* (2007). In December 1999, the United Nations General Assembly designated November 25 (the anniversary of the day of the murder of the Mirabal sisters) as the annual date for the "International Day for the Elimination of Violence Against Women."

There is also a 2009 documentary of the sisters that closely mirrors Alvarez's account, as well as a 1996 biography written by Miguel Aquino García. His work, *Tres heroínas y un tirano* (Three Heroines and a Tyrant) returns to Dede Mirabal as the primary source of information. Although it is described as "la historia vérdica" (the true story), this account too relies heavily on testimonial rather than historical documents. Indeed, in all of these examples, there is a fine line between myth and reality concerning the story of the Mirabal sisters that both contributes to and distracts from its value as a source of cultural and national identity for Dominicans.

It is this line between fact and fiction that concerns Ilan Stavans in his 1994 review of *In the Time of the Butterflies*. He argues that although the novel is an important recognition of the history of the Mirabal sisters, it risks mythologizing them further in large part because the story stops with their murder.[45] What may be needed, he suggests, is more detail about the 1962 trial of the sisters' killers, which could have placed them "more firmly in the *flux* of Dominican memory."[46] Stavan's insistence that the story beyond the lives and death of the sisters is important echoes what Dominic LaCapra would call a sense of "empathetic unsettlement," which does not reduce the *trujillato* to a period of time overcome by "spiritually uplifting accounts of extreme events from which we attempt to derive reassurance or benefit."[47]

There was, in fact, a trial of the five men accused of carrying out the murders, and they were found guilty and sentenced to prison. All five resorted to what Martin called the "Nuremberg defense—they had no choice but to carry out orders."[48] In the months leading up to the 1965 uprising, the Dominican government made arrangements to release the men, however, and several of them subsequently migrated to the United States. This blatant disregard for legal processes so outraged the family that even forty years later in her memoir, Dedé Mirabal asks, "¿Cómo consiguieron visas y residencias en ese país si eran prófugos de la justicia dominicana?" (How did they secure visas and homes in that country [United States] if they were fugitives from Dominican justice?).[49] With the majority of the accused in exile, as Dedé explains, "en la memoria colectiva de nuestro país pesará por siempre la vergüenza de que la mayoría de los que participaron en el crimen murieran en sus camas" (in the collective memory of our country the shame that the majority of those who participated in the crime would die in their beds would weigh heavily on us forever).[50] The exodus of these suspects further delayed the country's need to face the memory of the thirty-one years of repression and the resulting trauma that had crippled the national psyche.

By the 1990s, meanwhile, the United States' post–Cold War policy shift, away from political interference to economic and development concerns under the guise of the now infamous "Washington Consensus," was underway.[51] As John Williamson, who first proposed the idea in 1989, explains, the original consensus had three big ideas: "macroeconomic discipline, a market economy, and openness to the world (at least in respect of trade and FDI)."[52]

For the Dominican Republic's relationship with the United States, the Washington Consensus promised cooperation rather than intervention based on the shared goal of economic and social independence. Political stability, of course, is central to economic growth, especially on the global level proposed by the Washington Consensus. The Dominican economy, like the politics of the country, was still dominated by neo-Trujillo elements whose corruption and repressiveness offered little hope for an open and thriving macro- or microeconomic future.

The 1996 election of Leonel Fernández, however, seemed a positive indicator that these economic forces were taking hold. By all accounts, including an international commission headed by Jimmy Carter, the election was free and fair.[53] Thus, the Dominican Republic elected its youngest president and first "Dominicanyork."[54] It is telling, however, that shortly after his inauguration in August, the *New York Times* quoted one diplomat as saying, "People are disoriented. . . . They know that the old rules suddenly don't apply any more, but they don't yet know what the new rules are going to be."[55] The end of "Trujillismo without Trujillo" left the Dominican people with the uncertainty of a future already fragmented by decades of fear, repression, and intimidation. The sense of social continuity that usually is found in a nation, even in times of crisis, seemed absent, captured in the fear of not knowing "what the new rules are going to be." In his inaugural address, Fernández emphasized concepts such as *civil society*, *common good*, and *governability*, which, for him, depended on a tolerance for differing opinions and an end to corruption.[56]

Fernández began immediately to redefine Dominican nationhood. First, he retitled many of the old Trujillo monuments and created new memorials commemorating the struggle against the *trujillato*. One of the most salient examples of this shift would be the complete renovation of the obelisk Trujillo had built in Santo Domingo in 1935 to commemorate his patrimony. Measuring one-quarter of the size of the Washington Monument, the obelisk commands a central place on the malecón, the main boulevard between the Caribbean Sea and the edge of Santo Domingo. Until 1997, it was simply one more decaying memory of the *trujillato*, with no place in the national conscience. Indeed, it was in a perpetual state of disrepair. Then Fernández's government decided not only to renovate the monument but to turn it into a memorial to the Mirabal sisters. The original artist, Elsa Nuñez, entitled her work, "Canción a la libertad" (Song to Liberty), with the faces of the three sisters and a group portrait on the fourth side. Sponsored by the national phone company, Codetel, the rededication of the monument, according to the president of the company, was carried out both to eulogize the sisters' work as well as to atone for "the ignominious motive that gave birth to this monument."[57] In 2007, the obelisk was repainted although, clearly, the sisters were still the major theme of the work. It has, in fact, been repainted four times, with a fifth mural completed in 2012. Fittingly, the new mural is called "Alegoría a la libertad" (Allegory of Liberty); and this time, four artists, each working on one side of the obelisk, have created a monument to the Dominican Republic that includes "aspects of the Dominican flag and symbols of patriotism and faith," along with tributes to "the contributions of women to the nation through the arts, culture, economy and labor."[58] Yet there is a lingering concern about this most recent transformation inasmuch as the original design, clearly focused on the Mirabal sisters, is now a more generalized tribute to, once again, various "aspects of the Dominican flag and symbols of patriotism and faith." In Edward Said's powerful essay "Invention, Memory and Place," he notes that transformed places, and refashioned memories, especially in their "collective forms," provide people with "a coherent identity, a national narrative, a place in the world.[59] Trujillo's obelisk, then, devoid of meaning and memory after his death, reenters national memory. Nora insists that these transformations are what distinguish *lieux de mémoire* from "simple memorials": they "thrive only because of their capacity for change, their ability to resurrect old meanings and generate new ones along with new and unforeseeable connections (that is what makes them exciting)."[60] The reconceptualization of the obelisk illustrates how a "cold and solemn" official site can be transformed into a "dominated" *lieu de mémoire*, which, for Dominicans, means that the site no longer harbors the negative memory of Trujillo, but rather, is a place to remember and celebrate their collective past and present.[61]

During his second term (2004–2008), Fernández also authorized the creation of "The Memorial Museum of Dominican Resistance," and, on May 31, 2011, fifty years after Trujillo's death, the museum opened in the Colonial district of Santo Domingo. Composed of photographs and texts that take up the majority of the two floors of the small colonial home, the museum's mission is to "compile, organize, catalogue, preserve, investigate, disseminate and exhibit the tangible and intangible assets of national heritage related to the facts and consequences of the struggles of several generations of Dominican men and women during the dictatorship of Rafael L. Trujillo."[62] In many respects, the museum represents the culmination of years of memory work throughout the country as those involved in the museum's creation rewrite the legal, social, and cultural histories of the *trujillato*.

In addition to the physical museum, there is also an interactive website where not only can visitors learn about the years of the *trujillato* but, equally important, victims can add their testimonies, register the disappeared, read about current investigations into past violence and torture, and participate virtually in future actions.[63] The Mirabal sisters and the 14th of June Movement figure prominently in the museum. Along with a variety of photos and narration about their role in the resistance movement, there is a holographic re-creation of the sisters and a life-size mannequin representing Manolo Tavárez, Minerva's husband and the leader of the movement. There are also important investigations into many of the more egregious crimes committed by Trujillo's regime, such as the murder of the Mirabal sisters. In March of 2013, the museum took the lead in officially requesting that the Dominican government establish a Truth Commission to investigate the "thousands" of crimes committed during Trujillo's dictatorship and beyond. The museum director, Luisa de Peña

Díaz, announced that the museum "has collected 15,000 signatures to petition the Dominican government to create the commission" to address for the first time how many people were tortured and killed under the 1930–1961 rule of Trujillo and the early years of the Joaquin Balaguer presidency that followed.[64] Truth commissions are intended to expose abuses while allowing witnesses to speak without fear of prosecution; one might think of Argentina, Chile, Nicaragua, and Guatemala. An estimated 50,000 people were killed under Trujillo, including an estimated 17,000 Haitians massacred in 1937.

The journey from the original decision to create the museum until its inauguration, however, is emblematic of the continued struggle between the neo-Trujillo elements of the Dominican Republic and groups who are seeking accountability for the thirty-one years of Trujillo's reign and the subsequent decades of political oppression. In her article "La Historia del Museo Memorial de la Resistencia Dominicana" (The History of the Memorial Museum of Dominican Resistance), De Peña Díaz describes the difficult journey of establishing the museum, which met with resistance at every turn. Although the project had governmental support and international recognition, elements loyal to the Trujillo past were a vocal and legal force that succeeded in blocking the government from donating the colonial "Casa de las Fundaciones" to be the site for the museum.[65] In her essay on the founding of the museum, De Peña Díaz, in fact, notes that when she went to visit the Holocaust Museum in Washington, DC, she was told to steel herself against the coming onslaught of rumors, betrayals, and accusations, all of which, she remembered assuring the director, "no iba a pasar entre nosotros" (that was not going to happen between us), but which, as she later noted, proved to be true.[66]

In May 2011, the museum, along with the "Comisión Permanente de Efemérides Patrias" (Permanent Commission on National Anniversaries), published El juicio de los asesinos de las hermanas Mirabal (The Trial of the Assassins of the Mirabal Sisters) with the explicit purpose of countering the fifty-one-year denial by many of Trujillo's supporters that the dictator had been involved in their murder. In the prologue, the editor, Franklin Franco, explicitly refers to the continued "notorious influence" of Trujillo supporters in recent years, making it possible to "esconder la verdad (y) disfrazar la imagen de la tiranía . . . del trujillato" (hide the truth [and] disguise the image of the tyranny . . . of the trujillato).[67] Consisting of some three hundred pages, the book includes the testimonies of the five accused murderers, eyewitness accounts, and the transcript of the final sentencing. There are also photos of the trial in June 1962 as well as family photos of the Mirabal sisters, showing events from various times of their lives such as weddings and graduations. Indeed, the inclusion of the photos helps to remind the reader of the women victimized by this tragic event.

Yet history, myth, memory, and identity are more complex when these discourses are attached to nationalism or nationhood. And just as the museum and other Dominican governmental agencies have taken on the role of restoring the lost memories and histories of the past fifty years and beyond, there has been an equal amount of resistance to this narrative on the part of members of Trujillo's family and supporters. Most recently, Ramfis Dominguez Trujillo, grandson of Trujillo and son of Angelita, has undertaken an aggressive campaign, as he says, to "rescatar la memoria" (rescue the memory) of his grandfather.[68] In 2012, Ramfis and many of Trujillo's other followers created the "Fundación Rafael Leónidas Trujillo Molina" website, which mimics the Museo de Memoria's page in terms of history, events, and open forums.[69] Along with copies of his mother's book, the site purports to provide viewers with a complete picture of the "successes that Trujillo left to the country."[70] There is even a first-person account by Miriam Morales, supposedly the last person to see the Mirabal sisters alive, according to the site. As with Angelita Trujillo's account, here too the conclusion is that they were murdered by some unknown man who was seeking to discredit Trujillo.[71] The mission of the "Fundación," as the home page explains, is to "llevar a cabo el decoroso proceso de complementar los anales del siglo pasado con la justa restauración de los 30 años mutilados a nuestra historia patria correspondiente al periodo conocido como la 'Era de Trujillo'" (bring about the dignified process of enhancing the annals of [the] past with the just restoration of the 30 years that have been mutilated by those focused on what they call the 'Era of Trujillo' of our historical country).[72] The website's commemoration of Trujillo will remain virtual for now unless the family can change the 1962 law that specifically banned any kind of memorializing of Trujillo, a law that they unsuccessfully fought.[73]

Ultimately, opposing claims about who was responsible for the murder of the Mirabal sisters echo the competing assertions about who is and who is not a "true Dominican." Ramfis, in a March 2013 interview for the *Dominican Hoy*, argues convincingly, so he thinks, that his project will restore pride in Dominican identity through the recuperation of the positive works of his grandfather during that thirty-one-year-long period.[74] Yet, on the back cover of *El juicio*, the editors make a similar statement arguing that the publication of the 1962 trial transcripts contributes to the "gran valor histórico que resaltan la permanente lucha y sacrificios de nuestro pueblo por la conquista de su libertad y la democracia" (great historic valor which emphasizes the struggle and sacrifices of our people for their liberty and democracy).[75]

Conclusion: The Struggle for Memory and History Is at the Very Heart of Dominican National Identity

As Paul Ricouer observes in *History, Memory and Forgetting*, "national history and, with it, history as myth have made way for national memory," in which "a new concern with 'identity' resulted from the emergence of this historicized present."[76] Collective memory relies on consensus about the past between often disparate points of view held by a variety of individuals. Cultural identity too is the result of a complex and unending series of negotiations between individual and group experiences and expressions. For the Dominican Republic and the United States, especially in the wake of the Cold War, these ongoing, interrelated, tangled, and difficult negotiations have created multiple belongings for citizens of both countries that challenge commonly held notions of nationhood, identity, and community. Through memory, migration, immigration, economic and social interaction, and the exchange of cultural capital, Americans and Dominicans have a shared past and future rich in possibilities and nuanced in expression.

Whose history will be the defining source of future Dominican identity? Can a war of words and ideologies be fought solely through websites or, in the end, will a truth commission established by the Dominican government stabilize once and for all the view of the past and the present? On the surface, the presence of pro-Trujillo supporters suggests a vigorous and continual debate among competing voices that seems democratic in its scope and tone. Yet, these voices too must be balanced against the still emerging history of the *trujillato*. As late as June of 2015, the director of the Memorial Museum of Dominican Resistance, Luisa de Peña Díaz, was still advocating for the creation of the truth commission despite having collected 114,000 signatures and officially requesting its formation to President Danilo Medina on December 10, 2013.[77] In her 2015 interview for *Z-Digial*, Dr. de Peña argues that even now, the *trujillato* continues to influence Dominican politics, adding that the mere suggestion of such an organization has led many to ask her directly about "la necesidad de esta Comisión [que] implicaría tocar muchos nombres" (the necessity of this Commission [that] will implicate a lot of names).[78]

While in some areas of the Dominican government advances have been made, de Peña's observation about the continued presence of dictatorial structures within the country and the fear they continue to engender throughout Dominican society seems undisputed. It is hard to imagine how the crimes of the *trujillato* and its pro-Trujillo legacy can be fully interrogated when, in the present, sectors of the Dominican government continue to abuse human and civil rights, most recently with the threat of forced repatriation for tens of thousands of Haitian immigrants and Dominicans of Haitian decent.[79] The Dominican government's decision to abandon the Organization of American States' Human Rights court in November of 2014 is equally disturbing in its return to an isolationist policy regarding human rights.[80] In many respects, these current oppressive policies make the moral and ethical recovery of the legacy of the Mirabal sisters even more important. Without an open and continual commitment on the part of the Dominican government to investigate fully the overt and covert suppression of their lives and deaths, without a clear strategy for recovering the silenced traumas of many individuals and groups, the history and identity of the Dominican Republic as a nation and as a collective of citizens remains inextricably tangled in the web of repression and fear that defined and defines the *trujillato*.

Postscript

On October 23, 2015, Junot Díaz, along with the Haitian-American writer Edwidge Dandicat, publicly spoke out against the Dominican government's treatment of Haitian immigrants. In response, the General Council of the Dominican Republic in New York withdrew Díaz's "Order of Merit," awarded to outstanding citizens of the country, arguing that his denouncement of the forced repatriation of Haitians "demuestra que es antidominicano" (demonstrated that he is anti-Dominican).[81]

Notes

1. Junot Díaz, *The Brief Wondrous Life of Oscar Wao* (New York: Penguin, 2007), 324.

2. Freddy Matos, "Libro *Trujillo, mi Padre* aclarará la muerte de las Mirabal" (Feb. 21, 2013), http://dominicanoshoy.com/index.php?id=58&tx_ttnews%5Btt_news%5D=23778&cHash=5700e 61379d008b99cda740816e6784e.

3. James W. Booth, *Communities of Memory: On Witness, Identity and Justice* (Ithaca, NY: Cornell University Press, 2006), 67–69.

4. See http://www.fundaciontrujillo.org/content/.

5. Maja Horn, *Masculinity after Trujillo: The Politics of Gender in Dominican Literature* (Gainesville: University Press of Florida, 2014), 140–41.

6. Nicola Miller, "The Historiography of Nationalism and National Identity in Latin America," *Nations and Nationalism* 12, no. 2 (2006): 217.

7. Etienne Balibar, "Culture and Identity (Working Notes)," in *The Identity in Question*, ed. John Rajchman (London: Routledge, 1995), 173–96.

8. Benedict Anderson, *Imagined Communities: Reflections on the Origin and Spread of Nationalism* (New York: Verso, 2006), 181–82.

9. Pierre Nora, *Realms of Memory: Rethinking the French Past*, trans. Arthur Gold Hammer, "Preface to the English Edition" (New York: Columbia University Press, 1996), xvii.

10. "Lider Denuncia," cited in Dedé Mirabal, *Vivas en su jardín: la verdadera historia de las hermanas Mirabal y su lucha por la libertad* (New York: Vintage Español, 2009), 181.

11. Nancy P. Robison provides an excellent overview of the history of the Mirabal sisters in her article "Women's Political Participation in the Dominican Republic: The Case of the Mirabal Sisters," *Caribbean Quarterly* 52, no. 2 (June–September 2006): 141–61.

12. Miguel Aquino García, *Tres heroínas y un tirano: la historia verídica de las hermanas Mirabal y su asesinato por Rafael Leonidas Trujillo* (Santo Domingo: Editora Corripio, 1996), 121–22.

13. John Bartlow Martin, *Overtaken by Events: The Dominican Crisis from the Fall of Trujillo to the Civil War* (New York: Doubleday, 1966), 52.

14. Alan Cambeira, *Quisqueya la bella: The Dominican Republic in Historical and Cultural Perspective* (Armonk, NY: M. E. Sharpe, 1997), 187.

15. Martin, *Overtaken by Events*, 52, 72.

16. Eric Paul Roorda, *The Dictator Next Door: The Good Neighbor Policy and the Trujillo Regime in the Dominican Republic, 1930–1945* (Durham, NC: Duke University Press, 1998), 234.

17. G. Pope Atkins and Larman C. Wilson, *The Dominican Republic and the United States: From Imperialism to Transnationalism* (Athens: University of Georgia Press, 1998), 86.

18. John Bartlow Martin, sent to the Dominican Republic as the first post-Trujillo US ambassador (1961–1963), dedicates much of his memoir *Overtaken by Events* to his and the State Department's efforts to contain and coopt any possible "Castro/Communist" activity after Trujillo.

19. Bernard Diederich, *Trujillo: The Death of the Dictator* (Princeton, NJ: Markus Weiner, 2000), 13.

20. Roorda, *The Dictator Next Door*, 95, 97.

21. Foreign Relations of the United States, 1961–1963, "Memorandum for the President," vol. 3, Cuba (January 1961–September 1962), document 43 (2/11/61), http://history.state.gov/historicaldocuments/frus1961-63v10/d43.

22. Atkins, *Dominican Republic*, 120.

23. Arthur M. Schlesinger Jr., *A Thousand Days: John F. Kennedy in the White House* (New York: Greenwich, 1983), 769.

24. The term *Castro/Communist* appears in John Bartlow Martin's memoir of the early years following Trujillo's assassination. Martin uses the term primarily when discussing Dominican rebels who he feels are being directly influenced by the Castro government.

25. Arthur G. Neal, *National Trauma and Collective Memory: Major Events in the American Century* (Armonk, NY: M. E. Sharpe, 1998), 109. The crisis was equally traumatic for the Caribbean. See, for example, Antonio Benítez Rojo's discussion of its impact on his youth in Cuba in *The Repeating Island: The Caribbean and the Postmodern Perspective,* 2nd edition, trans. James E. Maraniss (Durham, NC: Duke University Press, 1996), 10.

26. Jorge I. Domínguez, "US–Latin American Relations During the Cold War and Its Aftermath," in *The United States and Latin America: The New Agenda*, ed. Victor Bulmer-Thomas and James Dunkerley (Cambridge: Harvard University Press, 1999), 42.

27. Jesse Hoffnung-Garskof, *A Tale of Two Cities: Santo Domingo and New York after 1950* (Princeton, NJ: Princeton University Press, 2008), 85.

28. Cambeira, *Quisqueya la bella*, 193.

29. Idelber Avelar, *The Untimely Present: Postdictatorial Latin American Fiction and the Task of Mourning* (Durham, NC: Duke University Press, 1999), 3.

30. Neil Larsen, "¿Cómo narrar el trujillato?" *Revista Iberoamericana* 56, no. 142 (1988): 89–98.

31. In 1962, for instance, Martin notes that he was often expected to provide visas to Dominicans opposed to the "Consejo" created in the wake of Trujillo's death (Martin 99). In 1965, along with hundreds of exiles, there were also, certainly, Dominicans removed from the island for political reasons. In 2015, the fifty-year privacy ban on the manifests of evacuees from the Dominican Republic in 1965 aboard US warships will expire and the National Archives is currently digitizing that information. Who exactly were aboard these ships could shed new light on the role of the United States in supporting neo-Trujillo policies.

32. Neal, *National Trauma*, 7, 4–6.

33. Migration Policy Institute, "The Dominican Population in the United States: Growth and Distribution" (2004), http://www.migrationpolicy.org/pubs/MPI_Report_Dominican_Pop_US.pdf.

34. Homi K. Bhabha, *The Location of Culture* (New York: Routledge, 1994), 2.

35. Antonio Benítez Rojo, *La isla que se repite* (Hanover: Ediciones del Norte, 1999), 1–29.

36. Silvio Torres-Saillant, "Diasporic Disquisitions: Dominicanists, Transnationalism, and the Community," *Dominican Studies Working Paper Series* 1 (New York: CUNY Dominican Studies Institute, 2000), 8.

37. Balibar, "Culture and Identity," 187.

38. Ibid., 188.

39. Christina Stokes, "Re-envisioning History: Memory, Myth and Fiction in Literary Representations of the Trujillato" (PhD diss., University of Florida, 2009), 87.

40. Julia Alvarez, *In the Time of the Butterflies* (Chapel Hill, NC: Algonquin Books, 1994), 325.

41. Julia Alvarez, "Chasing the Butterflies," in *Something to Declare* (Chapel Hill, NC: Algonquin Press, 1998), 197.

42. Alvarez, "Chasing the Butterflies," 203.

43. Ibid., 324.

44. All translations from the Spanish are mine.

45. Ilan Stavans, "Las Mariposas" *The Nation*, November 7, 1994, 556.

46. Ibid.

47. Dominick LaCapra, *Writing History, Writing Trauma* (Baltimore: Johns Hopkins University Press, 2001), 41–42.

48. Martin, *Overtaken by Events*, 53.

49. Mirabal, *Vivas en su jardín*, 261.

50. Ibid., 259.

51. For an excellent overview of the failures of the Washington Consensus and its impact on Latin America, see the article by Dr. Robin Broad of American University, "The Washington Consensus Meets the Global Backlash: Shifting Debates and Policies," *Globalizations* 1, no. 2 (December 2004): 129–154, http://www1.international.ucla.edu/media/files/42.pdf.

52. John Williamson, "Did the Washington Consensus Fail?" *Foreign Trade Information System*, http://ctrc.sice.oas.org/geograph/westernh/williamson.asp.

53. Atkins and Wilson, *The Dominican Republic*, 219.

54. "Dominicanyork" is a somewhat conflicted term. While it is often used to simply describe Dominicans who were either born in New York or grew up there, for some Dominicans, it is synonymous with delinquency and cultural corruption. (See, for instance, Hoffnung-Garskoff, *Tale of Two Cities*, 229–31.)

55. Larry Rother, "Dominicans Now Have a New Kind of Leader," *New York Times*, December 1, 1996.

56. Leonel Fernández, "Discurso de toma de posesión" (inaugural address, National Palace, August 16, 1996), *Archivo General de la Nación*, DB1418.

57. Larry Rother, "The Three Sisters, Avenged: A Dominican Drama," *New York Times*, April 15, 1997.

58. "New Painting on the Obelisk" (June 29, 2011), http://colonialzone-dr.com/colonialzone-news/2011/06/29/new-painting-on-the-obelisk/.

59. Edward Said, "Invention, Memory and Place," *Critical Inquiry* 26 (Winter 2000): 179.

60. Nora, *Realms of Memory*, 15.

61. Ibid., 19.

62. "Documentary Heritage on the Resistance and Struggle for Human Rights in the Dominican Republic, 1930–1961," *Memory of the World Register* (Ref: 2008-20), 2, http://www.unesco.org/new/fileadmin/MULTIMEDIA/HQ/CI/CI/pdf/mow/nomination_forms/Documentary%20Heritage%20on%20the%20Resistance%20and%20Struggle%20for%20Human%20Rights%20in%20the%20Dominican%20Republic%201930%201961%20Nomination%20Form.pdf.

63. See http://www.museodelaresistencia.com/.

64. Associated Press, "Dominicana: promueven comisión de la verdad," *El Nuevo Herald* (March 11, 2013), http://www.azcentral.com/lavoz/spanish/us/articles/us_193246.html.

65. Luisa de Peña Díaz, "Historia del Museo Memorial de la Resistencia Dominicana," http://www.museodelaresistencia.org/index.php?option=com_content&view=article&id=330&Itemid=247.

66. Ibid.

67. Franklin J. Franco, *El juicio de los asesinos de las hermanas Mirabal*, http://www.museodelaresistencia.org/libros/JUICIO_asesinos_MIRABAL.pdf.

68. José Pimentel Muñoz, "Nieto Trujillo insiste críticas Procuraduría," *Noticias dominicanas.* http://noticiasrepublicadominicana.blogspot.com/2013/04/notird-sabado-6-de-abril-de-2013.html.

69. Fundación Rafael Leonidas Trujillo Molina, http://www.fundaciontrujillo.org/content/.

70. Ibid.

71. María de los Angeles Trujillo de Dominguez, *Trujillo, Mi padre* (Miami: MATD Endevours, 2010), 424.

72. Fundación Rafael Leónidas Trujillo Molina, "La Fundación," accessed November 22, 2015, http://www.fundaciontrujillo.org/content/index.php?option=com_content&view=article&id=12&Itemid=27.

73. "Authorities enforce law banning praise of Trujillo," *Dominican Today*, March 23, 2013, http://www.dominicantoday.com/dr/local/2013/3/23/47103/Authorities-to-enforce-law-banning-praise-of-Trujillo/.

74. Luis José Ramfis Rafael Francisco Miguel Domínguez Trujillo, interviewed by Rosario Fausto Adames, "51 años después: Ramfis Trujillo defiende a capa y espada a su abuelo" (May 30, 2012), http://www.acento.com.do/index.php/news/16539/56/51-anos-despues-Ramfis-Trujillo-defiende-a-capa-y-espada-a-su-abuelo.html.

75. Franklin J. Franco, *El juicio de los asesinos de las hermanas Mirabal*, República Dominicana: Comisión Permanente de Efemérides Patrias, 2011.

76. Paul Ricoeur, *Memory, History, Forgetting*, trans. Kathleen Blamey and David Pellauer (Chicago: University of Chicago Press, 2004), 635.

77. "Afirman sigue en pie iniciativa de crear Comisión de la Verdad," *Zdigital*, June, 31, 2015, http://zdigital.do/app/article.aspx?id=164291.

78. Ibid.

79. Azam Ahmed, "Dominican Resort is a Refuge Twice Abandonded," *New York Times*, July 30, 2015, http://www.nytimes.com/2015/07/31/world/americas/dominican-resorts-fate-at-center-of-debate-over-haitians-and-immigration.html?ref=topics&_r=0.

80. "Dominican Republic Withdraws from OAS Human Rights Court," *Panam Post* November 5, 2014, http://panampost.com/panam-staff/2014/11/05/dominican-republic-withdraws-from-oas-human-rights-court/.

81. Panky Corcino, "Cónsul de Dominicana en Nueva York define a Junot Díaz como 'antidominicano,'" *El Diario*, October 23, 2015, http://www.eldiariony.com/2015/10/23/consul-de-dominicana-en-nueva-york-define-a-junot-diaz-como-antidominicano/.

PART II

Borders Within
Regional Communities and Resistant Identities

Brief Introduction

T his segment of *Area Studies in the Global Age* focuses on borders, place, and community-building and -destruction inside two of the world's economic powers, China and Russia.[1] Although only partly linked to trends of democratization since 1990, both are closely tied to the global economy and processes of globalization. Neither country has a democracy, though both have taken economic advantage of newly opened international borders. These economic developments have accelerated urbanization in China, the exploitation of oil and gas in remote regions of Siberia and the North Caucasus, and the centralization of Russia's wealth in Moscow.

Part II investigates groups who perceive themselves to have been left behind, or, at least, whose concerns have been ignored, in the new economic order. All three communities are to one degree or another peripheral to the interests of the power center. These people typically are not enjoying the benefits of an enriched China in the global economy or the increasingly closely held political and economic resources in the newly authoritarian Russia. People on these edges are "liminal" in the sense that they have little access to legal, policy, and material resources, could develop an "outsider" identity, and thus in the course of time could potentially become a problem for those in power.

In their chapter on urban villages, Dan Chen and John Kennedy deal with the serious spatial divisions being caused by Chinese urbanization and the potentially divisive identity issues involving aggressive urban appropriation of rural village land. Over the last few decades since 1982, the Chinese urban population has grown from 20 percent of the total population to 51 percent. In discussing the effects of this massive shift on perceptions of identity and community, Kennedy and Chen focus less on "national identity" than what they call "institutional identity" and "place identity." Based on their field research of two "urban villages" (rural enclaves) surrounded by the city of Xi'an, they find that, although national identity has remained relatively stable, institutional factors (for example, the government policy on household registration) and place identity (for example, rural or urban) show troublesome differences. Property rights and economic opportunities of villagers are changing, including the household registration system. China is more than just one of the great success stories, it is *the* success story in the global economy that developed in the 1990s. Inside the People's Republic, however, significant identity and community gaps have developed as the country grows economically and transfers to a largely urban environment.

In her treatment of debates about post-Soviet identity, Edith Clowes shows the renewal and further development of a long-standing regional identity in Siberia, where ethnic Russians see themselves as fundamentally different from European Russians. Although center-oriented discourse stresses historical Siberian simplicity and stoicism and Siberian heroism in World War II, a study of discussions about identity in a broad array of Siberian newspapers shows robust, multipronged criticism of Russian economic and cultural policy and resistance to the center's treatment of Siberia as a colony offering only raw materials that mainly enrich the center. Two major issues in this study concern the frustration on the part of educated Siberians who feel that their voices are not heard outside their own Siberian city or in the halls of power in Moscow, as well as the spatial difficulty of building Siberian community beyond the level of individual cities in a territory that is so vast and difficult to travel.

Austen Thelen's chapter gives a picture of identity and community formation among the rising generation in the ethnically complex and heavily contested territory of the North Caucasus. His work deals with two federal units, the ethnically Russian Stavropol "krai" and the ethnically other, non-Russian Republic of Karachay-Cherkessia. Each enjoys different kinds of legal rights, particularly regarding language use. The research, consisting of field interviews and surveys among 357 young adults aged eighteen to thirty, was completed in 2009, about ten years after the Second Chechen War. Thelen shows the complexity of scale (local, regional, national) and overlapping perceptions among residents of these two federal territories, who perhaps perceive themselves to be "in place" at a local scale but "marginalized" or "out of place" at a regional or national scale. He implies that this more nuanced understanding of place-based identity construction sheds light on difficult center-periphery relations in this part of the world.

Noteworthy in this and the following parts of *Area Studies in the Global Age* are widely divergent conceptual contexts in which each chapter couches its analysis. In contrast to part I, where the chapters worked primarily within the methodology of memory studies, the chapters in parts II and III particularly may seem to be more disjointed. The reason has to do with theoretical context. Diverging from the relative homogeneity of approach in part I, parts II and III present a fruitful combination of theoretical methods dealing with place, identity, and community: social theory (Chen/Kennedy), discursive-cultural theory (Clowes), and human-geographical theory (Thelen). At these junctures, when chapters offer contrasting approaches to allied topics, one finds synergetic concepts and terminologies. Here one can begin to work out points of mutual enhancement between various disciplinary traditions. The result is a truly interdisciplinary approach to studying and interpreting identity and community in the context of area studies.

Notes

1. These countries are often called the BRIC countries, comprising Brazil, Russia, India, and China.

Urbanization and Urban Villagers
Institutional Factors and Social Identity in Urban China

DAN CHEN AND JOHN JAMES KENNEDY

Introduction

Social identity defines how people perceive themselves based on their group membership.[1] Similar place, religion, and ethnicity can play an important role in shaping community membership and perception of self. Indeed, the physical environment has a significant influence on social identity.[2] According to Tajfel,[3] identity in relation with the community is defined as the individual's knowledge that "he belongs to certain social groups together with some emotional and value significance."[4] In cognitive terms, a community or social group can be defined as "two or more individuals who share a common social identification of themselves or, which is nearly the same thing, perceive themselves to be members of the same social category."[5] Here Tajfel refers to the basis of a social category as a social identifier. Sharing a common place is also a social identifier. Thus, the local environment is a strong predictor, and a significant change in place, such as a move from the countryside to the city or rapid urbanization, will dramatically influence the way people perceive themselves. However, social context and institutional factors may have a greater effect than the immediate physical environment.[6] Social and political categorizations are also personal identifiers that can form individual and group identity. Thus, the question is whether the institutional (contextual) factors or the physical environment have the greatest influence on social identity. In this chapter, social identity that is determined by institutional factors, rather than nationalism, cultural orientations, or other factors is referred to as institutional identity. Social identity that is determined by place origins through relations with "the physical environment by means of a complex pattern of conscious and unconscious ideals, beliefs, preferences, feelings, values, goals, and behavioral tendencies and skills relevant to this environment" is referred to as place identity.[7]

While regional and cultural variations can shape the debate, rapid urbanization in China provides an excellent case in which to examine the institutional and environmental factors. In fact, China's population demographics have gone from 20 percent urban in 1982 to 51 percent in 2012. This is one of the most rapid urban transformations in modern world history. It has created significant change in the physical environment for millions of villagers, who have lost their farms and traditional housing to urban expansion. At the same time, China still has an extensive national household registration system that determines whether an individual is considered an urban or rural resident. The rapid urbanization has created urban villages, usually nestled between high-rise buildings, within the expanding cities, where the original rural residents experience a dramatic change in living conditions and environment, but do not have official urban registration. Thus, does the change from rural to urban environment influence the way urban villagers view themselves? That is, do they consider themselves urban, rural, or somewhere in between?

This chapter examines this question using a unique case study from two urban villages in Xi'an, China (a city of four million). The first section introduces the concept of the "household registration system" and how it influences social identity in China. This section also includes an overview of China's urbanization and demographic change. The second section presents the urban village in China and shows how these villages are a reflection of place identity. The third section reviews the research methodologies used for this study. The fourth section describes an in-depth case study of two urban villages from Xi'an, China, followed by the final section, which evaluates the questions of place identity and social context.

Institutional Household Registration and Urbanization in China

For almost thirty years, the central government in China has managed to restrict internal migration through a strict household registration system.[8] From 1960 until the late 1980s, it was nearly impossible for a rural resident to find a job or a place to rent in the city without an urban registration card. However, in the 1990s, the central and local governments began to loosen the residency restrictions, especially in the major cities, where rural migrant labor was needed for new construction and infrastructure development.[9] Rural migrants do not have urban registration cards and it is difficult to rent apartments legally. As a result, they typically have three possible options for living space. First, they live at the factory where they work, in company dorms or temporary structures (like Quonset huts) that are built on the construction sites. Second, they might live in suburban communities with rural migrants from similar provinces or regions.[10] Living on the outskirts of the city makes it easier to build or rent homes without the urban registration. Finally, a significant number of rural migrants tend to rent relatively cheap apartments or live in boarding houses within the city, in urban villages where it is easier to overlook the migrants' household registration status.

The institutional categorization of Chinese citizens as either rural or urban was established during the Maoist era (1949–1976), when the central government set out to industrialize China. In the 1950s, China was an agrarian society, and the goal for the Chinese Communist Party (CCP) was to rapidly expand Chinese industry. However, the government had little capital to invest in heavy industry. To resolve this problem, the central government used agriculture to pay for urban industrial development through a system known as the "price scissors effect" in which the central government controls the market and labor migration to develop heavy industry.[11] To accomplish their goal, the government placed price caps on agricultural products so that farmers had to sell their grain at below market prices while, at the same time, selling industrial products, such as trucks and tractors, to collective farms for a higher than market price. Thus, the government provided cheap grain and agricultural products for urban workers. However, using agriculture to pay for urban industrialization required villagers to stay on the farm. Massive rural-to-urban migration would result in less agricultural output and slow down the industrialization process. To stem this migration, the central government enacted a household registration system (*hukou* system) in 1960 that restricted the free movement of labor.[12]

The household registration system categorized citizens by place of birth (village/town/city) and occupation (agricultural/nonagricultural). All social services, including land, housing, education, and employment were dependent on the type of registration card an individual held. Urban residents (with a nonagricultural *hukou*) were subsidized through the Iron Rice Bowl or work unit system, in which the urban factory or enterprise, such as a university or government office, supplied housing and food coupons to be spent at state stores. Thus, if a rural resident (with an agricultural *hukou*) came to the city to look for work in 1980, he or she would be unable to find employment or housing. For over two decades, the system maintained a rural/urban divide that discriminated against the rural population.[13]

The introduction of market reforms in the 1980s and especially after 1992 meant that rural migrants could come to the cities, work in private enterprises, and buy food at private stores. Nevertheless, the household registration system remained in effect. Throughout the 1990s and after 2000, many migrant work-ers could find places to rent, but their children could not attend local schools without the correct registration.[14] Many rural migrants moved to the cities without their spouses or children for years at a time, only to return home once a year for Chinese New Year. It is estimated that over 200 million migrant workers travel home during the New Year.[15] Moreover, a number of villagers are still tied to the land for both economic and psychological reasons. While villagers do not own the land, they do have thirty-year land use contracts with the village committee. Thus, unlike villagers in other developing countries, such as Mexico, Brazil, and Egypt, China's villagers cannot sell their land and move to the cities. Indeed, collectively owned land is one of the last vestiges of communism in rural China.

The institutional argument of social identity suggests that rural residents who come to live in the city, even for years at a time, continue to face discrimi-nation as nonurban residents.[16] It is not the place that defines them as much as the government identification and social (urban) definitions. Rural residents who live in the city are constantly reminded of their "outsider" existence. Even the local municipal press (government-owned) continues to describe the rural migrants as a "floating population," and increasing local crime rates are blamed on unruly "outsiders." The media reports as well as urban citizens target urban villagers as the source of the "problem." Both the rural migrants living in the urban villages and the original urban villagers, who became part of the city by default through urban expansion, are lumped into the group of "outsiders."[17]

Although most of the research on urban villages tends to focus on rural migrants, few studies have closely examined the urban villagers from their own perspective. Both groups of villagers are going through a transitional stage within the same community (urban village), but urban villagers are in a unique position where they experience dramatic change in their physical environment without migration. Unlike rural migrants, urban villagers can-not return to the land and the home village in the countryside. Institutionally, urban villagers have household registration cards that are agricultural (rural), or they receive a new categorization as "transitional residents"—neither rural nor urban. As a result, the institutional factor of household registration points to a more rural rather than urban social identity. Thus, if the institutional factors play a greater role in shaping identity, then one would expect urban villagers to identify themselves more as rural rather than urban residents. Controlling for population density and years spent living in urban dwellings, the institutional hypothesis suggests that most urban villagers do not perceive themselves as urban.

Urban Villages in China: Social Identity and Place

A number of authors suggest that social identity is shaped by the physical environment, especially in urban settings.[18] There is a clear distinction between rural and urban identity, and it is the environment that plays a significant role in social identification.[19] However, there is also a difference between "native place" identity and place identity. Native place identity is associated with a connection with a specific home province or county. This is a broad community identification for migrant workers, not unlike the home country association of American immigrants, such as Irish or Italians, at the turn of the twentieth century. A more recent example is the description of Latino migrant workers within the United States. These are US citizens who follow a circular route each year working in various crops. However, because of the work they do and their ethnicity, they are still not considered "Americans." Most scholarship on rural migrants tends to focus on studies of native place identity such as Zhang[20] and the research on "Zhejiang village." These are urban settlements made up of rural migrants coming from other provinces to major cities such as Beijing or rural migrants from specific counties migrating to the provincial capital. These tend to be settlements nested between the urban suburbs and the countryside (peri-urban). For this study, place identity is associated with a more immediate urban environment and the influence that urbanization has on rural residents who become "urban residents" without migration. Instead, rural villagers remain on the original site (land), and the landscape changes from rural to urban before their eyes.

Indeed, as cities in China expand outward, many villages are enveloped by thirty-story office buildings and apartment complexes. As cities expand into the adjacent countryside, municipal governments negotiate with the village community over compensation and new land rights. Then villagers receive housing subsidies to build new homes in a designated area.[21] The new village community consists of densely packed two- to four-story buildings built close together. After the land use rights are transferred from the villagers (farmland) to the municipality, the local government leases the land to developers and the high-rise construction begins. The urban villages are nestled between these high-rise apartments and office buildings.

Although few studies explicitly examine social identity of urban villagers, some scholars suggest that the urban environment can influence self-perception and the transition from rural villager to urban resident.[22] For urban villagers, the change in the physical environment, such as loss of farmland, and the move into three- to four-story apartments surrounded by high-rises, is also accompanied by a new urban market economy. This includes nonagricultural employment at stores, restaurants, and factories as well as shopping at super-markets and stores for basic food items (rather than growing one's own). The urban post-socialist experience can change social identity and perceptions of self beyond state classifications.[23] While the urban villagers do not typi-cally live and work with official urban residents as colleagues and immediate neighbors, they do begin to adapt and adopt urban practices and lifestyles. As Bach[24] suggests, they begin as peasants but they become urban citizens. Thus if the physical urban environment plays a greater role in shaping identity, one would expect urban villagers to identify themselves more as urban rather than rural residents. Controlling for population density and years spent living in urban dwellings, the environmental (place) hypothesis suggests that most urban villagers perceive themselves as urban.

Methodology

This study uses a qualitative approach to address the research question. Interview data, participant observation, and analysis of media reports are needed to answer the question of whether or not the change from rural to urban environment will influence the way urban villagers view themselves. We are interested in the factors that influence self-perception and its links to the dynamics of urbanization. The ethnographic method is appropriate when studying social interactions over time, especially in developing countries.[25] Open-ended interviews of urban villager households collecting individual and family histories over time are most suitable for this type of study.[26] Over the period from 2009 to 2012, we collected twenty in-depth open-ended villager interviews from two urban villages, including one village committee member (village cadre) from each urban village, as well as over fifty interviews with urban residents, migrant workers, and other urban villagers.

We selected two urban villages as the cases, based on the length of time these villages became "urban" with a changed household registration status and how they fit into the municipal urbanization plan. Xi'an municipality was chosen as the city case because of the rapid urbanization plan and our relationship with the major university in the area. The city is located in Shaanxi province and is the provincial capital. Two urban villages were selected in 2009, and we observed the communities for three years. There are also other urban villagers that we have observed in Xi'an, but we only returned to two villages.

The villagers for the in-depth interviews were selected using snowball sam-pling, which has advantages because the researcher can get insider access to specific communities and organizations that might otherwise be inaccessible.

However, there are also drawbacks to the method, because relying on one initial informant can create an unwanted bias. One informant may introduce the researcher to like-minded people within a small subgroup of the intended sample. One way to avoid this bias is to include several initial informants. This is the procedure we followed for our study. Moreover, we paid close attention to varying the age, gender, and occupation of participants in the in-depth interviews as much as possible. The sample was all Han ethnicity, and six of the twenty in-depth interviewees were women.

Within urban villages, inhabitants made a definite distinction between the original residents and the rural migrants. We also interviewed migrant workers living in the urban villages and official urban residents who lived near the urban villages. These were not random samples but rather convenient samples. Although the convenient samples were not representative, we used these interviews in conjunction with the public media reports on urban villagers.

Finally, we use qualitative content analysis of publicly available reports from Xi'an's major newspapers. The major newspapers reflect the municipal and provincial party-government position on urban villages. Of course, the Chinese media are state-controlled at the national, provincial, and municipal levels. While there are specific national topics about which it is either prohibited or required to publish, provincial and municipal media have developed more autonomy to attract a local audience and advertisers. In this study, we use the media reports as a reflection of the local official position on urban villages as well as the state attitude toward urban villagers as rural, urban, or transitional residents (i.e., as urban residents or as "outsiders").

Urban Village Case Studies: Transformation and the Urban Environment

Xi'an municipality is located in the northwest province of Shaanxi. In 2010, Xi'an municipality consisted of nine districts and four counties with over three thousand villages. The population of the whole municipality is 7.8 million, and that of the concentrated urban district is 3.9 million. However, the official population statistics divide the population by official household registration status, as either agricultural (rural) or nonagricultural (urban). In the municipality including the counties, only 49 percent of the population is considered urban and the rest have an agricultural registration. In Xi'an city about 65 percent of the population is urban. Thus, there is a clear distinction between rural and urban even within the urban districts. This difference is due to urban expansion over the last twenty years. Rural counties within the municipality have been redesignated as districts, with little change in the rural and urban composition of the population over the last ten years. For example, when Chang'an County became a district in 2002, 80 percent of the population was rural; in 2010 the official population division was essentially the same with 78 percent rural. Municipal governments change the designation in order to have greater control over land use rights, which in turn facilitates the urbanization process.

In the early 1990s, Xi'an municipal urban districts began to expand beyond the city center through the introduction of new High-Tech Industrial Development Zones and expanding existing urban districts. The most successful case is the Gaoxin District in Xi'an, which began in 1992. The area covers 107 square kilometers of development, with an expansion after 2012 to 200 square kilometers. It is a city within a city, and it is about the size of Lincoln, Nebraska. In 2012, the district had over a dozen urban villages, and the number had fluctuated over the years due to the incorporation of new villages in the expansion process and the demolition of the older villages. The same process is occurring in the older districts that are expanding outward from the city center. For example, Xincheng (New City) district started to develop beyond the traditional city walls and to include villages in the urban district in the late 1980s and early 1990s. Xincheng district has 31 square kilometers and has 89 urban subdistricts (neighborhood committees) and 13 urban villages. This district is closer to the urban core and more densely populated than Gaoxin, but it has about the same number of urban villages. For both districts, the legal transformation from a rural (agricultural) to an urban (nonagricultural) household registration takes about ten to twenty years and includes consolidation of rural homes, urban development (urban village status), and then demolition of the urban village and relocation into a high-rise apartment complex.

The two urban village cases are Zhao family village (Zhaojia cun) in Gaoxin District and Hansenzhai village in Xincheng district. The change from rural county to urban districts began around the same time in the early 1990s for both villages. Moreover, both villages have gone through the same process of urbanization. The main difference is that in 2012, the Zhao family village was demolished and the new high-rises began construction later that year, whereas the Hansenzhai villagers are still waiting for the demolition and new high-rises for the official "village" residents in 2014. The physical environment in Hansenzhai and Zhao family villages went through a dramatic change from a traditional rural setting to densely populated urban district within a two-to-three-year period. It is this intense transformation of the immediate living conditions that can have a strong influence on social identity.

According to a village committee member, about 10,000 original villagers live in Hansenzhai, with an additional 20,000–25,000 migrant workers living in the urban village. Of course, it is difficult to get an accurate count of migrant villagers, but the original villagers make up about one-third of the current population. The living space and shopping areas within the village are crowded. On a typical day the narrow streets are filled with residents buying food, running errands, and making use of local services from haircuts to clothing repair. However, it is clear that the large majority of migrant workers live and work in the urban village except during the Spring Festival (Chinese New Year). During the week-long celebration, most migrant workers return to their home villages. For example, in 2012, there were over 250 million migrant workers returning home for the holiday in a massive rush on rail lines and bus routes.[27] As a result, many of the urban villages, including Hansenzhai village, were ghost towns for a week.

Hansenzhai village is an urban environment teeming with life during the day and early evening, with rows of open food stalls and storefronts lining the narrow alleyways and streets. The urban village economy is based on the provision of local services for residents, both original villagers and migrants. The owners of the small stores and service providers are also a mix of local villagers and migrants. Unlike other urban neighborhoods, Hansenzhai village offers a wide range of stores and services that cater to lower-income families and individuals. There is a larger percentage of Internet bars, because few people in urban villages own home computers compared to average urban residents. There are also more public showers because many of the rental units in the village do not have shower facilities. In addition, clothing repair, from patches to buttons and zippers, as well as bicycle repair stands, are common in Hansenzhai. In the 1990s and after 2000, there were clothing and bicycle repair stands all over the city of Xi'an, but after 2002 there was a dramatic rise in private cars and more disposable personal income among urban residents. As a result, there were fewer bicycles and less demand to repair older clothes. However, within the urban villages, migrant workers and original villagers did not experience the same increase in incomes, and many families still depend on the more "traditional services."

One of the main reasons that large numbers of migrant workers live in urban villages is the availability of cheap housing and less restrictive enforcement of the household registration system when renting a small apartment or room. In 1994, after villagers had to sell their land use rights, the village was consolidated into an area with the size of several large city blocks, and each family was given a relatively large living space in four- to five-story buildings. Although these are not high-rises, villagers moved from small rural single-family homes into larger urban housing units. Most villagers converted their larger homes into apartments and boarding houses. While most migrant workers rely on manual labor in urban stores and restaurants, many Hansenzhai villagers have become dependent on rental fees and boarding house revenues for their income. Thus there is a mutual dependence between the rural migrants and the original villagers. In addition, it is technically illegal to rent an apartment or a room without registering the occupants with the local public security office, but villagers rent out rooms without the formal registration. In an attempt to see how this system works firsthand, one of the authors (Kennedy) rented several rooms at different boarding houses. He found that it is easy to rent a room, even for a foreigner. In 2011, the general boarding room price was 35–50 yuan a day (five-fifty to eight dollars). When asked the price in the first boarding house, the landlord answered, 30 yuan a day without a toilet in the room and 40 with a bathroom. After we agreed on the room, the attendant asked for Kennedy's passport, upon which Kennedy answered that he did not have it. The attendant still agreed to rent the room, but the price changed to 50 yuan a day. While renting a room to a rural migrant without officially registering the occupant is legally risky, renting to a foreigner without registering is downright dangerous. However, in visits to three boarding houses in Hansenzhai village, the same interaction occurred, except that the prices varied (but were still under 60 yuan per day).

Converted apartments and boarding houses in urban villages are unofficially allowed to operate. An interview with an urban village committee member indicated that the local police know that the apartments are "illegally" rented out, but these actions are tolerated for two reasons. One is that the concentration of rural migrants within a specific community makes it easier for the municipal police to monitor and control it. It is difficult to stem the inflow of migrant workers to cities such as Xi'an, but monitoring a community with a known concentration of rural migrants is easier than having them unevenly spread throughout the city and the suburbs. Second, it is important for the original villagers to have a steady source of income. The village committee member admitted that, in the beginning, more than half the villagers were not happy with the loss of farmland, even though they received monetary compensation, larger housing, and the promise of an urban registration card for themselves and their children. Over time, villagers spent the initial compensation. Allowing them to rent out rooms and small apartments is a way to provide them with a continued unofficial subsidy for giving up their farmland. Moreover, for the municipal public security bureau, social stability is the most important policy goal. And allowing greater income opportunities for urban villagers can also offer a way to monitor rural migrants in the city.

For the original urban villagers, the distinction between themselves and rural migrants is an indication that the urban environment can influence social identity. From our interviews and observations, the original villagers feel no solidarity with the rural migrants, and they see themselves as "permanent" residents as opposed to the more transitory migrant population. However, recognizing a difference between themselves and the rural migrants does not mean they view themselves as urban (and migrants as rural). Indeed, most of the Chinese news reports do not make the distinction between the original urban villagers and rural migrants, which can influence the general public perceptions, as well as urban villagers.

Media Perceptions of Urban Villagers and Migrants

Media perception of the urban villages is an important measure of how local and national government perceives urban villages. In addition, the state-run media outlets can all influence urban public perceptions of urban villages. We analyzed national and local (Xi'an City) newspapers, and we uncovered two distinct media depictions of urban villages and their inhabitants.

First, the state media rarely distinguish between rural migrants and the original farmers. As a result, both the local and national media frequently refer to all residents in the village as "urban villagers" and "outsiders." For example, a story in *Workers' Daily*, an official national newspaper, reported that the police arrested two suspects for counterfeiting train tickets and other certifications in an urban village in Guangzhou, without specifying whether these suspects were rural migrants, local farmers, or other people living in the urban village.[28] Another story in the *Wuhan Evening Newspaper* reported that an express mail postal worker was beaten while attempting to deliver a package in an urban village.[29] In self-defense, the postal worker stabbed another man. The postal worker complained that the addresses in the urban village were confusing and difficult to find and, as a result, he knocked on the "wrong" door. Again the story did not specify whether the man involved in the fight was a rural migrant or a local villager.

Second, the state media show negative bias against urban villagers. The media tend to profile urban villagers as unruly outsiders and the urban village as a hotbed of criminal activity. While there are many police operations across the city, the press tends to focus on police activity in urban villages. For example, the Xi'an newspaper *San Qin Capital City Report* (*Sanqing Dushibao*) published a story on a surprise police inspection in an urban village as part of the fight against criminal activities such as prostitution.[30] Although there were raids in other parts of the city, this report refers to hotels, hair salons, and poker rooms in a specific urban village. Urban villages are also referred to as "complicated places," different from other urban areas because of the various criminal activities and "unhealthy social practices" that occur. This reporting creates a widespread negative perception of the people who live in urban villages. A report from a local Xi'an newspaper, the *Chinese Business Report* (*Huashangbao*), described how a citywide police sting in Xi'an to confiscate illegal guns focused exclusively on urban villages as the source.[31] This focus clearly assumed that urban villages are the places where crimes prevail, whether or not these assumptions were backed with sufficient evidence. Similar news stories from national media such as *sina.com* and *people.com.cn* have reported on criminal activities in urban villages, such as rape and robbery.[32] The implication is that the state media perpetuate the negative perceptions of urban villagers as unruly outsiders from the countryside.

Still, some reports adopt a more sympathetic tone toward urban villagers, which is also based on the implicit perception that urban villagers are outsiders who come to the cities hoping for a better life but end up in an unfortunate situation. One type of report focuses on personal security concerns related to antiquated facilities and insufficient infrastructure in urban villages. For example, in December 2012 the local press reported a story about an 18-year-old man living in an urban village, who was poisoned to death by carbon monoxide when using a coal stove in a poorly ventilated room.[33] Stories about forced removal from the urban village marked for demolition, and conflicts between urban villagers and the local governments, also appear in the local and national press. For example, in 2012 the *Xi'an Chinese Business Report* detailed the harrowing experience of a family who refused to leave home after their whole village was forced to leave and their home was the only one left standing.[34] In China the state media call these "nail households" (*dingzihu*) because of their stubborn refusal to go along with a local policy or project. In fact, this is a typical tactic for rural villagers, and in most cases the villagers use the national laws, such as property rights and land use rights, to protect their local interests. These are also known as "rightful resistance."[35] In this case the nail household lost. Their home was demolished, the family was beaten, and the furniture was buried in rubble. The national news media Xinhua News Agency carried a number of similar reports of urban villagers who were violently evicted from their houses in 2012.[36] These reports adopted a sympathetic tone toward the urban villagers, describing the violence they have endured as a result of forced removal and demolition. However, such reports may also perpetuate the distinction between rural and urban populations as well as the biased perception that urban villagers are outsiders and do not belong to the cities. Such violent incidents of removal rarely occur for urbanites. While official urban residents have been moved from older government-subsidized housing to newer high-rises, this type of removal is less controversial.

Finally, the state media often depict urban villagers as uneducated in the ways of urban life and needing to learn how to operate within the urban environment. Local law-enforcement personnel typically prefer methods of "persuasion" or "education" to violence against urban villagers in order to enforce zoning or local regulations. For example, a news report from the Xi'an government website remarks that local police were used to persuade and educate urban villagers on how to operate their business activities such as street stalls and storefronts, where store owners set up tables and sell items on the front sidewalks. For those urban villagers who refused to comply with the regulation, law-enforcement personnel cleared up and confiscated the goods.[37] This type of report suggests the difficulty municipal governments have with "uneducated" outsiders from the countryside even if they are the original urban villagers.

Urban Villager Self-Perceptions

While the state media refer to urban villagers as outsiders, it is unclear whether the original urban villagers view themselves as rural or urban. For rural migrants, it is clear that they consider themselves outsiders. In Chinese, the word *outsider* (*waidiren*) is made up of three characters—outside (*wai*), place (*di*), and person (*ren*). This term has very real social significance in Chinese society, and being an outsider does not only mean being rural or urban; the term is also used for people from different cities or rural areas. For instance, a farmer from village *x* may view a person from village *y* as an outsider because they are not from the same village or township. The irony is that in the urban villages we studied, the original urban villagers viewed rural migrants residing within the village as outsiders, but the general urban population (through the state media) perceived all urban villagers as outsiders. According to our interviews, the time spent living in the urban village does not change the self-perception. For example, a migrant worker from the neighboring province of Henan said that he has lived in Hansenzhai village for over eight years, but he still considers himself a nonresident of the village. He perceives himself as an outsider, even though his two sons and wife also live in Hansenzhai. Every interview with migrant workers provided the same general response in both Zhao family village and Hansenzhai.

During our field study, original villagers were initially hard to identify and we had to use the snowball sampling method to meet with these residents. Over a couple of months in 2010, we were able to meet with and interview over twenty original village residents. The age groups varied from thirty-five to seventy years old and the older villagers (over forty-five) provided the greatest detail regarding the change in their household registration status. One of the most striking revelations from our interviews in both urban village case studies is that many of the original villagers still consider themselves outsiders, even some of the younger respondents who have spent nearly half their lives in the urban village. An older villager shared his thoughts on the irony of complaining about the outsiders (rural migrants) taking over their urban village, while still feeling like an outsider himself within the urban district. In this respect, being an outsider in the city is a social identity that the original villagers and the rural migrants have in common. This perception also follows the state media depiction of all residents of the urban village. Yet the main variation among the respondents is whether their self-perception is rural or urban. Some of the younger respondents believed they were more urban, while some of the older respondents still held on to some of the more traditional rural values and perceptions. However, the term "rural and urban" is not so clear-cut for the original residents.

Our research question (and two hypotheses) is whether (1) the physical urban environment or (2) the institutional categorization plays a greater role in shaping social identity. The interviews suggest that the household registration has a greater influence. Most of the original urban villagers we interviewed identified themselves in accordance with the status of their household registration. However, age and occupational experience also play a role in shaping social identity. When we asked villagers whether or not they considered themselves urban, we received an unexpected answer from most respondents. The common answer was neither rural nor urban, but in the middle or as one villager put it, "we are urbanites in waiting." This is because in both village case studies, the original villagers were in the process of changing household registration status from agricultural to nonagricultural, which can take up to twenty years. In the interim, they literally have rural transfer registration cards. As soon as the municipal government proposes future plans to demolish the urban village and construct high-rises and new housing for the original villagers, then a change in their registration status begins. Thus, the original urban villager identity is shaped more by the institutional categorization as "middle" or "transfer" people than by the immediate urban environment. Some may argue that one of the reasons why the original villagers feel superior to the rural migrants is that they can stay in the same place and enjoy the benefits that rural migrants do not have. But this is precisely a result of institutional arrangements rather than place identity, because the material benefits are part of institutional change in registration rather than place of origin.

The complete transfer from agricultural to nonagricultural status is a long process due to the negotiations between the urban village committee (local governing body) and the municipal government. The village committee is the legal "owner" of the land and literally controls the land use contracts. They work with municipal government on two main agreements. First is the initial "sale" of the land use contracts and transfer of the land to the urban district. Second is the move to a new high-rise where the village gets a high-rise apartment complex and can "buy" a subsidized apartment. The second process can drag on for over a decade. For example, one urban village in Xi'an that was not included in the case studies is known as the "nail village" (*dingzi cun*) because of the village committee's reluctance to accept the municipal government's new high-rise plan. According to a local researcher who investigated the case, village residents were very unhappy with the new location of the apartment complex to be built more than three kilometers (two miles) away from the village site. The most interesting aspect of this case is that neither the local government nor the construction company hired to build on the urban village site has made an attempt to forcefully remove the original residents or the rural migrants. As of 2012, negations are still ongoing.

In the twenty in-depth interviews and additional thirty short interviews in our sample, registration status has the greatest influence on social identity. This supports previous studies[38] and also demonstrates that this explanation fits within the Chinese context, where institutional categorizations have had a significant influence on two generations of Chinese citizens. However, occupational experience and age also have a significant effect on an urban villager's perceptions of the process as positive or negative. Both male and female interviewees younger than forty-five years old tend to have a relatively optimistic view toward the change in registration status. For example, several of the younger respondents believe that once they receive the official nonagricultural urban status and move into the new high-rise, they will become urban. Indeed, for younger urban villagers, achieving an urban status is an important goal. In the Chinese media and official propaganda, modern social development is closely linked to urbanization. Of course, there is a rich discourse on modernity in North American and Western European history, but this desire to achieve a modern urban status at the individual and national level is associated with China's postsocialist development since the late 1990s. Thus social identity for this cohort is connected with the official and social recognition of being urban.

The older urban villagers tend to have a more negative view of the official transformation process. Unlike younger urban villagers we interviewed, older villagers worked on the land and remembered life on the farm. This is a key experience. Several respondents in Hansenzhai village remarked that the land is the most secure form of social insurance. For example, a sixty-eight-year-old gentleman said that his family received 24,000 yuan ($2,900) in 1992 to pay off their land use contracts to the city. His family had two mu of land (1 mu = 0.16 acre) and they grew wheat. He admits that his material life is better now than when he was a farmer, but he currently has no insurance (his quote was "no land, no insurance"). A sixty-three-year-old woman from the same village told a similar story. In 1992, her family received 24,000 yuan per mu, but she said this was not a fair price for villagers because the village committee sold the land for 100,000 yuan per mu to the city (1 USD equals about 6 Chinese yuan, and 1 mu equals approximately 667 square meters). When Chen asked her how she knew this information, she said she was a village committee member at the time. When Kennedy and Chen asked her about the change in registration status, she said that she did not want to be an urban resident. She also referred to the same problem about lacking social insurance and having no land (her quote was "no land, no grain insurance"). Among all the older respondents, the initial cash compensation seemed like a lot of money at the time, but it was not enough to invest in an urban apartment and it was spent after a few years. They missed the security of the land, only because, as opposed to cash, land is a relatively stable source of sustenance. The elderly urban villagers have already witnessed inflation and the rising cost of basic foods without the same official social insurance that elderly urban residents received from the government after retirement. Therefore, while the older urban villagers do not perceive themselves as rural because they are in the official transition stage, they also do not have the same desire to become urban that the younger villagers do.

The general urbanization process for both urban village cases in the Xi'an municipality has been underway for about twenty years. Before 1992, all villagers had an agricultural registration status, and each family had its own plots of land (known as rural contract land). In 1992, the Xi'an municipal government began urban expansion by redefining the administrative rural area as an urban district. Soon after the redistricting, the village committee negotiated the sale of land use contracts and then moved forward with the consolidation of village land and housing. In 1993, urban villagers received the agricultural transfer registration (neither rural nor urban), and the population dynamics within the urban village changed as rural migrants moved in. In 2011, the Zhao family village committee members finished the negotiations with the municipal government over the rest of the village land. In 2012, the Zhao family village was demolished, and rural migrants were forced to move out. Urban villagers received their nonagricultural registration card and subsidy for a rental apartment until their new high-rise apartment (con-dominium) was finished, scheduled for 2014 on the same site. In 2012, the Hansenzhai village committee members are negotiating with the municipal government. It is expected that the village will be demolished at the end of 2013 and the original urban villagers will receive their official urban regis-tration cards.

Conclusion

We define social identity as people's perception of themselves based on their group membership. While similar place and shared environmental setting can play an important role in shaping community membership and perception of self, we confirm that institutional categorization is one of the key factors in shaping social identity for the two Chinese urban village cases we observed. Although China is relaxing the household registration system and currently allows internal migration, the system still affects self-perceptions. Indeed, the state media perpetuate the rural/urban differences and the notions of urban "insiders and outsiders." Our findings suggest that the political and insti-tutional environment still has a deep influence on social identity in China, which is the legacy of the household registration system. Such institutional influence on social identity reinforces the differences between urban and rural residents and may even perpetuate discrimination against nonurban groups. As urbanization continues, the mingling and interaction between the rural and urban population will only become deeper and more prevalent. Sharp dif-ferences in social identity thus have important implications for the relations between rural and urban social groups, the identities of whom are strongly influenced by political institutions.

Nevertheless, social identity is complex and is shaped by a number of fac-tors. With the constantly changing landscape of Chinese migrants, we should also take into account the impact of social identifiers such as place identity, which includes more specific factors such as age and life experience. The influ-ence of place identity that we found also confirms much of the literature. The inertia of the psychological bond with the place where individual life is lived stands against the influence of the political institutions, which reflects the rapid change in the process of urbanization. How these different sources of influence affect social identity will depend on the interaction between contex-tual and individual-level factors.

While our findings are suggestive, they are also limited to a small sample. There are a large number of other urban villages in wealthier eastern cities where villagers have different opportunities. Improved economic conditions also provide different life experiences, which in turn influence group dynamics and social identity. Future research on urban villages and social identity will examine the economic and geographic variation in urban villages to determine the strength of institutional factors.

Notes

1. Henri Tajfel, *Human Group and Social Categories: Studies in Social Psychology* (Cambridge, UK: Cambridge University Press, 1981); Henri Tajfel, ed., *Social Identity and Intergroup Relations* (Cambridge, UK: Cambridge University Press, 1982).

2. Gerard Kyle, Alan Graefe, Robert Manning, and James Bacon, "Effects of Place Attachment on Users' Perceptions of Social and Environmental Conditions in a Natural Setting," *Journal of Environmental Psychology* 24 (2004): 213–25; H. M. Proshansky, A. K. Fabian, and R. Kaminoff, "Place-Identity: Physical World Socialization of the Self," *Journal of Environmental Psychology* 3 (1983): 57–83; G. Speller, E. Lyons, and C. Twigger-Ross, "A Community in Transition: The Relationship between Spatial Change and Identity Processes," *Social Psychological Review* 4 (2002): 39–58.

3. Henri Tajfel, "The Psychological Structure of Intergroup Behavior," in *Differentiation between Social Groups: Studies in the Social Psychology of Intergroup Relations*, ed. Henri Tajfel (London: Academic Press, 1978), 67.

4. J. C. Turner, "Towards a Cognitive Redefinition of the Social Groups," in *Social Identity and Intergroup Relations*, ed. Henri Tajfel (Cambridge, UK: Cambridge University Press, 1982), 21.

5. Ibid., 15.

6. J. C. Turner, M. A. Hogg, P. J. Oakes, S. D. Reicher, and M. S. Wetherell, "A Self-Categorization Theory," in *Rediscovering the Social Group: A Self-Categorization Theory*, ed. J. C. Turner et al. (Oxford: Basil Blackwell, 1987).

7. Harold M. Proshansky, "The City and Self-Identity," *Environment and Behavior* 10 (1978): 147–69, 155.

8. Fei-Ling Wang, *Organizing Through Division and Exclusion: China's Hukou System* (Stanford, CA: Stanford University Press, 2005).

9. Kam Wing Chan, "The Chinese Household Registration System and Migrant Labor in China: Notes on a Debate," *Population and Development Review* 36 (2010): 357–64.

10. Li Zhang, *Strangers in the City: Reconfigurations of Space, Power, and Social Networks* (Stanford, CA: Stanford University Press, 2001).

11. Justin Yifu Lin and Mingxing Liu, "Rural Informal Taxation in China: Historical Evolution and an Analytic Framework," *China & World Economy* 15 (2007): 1–18; Raaj Kumar Sah and Joseph E. Stiglitz, "The Economics of Price Scissors," *American Economic Review* 74 (1984): 125–38.

12. Z. Liu, "Institution and Inequality: The Hukou System in China," *Journal of Comparative Economics* 33 (2005): 133–57; Lin and Liu, "Rural Informal Taxation in China."

13. Wang, *Organizing Through Division and Exclusion*.

14. Zhang, *Strangers in the City*.

15. Xinhua News Agency, "Tens of Millions on the Move as China Spring Festival Travel Season Starts," *Xinhua News*, January 8, 2012, accessed March 12, 2013, http://news.xinhuanet.com/english/china/2012-01/08/c_131348789.htm.

16. Dorothy J. Solinger, "China's Floating Population: Implications for State and Society," in *The Paradox of China's Post-Mao Reforms*, ed. Roderick MacFarquhar and Merle Goldman (Cambridge, MA: Harvard University Press, 1999); Zhang, *Strangers in the City*; Wang, *Organizing Through Division and Exclusion*.

17. Yuting Liu, Shenjing He, Fulong Wu, and Chris Webster, "Urban Villages under China's Rapid Urbanization: Unregulated Assets and Transitional Neighborhoods," *Habitat International* 34 (2010): 135–44.

18. Kyle et al., "Effects of Place Attachment," 213–225; Proshansky et al., "Place-identity"; Speller et al., "A Community in Transition."

19. Jonathan Bach, "They Come in as Peasants and Leave as Citizens," *Cultural Anthropology* 25 (2010): 421–48; Dorothy J. Solinger, *Contesting Citizenship: Peasant Migrants, the State and the Logic of the Market in Urban China* (Berkeley: University of California Press, 1999).

20. Zhang, *Strangers in the City*.

21. Liu et al., "Urban Villages under China's Rapid Urbanization"; S. J. He, Y. T. Liu, C. Webster, and F. Wu, "Property Rights Redistribution, Entitlement Failure, and the Impoverishment of Landless Farmers," *Urban Studies* 46 (2009): 1925–49.

22. Bach, "They Come in as Peasants and Leave as Citizens"; Mary Ann O'Donnell, "Becoming Hong Kong, Razing Baoan, Preserving Xin'An: An Ethnographic Account of Urbanization in the Shenzhen Special Economic Zone," *Cultural Studies* 15 (2001): 419–43.

23. Li Zhang and Aihwa Ong, *Privatizing China: Socialism from Afar* (Ithaca, NY: Cornell University Press, 2008).

24. Bach, "They Come in as Peasants and Leave as Citizens."

25. Wayne Fife, *Doing Fieldwork: Ethnographic Methods for Research in Developing Countries and Beyond* (London and New York: Palgrave Macmillan, 2005).

26. Elizabeth Francis, "Qualitative Research: Collecting Life Histories," in *Fieldwork in Developing Countries*, ed. Stephen Devereux and John Hoddinott (New York: Harvester Wheatsheaf, 1992); D. K. Kondo, "How the Problem of 'Crafting Selves' Emerged," in *Contemporary Field Research: Perspectives and Formulas*, ed. Robert Emerson (Long Grove, IL: Waveland, 2001).

27. Xinhua News Agency, "Tens of Millions on the Move."

28. C. Huang and X. Ye, "Guangzhou Railway Police: Two Major Crimes of Counterfeiting and Selling Fake Tickets Were Cracked Down in One Day," *Workers' Daily*, January 19, 2013, accessed March 15, 2013, http://acftu.people.com.cn/n/2013/0119/c67502-20256350.html.

29. W. Dai, "A Wuhan Delivery Man Stabbed Another Man's Neck Vein Using Knife," *Wuhan Evening Newspaper*, November 25, 2012, accessed March 15, 2013, http://info.wuhan.net.cn/pub/2012/1125/118072.shtml.

30. Y. Li and J. Wang, "Yanta Police's Raid on Urban Village Last Night," *Sanqin Capital City Report (Sanqin Dushibao)*, November 30, 2012, accessed March 15, 2013, http://www.sanqindaily.com/News/20121130/212851.html.

31. D. Yang and T. Dang, "Lianhu Police Confiscated 43 Guns," *Huashang Newspaper (Huashangbao)*, November 29, 2012, accessed March 15, 2013, http://media.hsw.cn/system/2012/11/29/051547594.shtml.

32. Beifang Web, "Temporary Worker Committed 21 Rape Cases Involving 7 Victims in 6 Months," *Beifang Web*, January 4, 2013, accessed March 15, 2013, http://news.china.com/social/1007/20130104/17611213.html; H. Ju, "Police Arrested a Criminal in an Urban Village," *Taiyuan Evening Newspaper*, January 1, 2013, accessed March 15, 2013, http://news.sina.com.cn/c/2013-01-01/013925936691.shtml; Y. Zuo, "Taiyuan: Serial Robbery and Rape Cases in Urban Villages Cracked," *Shanxi Daily*, January 16, 2013, accessed March 15, 2013, http://sx.people.com.cn/n/2013/0116/c189147-18027924.html.

33. L. Wen, "18-year-old Man Dead in a Rented Apartment, Coal Stove Suspected to Be the Reason," *Huashang Web*, December 7, 2012, accessed March 15, 2013, http://news.hsw.cn/system/2012/12/07/051552949.shtml.

34. Y. Liu, Y., "The Worst Nail House in Xi'an City Chang'an District," *Yan'an Express*, December 11, 2012, accessed March 15, 2013, http://yanan.hsw.cn/system/2012/12/11/051555911.shtml.

35. Kevin O'Brien and Lianjiang Li, *Rightful Resistance in Rural China* (Cambridge, UK: Cambridge University Press, 2006).

36. Z. Liu and X. Hu, "Wuhan Urban Villagers Violently Forced to Demolition, Urban Villagers Beaten When Police Arrived," *Legal Daily (Fazhi Ribao)*, December 29, 2012, accessed March 15, 2013, http://news.xinhuanet.com/local/2012–12/29/c_124166401.htm.

37. Chang'an District Government, "Chang'an District Weiqu Street Started Remediation Activities in Urban Villages," *Xi'an Government*, December 26, 2012, accessed March 15, 2013, http://www.xa.gov.cn/ptl/trs_ci_id_543676.html.

38. See, for example, Turner et al., "A Self-Categorization Theory."

Place, Scale, and Self-Reliance

Issues of Identity and Community in Contemporary Siberia[1]

E D I T H   W.   C L O W E S

From the standard point of view of a European Russian, the stereotypical Siberian is a simple but good kind of person. Siberians' canonical resilience and good will have been forged by geo-meteorological conditions—bone-chilling cold and vast, unforgiving terrain. To quote Petr Pridius, the author of a post-Soviet book on the Trans-Siberian Railroad, Siberians are "strong, stalwart [*muzhestvennyi*] people . . . made that way by the harsh climate. [Composed of] many different ethnic groups, [Siberians] are one in spirit, toughness, and persistence."[2] This stereotype of the tough, honest Siberian is promoted on a regular basis by Russia's president, Vladimir Putin, who equates "Siberia" with the "Siberian character," "stalwart," and possessing the "ability to overcome hardship, to reach goals, and under difficult circumstances to achieve bright, positive results."[3] Putin considers the Siberian character "one of the main resources in Russia," which will help Russians "reach all our goals and resolve all our problems."

In his autobiographical novella, *Rivers* (*Reki*, 2005), Siberia's most popular post-Soviet writer, Evgeny Grishkovets, reaffirms the theme of Siberian "stalwartness," as well as the moral traits of fairness and generosity, though with a difference. Lest anyone suspect that Siberians are less than bright or are easily duped, Grishkovets pointedly uses the Siberian as the ultimate judge of political and economic ethics: the Siberian "hates dirty dealing [*verolomstvo*] and never forgets lies, duplicity, and meanness. He cannot bear greed and calculated pragmatism. In any quiet, neat teetotaler a Siberian espies craftiness, greed, and disdain toward himself."[4] This new addition to the Siberian character is a clear criticism of Putin himself, who is reticent, neat, and a teetotaler.

In contrast to traditional area studies, which focus on centers of power—their rhetoric, decisions, and actions,—the goal of this and a number of other chapters in this book is to hear voices on the "periphery" in the context of the big themes of the early twenty-first century, particularly democratization.

At the heart of this chapter is a consideration of the Siberian vocabulary of identity and a range of Siberian opinions about being Siberian and Siberians' relationships to other Siberians. Examining the reasons why Grishkovets might be criticizing Putin, even in this indirect way—and what else Grishkovets has to say about Siberia per se—highlights a new Siberian literary-political activism and its significance for Siberians' sense of identity and community. More broadly, this chapter investigates public discourse about being Siberian and forming Siberian community since 2000, when Putin became president. The decade between 2000 and 2010 had particular significance for the development of Siberian consciousness because it saw the curtailment of the relative political autonomy proffered to Russia's regions by the Yeltsin administration in the 1990s. At mid-decade President Putin put all Russia's regions under seven centrally appointed and controlled "governors." Against this background I focus on the case of Evgeny Grishkovets, a young post-Soviet writer and public celebrity, who has articulated crucial issues of the type and scale of community formation shared by many educated Siberians.[5] Among these issues are the difficulty of defining Siberia as a meaningful place, a place where residents cherish hopes for business, artistic, educational, and other kinds of opportunity. After briefly summarizing the historical and social context for understanding contemporary Siberian identity, I probe Grishkovets's autobiographical novella, *Rivers*, which I view as at once a critique of the stereotypical Siberian myth, an alternative conceptualization of "being Siberian" that resonates with themes more broadly heard in the Siberian press. It is finally an expression of resistance to specific initiatives of the Putin government.

Definitions of Identity, Place, and Community

Identity may be defined as the self-awareness and sense of belonging of a person with relation to a group or community—whether articulated or not. Definitions of identity and community have split along two lines: traditionally essentialist models (based on traditional categories, for example, of genetics, gender, and ethnicity) and constructivist models (based on more mobile concepts, among others, of class, constitution, and choice).[6] Although democratizing movements often operate with a concept of identity based on grassroots formations and claims to autonomous self-expression, new states work to shape identity "top-down" through the press, language policy, education, census-taking, and citizenship.[7] Whether state-initiated or grassroots, these forms of identity can be based on either line of thinking, essentialist or constructivist.

Over the last three or four decades digital technology, economic globalization, and massive migrations across national borders have challenged state constructions of identity and community, as grassroots "independent" media and international nongovernmental organizations of all kinds have blurred those borders and offered other modes of self-understanding.

Another important feature in recent thinking about mass self-awareness is an emphasis on physical space—whether built space, geographical area, or geopolitical territory. "Space," as geographers conceive it, becomes "place" when resident individuals and communities frame territory in symbols, rituals, and narratives of identity.[8] This chapter probes the tension between recent grassroots and state efforts to mold the definition and social-political impact of Siberian identity. Concepts of identity and community examined here are grounded in Siberians' articulated self-identification, that is, in the ways in which Siberian stakeholders form and use a Siberian discourse to define themselves and their region, and shape physical space into cultural and social place.

Methodology

The approach to area studies used here assumes that ideas matter when they are articulated in language that resonates in a community and promotes significant change in thinking and behavior. In probing the nature of regional identity and community, this chapter employs a number of humanistic strategies—focusing on a large number of individual voices and views and using the written record to mark changes in opinion and action. The social sciences define "normal" opinion and behavior gleaned through polls, surveys, and other instruments from massive numbers of the population. The humanities, in contrast, examine "discourse," that is, the range of articulated possibilities for identity, the language in which they are expressed, and their claim to authenticity and authority. In these utterances vocabularies of identity are created and consciousness is formed.

To gain a clear picture of contemporary Siberian self-awareness, this chapter uses the concept of "imagined geography" embedded in the writing culture. Imagined geography finds expression in metaphors of place that convey implied systems of value.[9] Literary scholar Edward Said's concept of "imaginative geography" has gained wide acceptance as a tool to examine the articulations of the exotic, colonized "other" by writers and artists representing the view from a colonizing center of power.[10] In contrast, chapters in this book by geographers Smiley and Thelen base their analyses on "mental mapping" and "cognitive geography," techniques that use visual maps drawn by local and regional informants to probe those informants' geographical or geopolitical concepts of significant "place," such as "home" or "homeland," "belonging" or "being alien." With the term "imagined geography" I foreground two features: (1) the predominant patterns of metaphor conveying geographically and geopolitically located identity, used by regional or central political leaders and other creators of public opinion (celebrities; popular writers and artists; print, radio, and Internet commentators), as well as anonymous voices on Internet sources (for example, blogs, news sources, video sources); and (2) the relation—explicit or implied—of those places to crucial systems of value and to specific issues of self-understanding and self-image (such as home, community, otherness [we vs. them], nature vs. created environment, and territorial scale [village, city, region, country]). This approach lends itself well to the topic of Siberian identity because Siberians are traditionally seen and often view themselves in clear territorial, geo-economic, and geopolitical terms, and because it can guide us in thinking about issues of political and economic development and demographic shifts that confront the Putin government, following actions taken in 2005 to curtail regional autonomy and regional unity.

Because it both resonates with and articulates crucial Siberian issues, Grishkovets's novella, *Rivers*, is the focal point of this chapter. To set the context of debate about Siberian identity, I examined documents and materials that represent contemporary Russian-language Siberian writing culture, broadly understood—aside from fiction, contemporary social commentary and journalism became crucial sources. Using the East View database of 112 Regional Russian Newspapers that covers at least 27 Siberian newspapers dating back to 2000, I selected articles showing the Cyrillic keywords "*sibiriak*" (сибиряк, person from Siberia), "*sibirsk**" (сибирск*, Siberian, adj.) and "*pisatel'*" (писатель, writer). This search produced over 1,600 articles, of which I selected 93 for their focus on issues of identity, community, and expressions of imagined geography. In addition to those articles, I found blogs and other articles online, not collected in the East View database, and have obtained over twenty works of recent Siberian fiction and collected essays on Siberian identity and community by Siberian media celebrities.

Historical and Social Context

Across its almost five-hundred-year history as part of the Russian state, Siberia has been at different times the treasure house of the Russian capital, its prison house, and its ethnographic field station for the study of its many

native peoples and their cultures. In the second half of the nineteenth century, Russian Siberians, most notably Grigory Potanin and Nikolai Iadrintsev,
started to articulate an anti-colonialist Siberian identity distinct from that
of European Russia.[11] Since 2000, readers have been particularly interested
in the writings of historical activists and famous exiles to Siberia, their anti-
colonialist narratives and themes, and their demands for greater attention
from the capital to Siberia's needs.

The Putin era (2000–) has been a time of limiting the autonomy of Russia's regions. Siberian activities in this period are typically ignored and on
occasion repressed when they challenge the central government's discourse
of identity or the center's perceived exploitation of Siberia. In the history of
Siberian regionalism, which dates back three hundred years to the reign of
Peter the Great, one finds waves of occasional separatism, and much more
frequent expressions of regionalist pride and demands that Siberians be heard
and treated as more than the residents of a colonized territory. When they
start to gather any political steam at all, these movements are typically side-
lined or repressed.

What do surveys in the early twenty-first century tell us about Siberians?
The image of Siberian identity produced through polls and other statistical
studies gives us a good background for a discussion of contemporary imagined geography and identity. The Levada Center in Moscow has produced
reliable sociological and political polls since the early 1990s, when Russia's
regions had more autonomy than they have at present. The Levada polls
from the mid-1990s show stronger than average *antireformist conservatism*
throughout Siberia. In other words, in the 1990s Siberians generally held
to the model of a centralized state to which Siberia belonged. This attitude
was explained partly through many Siberians' economic dependence on the
Soviet-era model of urbanization around one industry that gave employment opportunity with poor or nonexistent social and cultural infrastructure.[12] This conservatism appears to confirm another feature of the Siberian
stereotype, the belief that the Russian state has been responsible for giving
shape to Siberia through building transportation networks through the
taiga, originally the Siberian highway (*trakt*) and later the Trans-Siberian
railroad. From that belief springs a tradition of Siberian support for the central government and resistance to change.

Expressing the opposite view, on the other hand, the 2010 census saw a
movement among blog writers to urge Siberians to express a separate identity.
The blog "Real Siberians" (*Nastoiashchie sibiriaki*) pressed Siberian residents
to note their nationality as "*sibiriak*" (Siberian) when filling out the census
document, in order to distinguish themselves from European Russians.[13] And

indeed, the 2010 census did show a significant number of Siberians marking their nationality as *sibiriak*.[14] Some observers hope that the next census in 2020 will list a "new nationality" of Siberian.[15] The published results of the census, however, lumped "sibiriak" with a large array of twenty-nine different Russian-identifying groups, including various religious sects, which could not be viewed as a "nationality," suggesting that "Siberian" may well not appear in 2020 as a separate ethnic choice.[16]

Putin-era Siberian writing culture features a vocal articulation of "region-alist"—though not "separatist"—interests and a clear pride in Siberian history. The press regularly highlights the importance of regional literary and cultural pride and confronts the deafness of the center to Siberian economic and political needs.[17] Of particular concern are issues of Siberian poverty, exploitation of natural resources, and economic underdevelopment.[18] Siberian writers and journalists have used a number of means to arouse Siberian pride—the recovery and memorializing of the pre-Soviet history of Siberia, thus establishing a "usable history" that could serve as a model for Siberians going forward; the rediscovery and celebration of repressed Siberian-themed art; the interrogation of Siberian stereotypes; and the search for models of successful business and community building.

At the outset, it is important to emphasize that Siberian identity suffers from issues of scale. Writers often show a preference for building local identity around the city where they reside rather than emphasizing Siberia-wide accomplishment. While many Siberian commentators define regional interests broadly, in terms of the whole of Siberia, many promote the superiority of a particular city, a sentiment that complicates efforts to articulate common interests across the region.

Identity and Community in Siberian Writing Culture

While the process of journalistic recovery of a usable history has kept pre-Soviet historical experience in the public eye, fiction has played a crucial role in a more thorough articulation of what it means currently to be Siberian. Before discussing Evgeny Grishkovets's work in greater depth, a number of writers deserve commentary. To start with, it will help to sketch out the array of attitudes among writers about Siberia—from ultraconservative to moderate to strongly pro-reform. A number of Soviet-era writers, including Valentin Rasputin from Irkutsk, have turned to what might be called a conservative, Russian-nationalist attitude of "Siberia for ethnically Russian Siberians." Another writer, Mikhail Shchukin (1953–) from Novosibirsk, is engaged in the development of a Russian Orthodox, patriotic, family-oriented piety, which he terms "enlightenment."[19] Shchukin writes historical fiction and owns the publishing house Siberian Cenacle (*Sibirskaia gornitsa*).

At the other end of the political spectrum is the young writer from Irkutsk, Vasily Avchenko, currently a political activist in Vladivostok, who is highly critical of Putin's authoritarianism. His 2009 documentary novel, *Driving on the Left* (*Pravyi rul'*), makes the typically Japanese right-hand steering wheel (found on cars imported from Japan to Russia's Pacific coast region) into a metaphor for Siberian and Far East "otherness" and Moscow's misunderstanding of its provinces. He reiterates the often-heard criticism that opinion from Siberia and the Far East receives no attention from the center: "They [the state] consider us to be 'incorrect.' They accuse us of not being patriotic enough, because of our love of the [Japanese, imported] right-side steering wheel, while in the same moment the federal government calmly hands islands in the Amur River over to the Chinese, and our protests have no effect. As before, our voices are muted and hard to hear."[20] It is worth noting that, of current Siberian writers, Avchenko has been among the most politically active. In 2010 he signed a document of the anti-Putin opposition entitled, "Putin Must Go" ("Putin dolzhen uiti").[21]

Somewhere in the middle between the traditionalist and reformist poles is the prolific Tiumen' writer, radio personality, and television entrepreneur, Anatoly Omelchuk. Omelchuk draws parallels between the present and key moments of identity formation and regional activism in the eighteenth and nineteenth centuries. In his essays he combats the view that Siberians should be satisfied with what they have and not think about what makes them different and worthy of a better life: "Today, just as 100 and 200 years ago, the very thought that Siberia's future should be different from what it has been is being suppressed." Omelchuk continues: "It is being suppressed not as Peter did, through hanging ... not as the [nineteenth-century] 'regionalist' Iadrintsev was treated, by being exiled from Siberia to European Russia, ... not as in Soviet times through suppression of the *Soviet Encyclopedia*, but in a new style of ignoring [Siberian concerns]."[22] Omelchuk insists on the necessity of always speaking up.

No separatist, Omelchuk's vision of Siberia is inclusive and embracing, promoting on one hand the non-Russian cultures of northern indigenous peoples of Siberia and, on the other, the importance of Siberia for Russia as a whole. He argues for the importance of the Siberian myth for Russian national identity: "Siberia the myth is more powerful than Siberia the landmass ... because those expanses make the Fatherland great. It is precisely Siberia that makes Russia unfathomable."[23] Finally, his writing has a pragmatic purpose, to hold before the eyes of Russia's rulers the persistent problem of Siberian poverty: "An impoverished Siberia is a black mark not just on Russia but on all humanity."[24]

Possibly more than any other contemporary writer, Evgeny Grishkovets (1967–) has injected new notes into the discourse about Siberian identity and has succeeded in reaching a broad audience across Russia. Although Grishkovets, who was born in the Siberian city of Kemerovo, left Siberia in 2007 at the age of thirty, he is proud to call himself a "Siberian who doesn't live in Siberia."[25] He admits that he chose to move away from Siberia to overcome perceived obstructions that many Siberians find annoying and to build a wider audience beyond Siberia. Grishkovets's main Siberian work is the autobiographical novel, *Rivers* (*Reki*, 2005), written shortly before his move. As the title suggests, Grishkovets foregrounds rivers as the defining topographic feature of Siberian imagined geography, just as they have been the geographical focus for many Siberian so-called "village" writers of the last Soviet decades, including Viktor Astaf'ev and Valentin Rasputin. For them, Siberian rivers signal a grand, violent natural force. In contrast to the older village writers, Grishkovets is proudly Siberian and yet does not love the boundless taiga, finding the wildlife and villages of the taiga less than interesting. Instead, he redefines the image of the river to urge reconsideration of the traditional Siberian myth. In his novella Grishkovets undermines these and other Siberian stereotypes but lends a fresh, culturally oriented meaning to the idea of the river.

Having dispensed with the usual Siberian themes of nature, hunting, and farming, Grishkovets leaves his imprint on what for him is the most important issue, the problem of his own Siberian imagined geography and how it has influenced his creative process. For him, Siberia is essentially a featureless expanse, a form of "nowhere" that can hardly even be mapped because of the lack of natural borders: "you can't depict a map of Siberia because it, the map, probably doesn't even exist. Because there are no clear borders. . . . Where does it begin and where does it end?" Grishkovets's narrator envies a country like Italy, which has a very clear shape and is in an important place with lots of famous buildings and historical events. Instead, the narrator highlights an urban definition of Siberia that emphasizes its cities as its critical feature. The narrator is from a city on a river, both of which remain nameless, suggesting that it could be any and every Siberian city. Through its very nameless generality this city becomes the model for post-Soviet Siberian place in which identity and community emerge. The idea of "Siberia," the narrator argues, is created by the people who live in Siberia's widely dispersed cities. Grishkovets's narrator remarks that a "resident of Omsk [in Western Siberia] can tell someone from

Irkutsk [in Eastern Siberia] if they meet up at some Black Sea resort. . . . He'll call him a 'fellow Siberian!' And the guy from Irkutsk won't mind, in fact, he'll be glad. They are both Siberians, even if the whole of Europe from Finland to Portugal can fit between their cities." In fact, as one often sees in Siberian newspapers, which are located in a certain city and help to define that city's cachet, cities are the crucial feature on the otherwise flat, featureless Siberian landscape.

The narrator also resists the often-heard view that the Trans-Siberian Railroad defines Siberia by linking Siberia's cities like pearls on a necklace. The Trans-Siberian, in his view, is more about time than space: "Where is Siberia in all that [the train]? What can I grab onto in order to feel like I'm connected to something concrete? I can't get a sense of Siberia's open spaces, I just feel . . . time zones." The Trans-Siberian is measured not by discernible, definable space but by the passage of time between Moscow and any given Siberian or Pacific coast city. In no way does it help to make the space of Siberia—its taiga, rivers, and mountains—into meaningful cultural, historical place.

Grishkovets's narrator yearns for a creative space of Siberia. The landscape itself is empty and invites no fantasies about the past since there is none of what architects call "built space" or human geographers call "place"—no meaningful definition of the natural, physical space of Siberia that speaks of human strivings of the past. As the narrator puts it, there are "no castles." To repeat, in Grishkovets's imagined geography, the river and the city are the key features of Siberia. The city is Grishkovets's main scale for measuring community—it is the place where the narrator grew up and found meaning, particularly through his grandfather, although it also becomes that place that eventually he desires to escape to find a wider world of creative opportunity. With the image of the river, Grishkovets invokes the main point of his geography. The river links the city and the young boy to the much larger Siberian map and to the rest of the world, making the boy part of much greater natural and human forces. The thought that the river flows up north into eternal ice brings Grishkovets to the conclusion that Siberia is not linked to any possibilities for a creative, imaginative process but rather suggests a creative dead end. In many ways, this long meditation on rivers explains Grishkovets's decision to move away from Siberia—he felt the need for greater stimulation and human contact. *Rivers* is less about demythologizing Siberia than it is about reaching out—connecting to broader human experience, to human community—and overcoming isolation.

Despite Grishkovets's complaint that Siberia is culturally empty, the last decade has witnessed many efforts at strengthening cultural and social life. Various projects now include building historical memory, from erecting monuments to famous Siberians in Novosibirsk, to bolstering writing culture through publishing ventures and enhancing cultural identity by including Siberian cultural-historical components in the school curriculum. One of these projects, a 2006 anthology of Siberian writers for the Irkutsk school system, garnered significant political support through the then pro-Siberian Irkutsk governor, Boris Govorin.[26]

The Internet has become an enormous boon for overcoming the challenges of space in Russia's provinces, and especially Siberia. Again note the importance of the Live Journal (*zhivoi zhurnal*) blog, "Real Siberians" (*nastoiashchie sibiriaki*), which rallied Siberians to mark their identity as "*sibiriak*" in the 2010 census and which now offers readers a library of writings of Siberian interest.[27] Internet projects are enhancing provincial literary life. For example, in coordination with the yearly event, Krasnoiarsk Book Culture Market, there has been an "Online Internet Conference." A more far-reaching project is the fascinating website "The New Literary Map of Russia" (Novaia literaturnaia karta Rossii, http://www.litkarta.ru), started in 2007, funded by the Astaf'ev Fund, and still vibrant and vital today. New and established writers post and discuss their work on this site. The blogosphere has become crucial for building creative community across the wide Siberian spaces, perhaps too late for Grishkovets but soon enough to attract the next big Siberian talent.

Conclusion

Siberian administrations worry about the very issue that Grishkovets has so poignantly articulated—the downward direction that the basic demographics of the Siberian population is taking and the trend among some Siberians to leave their homeland in search of greater opportunity. As prime minister, Putin has visited Siberia and held forums and conferences on Siberian development. In addition, he has offered some modest start-up money to pay families to move to Siberia.

One of the problems, among many others, is that Putin has a tin ear and, willfully or not, has ignored the shift in Siberian discourse. His rhetoric only repeats the old, stolid stereotypes of Siberians, showing that he has little insight into or care for their contemporary concerns. It is instructive to revisit Putin's vacuous comments from 2012 that "Siberia" means the "fundamental idea of the Siberian character," by which he means the "ability to overcome hardship, to reach goals, and under difficult circumstances to achieve bright, positive results." Putin affirms the stalwart Siberian character as "one of the main resources in Russia that [will ensure we] reach all our goals and resolve all our problems."[28] As noted at the outset, Grishkovets has indirectly expressed his strong distaste for Putin through juxtaposing the stereotypical "good Siberian" and the dirty-dealing leader of the new Russia.

In conclusion, we return to our original question: what defines Siberian consciousness in the early twenty-first century since the end of the relatively "democratic" regional autonomy of the Yeltsin years? Among the crucial elements of contemporary Siberian identity is the strong disaffection felt by many Siberians at having their land exploited economically and abandoned by the center without serious new investment for building infrastructure—communication and transportation networks—and social and cultural institutions.[29] Contemporary Siberians want to be heard in the rest of the country—including, of course, the capital—and to be included as stakeholders at all levels of regional, national, and global life, in its culture, economy, and politics. This desire, as one sees in Grishkovets's writing, is balanced with strong frustration and a growing determination to migrate beyond Siberia in search of opportunity.

Siberia is diffuse and uncoordinated geographically, economically, and politically—facts that lead many to the overwhelming perception that it continues to be exploited and treated by the center as a colony.[30] The Siberian terrain is viewed not just as a defining feature but as a problem hampering community building and keeping the life of individual cities isolated in their own bubbles. Siberian leaders, as people living on the periphery, are grappling with the typical colonial/postcolonial bind—between striving for the attention of the center and the bigger audiences, and turning their attention to building audiences and communities across the lengthy but narrow strip of territory that holds the main population of Siberia.

Finally, is there a model for twenty-first-century Siberian identity substantially different from the old Soviet layered identity? In Soviet society it was understood that local, regional, and national identities coexisted in a hierarchy that placed a general Soviet identity at the top and then the "little" local and regional ethnic identities below, allowing them less weight and with time a diminishing "reality."[31] Although Siberians as a group certainly identify as ethnically "Russian" and view themselves in relation to the country as a whole, their local and regional identities are powerful and palpable—and not viewed necessarily as being "lesser" than their allegiance to Russia as a whole. The growing debate by Russian researchers and public intellectuals on the issue of authentic regional identity has created a groundswell that promises eventually to shift the strict division between capital as holder of all the resources, and region as impoverished, boring provincial backwater that has obtained for much of Russia's modern history.[32]

Notes

1. This chapter builds in part on material developed in my article, "Being a *Sibiriak* in Contemporary Siberia: Imagined Geography and Vocabularies of Identity in Regional Writing Culture," *Region* 2, no. 1 (2013), 47-67.

2. Petr Pridius, "Vostri, brat, glaz na vostok," *Kubanskie novosti*, September 18, 2001, 164, accessed June 24, 2012, http://dlib.eastview.com.www2.lib.ku.edu:2048/browse/doc/3309677.

3. Ravil' Geniatulin, "Politika i vlast': V Rossii nastupaet 'vremia Sibiri,'" *Zabaikal'skii rabochii* (April 3, 2012), accessed July 20, 2012, http://dlib.eastview.com.www2.lib.ku.edu:2048/browse/doc/26868356.

4. Evgenii Grishkovets, *Reki* (Moscow: Makhaon, 2005), accessed July 14, 2012. Here and below all quotations come from this source. All translations are my own.

5. Grishkovets is certainly a well-recognized figure outside his home city of Kemerovo. A small survey of 90 Tiumen' students and faculty conducted in fall 2013 shows that after Astafiev and Rasputin, Grishkovets is among the influential writers named by respondents who have helped to shape readers' image of their home region (Clowes survey on geographical and cultural markers of Siberian identity, October, 2013, unpublished material). In his book *Regional'naia identichnost' "Zemli tiumenskoi": Mify i diskurs*, the well-known Tiumen' political philosopher, Vladimir Bogomiakov, reiterates Grishkovets's question from *Reki*, "Where is Siberia?" (107).

6. See, for example, Eric J. Hobsbawm, *Nations and Nationalism Since 1780: Programme, Myth, Reality* (Cambridge: Cambridge University Press, 1990); Ernest Gellner, *Nations and Nationalism* (Oxford: Blackwell, 1983); Benedict Anderson, *Imagined Communities: Reflections on the Origins and Spread of Nationalism* (London, New York: Verso, 1991). For a good overview on defining and studying identity, see Rogers Brubaker and Frederick Cooper, "Beyond 'identity,'" *Theory and Society* 29 (2000), 1-47. For a useful volume of readings on the current debate about national identity, see *Mapping the Nation*, ed. Gopal Balakrishnan (London: Verso, 2012).

7. For the former, see Hobsbawm, *Nations and Nationalism*. Studies of Soviet state efforts to build identity include Ronald Suny and Terry Martin, eds., *A State of Nations: Empire and Nation-Making in the Age of Lenin and Stalin* (Oxford: Oxford University Press, 2001); Francine Hirsch, *Empire of Nations: Ethnographic Knowledge and the Making of the Soviet Union* (Ithaca, NY: Cornell University Press, 2005).

8. See, for example, Robert D. Sack's short summary, "The Power of Place and Space," *Geographical Review* 83, no. 3 (July 1993): 326-29.

9. Edith W. Clowes, *Russia on the Edge: Imagined Geographies and Post-Soviet Identity* (Ithaca, NY: Cornell University Press, 2011).

10. Edward Said, *Orientalism* (New York: Pantheon, 1978); Susan Layton, *Russian Literature and Empire: Conquest of the Caucasus from Pushkin to Tolstoy* (Cambridge: Cambridge University Press, 1994); Mark Bassin, "Inventing Siberia: Visions of the Russian East in the Early Nineteenth Century," *American Historical Review* 6, no. 3 (June 1991): 763-94.

11. Stephen Watrous, "The Regionalist Conception of Siberia, 1860-1920," in *Between Heaven and Hell: The Myth of Siberia in Russian Culture*, ed. Galya Diment and Yuri Slezkine (New York: St. Martin's, 1993), 113-32.

12. Yuri Levada, "Sociological Essays 1993-2000," *Levada Center*, accessed August 15, 2012, http://www.levada.ru/books/yurii-levada-sotsiologicheskie-ocherki-1993-2000.

13. Austin Charron, "The *Sibiriak* Movement and the Roots of Modern Siberian Regionalism" (2011), accessed August 5, 2012, http://www.crees.ku.edu/~crees/funding/laird-essay.shtml.

14. Ibid.

15. Federal State Statistics Service, "Volume 1: The Size and Distribution of the Population," accessed September 6, 2012, http://www.perepis-2010.ru/news/detail.php?ID=6390.

16. Federal State Statistics Service, "National Population Census 2010: National Composition of Population," accessed October 7, 2014, http://www.gks.ru/free_doc/new_site/perepis2010/croc/Documents/Vol4/pub-04-01.pdf.

17. Vasilii Popok, "Pisatel' neskol'kikh pokolenii," *Kuznetskii krai* (May 29, 2004), accessed July 2, 2012, http://dlib.eastview.com.www2.lib.ku.edu:2048/browse/doc/6314240.

18. Anastasiia Bazhanova, "Otkuda poshla Sibir," *Sovetskaia Sibir'*, May 4, 2007, accessed July 5, 2012, http://dlib.eastview.com.www2.lib.ku.edu:2048/browse/doc/11960100.

19. Anastasiia Obizhaeva, "Kuptsy, iamshchiki, konokrad i poruchik leibgvardii," *Sovetskaia Sibir'*, no. 193, October 3, 2008, accessed July 07, 2012, http://dlib.eastview.com.www2.lib.ku.edu:2048/browse/doc/19023241.

20. Quoted in Mikhail Tarkovskii, "Pochemu federal'nyi tsentr spokoino otdaet Kitaiu ostrova na Amure," *Krasnoiarskii rabochii*, June 23, 2010, accessed July 9, 2012, http://dlib.eastview.com.www2.lib.ku.edu:2048/browse/doc/22034395.

21. See Bukvaved.org, "Basil O. Avchenko Biography," accessed September 6, 2012, http://bukvaved.org/biography/68271-biografija.html; "Avchenko, Basil O.," Wikipedia.org, accessed August, 5, 2012, http://ru.wikipedia.org/wiki/Авченко,_Василий_Олегович.

22. Anatolii Omel'chuk, "Novye knigi: Chastnoe otkrytie Sibiri," *Kuzbass*, March 30, 2007, accessed July 5, 2012, http://dlib.eastview.com.www2.lib.ku.edu:2048/browse/doc/11956332.

23. Ibid.

24. Ibid.

25. Andrei Sotnikov, "Evgenii Grishkovets: 'Ia sibiriak, kotoryi v Sibiri ne zhivet,'" *Samarskie izvestiia*, March 2, 2007, accessed July 5, 2012, http://dlib.eastview.com.www2.lib.ku.edu:2048/browse/doc/11715049.

26. I. Tsyplakov, "Pervoprokhodets," *Sovetskaia Sibir'* (March 17, 2006), accessed July 4, 2012, http://dlib.eastview.com.www2.lib.ku.edu:2048/browse/doc/9189480.

27. http://real-siberian.livejournal.com/315465.html, accessed July 31, 2012.

28. Geniatulin, "Politika i vlast."

29. This sentiment comes through particularly strongly in a recent sociological survey on Siberian identity by A. A. Anisimova and O. G. Echevskaia, *Sibirskaia identichnost': predposylki formirovaniia, konteksty aktualizatsii* (Novosibirsk: Novosibirskii gos. univ., 2012), 75-79.

30. Vladislav Mikhailov, "All Siberia Believes That Moscow Refers to It as a Colony," *Expert Online*, accessed August 10, 2012, http://expert.ru/siberia/2012/31/vsya-sibir-schitaet-chto-moskva-otnositsya-k-nej-kak-k-kolonii/.

31. See, for example, Dmitry Baranov's chapter on the ethnographic museum in Mark Bassin and Catriona Kelly, eds., *Soviet and Post-Soviet Identities* (Cambridge: Cambridge University Press, 2012).

32. Vladimir Bogomiakov (see note 4), Urals cultural geographer Dmitrii Zamiatin, and culturologist Madina Tlustanova are just three voices in the growing debate.

The Post-Soviet North Caucasus

Factors of Contemporary Ethno-National Identity and Community

AUSTEN THELEN

The goal of this chapter is to examine concepts of collective ethno-national identity among young adults in the North Caucasus, focusing on issues of place and territory, in order to understand how identity is constructed in the communities inhabiting two of the region's federal territories: Stavropol *Krai* and the Republic of Karachay-Cherkessia. A comparison of these two territories is potentially illuminating for understanding Russia's regional and ethno-territorial identity dynamics. Of central interest here is the focus of these communities on social and place-based factors within their collective constructions of national identity.

The North Caucasus is extremely diverse by virtue of its numerous local languages, ethno-national groups, and religious communities, as well as the multiple scales of territorial division to which the population can ascribe meaning. Stavropol *Krai* and the Republic of Karachay-Cherkessia share a border and are functionally part of Russia's North Caucasus Region; however, these territories are administered according to two different levels of federal autonomy, falling under the common descriptions of ethnic Russian territory, in the case of Stavropol *Krai*, and non-Russian territory, in regard to Karachay-Cherkessia. How people relate to the territories where they live plays an important role in the construction of group identities and conceptions of community because such relations work to contextualize many other identity-building attributes. Through ascribing meanings to places and portraying them via borders and boundaries so as to signify idealized containers for group identity, communities are able to form a set of social norms that dictate which attributes should be considered *in place*, or socially definitive of a given community's territory, as opposed to *out of place*, not fitting the context.[1]

In the North Caucasus, the meanings associated with ethno-national, linguistic, and religious identities have become deeply imbricated in a variety of

territorial constructions. When individuals can be part of multiple community groups, the territories in which their various communities are *in place*
might differ depending on social and political contexts. Communities in the
North Caucasus vary in the ways they identify with the state (Russia), their
region (the North Caucasus), and the other territorial divisions where they
reside. By examining which territories are important to which communities
and why, one may gain an understanding of how these communities spatially
contextualize their identity constructions, which is important when researching relations among communities in a geopolitical sense. In this project, I propose a methodological approach for researching the role that territory plays in
constructing collective identity. This methodology is applicable to the study of
communities impacted by scalar territorial divisions, which takes into account
the various levels of power distribution and organization that define a hierarchy
of places within the sociopolitical context of contemporary Russia, and aims to
assess how strongly various communities identify with these places.

This chapter is based on field research I conducted in the North Caucasus
region of Russia during the summer of 2009.[2] I selected the North Caucasus as
a research area because its residents might be expected to have identities associated with territorial units.[3] The region is located on Russia's southwestern
periphery and constitutes a cultural crossroads between historically Russian
and non-Russian lands, between steppe lands and mountains, and between
Christianity and Islam.[4] Scholars and media outlets, both in Russia and
abroad, have focused on the North Caucasus as the setting of numerous conflicts, especially those dealing with security and geopolitical instability. This
study provides some geographically oriented insights into collective notions
of identity and community that prove useful for research ranging from linguistic and religious policies, to political activism, to peace and conflict studies and other spatially contextualized issues.

"Community" and "Identity" in Geography

According to the *Dictionary of Human Geography*, "community" is defined
as "a group of people who share common culture, values, and/or interests,
based on social identity and/or territory and who have some means of recognizing, and (inter)acting upon, these commonalities."[5] Thus, geographers
tend to emphasize in the notion of community a linkage of society, identity,
and territory. How particular geographical communities are defined often
depends on spatial proximity among their members in relation to those not
included within a given community. Community, as understood in terms of

territorial sovereignty and jurisdiction, cannot be divorced from territory, regardless of scale. This notion is especially valid within democratic and federal systems (like Russia), where citizenship, meaning "the rights and duties relating to an individual's membership in a political community,"[6] is ascribed via geographical location within defined political borders, having differing connotations at multiple scales.

The issue of "identity" is also a major topic in geography, especially for political geographers who are interested in understanding the ways populations separate themselves according to geographic divisions, how these divisions are used to meet political ends, and how identity is related to places and territories.[7] Geographies are socially produced when space becomes defined via collective organization. This process takes different forms, depending on who is doing the organizing. Therefore, the territories, places, and locales that constitute any given geography are in constant flux in terms of their roles in the meanings and preferences held by different groups of people at any given time, making them inherently subjective. Within any geography, such notions of "subjective territorial identity" are constructed when territories are ascribed meanings in their own unique contexts, such as politics, work, or the activities of everyday life.[8] When these various notions of identity become salient among groups of people, they work as a set of criteria by which group members can differentiate between *others* and their own. Therefore, territory, which can be understood as space under power, plays a critical role in how identities become defined spatially, prompting geographers to take issues of identity and territory very seriously.

Territory is a key component to many collective identities, nations for example, because it establishes tangible evidence for a group's existence, often giving credence to ideas of collective primordial existence in a particular place and long-established territorial legitimacy in the form of *homeland*.[9] However, it is also important to recognize that within any geography, there exists a "hierarchy of geographically based identities," which may contend for groups' adherence.[10] In the context of the Russian Federation, a city like Moscow has a variety of meanings among Russia's various communities. The city is viewed as a holy place by the Orthodox Christian community. It can be seen as a source of ethno-national culture and power by ethnic Russians and/or any citizens who hold an affinity for the Russian Federation. For Chechens, or other non-Russian ethno-national groups, Moscow could represent oppression and subjugation. In Moscow, one sees a single defined place as a point of cohesion that is identified within group narratives on identity. However, Moscow provides distinctly different meanings and emotive forces when taken in the context of different identities. For geographers, identity represents a socially constructed continuum of qualities or standards that people use to organize and self-ascribe their own conceptions of substantive cohesion within groups. Because places are also ascribed qualities within any given identity, it is the work of geographers to ascertain the reasons why particular places become defined the way they are, point out alternative voices from within the multiplicity of meanings ascribed to places, and analyze the role of these places within spatial discourses.

The concept of geographic "scale," which refers to the use of parameters to define levels of focus and definition in regard to space or processes, is helpful in researching and understanding the spatial aspects of identity and community. Scale is a tool used to make sense of space in particular contexts. It differentiates among levels within a given spatial hierarchy, such as local, regional, and national, on which phenomena are constituted.[11] Scales are always established. They are also subject to change reflecting sociospatial dynamics, thus defining spatial extents of processes and denoting the comprehensible levels at which these processes function.[12] It is therefore important to view scale as something socially constructed, rather than as natural or predetermined. Issues of scale are fundamental to understanding communities in a geographical perspective because communities exhibit a variety of meanings at different scales within their given societies.[13] A community could be considered to be *in place* at a local scale, but might become marginalized, or *out of place*, at less refined scales. For example, Russia's Islamic community is a minority at the federal scale, but constitutes a majority at several more localized scales, such as in Karachay-Cherkessia. Therefore, through the context of geographic scale, the scope of identity might be narrowed to exclude others and become more cohesive in a more localized territorial context. Certain identities have the potential to be salient at a grand scale, such as one's identity as citizen of the Russian Federation, while other identities may only come into significance under more narrow focus. Comparing how individuals and groups react to some of these scalar notions of territorial identity allows one to get a glimpse of how they construct meanings and set priorities when forming understandings and preferences about how to identify themselves (and *others*) in spatial terms.

The Study Area

Throughout the Caucasus's history, ever-changing borders, states, and sources of power and authority have had a profound influence on regional peoples' understanding of meanings associated with territory and political

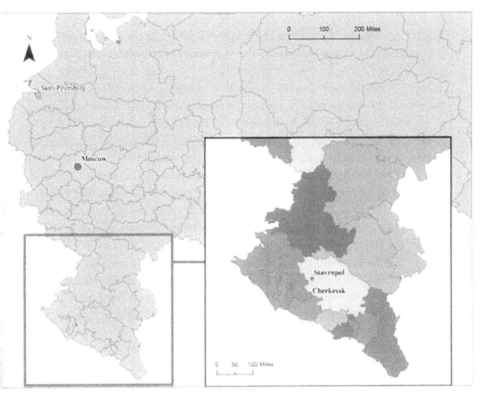

FIGURE 1. Map of the study area.

legitimacy within territorialized contexts.[14,15] People in the contemporary
North Caucasus are faced with the various territorial designations that define
their region vis-à-vis the context of Soviet legacy and contemporary Russian
ethno-federalism, where territories are defined and governed according to
distinct ethno-national homelands. Ethno-national groups living in territories designated for their groups are known as titular, or are said to have
titular status.[16] Therefore, Russians in majority ethnic Russian territories,
such as *krais* and *oblasts*, would be considered titular, while Karachays and
Cherkess would be considered titular ethno-national groups in the Republic
of Karachay-Cherkessia. Russian policies such as these have worked to dis-
cursively define and reinforce an array of meanings regarding ethno-national
groups and their territories.

The North Caucasus's contemporary political geography is made up of
two types of federal territories: *krais* and republics. *Krais* are majority ethnic
Russian territories, governed under Moscow's direct jurisdiction. Republics
exhibit majority non-Russian populations and function with some autonomy

from Moscow. Republics have non-Russian official languages and individually specific constitutions, granting them the right to enact legislation specific to their semiautonomous territories. The individual *krais* and republics are also grouped together into subfederal units called "federal districts" (*federalnye okrugy*). While *krais* and republics function as separate political entities at the provincial scale, they must function as part of a single unit, a federal district, at the subfederal scale. All the territories in Russia are ultimately subordinate to Moscow at the federal scale. Thus, people living in the North Caucasus can identify with multiple scalar territories simultaneously.

I used two bordering territories as data collection sites: Stavropol *Krai* and the Republic of Karachay-Cherkessia. In terms of official ethno-federal designation, Stavropol *Krai* constitutes an ethnic Russian territory. Russians are therefore titular in Stavropol *Krai*, while other ethno-national groups are non-titular. Karachay-Cherkessia comprises a majority non-Russian population, having two titular groups for which it is named: Karachay and Cherkess. The border between Stavropol *Krai* and the republics to its south, including its border with Karachay-Cherkessia, is important because it represents a transition between Russian and non-Russian space, and also between areas that have collective Christian majorities as opposed to collective Muslim majorities. Throughout this chapter, I analyze how these differences, at various scales, factor into conceptions of collective identity and community among young people in the North Caucasus.

Methodology and Data Collection

To examine how notions of territory factor into constructions of identity and community among the young adults in the North Caucasus (individuals 18–30 years of age), I employed a mixed methodological approach, incorporating quantitative and qualitative data. Integrating qualitative and quantitative analyses is useful because it lets a researcher make observations about group differences that are supported by statistics (quantitative analysis), and also allows one to explain (qualify) these findings by gathering in-depth information from community members. I collected survey data from 357 individuals in Stavropol *Krai* and Karachay-Cherkessia, where participants provided biographical information and ranked various factors of ethno-national identity in terms of importance (see tables 1 and 2). I also conducted oral interviews with forty of the participants, compiling more detailed information about how they answered the survey. More important, inquiring about participants' opinions regarding

ndependent Variables	Categories	Categories 2
Nationality	Russian (N=145)	Non-Russian (N=212)
Gender	Male (N=96)	Female (N=261)
Titular Status	Titular (N=246)	Non-Titular (N=111)
Religion-Type	Islam (N=194)	Christianity (N=163)
Religion-Practice	Practicing N=76	Non-Practicing (N=281)
Birthplace	Urban (N=97)	Rural (N=260)
Place of Residence	Urban (N=191)	Rural (N=166)
Lineage in Place of Residence	Multiple Generations (N=180)	First Generation (N=177)
Parents' Nationalities	Different (N=30)	Same (N=327)

TABLE 1. Independent Variables and Categories for MANOVA

Dependent Variable	Overall Mean Score (N=357)	Categories Showing Significant Preferences
Birthplace	3.42	Titular, Multiple Generations
Living in the Russian Federation	3.52	Russian, Christian, Multiple Generations
Living in a Federal District	3.33	Islam
Living in the North Caucasus	3.64	Islam, Non Titular
Living in the Krai or Republic	3.58	Islam Multiple Generation
Religion	4.33	Practicing
Native Language	4.59	
Ancestry	4.41	Non-Russian, Male, Multiple Generations

TABLE 2. Mean Scores Regarding Importance of Dependent Variables to Ethno-National Identity and Categories Displaying Significance Regarding Each Dependent Variable as Indicated by MANOVA

identity and community provided them with the chance to raise questions that were not discernible via the survey data alone.

When coordinating my field study, I relied heavily on connections and relationships I had established previously in the study area. My contacts included faculty and students at four local universities: Stavropol State University, Stavropol Medical College, Stavropol State Agrarian University, and the State University of Karachay-Cherkessia. Two cities, Stavropol and Cherkessk, served as bases for data collection. I selected them because the universities in these urban areas attract students from throughout the North Caucasus, thus widening the geographical scope of the study to include participants from the entire region.

Through these contacts, I used a data collection strategy called "snowball interviewing." Also known as "referral sample," snowball interviewing, or "snowballing," relies on personal contacts and introductions from participants. New participants are referred to the interviewer by other participants, thus establishing contacts and credibility. This technique has been cited as an efficient way to sample data in Russia, where access to information is often lacking and potential participants tend to be apprehensive toward foreigners.[17] Several of my contacts, including two university professors, allowed me to conduct my project with their students. This approach provided me with a large volume of contacts, especially non-Russians. Several other contacts served as proxies, distributing surveys to individuals whom they knew to be within the target age group for the study. I also personally gathered data from over one hundred individuals directly through interactions in public places, in or around Stavropol and Cherkessk and their surrounding villages. I conducted oral interviews with forty survey participants (in Russian).

Through participants' biographical data, I could identify their ethno-national groups, religions, native languages, places of birth, and places of residence. They also provided the same information about their parents, which allowed me to gain some understanding into their families' historical lineages in terms of place. These categories constituted the basis for my project's independent variables (see table 1). I based these selections on the works of several scholars, including Weber[18] and Smith,[19] who have acknowledged language, ancestral lineage, and religion as the overriding factors important for building and ascribing to notions of collective identity. Participants were asked to evaluate their association with eight dependent variables (see table 2) in terms of relevance to their own personal conceptions of ethno-national identity. This evaluation was conducted using a Likert-style (5-point) scale, where "1" meant "absolutely not important" and "5" meant "very important."

To analyze these data, I drew on a statistical method called "multivariate analysis of variance" (MANOVA), which tests for significant differences among group responses in situations where there are multiple dependent variables.[20] MANOVA has been cited in previous studies as a technique useful for measuring group differences regarding ethnic identity.[21] The results of a MANOVA show the researcher whether differences between categorical group responses occur at random. If differences are indicated at the $p < .05$ level of significance, then statistically a researcher can say that there is a 95 percent probability that the difference is not random, therefore rejecting the null hypothesis of no difference.

In order to perform a MANOVA, data must meet several requirements, one of which is that they are normally distributed.[22] I evaluated the distribution of each of the variables for normality based on their standardized skewness scores (skewness divided by standard error), which analyzes asymmetry in a given data set and is a common method for determining whether data are normally distributed. Any variable's distribution having an absolute standardized skewness score of greater than 3.09 (p < .001, two-tailed) was considered not to be normally distributed and therefore needed to be transformed for analysis. I performed the MANOVA using the statistical software program SPSS. Because I deemed each independent variable important enough to include in the study, I anticipated possibly rejecting the null hypothesis of no difference in the case of each one.

Results and Discussion

A comparison of the overall mean scores among dependent variables suggested several important trends for young people's conceptions of ethno-national identity in the North Caucasus. First, it is important to note that none of the dependent variables registered an average mean score lower than 3.0 (see table 2), showing that each one is considered to be important among the population. Therefore, each dependent variable performs some role in the construction of ethno-national identity. Three dependent variables, "native language," "ancestry," and "religion" respectively, received the highest overall mean scores. These three variables are social in nature, reflecting distinct roles within participants' communities and suggesting group interaction and community differentiation.

"Native language" was the highest-ranking dependent variable (M = 4.59, where M is the mean of all responses), signifying that a majority of the participants hold their native language to be "very important" in their personal conceptions of ethno-national identity. Furthermore, based on the MANOVA, none of the independent variables registered significant effects between categories regarding native language. Of the various factors one could use to understand his or her sense of community, native language is an especially striking factor.

The data in this study suggest native language to be the most important factor in ethno-national identity, which perhaps is not surprising. Since the use of vernacular languages in print media became common, native language has generally replaced religion as the simplest way for people to identify members of their own ethnic groups and members of other groups.[23] Participants declared several reasons for ranking their native language highly. One dominant reason was the belief that language restricts one's thought process. That is, if one speaks Russian, he or she is essentially forced to think like a Russian and would thus demonstrate a Russian mentality. Participant number 40, a Russian from Stavropol, noted that "Not having Russian language would be very problematic. . . . It is connected to one's mentality. Russian language, in my view, is a designating factor."[24]

Although native language is often considered requisite for belonging to a national group, in Russia it is connected to another important identity factor: "the Russian soul (*russkaya dusha*)." It is widely believed that without the Russian language, it is impossible to possess this crucial element of Russianness due to its necessity for understanding and expression. Participant 193 added: "To be Russian, one must speak Russian. However, one can speak Russian without being Russian. If someone immigrates from abroad and learns Russian language, it does not make him Russian just due to language. One's soul needs to be Russian. If he has Russian language and a Russian soul, and considers himself Russian, then he can be. It does not matter even if he is black or white."[25]

Beyond the uses of language as a means of communication and structure for one's thought process, the use of particular languages in the North Caucasus is politically linked to territorial understandings of identity. While Russian is an official language anywhere in the Russian Federation, republics, like Karachay-Cherkessia, have special language rights under the Russian Constitution. Because the republic is an officially designated homeland for the Karachay and Cherkess populations, the use and prevalence of these groups' respective native languages not only constitutes a de facto means of communication among their populations, but is in fact politically encouraged via their territory's republic status. In Stavropol *Krai*, Russian is the only official language, as the territory operates directly under Moscow's federal authority. Therefore, in the entire study area, some languages are automatically given state-backed *in place* status, while languages spoken by the many other minority groups in the area are not recognized with official support. The importance of one's native language to his or her sense of identity could be bolstered by official language status, or could work to create a sense of marginalization without such recognition, serving as a reminder that speaking an unofficial language could put a community *out of place.*

"Ancestry" was the second-highest-ranking dependent variable (M = 4.41). Unlike native language, which displayed no significant differences among independent categories, ancestry is significant for non-Russians, males, and people with multiple generations from the same area. Non-Russians (M = 4.64) significantly favored it to Russians (M = 4.08), and interviews provided insight as to why the difference occurred. First, Russians recognize the effects of the Russian imperial legacy on the country's ethnic geography and acknowledge

their population's historical interaction with other ethno-national communities. Many Russian participants said they were either unsure of their own
ancestors' nationalities, or were fairly certain that other ethnic groups existed
in their family lineage. According to Participant 177, "Pure-blooded people
never occur among us. There will of course be different nationalities among
our ancestors. Therefore, it does not play the most important role."[26]

Non-Russians, especially males from Karachay-Cherkessia, tended to be
extremely aware of their ancestral lineages. According to participant 128, a
man from an *aul* (village) in Karachay-Cherkessia, "We Karachays consider
that to be one of us, a person needs to have seven generations of Karachay
ancestors, without exception. For example, I know for a fact that for at least
seven generations of my family, we have been fully Karachay. This is the reason why marrying a Karachay woman is important. I want my children to be
Karachay, like me. It is very important to me and the rest of my family."[27]

The differences between prevailing Russian and non-Russian attitudes in
regard to the importance of ancestry provide a different insight into the various ethno-national senses of community found in the study area. For Russians, ancestry is based more on a sense of culture and ideas than on notions
of bloodlines and genetics. Conversely, non-Russians seemed much more
focused on knowing exact family histories and birthplaces. As an identity factor, Russian ancestry has more room for choice and preference, rather than
relying heavily on from where, or from which group, one's forefathers originated. While not all of the Russian participants in this study expressed support for an inclusive sense of Russian identity, the idea of nationality by birth
was far less stressed as a prerequisite for membership in the greater Russian
community. However, non-Russian participants seemed much more focused
on ancestry as a vital factor for group membership.

Traditional gender roles and patriarchal traditions among many of the
non-Russian ethnic groups in the study area likely influenced participants'
feelings about the concept of ancestry. Patriarchal traditions are important
for men in the Caucasus and are common throughout the region, especially
among Islamic populations.[28] Among ethno-national communities with relatively small consolidated populations, like the Karachays, the availability of
ethnically acceptable spouses can become an issue. Fathers and husbands also
determine where their daughters will study and eventually live, and because
of the cohesiveness of their family units, young women are likely to stay in the
North Caucasus. Therefore, encouraging ethnic purity discourages outmigra-
tion and results in long lineages and traditional localized family homelands.
It is not surprising that individuals from these communities also prioritized
ancestry in their responses.

Religious beliefs are vital in the context of the North Caucasus because the region serves as a long-standing crossroads between Christianity and Islam, fixing notions of religious identity to territory. However, as a factor of identity, participants tended to rely more on community associations when claiming to be "Orthodox" or "Muslim," rather than on religious observance or practice. Religion, unlike native language, has the potential to manifest itself in a social binary in the study area, as the vast majority of its population are culturally connected to either Christianity or Islam. In Stavropol *Krai*, a large Armenian presence makes Christianity more than simply about being Russian, while most of the area's other significant minority populations are united by a shared sense of Islamic heritage.

As a dependent variable, "religion" was important overall (M = 4.33), but those individuals who self-identified as practicing their religion significantly favored its importance. Considering that only 23 percent of Russian participants said that they went to church regularly, Orthodox Christianity, at least as a social process, did not seem to play a major role in identity among ethnic Russians. However, identifying with the Church does provide a connection to a greater sense of belonging, which is reinforced by geography, vis-à-vis the presence of sacred Orthodox Christian spaces throughout the landscape. Such landmarks, which include churches, holy areas, and local sites of pilgrimage, serve as a constant reminder to Orthodox Christians that they are *in place* in their own Orthodox space, and work to ascribe social meaning to Stavropol as an Orthodox place. Despite the fact that there is a noteworthy Islamic population in Stavropol, Muslims there must leave this Christian-dominated environment in order to worship, since the only mosque in town was made into an art gallery. Christians in Karachay-Cherkessia do not face this problem because there are many churches in the republic. Being part of the Russian Federation means that Russians in Karachay-Cherkessia can be connected to the greater notion of Christian space. Politically, they can also lobby Moscow for funding support in building churches.

"Birthplace" can often prove to be a socially deterministic place-based identity factor. Where one is born often plays a part in defining his or her status in community membership. People are likely to carry with them the stereotypes associated with their birthplace, and perhaps also its accents, customs, and even mentality. Birthplace can bring with it social expectations, especially in a cultural crossroads like the North Caucasus.

In the context of Russia, being born in one's ethno-national homeland is important. Participants with titular status significantly favored birthplace (M = 3.52) over those who are nontitular (M = 3.17). Participants having multiple generations of family lineage in the same place (M = 3.74) also ranked "birthplace" significantly higher than first-generation residents (M = 3.08). However, when asked to comment on the role of birthplace in ethno-national identity, many of the participants noted its importance in terms of citizenship and the law, emphasizing the tendency to draw on symbols of the nation-state, as would be expected.[29] Participant 144, a Russian from Stavropol, said, "The nationality of one's parents is a more important factor than birthplace, but by law, if you are born outside of Russia, you are not fully Russian."[30]

Despite being a dependent variable to which every participant in the study could relate, "Living in the Russian Federation" received an overall mean score of 3.52, ranking third in importance among all of the place-based variables. However, this variable was prioritized by Russians, Christians, and participants with family lineage in one place. "Living in the Russian Federation" denotes recognition of Russian society at the state level, representing what Knight[31] would call a high level of authority over social order. Federal authority is the highest level of social order within the Russian state. Living in Russia also matters for human security. State authorities are ultimately responsible for making policy decisions that will directly affect the human security of the populace of the state.[32] These authorities are also responsible for providing economic security in the North Caucasus, as half of the republics' income is received in the form of federal subsidies.[33]

Russia, as a state, also has a monopoly on discourses involving membership within the Russian federal (*Rossiiskoe*) civic community. The Russian state controls borders, print media, national broadcasting, currency, law, and citizenship policies. Perhaps more important, the Russian Federation represents space that is not hostile to ethnic Russians, its majority ethno-national group. Theoretically, Russians could feel *in place* anywhere in Russia. In contrast, in terms of ethno-national territory and ethnic homeland, non-Russians may not identify with all of Russia, causing them to be *out of place*. Republics, such as Karachay-Cherkessia, reflect a concept known as "national cultural autonomy," where national minorities exist with some degree of freedom from a state's dominant group, but remain within said state's sovereign borders.[34] For example, adherence to Islam places one in a minority community in the Russian Federation at the state level. Ethnic Russians, as a "state-bearing" nation, are the dominant group that establishes and enforces social and political norms,[35] and they mostly identify with Orthodox Christianity, the state's most commonly practiced and best-publicized religion. Thus, as the data from this study indicate, Muslims are likely to identify with more localized scales of territory in regard to their community associations, while Christians feel more comfortable at the state level.

The Southern Federal District (SFD) received a relatively poor comparative ranking (M = 3.33) compared to other factors. However, Muslims (M = 3.64) significantly favored the SFD over Christians (M = 2.97). Interestingly, the difference between ethnic Russians and non-Russians was not significant concerning this factor. Being a federal district, the SFD is directly subordinated to Moscow, acting as the first line in the regional chain of command. Therefore, if the SFD were recognized in terms of ethno-national authority, Russians would likely have prioritized it higher than non-Russians. However, Muslims found the SFD more favorable because it has a relatively high percentage of Islamic residents compared to Russia's other federal districts. According to Participant 21, a man living in Stavropol: "I am a Muslim and could thus live in other countries . . . in the United Arab Emirates, or in Turkey for example. As for Russia, it is better to live in the Southern Federal District because, out of all the regions, it is the best for my religion."[36]

"Living in a Particular *Krai* or Republic" was another dependent variable favored by Muslims over Christians, furthering ideas of a break in religious space. The non-Russian titular groups in republics have a very limited amount of territory that they can fully claim as their own, in terms of officially recognized homeland, leading to strong associations with their republics. Minority groups without titular status technically have no territory to claim, leading them to associate with nonplace-based dependent variables, in this case, Islam.

Russians did not seem to favor the importance of *krais* and republics to their ethno-national identity. In fact, living in a particular *krai* was the second-least-important factor for Russians overall, only more important than living in the North Caucasus. This result is not surprising because Russians have many federal territories where they are the majority group and that are officially considered ethnic Russian territory: *krais* and *oblasts*. However, they seemed more aware of the differences between Russian and non-Russian territory, having lived in the latter. Participant 78 is a Russian from Karachay-Cherkessia. Having lived seventeen years in the republic and only three and a half years in Stavropol, she remarked, "I am from Karachay-Cherkessia, but I do not really like it there. I like it here better, in Stavropol. I was born in Stavropol, but we moved to Karachay-Cherkessia when I was half a year old, so I actually consider myself to be from Stavropol."[37]

Hesitating to claim that one is fully from Karachay-Cherkessia is not uncommon among Russians in Stavropol. Being from a non-Russian territory is seldom glorified; it suggests that someone is uncultured, similar to stigmas about rural populations.

With an overall average mean score of 3.64, "Living in the North Caucasus" was the most important place-based dependent variable. Although the North Caucasus is a cultural crossroads, it is also a border region, as it marks the break between Russia's federal borders to the south, encompasses several autonomous republics and two *krais*, and demarcates where majority Russian and Christian populations end and majority non-Russian and Islamic populations begin. This geopolitical position works to facilitate regional conceptions of identity shared by members of each community. Living in the North Caucasus was significantly preferred by Muslim and nontitular participants, both of whom constitute minority communities.

Living in the North Caucasus was more important to Muslims (M = 4.29) than Christians (M = 2.88), further emphasizing the *cultural shape*[38] of the region in terms of Islamic space. Christian participants consistently rated living in the North Caucasus lower than the other place-based dependent variables. This trend shows Christians relating to concrete federal territories, rather than to a somewhat ambiguously defined subregional construct. However, several participants noted the prevalence of a North Caucasus regional idea within official state and popular discourses. Participant number 40, an ethnic Russian, rated living in the North Caucasus "5" because she felt that the idea of the Caucasus was often used in local culture, society, and government. She said, "The North Caucasus is important because everyone emphasizes this fact here. They always say that we are in the Caucasus. This is our place . . . where we live."[39]

Some participants, especially Russians, also associated with the North Caucasus for aesthetic reasons, particularly a love of the area's natural beauty. Participant 20 said, "I love the mountains, nature is beautiful there. I really like to relax, and Dombay [a mountain resort town in Karachay-Cherkessia] is a very relaxing place."[40]

For Muslims, the North Caucasus often represents not only a stronghold for Islam, but also an environment in which their ethno-national groups have established histories and geographies. Muslims associated more strongly with the North Caucasus region than with any particular republic. This trend suggests prioritization of family and social connections among Muslim communities throughout the region over official state territorial markers. Participant 192, a Muslim woman from Stavropol, explained, "For me, it is really important where I was born, but living in the Russian Federation is not so important . . . living in the North Caucasus is very important! It is where my family is from, and I have a large circle of acquaintances there."[41]

This comment demonstrates clear identification with the North Caucasus as opposed to Russia, with justification through personal connections, suggesting the importance of a regional scale sense of meaning through lived experience, without focusing on broader scales, which may not be seen as directly meaningful for the participant's life. Such feelings show the North Caucasus, not Russia, as where community interactions occur, pointing to familiarity as important for identifying with a particular place.

Conclusion

The results of this study reveal several trends regarding ethno-national identities and communities among young adults in the North Caucasus. Participants' overall high ranking of native language, ancestry, and religion speaks to the population's social consciousness. The prioritization of native language in particular, and the fact that there were no significant categorical differences in regard to it, demonstrates the importance of language as a factor of identity. However, participants were not indifferent in their treatment of place-based factors of ethno-national identity. Territorial identity factors, in almost every case, were favored significantly by those participants having multiple generations living in the same place, which emphasized the strong sense of place among those with geographically established families.

Ideas of Russian versus non-Russian space were also prevalent among participants, as were notions of Christian versus Islamic space. While Russians preferred to identify with territories at wider scales, non-Russians, Muslims in particular, favored a much more regional scope, especially in regard to ideas that present the North Caucasus region and the Southern Federal District as the spaces most preferable for themselves and their communities within the Russian federal context. These trends in ethno-national identity and community reflect on the diversity of the North Caucasus, and will certainly continue to influence the region's geography in the future.

By examining both territorial and non-place-based elements, notions about which factors of identity are most important, and how identity is spatially contextualized among the North Caucasus's major territorial constructs, are illuminated in this study. Such understandings are generally important because they help make sense of complex landscapes and provide insights into which spaces are claimed and constructed by various communities. Through fieldwork and analysis, I have presented empirical data suggesting spaces in which certain aspects of ethno-national identity are normalized or marginalized in the territorial context of the North Caucasus. This study provides insight into how these spaces exist in terms of scale, and also into their relations among spaces at other scales within broader geographies. Understanding sociospatial aspects of community is important for area studies in general because it helps to define the territorial extent of the particular processes and identities that exist in any territorial context.

How various communities understand their territories depends on many factors, but it is important to note the multiplicity of meanings that notions of territory may exhibit among members of any given community. Seeing the North Caucasus from the gaze of the ethnic Russian community conjures images that are different from perspectives held by localized groups of people indigenous to the region, who have identity narratives connected to times and geographies existing before Russian forces began to dominate the region in the 1700s. Despite their differences, however, there remains the sense of a greater North Caucasus community, which includes members of all ethno-national and religious groups. Economic motives, state discourses, and geopolitical agendas tug and pull at the North Caucasus community from a variety of different angles, but ultimately the people in this region must view their experience through their everyday lives. Their expression of identity and membership within their various communities has an impact on many important aspects of their lives, ranging from where they might venture, where they work, and whom they might marry. Participants in this study are conscious about where they live and about where they fit into the North Caucasus and the greater Russian cultural montage. Therefore, understanding difference among the various social divisions in the North Caucasus is critical not only for understanding individual groups, but for understanding the region as a whole. Questions regarding what Russian identity means in a territorial sense continue to be relevant throughout post-Soviet space, and defining Russian communities as either *in place* or *out of place* may lead to conflicting claims to legitimacy, while at the same time influencing geopolitical agendas both inside Russia and beyond its borders.

Notes

1. L. Staeheli, "Place," in *A Companion to Political Geography*, ed. John Agnew, Katharyne Mitchell, and Gerard Toal (New York: Blackwell, 2003), 158–70.

2. This project was partially funded by the University of Kansas Geography Department's "Kollmorgen Fund."

3. V. Belozorov, V. Tinkov, and N. Panin, "Atlas and Information Systems for Studying Ethnodemographic Processes in the Stavropol Krai," in *Ethnic Atlas of the Population of Stavropol Krai* (Stavropol: Stavropol State University, 2008), 39–44.

4. Susan Layton, *Russian Literature and Empire: Conquest of the Caucasus from Pushkin to Tolstoy* (New York: Cambridge University Press, 1994); Michael Khodarkovsky, *Russia's Steppe Frontier: The Making of a Colonial Empire, 1500–1800* (Bloomington: University of Indiana Press, 2002); Edith W. Clowes, *Russia on the Edge: Imagined Geographies and Post-Soviet Identity* (Ithaca, NY: Cornell University Press, 2011).

5. D. Gregory et al., *The Dictionary of Human Geography* (Oxford: John Wiley and Sons, 2011).

6. Ibid, 119–20.

7. J. Agnew et al., *A Companion to Political Geography*.

8. John Agnew, *Place and Politics: The Geographical Mediation of State and Society* (Boston: Allen and Unwin, 1987), 28–29.

9. Guntram Herb, "National Identity and Territory," in *Nested Identities*, ed. Guntram Herb and David Kaplan (Lanham, MD: Rowman and Littlefield, 1999), 9–30.

10. David Kaplan, "Territorial Identities and Geographic Scale," in *Nested Identities*, 31–50.

11. D. Delaney, "The Political Construction of Scale," *Political Geography* 16, no. 2 (1997): 93–97.

12. S. Marston, "The Social Construction of Scale," *Progress in Human Geography* 24, no. 2 (2000): 219–42.

13. D. Knight, "Identity and Territory: Geographical Perspectives on Nationalism and Regionalism," *Annals of the Association of American Geographers* 72, no. 4 (1982): 514–31.

14. S. O'Lear, "Azerbaijan's Resource Wealth: Political Legitimacy and Public Opinion," *The Geographic Journal* 173, no. 3 (2007): 207–23.

15. V. Belozorov et al., "Atlas and Information Systems," 39–44.

16. Walter Richmond, *The Northwest Caucasus: Past, Present, Future* (New York: Routledge, 2008), 119–120.

17. S. Rivera, P. Kozyreva, and E. Sarovskii, "Interviewing Political Elites: Lessons from Russia," *PS: Political Science and Politics* 35, no. 4 (2002): 683–88.

18. Max Weber, *Economy and Society* (1922; repr., Los Angeles: University of California Press, 1968), 385–395.

19. Anthony Smith, *The Ethnic Origins of Nations* (Oxford: Blackwell, 1986), 174–240.

20. Craig Mertler and Rachel Vannata, *Advanced and Multivariate Statistical Methods* (Glendale, CA: Pyrczak, 2005), 13–22.

21. E. Dunbar, "The Personal Dimensions of Difference Scale: Measuring Multi-Group Identity with Four Ethnic Groups," *International Journal of International Relations* 21, no. 1 (1997): 1–28.

22. Peter Rogerson, *Statistical Methods for Geography* (London: Sage, 2001), 65–81.

23. Benedict Anderson, *Imagined Communities* (New York: Verso, 1983), 67–82.

24. Participant 40, interview with author, Stavropol, Russia, June 9, 2009.

25. Participant 193, interview with author, Tashla Neighborhood in Stavropol, Russia, June 19, 2009.

26. Participant 177, interview with author, Stavropol, Russia, June 7, 2009.

27. Participant 128, interview with author, City of Cherkessk, Republic of Karachay-Cherkessia, Russia, June 17, 2009.

28. F. Aliyev, "Framing Perceptions of Islam and the 'Islamic Revival' in the Post-Soviet Countries," *Journal for the Study of Religions and Ideologies* 2, no. 7 (2004): 123–36.

29. Anderson, *Imagined Communities*.

30. Participant 144, interview with author, Stavropol, Russia, June 8, 2009.

31. D. Knight, "Identity and Territory: Geographical Perspectives on Nationalism and Regionalism," *Annals of the Association of American Geographers* 72, no. 4 (1982): 514–31.

32. S. O'Lear, "Azerbaijan's Resource Wealth," 207–23.

33. V. Belozorov et al., "Atlas and Information Systems," 39–44.

34. Kaplan, "Territorial Identities and Geographic Scale," 31–50.

35. R. Brubaker, "National Minorities, Nationalizing States, and External Homelands in the New Europe," *Daedalus* 124, no. 2 (1995): 107–32.

36. Participant 21, interview with author, Stavropol, Russia, June 11, 2009.

37. Participant 78, interview with author, Stavropol, Russia, June 10, 2009.

38. Anssi Paasi, *Territories, Boundaries and Consciousness: The Changing Geographies of the Finnish-Russia Border* (Hoboken, NJ: Wiley-Blackwell, 1996).

39. Participant 40, interview with author, Stavropol, Russia, June 9, 2009.

40. Participant 20, interview with author, Izibilnyi, Stavropol Krai, Russia, June 14, 2009.

41. Participant 192, interview with author, Stavropol, Russia, June 13, 2009.

PART III

Civil Society and Its Discontents
Freedom of Religion, Human Rights, and Free Speech

Brief Introduction

Over the last twenty-five years, the processes of globalization and democratization have diminished the lives of many of the world's poorest people instead of fostering real economic opportunity and legal well-being among the world's populations. As Nobel Prize–winning economist Joseph Stiglitz has shown, so-called open borders are by no means open borders for everyone but rather a membrane through which goods and products move in one direction, and money moves in the opposite direction—mainly for the benefit of the world's richest countries, companies, and individuals. Similarly, many initially democratically minded initiatives have stalled as "halfway houses" between some form of popular representational rule and dictatorship.[1] Other initiatives have moved clearly toward authoritarian rule or toward chaos and civil war. Political research on democratization, it has been noted, has produced "largely a literature about the choices political leaders have made and the consequences of those choices."[2] A task considerably more difficult than creating overly generalized models and definitions is to examine the complexities of exercising choice, free speech, and other civil and human rights on the ground—the actual performance of these rights, and the costs and limiting factors working against those who undertake such performance, such as violent militant reaction, police reprisal, renditions, and other actions in the unaccountable or less accountable sectors of an otherwise "democratic" government. This complexity can be found in many places of the postcommunist and postcolonial world.

Relatively lacking in the area studies scholarly conversation has been consideration of ordinary people's voices. These are the people most affected at the receiving end by apparent "liberation" from dictatorship, which, in some cases, was turned into other forms of suffering—civil war, religious oppression, and sexual violence, to name a few. Such experiences could become sources of eventual radicalization for those without a voice in the official structure. The examples investigated in part III show a number of different scenarios in which the ruling elites have failed to support and assure the human rights— and civil rights—of their citizens. As in other parts of *Area Studies in the Global Age*, the communities studied here are by definition "liminal"—they are in politically or culturally contested places, and their identity is in flux.

In her chapter on the rebirth of Islam in the new states of Central Asia, Mariya Omelicheva creates a typology of new Islamic formations, based in part on her field research conducted in 2010 and 2011. The three types are identity-oriented, theology-oriented, and politically oriented Islam. Her typology helps to clarify where Islam can be viewed through the lens of a civil right, "religious freedom," and where it is better viewed as a coercive, limiting practice by a leader or elite community in power. Omelicheva's treatment shows noteworthy rifts among local communities and between local and national Islamic discourses; and between local identity-oriented and more doctrinaire forms of Islam. Of particular interest here, also, is the overall moderate nature of the many forms of Islam in Central Asia, although, as Omelicheva notes, area governments' inept, heavy-handed treatment of competing forms of Islam is a source of resentment among Central Asian communities.

While Omelicheva's chapter gives an overview of the Islamic awakening and accompanying contestation of religious identity in the regional context of Central Asia, the remaining three chapters focus on one or at most a few socially committed creative productions that magnify and illuminate the failure of human rights in three countries, Congo, Romania, and Russia. Marike Janzen treats the complete failure of community in the context of civil war—and through that experience, she examines the historical shift in concepts of human community from the now latent Marxist/Soviet idea of "solidarity" (based on economic equality) to the current "human rights paradigm" operative in international law (based on the very abstract concept of an inherent right in each human). Janzen's lens is an unusually personal, though also international, play by US playwright Lynn Nottage about rights issues and Congolese women's experiences of "rape as warfare" in the Congo's civil war. She focuses on Nottage's project as an effort to raise awareness in the English-speaking world of these crimes against humanity. Nottage traveled to Uganda in 2004 and interviewed women who had fled civil war and were now subsisting in the Ugandan refugee camps. Out of this set of interviews came the determination to carry these voices to the broad public in the form of a play, *Ruined*, first staged in 2008 in the United States and since then staged in many parts of the English-speaking world, including in Congo. Modeled on Bertolt Brecht's play *Mother Courage and Her Children*, also about a non-combatant creating a civil-war economic community during the seventeenth-century Thirty Years War, *Ruined* focuses instead on the contemporary human rights community. Nottage takes it as her goal to expose the weakness of the UN human rights paradigm and to move the international human rights community to take positive and helpful action.

Janzen's chapter treats a US writer working outside of Africa to raise international consciousness about the human rights crisis in Congo. Other uses of art to raise political consciousness *inside* an authoritarian regime are the topics of the last two chapters. Art as the voice resisting political suppression of free speech and human rights is nothing new, though the hope of recent democratization was to obviate that role. Now, once again artistic production within increasingly oppressive political regimes has become an outlet for exposing overbearing censorship and abuse of police power, one in Romania with its lingering secret police power and one in Russia with its reempowered police.

Corina Apostol examines what she terms the "self-historicizing" project of Romanian artist Lia Perjovschi. Through becoming aware of the impact of past censorship, viewers of Perjovschi's artistic archive are urged actively to remember their own past, to correct official versions of Romanian history, and to think about the concepts of "solidarity" and "community" and their possible new meanings in a Romanian culture highly suspicious of such words. Perjovschi's artistic archive of books, slides, photocopies, files, postcards, printed matter about international as well as Romanian contemporary art in its historical context, and her related project "The Knowledge Museum," represent spaces of resistance against reactionary state institutions. Her open Archive of Knowledge is the polar opposite of the infamous "Securitate" (Secret Police) Archive, a place in which official history was crafted and competing narratives suppressed during the dictatorship. The continued stranglehold of the security police on citizens' lives and consciousness, Apostol argues, portends the lingering weakness of Romanian civil society.

In his chapter on Russian performance art collectives, Patrick Callen investigates the figure of the policeman in post-Soviet poetry and art, focusing particularly on conditions of civil rights abuse under Putin and Medvedev in the early twenty-first century. He deals largely with the work of the famous music group Pussy Riot and the less well-known but related collectives, Chto delat' (What is to be done?) and Voina (War). Since the rule of law and the press have been muzzled, such groups have worked to engage the public through outrageous satires of institutions of power—particularly the police. Their "theaters" are public venues—the streets and the metro stations of Russia's

largest cities. Through their performance art they have transformed St. Petersburg and Moscow by making everyday life into a work of lived political art.
All four cases treated here deal with instances of cultural resistance in the
context of failed efforts to enact civil rights. Public art and ritual are more
than mere reactions to or reflections on repressive initiatives taken by centers
of power. Instead they urge critical thinking and aggressive social action on
the part of ordinary people to create a form of grassroots "people power" to
challenge power elites.

Notes

1. Matthias Basedau and Patrick Köllner, "Area Studies and Comparative Area Studies: A
Primer on Recent Debates and Methodological Challenges," *Japan aktuell* (2007): 4.
2. Valerie Bunce, "Rethinking Recent Democratization: Lessons from the Postcommunist
Experience," *World Politics* 55 (2003): 188.

The Multiple Faces of Islamic Rebirth in Central Asia

MARIYA Y. OMELICHEVA

n the years preceding the breakup of the USSR, the Central Asian republics of Kazakhstan, Kyrgyzstan, Tajikistan, Turkmenistan, and Uzbekistan
experienced a revival of Islam. Variously labeled as "re-Islamicization,"
"Islamic renaissance," and "secondary Islamicization," the process accelerated
following the Soviet Union's breakup, as Islam always has had deep roots in
the region with a rich Islamic heritage, developed religious infrastructure,
and the presence of progressive Muslim clergy. Following the inception of the
US-led "war on terror" in 2001, images of radical Islamic groups seeking jihad
(holy war) against non-Muslim states and peoples permeated the references
to Islam in the Western media and public discourse. Against the backdrop of
the pervasive discourse about the Islamist threat, the discussion of Islam in
Central Asia has also focused on the emergence of radical Islamic groups with
political goals and agendas, while many other sides of the Islamic rebirth in
Central Asia have been overlooked.

This chapter seeks to contribute to a more comprehensive study of the
Islamic revival in Central Asia by pointing out the multiple "faces" or manifestations of the Central Asian Islamic rebirth. To achieve this goal, the chapter focuses on three overlapping expressions of the Islamic revival, namely,
identity-oriented, theology-oriented, and politically oriented forms of Islamic
rebirth. The identity-oriented rebirth of Islam describes the return of Central
Asian Muslims to the Islamic faith as part of the rediscovery of their national,
ethnic, and communal identities, and accompanying this process, the reintro-
duction of Islam into their daily lives. The theology-oriented revival denotes
growing interest in the sources of Islamic knowledge as well as renewed religious debates among representatives of various expressions of Islam in Central Asia. The politically oriented rebirth of Islam refers to the emergence and
activities of Islamist movements. These concomitant processes of Islamic revival
both illustrate and elucidate the multiple and continuously changing Islamic
identities and communities in Central Asia. What is Islamic—a defining element of an Islamic identity made up of the body of principles, norms, and

practices derived from the scriptures and tradition—is what purposive actors (governments, muftis, religious leaders, and ulema [Muslim scholars]) make of it, and this "making" and presentation of all things Muslim is not independent of sociopolitical circumstances and traditions.[1] Muslim identity, therefore, is never static or unitary but embodies the wealth of cultural artifacts and knowledge stemming from social relations, which are interpreted against the backdrop of the changing social and political landscape and, therefore, are deeply affected by it.

Several types of methods and strategies for collecting evidence were employed in research for this chapter. Descriptive statistical evidence of various aspects of religious observation and practices in Central Asia and survey data were used for charting the identity-oriented Islamic rebirth. To examine religious debates, this study relied on primary and secondary religious sources, including published excerpts from teachings and written exchanges between Muslim clergy and statements of religious groups discussing doctrinal questions of Islamic theology in Central Asia. The study of political Islam relied on anthropological research carried out in the region, in addition to public statements and publications of the Islamist movements and the author's field research in Central Asian states.

Identity-Oriented Islamic Rebirth in Central Asian States

Although Arab armies brought a new religion, Islam, to a territory demarcated by the Amu Darya and the Syr Darya Rivers in the seventh century, it took more than a millennium for the Islamic faith to spread across the region. The present-day Kazakhs and Kyrgyz were converted to Islam by the end of the nineteenth century, while the ancestors of modern Tajiks and Uzbeks adopted the Islamic faith much earlier. The Bolshevik government that came to power in 1917 launched a ruthless attack on religion, which was perceived as an enemy of communism. This campaign for atheism and the rooting out of what Karl Marx had labeled the "opium of the people" endured through the first part of the twentieth century.[2] Following the Second World War, the Soviet government removed some restrictions on religious practices. Soviet policy on nationalities permitted religious identification, observance, and education, which were treated as important markers of the peoples' cultural heritage. At the same time, the Soviet authorities discouraged mosque visitations and public prayers as "extreme" religious manifestations incompatible with the ways in which the Soviet people defined their Muslim identity.[3] As a result, many Muslim believers preferred to conceal their faith by limiting their religious practices to certain religious rituals at weddings, funerals, and circumcisions. Even with restrictions, however, the ability to practice these Islamic customs laid the basis for the return of Islam as a way of life in the postindependence Central Asian Muslim communities.[4]

By the late 1980s, the effects of perestroika (the major political and economic reforms initiated by General Secretary of the Communist Party of the USSR Mikhail Gorbachev in Moscow) trickled down to the Central Asian region, where local authorities finally curbed the persecution of religious activities. The following years saw a record increase in Islamic identification among Central Asian peoples, in part because they finally had an opportunity to manifest their commitment to the Islamic faith (see table 1). Today, different estimates show that Muslims constitute 52–65 percent of the population in Kazakhstan, and 90–93 percent in Turkmenistan. In Kyrgyzstan, 75–86 percent of the population identifies with Islam, and around 88–90 percent of Uzbeks and 90–98 percent of Tajiks are Muslims. The majority of Central Asian Muslims are Sunnis of the Hanafi School, one of the most liberal schools of religious legal thought (*madhab*) among the existing four schools of law within Sunni Islam. Throughout all of the Central Asian republics there are also adherents to Sufism, combining a variety of mystical forms of Islam that profess direct personal experience and knowledge of God. Shiite minorities (about 2–5 percent) are present in the mountainous regions of Tajikistan and Uzbekistan's cities of Bukhara and Samarkand.[5]

The religious opening also has prompted growth in religious infrastructure. The governments of the Arab states, Turkey, Pakistan, and the Central Asian republics provided funds for new mosques and reconstruction of the old ones. In the 1950s, there were only 202 mosques in Uzbekistan, 18 in Kazakhstan, and 4 in Turkmenistan.[7] By 1992, Uzbekistan had about three thousand

Table 1 — Muslims in Central Asia

Republics	Muslims (% of population)[6]		
	1959	1979	2010
Kazakhstan	13.2	14.2	52–65
Kyrgyzstan	4.8	5.2	75–86
Tajikistan	6.5	7.5	90–98
Turkmenistan	4.7	5.3	90–93
Uzbekistan	26.4	30.0	80–88

mosques,[8] while two thousand new mosques opened their doors in Tajikistan during 1989–1991. By 1995, Kyrgyzstan had one thousand mosques, and Kazakhstan counted 1,402 mosques by the late 1990s.[9] Numerous religious sites reopened in all Central Asian states, and homage to the tombs of saints or revered ancestors has increased considerably.[10]

The spread and intensity of the Islamic rebirth has varied across Central Asia. In Kyrgyzstan, for example, it has been more widespread in the southern Osh and Jalalabad provinces (oblasts). In Kazakhstan, the Chimkent oblast bordering northern Uzbekistan is the most religious region. The residents of the Uzbek part of the Fergana Valley have been known for their greater religiosity than other Uzbek Muslims. A survey conducted by Ro'i and Wainer (2009) in four Central Asian states revealed that there are more Uzbeks who pray five times a day, regularly attend religious lessons and mosques, read Islamic literature, and perform Islamic rituals, compared to Kazakhs and Kyrgyz (see table 2).[11] Regional diversity with regard to religious practices and identification can be found in both Tajikistan and Turkmenistan. Sizable populations of the major urban centers in Central Asian countries, however, continue to have little interest in Islam.[12]

Much of the regional variation in Islamic practices and identification has deep historical roots. The sedentary life of the ancestors of modern Tajiks and Uzbeks was an important factor in the early adoption and stricter observance of juridical Islam by the Uzbek and Tajik settlers compared to the Kyrgyz and Kazakh nomads.[13] The policies of the Soviet government had both lessened this religious distinction and strengthened the national-religious identification by encoding religious practices as part of the national minorities' cultural traditions. The strong association between religion and ethnicity has

Table 2. Islamic Practices in Central Asia

	Pray 5 times a day (%)	Read Islamic literature or attend religious lessons regularly (%)	Attend mosque every Friday or 5 times a week (%)	Perform circumcision, nikah (marriage), and funeral (%)
Kyrgyz	8.3	32.1	23.1	30.8
Kazakh	12	29.9	19.2	7.8
Uzbek	32	32.6	24.9	53
Tajik	41	41.9	21.6	55.1
Turkmenistan	No data	No data	No data	No data

been reinforced in the post-Soviet context by the governments and religious authorities in the Central Asian states. Today, as a century ago, "Muslim-ness" is viewed as natural and intrinsic to the peoples of Central Asia. For the Kazakhs, Uzbeks, and, to a lesser degree, Kyrgyz, ethnic identity is a Mus-lim one.[14] Therefore, many Central Asian Muslims do not regard scriptural knowledge or the practice of the Five Pillars of Islam as the exclusive markers of Muslim identity. Instead, their Muslim identity is defined by virtue of birth into a family of Muslims and through the lineage in the communities where Islam constitutes a central component of life.[15]

Because of this strong association between religious and ethnic identities and, most recently, the national identities that have been ethnicized by the governments of the newly independent states, some scholars contend that quantitative manifestations of religious observance are not tantamount to an Islamic rebirth in Central Asian states. Instead, these indicators are symbols of national self-expression and a means for reclaiming ethno-cultural identity.[16] This chapter takes a different view. The release of ethnocentric energy in the postindependence states of Central Asia has bolstered their Islamic rebirth, and the latter has furthered a national revival. The return to the open practice of Islamic rituals cannot be separated from the celebration of the achievements in national culture, poetry, and philosophy, many of which are deeply inter-twined with religious thought. The Islamic renaissance and national rebirth have become indivisible in the Central Asian states, resulting in a complex interplay of national and religious identities, searches for their meanings, and struggles for their individual conceptions.[17]

For the Central Asian governments, the revival of Islam has become a potent force for creating unity in the multiethnic and multiconfessional states, and a strategy for purging the vestiges of colonial rule and Russian cultural hegemony. Central Asian authorities have promoted certain official interpre-tations of Islam presented as authentic, inherently apolitical, and harmoniz-ing with the Central Asian cultural heritage. Both Muslims and non-Muslims contest these state-sponsored definitions of "national" Islam. Many faithful view them as impediments to the reintegration of Central Asia into the world of Muslims.[18] The revival of multiple local varieties of Islam also challenges the monolithic conception of "national" Islam.

All in all, the identity-oriented rebirth of Islam has been a complex and multidimensional process related to, but in no way equivalent to, national rebirth. Despite all attempts at achieving a degree of uniformity of Islamic thought and practice at the national level, the local level has seen a growing diversification and fragmentation of the religious field as well as the formation of ethno-religious communities. It is this merger of local traditions with the practice of Islam that accounts for a greater religious diversity within Central Asia. Various forms of "local" Islam have been competing among themselves, as well as with pre-Islamic religions such as Tengrism and Zoroastrianism and such modern religions as Christian Evangelism.[19]

Theology-Oriented Islamic Rebirth

Islamic rituals performed by ordinary Muslims during the Soviet era often lacked a theological basis or a deep religious understanding.[20] In the post-Soviet era, however, study of the basic principles of Islamic faith by ordinary practitioners of Islam, as well as the renewed debates between Islamic intellectuals about the essence of "true" Islam and the role of Islamic faith in society and politics, became a prominent feature of Islamic rebirth in Central Asia. Demand for greater theological knowledge led to an upsurge in religious schools across the region. Uzbekistan registered about four hundred *madrasas* (religious schools) in the mid-1990s, and several analysts recorded two- and threefold growth in their students' enrollment. These religious schools also became highly popular in Tajikistan.[21] During the Soviet period, mullahs (religious clerics) from Kyrgyzstan and Kazakhstan traveled to neighboring Uzbekistan for religious training. Following their independence, both republics established their own Islamic institutions of higher education. Officially sanctioned Islamic newspapers and other publications, including the main religious texts translated into the native languages, appeared in all Central Asian states.

For those unable to satisfy spiritual and intellectual needs at home, opportunities emerged for receiving formal religious education abroad. Grants and scholarships from other Muslim governments and foreign charitable foundations, as well as a few scholarships from the Central Asian governments, enabled Central Asian Muslims to study at major religious schools. Medina University in Saudi Arabia and Al Azhar in Egypt have become the most popular destinations for Central Asian students because of their outstanding reputation in the Muslim world, free education, and financial support to students. Other Central Asian Muslims travel to religious schools in Syria, Pakistan, and Iran. The numbers of those seeking religious knowledge abroad were higher in the 1990s, but declined after 2000 due to the increased security concerns and Central Asian governments' attempts to regulate the movement of their citizens.[22]

The growing interest in various theological aspects of Islam and broader access to religious knowledge and information also have revived debates on different aspects of Islamic orthodoxy and praxis. During the years surround-ing the breakup of the Soviet Union, these debates were carried out on the pages of religious publications, in declarations of Central Asian theologians, and through statements of newly founded religious groups. Many diverse aspects of religion, including some ritual practices and interpretation of scrip-tures, were touched upon in these written and verbal exchanges. However, the main lines of the divide have been over the broader questions related to the compatibility of local Islamic practices with orthodox Islamic traditions, the coexistence of Islam and a secular state, and the relationship between Islam, on one hand, and innovation, modernity, and other religious faiths, on the other hand.[23] Throughout the 1990s and early 2000s, all Central Asian gov-ernments heightened their control over the clergy. Surveillance of religious practices and censorship of religious information in Uzbekistan, for instance, has stifled theological discussion.

Most Central Asian Muslims, including the official clergy, subscribe to the teachings of the Hanafi theological-juridical school. When it was reintroduced in the 1940s, following decades of antireligious purges, the new religious authorities attempted to accommodate Islam in the context of the Soviet sec-ular state with its atheist views. The Soviet era muftis (religious scholars), for instance, issued a series of fatwas (juridical rulings concerning Islamic law), which legitimized the separation of the secular state and religion, declared the possibility of the coexistence of Muslim communities with non-Islamic states, and permitted practices and traditions inconsistent with Sharia law. Consid-ered by the Muslims as the infallible law of God (Allah), Sharia is both a code of moral conduct and a law dealing with a variety of personal matters includ-ing diet, prayer, and gender and family relations in addition to many topics commonly addressed by secular law. Many Central Asian muftis supported the fatwas issued by the Central Asian Muftiate, the highest Islamic managing body in the region, during the Soviet era.[24]

Among the most fervent critics of Hanafism, in general, and the Central Asian official Islamic jurisprudence and local Islamic practices, in particular, are a diverse group of devout Muslims, who are frequently referred to as Isla-mists, Salafists, and Wahhabists. While there are important differences between Salafists, Wahhabists, and other fundamentalist varieties of Islam (Salafists, for example, reject all four schools of Islamic jurisprudence, and Wahhabists are the followers of the ultraconservative orientation within Salafism inspired by the teachings of the Saudi Arabian theologian Abd al-Wahhab [1703–1791]), they are united in their quest for a return to an original doctrinal Islam that existed in the medieval era of the Prophet Muhammad and the four righteous caliphs who ruled after his death.[25] The adherents of the fundamentalist views call for

purification of Islam from all innovations and purging of superstitious prac-
tices, such as the cults of saints, shrine visitations, and homage to ancestors.
However, the latter practices, which are derived from the tradition rather than
the Quran, and therefore are considered to be inconsistent with the orthodox
Islamic tradition, continue to shape the religious identity of many Central
Asian Muslims. The critics of traditional Islamic practices prevalent across
Central Asia insist that a return to "pure" Islam can only be achieved through
the re-Islamicization of the society and the establishment of an Islamic state.[26]

Central Asian fundamentalists hold conflicting views on a variety of questions in Islam, including the meaning and role of jihad and the relationship of
Islam to modernity and innovation. Some Islamists, known as conservative or
protective Salafists, completely discount the possibility of innovation within
Islam and strive for its protection from modern influences, especially those
originating in non-Islamic societies. The Salafists of the modernist or reformist variety, meanwhile, welcome scientific and technological progress as long
as it can be used to the advantage of Muslim societies. They share the same
goal of restoration of Islam in its pure form, but also call for the reform and
modernization of religious education.[27]

In practice, the boundaries between Salafi conservatives and modernists,
as well as between Salafists and Hanafites, are rather blurred. Salafists and
Hanafites agree on certain issues of dogma and ritual, and it is possible to find
conservatives and reformists among traditionalists within the Hanafi school.
Modern influences are unacceptable for both Salafi and Hanafi conservatives,
whereas modernizing and educational tendencies and ideas constitute the
core of the reformist movements' religious doctrines. Yet both conservative
and modernist varieties of Salafism will disagree with the Hanafi traditionalists on the place and role of Sufism in Islam.[28] If many Hanafis view Sufism
(mystical Islamic belief concerned with the purification of the inner self) and
Hanafism (school of law concerned with the external self) as complementary,
Salafists see Sufist ideas and practices as anathema.

An understanding of Islam in Central Asia would be incomplete without
considering Sufism, a mystical form of Islam with deep historical roots in
Central Asia. According to a broadly accepted interpretation, the word *Sufism*
is derived from the Arabic *suf*, "wool." Hence, Sufi denotes a person wearing an austere woolen garment.[29] Sufism is unrelated to the Sunni/Shia split
in Islam and is distinguished by its focus on the spiritual purification of its
followers. Sufism places emphasis on the personal connection of the faithful to Allah through mystic and ascetic discipline.[30] Four Sufi orders (schools
of thought) that originated in Central Asia are Yasawiya, Naqshbandiya,
Kubrwiya, and Qadiriya.[31] The Ferghana Valley has been the stronghold of

Central Asian Sufism, but the places of pilgrimage to the revered Sufi teachers and poets can be found in Turkestan (Kazakhstan) and beyond. The rebirth of Sufism occurred against the backdrop of Islamic revival in the region. The Naqshbandiya order, which historically played an important role in the politics and social relations of pre-Soviet Central Asian khanates, for instance, experienced a revival in Uzbekistan, and indigenous Sufi brotherhoods with links to the Yawawiya order appeared in Kazakhstan. However, the new Sufi movements represent a distant replica of the original philosophical and mystical Sufi tradition that was interrupted a long time ago. The modern forms of Sufism in Central Asia retained their outward association with the indigenous Sufi traditions but not the essence of their spiritual teachings.[32]

Rebirth of Political Islam in Central Asia

The spread of fundamentalist ideas in parts of Central Asia precipitated the emergence of Islamist groups and movements in these states. The origins of the Islamist groups can be traced to underground mosques and informal religious schools that operated in Uzbekistan and parts of Tajikistan in the late 1960s and 1970s. The educational efforts of unofficial mullahs teaching in the clandestine religious circles gave rise to a new generation of modern Muslim theologians. Two Islamic teachers—Muhammad Rustamov Hindustoni (1892–1989) and Abdulhakim Qori (b. 1896)—stand out, in particular, for training and inspiring numerous Muslim activists who played an indispensable role in the Islamic rebirth in Central Asia.[33] Said Adbullo Nuri, one of the founders of Tajikistan's Islamic Renaissance Party (IRP), was a student of Hindustoni, while Juma Namangani, the leader of the Islamic Movement of Uzbekistan (IMU), studied with Abdulhakim Qori.[34]

Because of the many obstacles to the establishment of national and region-wide Islamic organizations, smaller and locally operated Islamist movements and groups became the primary form of organization of Islamic activism in Central Asian states. In 1991, the famous Adolat (Justice) groups appeared in Uzbekistan. They marked a synthesis of the local self-government, militia, and clergy. The militia units were directed to keep order in the streets; the local authorities provided material assistance to the poor and enforced *zakat* (charitable contributions); and the clergy engaged in religious propaganda.[35] Ideologically, Adolat groups were Salafi. Their religious leadership preached Islamic puritanism and advocated the establishment of an Islamic state deemed as the only solution to crime, poverty, moral degradation, and many other socioeconomic concerns. In the early 1990s, a radical wing of the "warriors of Islam," or Islom Lashkarlari, crystallized within Adolat. The "warriors" committed themselves to jihad, the violent struggle against a secular regime in Uzbekistan, in the name of Islam. By 1991, Adolat assumed political control of the city of Namangan by taking over the Communist Party building and establishing a shadow government. These actions prompted a backlash from the secular government of President Karimov in Uzbekistan. Several prominent members of Adolat were arrested and the group was disbanded by the state. Its leaders found refuge in Tajikistan, where they took part in the Tajik civil war and created a new Islamist organization, the Islamic Movement of Uzbekistan (IMU), around 1997.[36]

The IMU retained some characteristics of a conservative Salafi organization inherited from Adolat. Because its leadership had a weak theoretical background in Islam and considerable fighting experience, the IMU developed into a jihadist organization with a vague political agenda limited to toppling the Karimov regime in Uzbekistan and imposing strict observance of Islamic norms and prohibitions in this country.[37] The United States, Russia, China, Central Asian states, and other states designated the IMU as a terrorist organization because of a series of terrorist attacks in Uzbekistan, raids on Kyrgyzstan, and ties with the Al Qaeda and Taliban networks. Severely weakened in combat with the United States' and its allies' forces in Afghanistan, the IMU lost its political purpose and degenerated into a group of guerrilla fighters and criminals living off drugs and arms smuggling with little or no religious political agenda.[38] Quite possibly, after 2000, the fragments of IMU joined with other Islamists in Central Asia in a new loosely organized umbrella group called the Islamic Movement of Central Asia, which was implicated in militant and terrorist activities in the region.

An important milestone in the revival of political forms of Islam in Central Asia was an attempt to form national Islamic renaissance parties. In 1990, the Islamic Revival Party (IRP) of Tajikistan was formed. It became legal in December 1991 after the Tajik Supreme Council terminated the law prohibiting the formation of religious parties. The Uzbek authorities denied official registration to the Uzbek branch of IRP, and soon after, all other Central Asian states passed official bans on the formation of religious parties. From the standpoint of its religious positions, the IRP of Tajikistan was a moderate Islamic group, though by no means homogenous. Its goals laid out in the party's statutes included a spiritual revival of the citizens of Tajikistan, the spread of Islamic knowledge, and application of Islamic principles to the everyday life of Muslims. The party emphasized peaceful and electoral means as primary methods for accomplishing its political goals.[39] The radical fringes of the party wanted to launch rapid Islamicization of Tajikistan, even at the risk of violent confrontation with secular authorities.[40] Ideological factionalism, which persisted within the IRP, impaired its organizational strength in the long run. The Tajik civil war (1992–1997), in which the IRP members played a leading role as part of the opposition coalition fighting the Russian-backed Tajik government, weakened the party both ideologically and politically. The ghost of civil war violence and anti-Islamist propaganda tarnished its public image. The party has never been able to mobilize Tajik voters in the parliamentary elections or overcome the highly politicized regional factionalism in Tajikistan. As a result, the party has been marginalized in Tajik politics. The death of Said Abdullo Nuri in 2006, IRP's chairman and one of the leaders of the armed opposition during Tajikistan's civil war, exacerbated internal power struggles in the party. The radical/fundamentalist wing of the IRP, affected by the teachings and practices of other Salafist groups in Tajikistan, calls for the transformation of Tajikistan into an Islamic state, while moderates insist on peaceful participation of the party in the political life of Tajikistan.

Hizb ut-Tahrir (the Liberation Party) is another Salafist movement with a significant presence in the Central Asian republics. Although the exact numbers of Hizb ut-Tahrir followers are difficult to ascertain due to the highly clandestine nature of its activities, analysts estimate that the group had about fifteen thousand members in Uzbekistan in 2003, an increase from seven thousand followers in 1999. In Kyrgyzstan, where the group appeared in 1997, the membership was between one and two thousand in the early 2000s, and reached as many as seven to eight thousand by 2009. In Tajikistan, Hizb ut-Tahrir recruited more than one thousand members in the early 2000s. Numerous reports about the spread of Hizb ut-Tahrir membership in both Tajikistan and southern Kazakhstan appeared in recent years.[41]

Contrary to other Islamist groups in Central Asia, Hizb ut-Tahrir is not indigenous to the region. It originated in Jerusalem in 1953, and its current website is maintained on a British server. The group promotes a pan-Islamist agenda of establishing an Islamic state, or caliphate, uniting all Muslims worldwide. Hizb ut-Tahrir resists the ideas of democracy and nationhood and disseminates anti-American and anti-Semitic views. These and other themes have limited resonance with the majority of Central Asian Muslims.[42] What explains the party's success in the region is its ability to adapt the Hizb ut-Tahrir ideology to local contexts and avoid theological debates.[43] Furthermore, contrary to other jihadist movements, Hizb ut-Tahrir eschews violence and emphasizes inner jihad in pursuing personal self-improvement and aligning one's conduct and thought with the precepts of Islam. The presentations of jihad that portray it as part of internal, spiritual, and psychological transformation find broad resonance among Central Asian Muslims, many of whom join the group motivated by prospects of changing their own and other people's behavior that exhibits any signs of addictions and poor discipline.[44]

In the 1990s, a local variety of Hizb ut-Tahrir, namely, Akromiya, split from the movement. Founded in 1996 in Andijan, Akromiya shared with Hizb ut-Tahrir its goals but disagreed on the methods of work. Akromiya's founders proposed scaling down the party's activities to the local level, focusing on one town or community for accomplishing its goals on a smaller scale. Akromiya's members created their own material base, a range of small businesses, which contributed one-fifth of their profits to alleviate poverty in their communities. Since employees of these companies were required to participate in the study groups, the cells of Akromiya united individuals with similar professional backgrounds.[45] In 2004, the government of Uzbekistan unexpectedly imprisoned twenty-three local businessmen, who were charged with membership in what the government designated as the "extremist organization" Akromiya in May 2005. Following the verdict, thousands of Andijan residents gathered in a peaceful demonstration, upon which security forces opened gunfire, killing several hundred protesters. The Uzbek government's brutality, harshly condemned in the West, curtailed Akromiya's activities.

Akromiya's teachings and structure are similar to those of a number of moderate Islamic movements in the rest of the Muslim world, such as the Muslim Brotherhood in the Middle East and the Nurcu and Fetullah Gulen movements in Turkey. The latter two groups also have appeared in Central Asia. Similar to Akromiya, Nurcu takes as its goal the revival of individual Muslims' faith through modern education. The group has engaged with the Central Asian youth through the Turkish Lyceums established throughout Central Asia with the exception of Uzbekistan, where the schools were shut down in 2000. The educational curriculum of the Nurcu schools includes sciences and modern disciplines, but also subjects and elements of the classical Islamic school system.[46] Nurcu also strives to educate devout Muslims through charity and welfare work. Hundreds of small Nurcu enterprises operating in Central Asia contribute portions of their income to charity in this way, performing one of the five pillars of Islam incumbent on all Muslims. Zakat, or giving charity, is required of every financially stable Muslim and Muslim business or organization.

Akromiya, Hizb ut-Tahrir, IMU, the Nurcu movement, and other Islamic groups and movements practicing their faith outside state-sponsored religious institutions are viewed as pseudo-Muslim, or terrorist and extremist, by Central Asian governments and Muftiates (spiritual administrations of Muslims in Central Asian states, which are recognized as "official" by the public authorities in these republics). The government of Uzbekistan and, to a lesser extent, the governments of Kyrgyzstan and Kazakhstan have carried out arrests, trials, imprisonments, and executions of thousands of alleged Islamists in the name of combating terrorism and religious extremism.[47] These measures, however, have failed to diminish individuals' interest in various questions of Islamic religion and radicalized some moderate believers and ulema mistreated by the states. States' policies contributed to the weakening of religious authority of the official clergy and Muslim Boards and played into the hands of Salafists, who have exhibited deeper knowledge of Islamic precepts.

Conclusion

The Islamic rebirth in Central Asia has demonstrated an overall moderate character largely expressed in the growing interest in rediscovering Islamic roots, identity, and culture. This is due to the prevalence of the indigenous forms of Islam in the Central Asian communities. The fact that the Islamic rebirth took place against the backdrop of a national revival also contained the spread of radical religious sentiments. The emergence and spread of revivalist tendencies in Central Asia were offset by events and developments internal to the region. Although Central Asian Muslims have not been immune to influences from outside the Muslim world, their return to Islamic faith has been defined by the centuries-long ideas and practices that matured within the Central Asian religious milieu. These local beliefs and practices include legends and myths of the sacred origins of local Muslim communities, cults of sacred persons linked to patronage networks characterizing social relations in Central Asia, and visitations and pilgrimage to shrines that often define communal identity, among many other local ways of knowing Islam or being Muslim. These local varieties of Islam, departing from the strict interpretations of Quran, are hardly unique to Central Asia but can be found in many places around the world. These diverse ways in which individuals construe their Muslimness and relate to Islam support the notion of the inherent heterogeneity of Islam and the malleability of Islamic identities.

The perplexing diversity within Islam gives rise to inevitable tensions and contestations within the religion. As illustrated in this chapter, in Central Asia the so-called "local" or "cultural" varieties of Islam have been challenged by more "normative" or "orthodox" versions of Islam claiming adherence to strict interpretation of Islamic sacred texts. In Central Asia these extremist and fundamentalist Islamic ideas developed internally as well as through influences from the Middle East. These radical ideologies invigorated active campaigning and other activities of Central Asian Islamists in the postindependence context. Radicalization and militarization of Islamist organizations and some moderate Islamic groups followed the governments' assault on those manifestations of religion, which have been perceived as a threat to the states and their governing regimes.

Central Asian Muslim societies have never been fully isolated from the larger Islamic community. Even during the Soviet era the teachings of the leading Islamic theologians extended to the other side of the iron curtain. After the breakup of the Soviet Union, international influences on Central Asia have become even more pervasive. Islamic religious literature and foreign missionaries from the Middle East inundated these states. Foreign funds supported building new mosques and madrasas. The ascension of the Taliban to power in Afghanistan in 1996, the civil war in Tajikistan, and the Chechen war in Russia inspired and enabled the activities of Central Asian Islamists. These events also became a pretext for the Central Asian governments' anti-Islamist propaganda and restrictive religious policies. On the one hand, the Central Asian secular leadership embraced Islam through the commemoration of Islamic holidays, its support of efforts at the restoration of Islamic infrastructure, and its reverence for national Islamic heritage. On the other hand, the Central Asian authorities began treating the growth of religious communities unrecognized by the state and the Muftiate as a national security threat. The US-led global "war on terror" provided the Central Asian governments with the necessary context for resolving this marked contradiction and portraying their strict religious policies as support for the worldwide efforts to combat religious terrorism and extremism. Not a single Central Asian government has made an attempt to clearly define the "threatening" varieties of Islam, choosing to refer to very distinct groups and movements with the blanket term of "extremist" and Wahhabi. By suppressing diversity within Islam and controlling religious practices, these governments have cultivated resentment among Muslims and, inadvertently, have contributed to the emergence of social forces ready to embrace alternative expressions of Islam, which may eventually assume radical forms.[48] Thus, measures that were intended to prevent radicalization have provoked discontent and induced the transformation of religious conservatism into fundamentalism.

Notes

1. M. Hakan Yavuz, "The Patterns of Political Islamic Identity: Dynamics of National and Transnational Loyalties and Identities," *Central Asian Survey* 14, no. 3 (1995): 341.

2. V. I. Lenin, "Sotsializm i religiia," *Polnoe sobranie sochinenii*, 5th ed., vol. 12, 142–47. First published in *Novaia zhizn'*, no. 28, December 3, 1905.

3. Julie McBrien, "Listening to the Wedding Speaker: Discussing Religion and Culture in Southern Kyrgyzstan," *Central Asian Survey* 25, no. 3 (2006): 344.

4. Pinar Akcali, "Islam as a 'Common Bond' in Central Asia: Islamic Renaissance Party and the Afghan Mujahidin," *Central Asian Survey* 17, no. 2 (1998), 268.

5. Mehrdad Haghayeghi, *Islam and Politics in Central Asia* (New York: St. Martin's, 1995), 82.

6. Data for 1959 and 1979 are reported in Murray Feshbach, "Trends in the Soviet Muslim Population: Demographic Aspects," in *The USSR and the Muslim World: Issues in Domestic and Foreign Policy*, ed. Yaacov Ro'i (London: Allen & Unwin, 1984), 93.

7. Yaacov Ro'i, *Islam in the Soviet Union: From the Second World War to Gorbachev* (New York: Columbia University Press, 2000), 62.

8. Ludmila Polonskaya and Alexei Malashenko, *Islam in Central Asia* (Reading, UK: Ithaca Press, 1994), 115–16.

9. Emmanuel Karagiannis, "Political Islam and Social Movement Theory: The Case of Hizb ut-Tahrir in Kyrgyzstan," *Religion, State and Society* 33, no. 2 (2005): 143; Laura Yerekesheva, "Religious Identity in Kazakhstan and Uzbekistan: Global-Local Interplay," *Strategic Analysis* 28, no. 4 (2004): 584.

10. Krisztina Kahl-Bodrogi, "Who Owns the Shrine? Competing Meanings and Authorities at a Pilgrimage Site in Khorezm," *Central Asian Survey* 25, no. 3 (2006), 235–50; Maria Louw, "Pursuing 'Muslimness': Shrines as Sites for Moralities in the Making in Post-Soviet Bukhara," *Central Asian Survey* 25, no. 3 (2006), 319–39.

11. Yaacov Ro'i and Alon Wainer, "Muslim Identity and Islamic Practice in Post-Soviet Central Asia," *Central Asian Survey* 28, no. 3 (2009), 303–22.

12. Haghayeghi, *Islam and Politics in Central Asia*, 78–79.

13. Aurélie Biard, "The Religious Factor in the Reification of 'Neo-Ethnic' Identities in Kyrgyzstan," *Nationalities Papers* 38, no. 3 (2010): 323–35. Many religious preferences of Central Asians are conditioned by their ethnicity. Mosques in Central Asia are still designated as Kyrgyz, Uzbek, and so on. Imams often come from their eponymous ethnic groups.

14. Chris Hann and Mathijs Pelkmans, "Realigning Religion and Power in Central Asia: Islam, Nation-State and (Post)Socialism," *Europe-Asia Studies* 61, no. 9 (2009): 1524; Irene Hilgers, "The Regulation and Control of Religious Pluralism in Uzbekistan," in *The Postsocialist Religious Question: Faith and Power in Central Asia and East-Central Europe*, ed. Chris Hann & the Civil "Religion" Group (Berlin: Lit Verlag, 2006), 75–98; Biard, "The Religious Factor." Muslims in Kyrgyzstan tend to emphasize relationships with their own kin, rather than all other Kyrgyz Muslims. Divisions between clans and lineages supersede ethnic divisions in Kyrgyzstan, where kin ties are more pervasive than the common denominators of religion and ethnicity.

15. Ro'i and Wainer, "Muslim Identity," 306.

16. Z. I. Levin, " Islam i natsionalizm v SNG," in *Islam v SNG*, ed. A. Malashenko (Moscow: IV RAN, 1998), 58.

17. Ghoncheh Tazmini, "The Islamic Revival in Central Asia: A Potent Force or a Misconception?" *Central Asian* Survey 20, no. 1 (2001): 66.

18. Sébastien Peyrouse, "Islam in Central Asia: National Specificities and Postsoviet Globalisation," *Religion, State and Society* 35, no. 3 (2007): 245.

19. Mathijs Pelkmans, "'Culture' as a Tool and an Obstacle: Missionary Encounters in Post-Soviet Kyrgyzstan," *Journal of the Royal Anthropological Institution* 13, no. 4 (2007): 881–99; Peyrouse, "Islam in Central Asia," 252.

20. Tazmini, "The Islamic Revival in Central Asia," 67.

21. Haghayeghi, *Islam and Politics in Central Asia*, 96–97.

22. David M. Abramson, "Foreign Religious Education and the Central Asian Islamic Revival: Impact and Prospects for Stability," *Central Asia-Caucasus Institute Silk Road Studies Program*

(Washington, DC: Johns Hopkins University, 2010), accessed July 1, 2011, http://www.silkroadstudies. org/resources/pdf/SilkRoadPapers/2010_03_SRP_Abramson_Central-Asia-Islam.pdf.

23. Translated religious texts and excerpts from the teachings of the Central Asian theologians can be found in Allen J. Frank and Jahangir Mamatov, *Uzbek Islamic Debates: Texts, Translations, and Commentary* (Springfield, VA: Dunwoody, 2006).

24. Bakhtiyar Babadzhanov, "On the Activities of *Hizb ut-Tahrir-al-Islami* in Uzbekistan," in *Islam in the Post-Soviet Newly Independent States: The View from Within*, ed. A. Malashenko and Martha B. Olcott (Moscow: Carnegie Foundation, 2001), 154–55.

25. For further discussion, see Martha Brill Olcott, *The Roots of Radical Islam in Central Asia* (Washington, DC: Carnegie Endowment, 2007), http://carnegieendowment.org/2007/01/17/ roots-of-radical-islam-in-central-asia/35w9.

26. For further discussion, see Vitalii V. Naumkin, *Radical Islam in Central Asia: Between Pen and Rifle* (Oxford, UK: Rowman & Littlefield, 2004).

27. Naumkin, *Radical Islam in Central Asia*, 5.

28. Ibid.

29. Razia Sultanova, *From Shamanism to Sufism: Women, Islam and Culture in Central Asia* (New York: I. B. Tauris, 2011).

30. For further discussion, see Martha Brill Olcott, *Sufism in Central Asia: A Force for Moderation or a Cause of Politicization?* (Washington, DC: Carnegie Foundation, 2007).

31. For further discussion, see Farhat Alvi, "The Significant Role of Sufism in Central Asia," *Oriental College Magazine* 84, no. 3 (2007), http://pu.edu.pk/home/journal/18/Volume_84_No_3_2009.html.

32. Olcott, *Sufism in Central Asia*.

33. Mchael Fredholm, "Islamic Extremism as a Political Force: A Comparative Study of Central Asian Islamic Extremist Movements," Research Report (Stockholm University, 2006), 9, accessed July 1, 2011, http://www.stintprogramcentralasia.org/Files/RR12.pdf; Muzaffar Olimov, "Islam in Contemporary Tajikistan: Role of Muslim Leaders," in *Religion and Security in South and Central Asia*, ed. K. Warikoo (Abingdon, UK: Routledge, 2011), 155.

34. Fredholm, "Islamic Extremism as a Political Force," 10.

35. Ibid., 19; Ro'i, "Islam in the FSU," 109.

36. Naumkin, *Radical Islam in Central Asia*, 96–97; Peyrouse, "Islam in Central Asia."

37. The IMU's statements have been replete with contradictory declarations (from the standpoint of juridical Islam) interspersed with jihadist rhetoric, scathing criticism of the Karimov regime, and anti-American and anti-Semitist themes (see, for example, excerpts from the IMU's statements in Khalid, *Islam After Communism*, 96-97; Naumkin, *Radical Islam in Central Asia*, 99–101).

38. For further discussion, see Murat Laumulin, "Islamic Radicalism in Central Asia," in *Religion and Security in South and Central Asia*, ed. K. Warikoo (Abingdon, UK: Routledge, 2011), 146.

39. Khalid, *Islam After Communism*, 88.

40. Naumkin, *Radical Islam in Central Asia*, 216.

41. Mariya Omelicheva, "Ethnic Dimension of Religious Extremism and Terrorism in Central Asia," *International Political Science Review* 31, no. 2 (2010): 167–86.

42. Khalid, *Islam After Communism*, 160; Naumkin, *Radical Islam in Central Asia*, 135–36.

43. For further discussion, see, for instance, Katleen Collins, "Ideas, Networks, and Islamist Movements: Evidence from Central Asia and the Caucasus," *World Politics* 60, no. 1 (2006): 64–96; Karagiannis, "Political Islam and Social Movement Theory."

44. Collins, "Ideas, Networks, and Islamist Movements," 78–79.

45. Laumulin, "Islamic Radicalism in Central Asia," 142.

46. Bayram Balci, "Fethullah Güllen's Missionary Schools in Central Asia and Their Role in the Spreading of Turkism and Islam," *Religion, State & Society* 31, no. 2 (2003): 151–77.

47. Mariya Y. Omelicheva, *Counterterrorism Policies in Central Asia* (New York and London: Routledge, 2011).

48. Peyrouse, "Islam in Central Asia."

Solidarity, Human Rights, and the Poetics of Connection

Articulating Community in Bertolt Brecht's *Mother Courage and Her Children* and Lynn Nottage's *Ruined*[1]

MARIKE JANZEN

Introduction

At the end of the Cold War, a human rights framework that articulates an ideal of one-to-one connection between individuals largely replaced solidarity as a model of human community. A poetic shift that I claim resulted in a loss of reflexivity about the way that individuals' historical positioning relates to their actions attended this political shift. In this essay, I trace the contours, and implications, of this larger political and poetic transition by focusing on the way that the US playwright Lynn Nottage reworked German playwright Bertolt Brecht's play *Mother Courage and Her Children* (1939) in her own piece, *Ruined* (2008). While Brecht's play defines human community in terms of economic relations that require and reinforce solidarity, Nottage's revision of his work implies that qualities inherent to all individuals justify their connection.

In 2004, Nottage traveled to Ugandan refugee camps with Brecht in mind. There, she interviewed women who had fled civil war in the Democratic Republic of the Congo (DRC) about their experiences. She planned to draw on her findings as the basis for an adaptation of Brecht's famous antiwar play, *Mother Courage and Her Children*, to publicize the plight of these women, whose abuse in the conflict was little known.[2] *Mother Courage*, which premiered in Zurich in 1941 and became a signature piece of Brecht's theatre in East Berlin after 1949,[3] explores a woman's work to support herself and her children within the context of warfare. Set in the Thirty Years War (1618–1648), in large part a conflict between European Protestant and Catholic states, Brecht's play follows Mother Courage, who sells wares to both Protestant and Catholic soldiers from a cart that she pulls through battlefields across

Europe. In this context, Courage aims to balance her need for war, which creates a market for her goods, and her desire to protect her children from harm. Ultimately, Courage decides that her survival depends on making sure that her cart—her capital—stays intact, rather than preventing her children from getting hurt.[4] Within the framework of Brechtian dramaturgy, Courage's denial of her children has a pedagogical purpose: her antipathetic character distances spectators from the protagonist and pushes the audience to reflect on the social and economic forces that shape individuals' choices.

When Nottage heard her Congolese interviewees describe their traumatic experiences in war, specifically the horrific rape that had become a tragic hallmark of the conflict in the DRC,[5] she decided that she could not replicate the "*Verfremdung*," or the alienation between audience members and characters on stage, that is the goal of Brechtian theatre.[6] Instead, in writing *Ruined*, she felt compelled to bring the audience close to the refugee women's stories.[7] Like Mother Courage, Nottage's protagonist Mama Nadi would consider peace to be bad for business. She depends on war in the eastern DRC to bring customers—soldiers—to her bar and brothel. Yet unlike Mother Courage, whose skepticism about the value of peace derives solely from her desire to profit from war, Mama Nadi's cynical attitude toward war grows out of the repressed personal trauma of rape, which, the play implies, can be healed through meaningful relationships. Even though Mama Nadi's body is scarred, her innermost self is not ruined. With this portrayal of a self independent from influence by political and economic spheres, Nottage rejects Brecht's abstract figures designed to foster audiences' rational analysis of social issues and replaces them with protagonists and imagined theatergoers imbued with the capacity for empathy.

Nottage's inversion of Brechtian theatre enacts a larger post–Cold War shift in conceptions of the way an individual relates to the human community that is referenced above. Accompanying this shift is a change in the individual's perceived role in effecting social critique and change. The demise of the Soviet Union and its affiliated "east bloc" states resulted in the waning influence of leftist conceptions of international solidarity. After the Cold War, what has emerged as the dominant framework for imagining global relations and obligations is what political scientist Jack Donnelly terms an "international human rights regime."[8] According to Donnelly, the Universal Declaration of Human Rights proclaimed by the United Nations General Assembly in 1948, as well as the International Human Rights Covenants adopted in 1976, have come to serve as the predominant norms by which governments as well as international nongovernmental organizations evaluate states' treatment of individuals.[9] Two examples serve to show the extent to which a human rights paradigm has come to dominate current modes of perceiving global relations in the past twenty years.

At the 1993 United Nations World Conference on Human Rights, representatives unanimously affirmed the position that "the universal nature of [human rights] and freedom is beyond question."[10] This widespread agreement on the relevance of human rights finds expression in the fact that in the past several decades, international law has come to be perceived as a field primarily dedicated to the moral project of "[protecting] individual human rights."[11] In other words, an idea of universal human rights has come to serve as the dominant concept in developing the theory and practice of global relations.

Furthermore, the diminishing salience of solidarity and the concomitant expansion of human rights as the paradigmatic framework for measuring global relations hold key implications for the way that people understand their relations to others and make sense of who they are. A framework that emphasizes solidarity measures human community in terms of all people's situation vis-à-vis historical economic forces. In this view, derived from Karl Marx and Friedrich Engels, the better community is one in which economic inequality is overcome and property is shared.[12] By contrast, a human rights paradigm evaluates human community in relation to inalienable rights inherent to each person, no matter their physical or economic context: an ideal community is one in which all people are able to exercise the rights they possess. Consequently, solidarity and human rights paradigms of community imply divergent definitions of individual identity as they locate that with which a person identifies—the struggle for economic equality or inalienable rights—as well as that which makes him or her "identical" to others, within either society or the individual.

Many scholars in the humanities and social sciences agree that a human rights framework provides a valuable tool for calling attention to injustice. However, they also offer a critique of this contemporary human rights regime that defines community in terms of all people's identical, inalienable rights. Drawing on the various emphases of their respective disciplines, these scholars show how evaluating human activity in universal terms can obscure consideration of past and present social and political forces that shape human connection. For example, literary scholar Walter Mignolo argues that a European-derived human rights discourse is only the most recent version of European expansionist and colonizing projects justified by Europeans' definition of what humanity holds in common.[13] In a similar vein, political scientists Adamantia Pollis and Peter Schwab point out that the idea of the individual who holds rights in spite of any connection to a social group, exists in tension with cultural traditions in which "the individual [is] conceived of as an integral part of a larger whole" such as "the kinship system, the clan, the tribe [or] the local community."[14] Indeed, as historian Samuel Moyn states in *The Last Utopia: Human Rights in History*, a human rights regime, far from being the only way of evaluating and enforcing an ideal of human behavior, is just the latest of many different kinds of utopian visions for a global community that have informed political work.[15] Finally, law scholars Makau Mutua and David Kennedy examine how human rights policies based on normative notions of the inviolable individual can obscure or even exacerbate social injustice. In an African context, for example, Mutua maintains that a human rights emphasis on curbing a "despotic state's" mistreatment of specific individuals sidesteps attention to the harm resulting from global patterns of economic injustice.[16] Kennedy notes the contradictions inherent in a human rights "elite" that speaks about what it imagines as universal issues, but which sees itself as "disconnected from economic actors and interests."[17] In sum, these scholars argue that the rhetoric and policy of a human rights regime locates human rights work as existing "above politics,"[18] and thus insufficiently takes into account external and structural factors that shape the condition of people's lives.

These critiques, as well as the political and poetic shift from solidarity to human rights to which they respond, are relevant for scholars in area studies. A human rights framework directly informs current post–Cold War US foreign policy, which in turn directly impacts area studies programs. As Jon Goss and Terence Wesley-Smith point out in their introduction to the volume *Remaking Area Studies: Teaching and Learning Across Asia and the Pacific*, "the institutional history of area studies is related directly to the international interests of the United States."[19] In the early Cold War period, as the United States competed with the Soviet Union for international allies, US politicians created legislation to fund area studies programs that would train Americans in histories and languages of the non-West.[20] In the post–Cold War period, national priorities continue to shape area studies even though US foreign policy goals have shifted from supporting anticommunism to focusing on international human rights. The State Department's "Bureau of Democracy, Human Rights, and Labor" reflects this change in priority.[21] It is also evident in the US military's use of humanitarian aid—a potential tool for allowing expression of human rights—as a key element of counterinsurgency efforts in Iraq and Afghanistan during the past decade.[22] Since the "Higher Education Act" that legislates funding of area studies centers "requires that the Secretary [of Education] consult with federal agency heads in order to receive recommendations regarding areas of national need for expertise in foreign languages and world regions," there exists a clear connection between a US approach to human rights and the shape and priorities of area studies programs.[23] It is important for area studies scholars to understand the political context of their programs in order to better understand what shapes the possibilities of their work, as well as the potential impacts their research may have.

Gayatri Spivak offers a way to make sense of the role of area studies programs in the context of a human rights regime. She cautions that thinking of global relations in terms of humans' universal similarities—their rights—minimizes the need to understand the specificities of, and inequalities between, communities' material conditions.[24] Area studies, even with its long "history of complicity with the national security project,"[25] can offer an important tool to combat the oversights that accompany an emphasis on universal rights. As Spivak argues, area studies programs are valuable and necessary precisely for their emphasis on deep knowledge about, for example, the linguistic traditions of minority populations.[26] Being attentive to specific histories, as well as thinking in terms of solidarity, can make us sensitive to people's material circumstances, even as we highlight universal rights as a point of connection in human community.

With these caveats about the connections between area studies and a human rights regime, I offer a comparative reading of Brecht's *Mother Courage* and Nottage's *Ruined*. My aim is to shed light on what "thinking community" in terms of human rights rather than solidarity looks like, and what is at stake when we tell stories of suffering and injustice in terms of either the social structures that foster injustice, or the pain of an individual's violation. While Brecht highlights how Mother Courage's actions relate to her position within the economy, rather than her innate human qualities, Nottage asserts a subjectivity or morality that exists in spite of, or outside of, the logic of capital and war. Nottage wants to bring us close to Mama Nadi, and, by extension, the largely unheard victims of violence in the DRC, by putting us in touch with her interiority. However, I argue that this "closeness" can paradoxically blind us to an awareness of the economic and historical forces that shape our relationships. Brecht's poetics, which push the audience to reflect on the need for solidarity, should thus not be abandoned.

In what follows, I situate the formal makeup of Brecht and Nottage's plays within this larger post–Cold War shift from solidarity to human rights ideas and discourse as outlined above. The aim is to demonstrate how, and why, these distinct views of the individual's historical position and the notions of human community that follow from them are expressed in each text through the trope of rational estrangement, or what I term a "poetics of distance," in Brecht, and empathic proximity, or what I call a "poetics of closeness," in Nottage. Next, I explore the implications of each text's form for spectators' identification with the work's protagonists and the political response they can imagine as a result. Walter Benjamin's observations on the politics of artistic form in his 1934 essay "Author as Producer" are valuable here to investigate the way that realistic representations of suffering serve to isolate the event of injustice from the conditions that can cause it. Finally, I argue for the need to remember Brecht, and the leftist framework for envisioning human community his dramaturgy represents, within a hegemonic international human rights regime that locates human connection within all individuals' internal similitude. As philosopher of law Costas Douzinas points out, measuring human behavior in terms of universal rights can help us take note of oppressive practices.[27] However, it ultimately runs the risk of dissociating the individual—and identity—from a material realm.[28]

Identity, Community, and the Aesthetics of Solidarity and Human Rights

The distinct emphases that Brecht's and Nottage's texts place on the relationship between individual and community structure can be understood in terms of the different ways that solidarity frameworks and human rights regimes implicitly define this relation. In a general sense, the term *solidarity* signifies people's identification with another group facing a struggle. In the history of leftist political engagement, solidarity more specifically references individuals' or groups' similar investment within a common, international struggle to transform economic arrangements in order to achieve greater social equality.[29] In the nineteenth and early twentieth centuries, workers across the world, the global proletariat, claimed solidarity in their goal to gain control of the means of industrial production through the creation of various international socialist organizations.[30] Lenin's 1916 assertion that industrialized nations relied on colonial expansion to procure raw materials and increase markets for their products, or that "imperialism" marked "the highest stage of capitalism,"[31] formed the theoretical basis for later twentieth-century iterations of international solidarity in the fight against "first world" exploitation of the "third world."[32] These conceptions of working-class and third world solidarity served as the cornerstones of official foreign policy in "East bloc" nations[33] and also galvanized political groups in the West.[34]

While now defunct communist states and projects specifically embraced and promoted the term *solidarity*, I believe it can still serve as an important marker of a particular way to conceptualize community in terms of connections to others that exist outside of the self. Douzinas offers a clear definition of solidarity in his discussion of a communist view of community. Following Douzinas, "Being in common is an integral part of being oneself: a self is exposed to the other, it is posed *in exteriority*, the other is part of the intimacy of a self. Being in community with others is the opposite of common being or of belonging to an essential community" (emphasis mine).[35] If the foundation of community is located in the individual's position to a world outside herself, according to Douzinas, it follows that social change must come from an understanding of the way individuals are shaped in relation to the outside world, to others, not the fulfillment of qualities already internal to herself.

Artists like Brecht worked to represent this notion of solidarity—a political stance based on an individual's position within a community—through formal means that could highlight the way that social change needs to occur on the communal, structural level, rather than on the level of the individual. Key features of Brecht's critical dramaturgy, what he termed "epic theatre," are elements that prevent insight into or investment in the interior lives of characters or audience members, but instead, foreground their social role. For example, by divulging the outcome of the story at its outset and blocking the buildup of suspense, Brecht disables the audiences' identification with the characters and the assumption of interior identity on which it relies.

Just as a conception of solidarity finds expression in a particular poetic form, literary texts reflect and reinforce a human rights framework. This is evident in the recent proliferation of narratives and films that draw attention to humanitarian crises and human rights abuses across the world.[36] These works often rely on a narrative arc structured on the potential for individuals to be rehabilitated, or rehumanized, based on the rights they theoretically possess.[37] That is, their descriptions and definitions of harm necessarily presuppose an intact human essence.

In his influential work, *Human Rights, Inc.: The World Novel, Narrative Form, and International Law* (2007), Joseph Slaughter identifies the historical connection between a human rights framework and the popular narrative trajectory of an individual person's violation and rehabilitation. Slaughter shows how the formal qualities of the Enlightenment coming-of-age-novel, the *Bildungsroman*, inform and reinforce notions of the rights-bearing individual. The *Bildungsroman* always traces the protagonist's exit or expulsion from the community, his pilgrimage that leads to maturation, and his productive reintegration into a community. In this genre, protagonists possess attributes to live successfully in community from the start—it is just that they must be developed. In a similar fashion, the rights-bearing individual always has rights, even though he or she may not be allowed to exercise them, or may not enjoy their protection. Within the *Bildungsroman* and a human rights framework, the individual with inherent qualities is the constant, and external circumstances may or may not allow their expression.[38]

This larger post-1990 political shift in conceptualizing community—from solidarity to human rights—variously shapes aesthetic reflections on social injustice and violence. Brecht forged literary forms to express a particular notion of subjectivity and community that I have identified as solidarity. Slaughter identifies a correlation between a particular narrative genre and a human rights framework that views community in terms of the way it permits the flourishing of the autonomous individual. In the next section, I follow the way that these communist-era and postsocialist visions of community are characterized through an emphasis on the individual's exteriority in Brecht, and the individual's interior life in Nottage.

Showing "Ruin" from Far Away and Close Up

Brechtian dramaturgy aims to demonstrate that characters' relationships are responses to historical circumstances and conditions. In *Mother Courage*, this view is shown in the way that the profit motive orders human interaction such as family bonds or nurturing acts. Within the context of the play, such points of connection that are typically viewed as one's "natural" human and humane responses to others do not serve as the foundation of human community. Instead, they serve as focal points for demonstrating people's alienation from each other within capitalism. Courage loses her children to save herself and her capital, while her daughter Kattrin saves others in danger, but loses her life doing so. By showing the alienating effects of a specific economic structure, Brecht defines solidarity negatively: it is that which is lacking among the characters. The play shows that structural relationships primarily shape the way people identify with others. It follows, then, that one must reorder structures, not merely uncover empathy, to overcome alienation and achieve equality.

Mother Courage evaluates all of her actions and relationships in terms of their potential effect on her finances, or, in the play's terms, the preservation of her cart and its inventory. Courage is not interested in the war's ideological fronts. Instead, she always hoists the flag of the winning side because she wants to stay in business.[39] As she says to her son, Swiss Cheese, "You don't ask tradespeople their faith but their prices."[40] When the Catholics have claimed victory after a battle and capture Swiss Cheese, the paymaster for the defeated Protestant regiment, Mother pawns her cart to collect enough funds to buy her son's freedom and stop his execution. Loathe to lose too much in the bargain, she negotiates for so long that the Catholic troops kill him before she can settle on the price she wants.[41] She does not want to give away her goods to those hurt by war. After a battle, the chaplain asks her for shirts that he and

Kattrin can tear into bandages for wounded civilians. Courage refuses: "I ain't tearing up my officer's shirts for that lot."[42] By the end of the play, Courage has managed to save her cart and save herself from financial ruin, but she is alone—all of her children have been killed in the war.

Unlike Courage, Kattrin—who is mute—possesses a humanitarian impulse uninhibited by financial "sense." In a setting in which success depends on extracting profit, this quality dooms her to failure. Kattrin's selflessness is fatal. In a move that foreshadows her death, Kattrin rushes into a burning house to save a trapped baby.[43] At the end of the play, while waiting for her mother near a farmhouse requisitioned by soldiers, she overhears their plan to attack a nearby village under cover of darkness. Kattrin climbs to the roof of the house with a drum, and bangs it loudly to wake the unsuspecting, sleeping villagers.[44] The soldiers order her to stop, and threaten to destroy her mother's cart if she continues drumming. She refuses, and the soldiers shoot her.[45]

Brecht shows nothing "more" to Mother Courage or Kattrin than their acts. Through actors' implementation of what Brecht termed *Gestus*, what Gitta Honegger describes as "a meticulously constructed, sparse language of gestures, posture, and speech patterns that [present] the character's social constructedness," the play reveals nothing hidden "inside" of the characters to explain their alienation.[46] All that readers are left with to interpret the characters' positions are their actions within a particular social arrangement. Indeed, by rendering Kattrin mute, Brecht gives the character no choice but to express her relationship to social forces via *Gestus*.[47] Brecht does not reveal Kattrin's personal reflection that could explain why she acts outside the logic of profit. Readers are left to wonder why, in this particular context, her heroism is not recognized and does not save her. If one similarly "reads" Mother Courage's actions as reactions to social forces, not as the expression of some hidden, internal motivation, her "moves" can be seen as reasonable responses to her circumstances: her means of survival depend on the fact that others negotiate with her for needed services. Specific social conditions explain the women's behavior and the community's responses to them. By implication, social conditions create alienation. Achieving connection, solidarity, would mean changing social relations and behavior, not uncovering a submerged, innate, extra-social humanness.

In *Ruined*, Nottage incorporates elements of Brechtian dramaturgy to historically situate her protagonists' actions.[48] For example, Nottage calls for the same actors to play the parts of two different militia groups that vie for control of the mineral-rich land in the Eastern Congo by raping women and thus terrorizing and fracturing communities. Through this formal device Nottage suggests a general framework of exploitation within which all characters function. Mama Nadi's position as a brothel owner, then, is not a reflection of her morality, but a response to a larger, regional, and historical practice of extracting profit from any and all available resources.

Despite this Brechtian move, however, the play is concerned with the way that exploitation can damage, or mask, a person's essential "core." Rather than articulating human community as the consequence of individuals' positions within a particular historical social arrangement, *Ruined* locates human connection within a quality of "humanness" identical to all. The play makes the claim that human connection exists outside of commerce, and outside of history, by building on a concept of personhood based on a framework of human rights dominant from 1990 on.

If Brecht focuses solely on characters' externality to illustrate that social relationships inform the way that humans are connected to each other, Nottage draws on what I term a "poetics of closeness" to assert humans' internal commonality. Indeed, it is her express goal to humanize, and make real, the "clinical language" of "human rights reports."[49] Throughout the course of the play, Nottage brings readers closer to Mama Nadi by formally removing a distrustful and cynical "shell" to reveal her "true" core, a vulnerable humanity that survives despite tragic circumstances. This development shapes the relationship between Mama Nadi and Sophie, one of the girls in her brothel (a relationship that formally echoes that of Mother Courage and Kattrin). When Mama Nadi's friend, Christian, asks her to take in his niece Sophie—a rape victim he feels will be safer with Mama Nadi than in her village—Mama Nadi is reluctant. Sophie is beautiful, but she is "ruined," a euphemism to describe that her rape resulted in a fistula, a tear in the wall that separates the rectum and vagina. As a result, Sophie can't generate income as a prostitute, and represents a body that will be a drain on Mama Nadi's resources. Nevertheless, Mama Nadi becomes a mother figure to Sophie. She houses her, acts protectively toward her, and decides to give her the raw diamond (her capital, parallel to Mother Courage's cart) that she has kept hidden in case of emergency so that Sophie can pay for surgery to repair her wound.

As one follows Mama Nadi's developing closeness with Sophie, one gains insight into Mama Nadi's emotional life. The play opens with a presentation of her as a brusque, "arrogant" businesswoman.[50] She is gruff with her supplier and friend, Christian, quick to chastise him for any delay that might hurt her income.[51] She mocks her "girls" for their interest in romance novels, telling them how the stories always end: "There'll be kissing, fucking, a betrayal, and then the woman will foolishly surrender her heart to an undeserving man."[52] Yet Nottage reveals Mama Nadi's own injuries, the way she, herself, has been taken advantage of within a patriarchal system, and shows that her tough manner is a self-defensive act to protect herself from further injury. Mama Nadi confesses to Mr. Harari, the diamond trader who assesses the value of her gem, that she will not leave her brothel: "Since I was young, people have found reasons to push me out of my home, men have laid claim to my possessions."[53] When Christian professes his love to Mama Nadi at the end of the play, she confesses to him that she, like Sophie, was raped and is "ruined."[54] In this context, it seems to be in her best interest to be skeptical of relationships and view them only in terms of their potential for personal gain and profit. Nevertheless, Mama Nadi's decision to take care of Sophie and be honest with Christian reveals an emotional vulnerability that is not self-destructive. If economic relations determine Mother Courage and Kattrin's mother-daughter relationship, *Ruined* argues that human relationships can transcend economic logic. This is why Mama Nadi and Sophie can bond like mother and child, and why Mama Nadi can accept Christian as her lover.

The particular crisis of rape as a tool of war in the Congo creates the need for this focus on women's interiority and human "sameness" as a way to make sense of and speak against their "ruin." The cultural and physical consequences of rape marginalize women. First of all, rape victims are often reluctant to speak about their trauma because they fear alienation from husbands, families, and communities.[55] Second, the brutality of rape frequently practiced by militia groups produces bodies that have no place in communities' sexual, reproductive, or social roles.[56] The fistula that results from the use of instruments such as sticks, knives, or guns in rape, if left untreated, allows the vaginal leakage of fecal matter and results in a bad odor that emanates from the woman.[57] Not only do victims of rape become unsuitable sexual partners, mothers, or wives, they can be seen as physically repugnant. Nottage's strategy to bring us close to marginalized bodies by revealing them to possess an emotional core offers a critical response to this expulsion of women's experiences and bodies from the community. The historical reality of what some call femicide in the DRC may call for the rooting of women's experience in a place outside of the female body or beyond its injuries.[58] In this way, Nottage's "poetics of closeness" can perhaps serve to critique violent acts in a way that Brecht's "poetics of distance," which offers no sense of an internal, and eternal, human core untouched by political contingencies, cannot.

It is unclear, however, whether the "core" that Mama Nadi and Sophie are shown to possess restores them to a position of historical agents within their community. At the end of the play, Sophie is still waiting for her surgery. Mama Nadi has asked Mr. Harari to take Sophie and the diamond to the city with him, and give Sophie the money he receives from the sale of the stone. Mr. Harari leaves with the diamond, but without Sophie. The bonds of Sophie,

Mama Nadi, and Christian based on mutual recognition of humanity hint at an alternate way of organizing community, but guarantee neither their wider social recognition nor the possibility for them to transform violent economic arrangements. By contrast, Mother Courage's daughter Kattrin, who, like Sophie, occupies a marginal position in the social order because of Kattrin's muteness, can engage and disrupt historical relationships.[59] By banging her drum and alerting a village about to be attacked, Kattrin participates in the political order in the only way she can.

Authors Producing an Audience: Reception and "Repair"

Though Brecht's "poetics of distance" and Nottage's "poetics of closeness" draw on distinct understandings of human community, they serve the same purpose of moving audiences to act, to work toward repairing the ruin that each text critiques. Yet the kind of audience response that each play advocates differs according to the way it situates spectators within the type of human community it wants to foster. Brecht, by setting *Mother Courage* in a context that was aesthetically and historically distant from the reality of German-speaking audiences, aimed to achieve a sense of alienation—or nonidentification—between the viewers and characters portrayed. In this way, Brecht resisted fostering a sense of common ground based on closeness to stories of suffering and instead aimed to promote critical thinking about conditions requiring solidarity.[60] Nottage's revelation of her characters' interior lives, by contrast, implies the possibility of connection between real rape victims, whose testimonies provide the source material for her narrative and audience members. There is an essential human-ness that connects the two groups that could form the foundation for viewers' intervention on behalf of Congolese women.

Walter Benjamin's reflections on the socially critical potential of art in his 1934 essay "Author as Producer" offer a way to evaluate the implications of the path to "repair" that each author's formal choice presents. Benjamin focuses part of his discussion on political art by comparing Brechtian dramaturgy with Alfred Döblin's novel, *Berlin Alexanderplatz* (1929). In his analysis, Benjamin explores issues related to the aesthetics of "distance" and "closeness" that I examine here. Benjamin is critical of Döblin's work, which employs a documentary realist style to describe (and decry) the problems of the Berlin working class during the 1920s. According to Benjamin, Döblin's realism, which brings the reader up close to workers' lives, fetishizes urban squalor.[61] In other words, Döblin's aim to reveal poverty in detail transforms the subject of his attention into an aesthetic object, and thus obscures readers' critical understanding of their own relationship to social ills. For Benjamin, Brecht's poetics are politically preferable because they push audiences toward social reflection, rather than limit them to a narrow admiration of an aesthetic object.

Benjamin's critique of Döblin's close-up representations of suffering raises important questions about what kind of repair a "poetics of closeness" can stimulate. The reception of *Ruined* closely aligns with the aims and reach of specific human rights institutions, just as Döblin's work fell within the fashion of "political" literature of the 1920s. Paradoxically, while both the play and the human rights regime assume a universal humanity, presenting their institutions as the proper recipients of support limits the horizons of response to the crisis in the DRC. Benjamin's pointed question about the reception of Döblin's work, whether feeding an aesthetic desire for empathy can obscure the need for structural, social change, applies to Nottage's play.

Both Nottage and nonprofit organizations doing work in the DRC make clear the close connection between the play and human rights institutions. For Nottage, staging the play in New York and Washington, DC, meant presenting it to a specific human rights audience: "I was really excited to bring this to the seat of power because the audience will be in a position to bring about some kind of change in the Congo . . . when we staged it in New York City we were very successful in bringing human rights organizations and NGOs and bodies like the United Nations in to see the play—and we found that [a] lot of those folks were moved to act."[62]

Further, a description of Nottage's play at the website for the nonprofit "Enough Project," an organization affiliated with the Center for American Progress and devoted to ending "genocide and crimes against humanity" in Africa,[63] concludes with the hope that seeing *Ruined* might "lead viewers to act."[64] Actions suggested on the "Enough Project" website include, for example, urging Congress to increase US aid to the project to help "[reform] Congo's security, justice, and economic institutions."[65]

Beyond relating to the work of specific organizations, *Ruined* also articulates with a United Nations human rights initiative, namely, the Convention on the Elimination of Discrimination against Women, or CEDAW, adopted by the United Nations General Assembly in 1979, and which had gained one hundred "states parties" by 1989.[66] In 2010, a conference of the committee on the status of women, the United Nations group that solicits reports and drafts recommendations from nations bound by CEDAW, held a gathering at which Lynn Nottage read from *Ruined*.[67] In this way, the play not only serves as a method by which to create a particular kind of activist audience, but it illustrates the kind of issues with which a certain audience is already engaged. There is a market for plays like *Ruined*.[68]

In her research on the reception of humanitarian narratives in Uganda, Laura Edmondson argues that the market for stories of humanitarian crises and interventions is global, and characterizes the creation and performance of "theatre of war" in Africa.[69] Specifically, Edmondson describes how children's performances about their abduction and rescue from the Lords' Resistance Army, organized in the context of drama therapy at the "World Vision Children of War Rehabilitation Centre" in northern Uganda, reflect an awareness of an international humanitarian audience.[70] The linear narrative of these performances that track a progression from children's violation to their liberation and rehabilitation by "World Vision," according to Edmondson, can be read as a "method of self-promotion," a way for the organization to make the crisis of child soldiers legible to a human rights regime that can offer humanitarian aid.[71]

Nottage's Congolese interviewees and government officials invited to view *Ruined* in Kinshasa in 2011 are participants within this international humanitarian market, either as recipients of aid at refugee camps or as elites likely charged with receiving and disseminating international assistance. Indeed, Nottage evaluates their roles as storytellers and listeners in terms of this market. Nottage reflects that the Congolese women's acts of telling stories were likely "cathartic" for them.[72] This implies that the women's storytelling facilitated the revelation of a purified, authentic self with which audiences would identify. Further, Nottage's invitation of Congolese government officials to see the play suggests an expectation that these viewers might have been spurred to "act" in the same way she hoped members of human rights organizations seeing the play in the United States would.

The humanitarian market that shapes the global reception of *Ruined* may, however, exclude modes of storytelling and listening. For instance, Nottage's description of interviewing women leaves unacknowledged the possibility that alternative conceptions of the individual's position within society—for example, as a member of a group rather than as a discrete self—may structure the play's "raw material." It would be important to note how the frameworks within which narratives of individual harm are formulated or circulated by women in Ugandan refugee camps may differ from Nottage's own understanding of the way these stories function.

The reason to consider such alternatives is that the play did not produce the same kinds of empathy among every audience. Nottage discusses how the play's reception in Kinshasa was different from what she witnessed when the play was staged in the United States.[73] During the latter production, Nottage saw a humanitarian worker weeping for the first time about the human rights abuses he had witnessed in the DRC. By contrast, those in the Kinshasa audience—many of whom were apparently "chatting [on their cell phones]"—seemed unmoved by the piece. Nottage attributes this response to a "very different theater-going culture."[74] Her observation may also suggest the need for a distinct form of presentation of the conflict that does not depend on individuals' empathic response, but expects the kind of engaged and critical audience that Brecht envisioned. Brian Crow's essay on Brecht's reception in sub-Saharan Africa lends credence to this line of thought. In his discussion of a specific African response to Brecht, Crow highlights the history of Brecht's tremendous influence on African playwrights in the postcolonial period.[75] He also describes a traditional dynamic between African performers and theater-goers characterized by spectators' direct commentary and evaluation of the people and events portrayed on stage that critics have called "Brechtian."[76] In other words, the alignment of *Ruined* with the parameters of a human rights regime, and its assumption of all individuals' shared interior life, may not bring the violation it describes closer to all audiences.

Further, the "close-in" poetics of *Ruined* turn the audience away from its historical connection to the kinds of markets the play references in both its content and form. The play does note the fact that worldwide demand for coltan, an essential element in cell-phone and computer production mined in the eastern DRC, fuels conflict in the region. However, *Ruined* does not focus on this story. As it emphasizes the *reality* of the atrocities it represents, for example, by publishing images of the tear-streaked faces of Nottage's Congolese interviewees in the script, the work suggests that spectators' primary reaction should be recognition of the protagonists' personhood, their humanity. Consequently, viewers may pay primary attention to characters' development, rather than making connections between the play's content and their own likely dependence on coltan in daily life.[77] As a result, the play moves away from suggesting the kind of "repair" that might follow from a solidarity framework, for example, regulation in electronics manufacturing that could prevent the immediate and structural violence related to coltan mining.

In *Ruined*, Nottage brings viewers up close to a real historical trauma to foster empathy. In this way, the play reinforces the hegemony of a human rights regime because it assumes that a particular view of the individual is the only mode for understanding what needs to be done to respond to the story that Nottage tells. I argue, in a vein similar to Benjamin's critique of Döblin, that Nottage's play misses an opportunity to reveal, and perhaps to repair, the historical forces that connect viewers to the action presented on stage. It is not enough to highlight the potentially universal inherent qualities of humans if there is no recognition of region-specific notions of human community, or no work is being done to address larger social and economic inequalities. For this reason, the challenge posed by a Brechtian "poetics of distance"—one that can lead to thinking in terms of "ruin" and "repair" from the perspective of solidarity—continues to be relevant.

Conclusion

Storytelling helps us make sense of our place in the world and identify with others. From a literary studies point of view, attention to form can make it clear that stories are not transparent reflections of reality, but rather, that narrative creates our self-awareness as well as our understanding of our relationship to others. For this reason, interdisciplinary research that examines the way narrative connects with major concepts driving public policy is crucial: the way we tell stories informs how we govern each other.

Conceptions of human rights push artists and scholars to think productively beyond regional and national boundaries, and to imagine human interconnection in new ways. However, by emphasizing all humans' identical possession of inviolable rights, Nottage allows viewers to feel a closeness with the oppressed without necessarily highlighting the economic and historical relationships between spectators and the subjects of her story. I do not mean to propose that Nottage's efforts to connect audiences with her subjects' suffering are without value. Yet Brecht's interventions continue to challenge us to examine the structural determination of identities and actions. Area studies, which foster the tools for investigation into specific cultural, linguistic, and historical traditions across the world, can help uncover such structures. In a time of hegemonic human rights regimes, as much as ever, the critical question of where and how to find solidarity remains urgent.

Notes

1. I would like to thank the students in my "Literature of Human Rights" and "World Literature" courses at the University of Kansas who have contributed their insights on the pieces in course discussions and have helped me deepen my understanding of both texts.

2. Celia McGee, "Approaching Brecht, by Way of Africa," *New York Times*, January 21, 2009, http://theater.nytimes.com/2009/01/25/theater/25McGee.html?_r=0.

3. Christa Hasche, "Through the Minefield of Ideologies: Brecht and the Staging of *Mutter Courage und ihre Kinder*," trans. Jutta von Zitzewitz, *Modern Drama* 42, no. 2 (1999): 187.

4. Frederic Jameson, *Brecht and Method* (London: Verso, 1998), 148–49.

5. Gillian Whitlock, "Remediating Gorilla Girl: Rape Warfare and the Limits of Humanitarian Storytelling," *Biography* 33, no. 3 (2010): 473.

6. McGee, "Approaching Brecht."

7. Ibid.

8. Jack Donnelly, "International Human Rights: A Regime Analysis," *International Organization* 40, no. 3 (1986): 605.

9. Ibid., 606.

10. José A. Alves Lindgren, "The Declaration of Human Rights in Postmodernity," *Human Rights Quarterly* 22, no. 2 (2000): 482.

11. Samuel Moyn, *The Last Utopia: Human Rights in History* (Cambridge, MA: Belknap Press of Harvard University Press, 2010), 176.

12. Costas Douzinas, "*Adikia*: On Communism and Rights," in *The Idea of Communism*, ed. Costas Douzinas and Slavoj Žižek (London: Verso, 2010), 85; Karl Marx and Friedrich Engels, "Manifesto of the Communist Party," 23, http://www.marxists.org/archive/marx/works/download/pdf/Manifesto.pdf.

13. Walter Mignolo, "Citizenship, Knowledge, and the Limits of Humanity," *American Literary History* 18, no. 2 (2006): 313.

14. Adamantia Pollis and Peter Schwab, "Human Rights: A Western Construct with Limited Applicability," in *Human Rights: Ideological and Cultural Perspectives*, ed. Adamantia Pollis and Peter Schwab (New York: Praeger, 1979), 8.

15. Moyn, *The Last Utopia*, 13.

16. Makau Mutua, "Human Rights in Africa: The Limited Promise of Liberalism," *African Studies Review* 51, no. 1 (2008): 30–31.

17. David Kennedy, "The International Human Rights Movement: Part of the Problem?" *Harvard Human Rights Journal* 15 (2002): 117.

18. Mutua, "Human Rights in Africa," 25.

19. Jon Goss and Terence Wesley-Smith, "Introduction: Remaking Area Studies," in *Remaking Area Studies: Teaching and Learning Across Asia and the Pacific*, ed. Terence Wesley-Smith and Jon Goss (Honolulu: University of Hawai'i Press, 2010), x.

20. "The Federal Role in Education," US Department of Education, http://www2.ed.gov/about/overview/fed/role.html.

21. "Bureau of Democracy, Human Rights, and Labor," US Department of State, http://www.state.gov/j/drl/.

22. Jamie A. Williamson, "Using Humanitarian Aid to 'Win Hearts and Minds': A Costly Failure?" *International Review of the Red Cross* 93, no. 884 (Dec. 2011): 1037.

23. "Laws and Guidance: National Resource Centers Programs," US Department of Education, http://www2.ed.gov/programs/iegpsnrc/legislation.html.

24. Gayatri Spivak, "Righting Wrongs," *South Atlantic Quarterly* 103, no. 2–3 (2004), 527.

25. Goss and Wesley-Smith, "Introduction: Remaking Area Studies," xv.

26. Gayatri Spivak, *Death of a Discipline* (New York: Columbia University Press, 2003), 9–10.

27. Douzinas, "*Adikia*: On Communism and Rights," 95–96.

28. Ibid., 94.

29. Eric Hobsbawm, "Opening Address: Working-Class Internationalism," in *Internationalism in the Labour Movement, 1830–1940*, ed. Frits van Holthoon and Marcel van der Linden (Leiden: E. J. Brill, 1988), 7.

30. Leonhard Wolfgang, *Völker hört die Signale: Die Anfänge des Weltkommunismus 1919–1924* (Munich: C. Bertelsmann Verlag, 1981), 37.

31. Vladimir Ilyich Lenin, "Imperialism, the Highest Stage of Capitalism," Internet History Sourcebook, last modified July 1998, http://www.fordham.edu/halsall/mod/1916lenin-imperialism.html.

32. Max Elbaum, *Revolution in the Air: Sixties Radicals Turn to Lenin, Mao and Che* (London: Verso, 2002), 326–27.

33. Peter Stobinski, "Nicaragua war uns wichtig: Zur Geschichte der Solidarität der DDR-Bevölkerung," in *Aufbruch nach Nicaragua: Deutsch-deutsche Solidarität im Systemwettstreit*, ed. Erika Harzer and Willi Volks (Berlin: Ch. Links Verlag, 2009), 62.

34. Werner Balsen and Karl Rössel, *Hoch die internationale Solidarität: zur Geschichte der Dritte Welt-Bewegung in der Bundesrepublik* (Cologne: Volksblatt Verlag, 1986), 404.

35. Douzinas, "*Adikia*: On Communism and Rights," 99.

36. Recent scholarly works that attest to the global emergence of such a genre include Kay Schaffer and Sidonie Smith's *Human Rights and Narrated Lives: The Ethics of Recognition* (New York: Palgrave Macmillan, 2004), and *Documentary Testimonies: Global Archives of Suffering*, ed. Bhaskar Sarkar and Janet Walker (New York: Routledge, 2010).

37. Paradigmatic of these narratives is the story of Ishmael Beah's experiences as a child soldier in Sierra Leone during the 1990s, *A Long Way Gone: Memoirs of a Boy Soldier* (New York: Gale Cengage, 2007). This work charts Beah's forced recruitment into the Sierra Leone army as a young adolescent, his transformation into a soldier able to kill ("it seemed as if my heart had frozen"), and his rehabilitation at a UNICEF-sponsored center (126, 131).

38. Joseph Slaughter, *Human Rights, Inc.: The World Novel, Narrative Form, and International Law* (New York: Fordham University Press, 2007), 52.

39. Bertolt Brecht, *Mother Courage and Her Children*, trans. Edmund Jephcott, ed. John Willett and Ralph Manheim (New York: Arcade, 1994), 30.

40. Ibid., 31.

41. Ibid., 42.

42. Ibid., 48.

43. Ibid., 49.

44. Ibid., 83.

45. Ibid., 85–86.

46. Gitta Honegger, "Gossip, Ghosts, and Memory: *Mother Courage* and the Forging of the Berlin Ensemble," *TDR: The Drama Review: A Journal of Performance Studies* 54, no. 2 (2008), 106.

47. Kim Solga, "*Mother Courage* and Its Abject: Reading the Violence of Identification," *Modern Drama* 46, no. 3 (2008): 342.

48. Sharon Friedman, "The Gendered Terrain in Contemporary Theatre of War by Women," *Theatre Journal* 62, no. 4 (2010): 600.

49. Dwyer Murphy, "History of Omission," *Guernica, A Magazine of Art and Politics*, May 1, 2013, http://www.guernicamag.com/interviews/history-of-omission/.

50. Lynn Nottage, *Ruined* (New York: Theatre Communications Group, 2009), 5.

51. Ibid., 6.

52. Ibid., 51.

53. Ibid., 91.

54. Ibid., 100.

55. "'They are Destroying the Female Species in Congo.' Congolese Human Rights Activist Christine Schuler Deschryver on Sexual Terrorism and Africa's Forgotten War," *Democracy Now!*, October 8, 2007, http://www.democracynow.org/2007/10/8/they_are_destroying_the_female_species.

56. Ibid.

57. Ibid.

58. Ibid.

59. Solga, "*Mother Courage* and Its Abject," 342.

60. Christa Hasche describes how Brecht changed the final scene of *Mother Courage* from one that had shown Mother Courage together with the dead Kattrin, to one that he felt expressed less pathos: Mother Courage pulling her cart, alone. He made this revision to prevent viewers from seeing Mother Courage as a "suffering mother in an unchanging scene of war." See Christa Hasche, "Through the Minefield of Ideologies: Brecht and the Staging of *Mutter Courage und ihre Kinder*," trans. Jutta von Zitzewitz, *Modern Drama* 42, no. 2 (1999): 187, 189.

61. Walter Benjamin, "Author as Producer," in *Reflections: Essays, Aphorisms, Autobiographical Writings*, trans. Edmund Jephcott, ed. Peter Demetz (New York: Schocken, 1978), 229–30.

62. Dayo Olopade, "The Root Interview: Lynn Nottage on 'Ruined' Beauty," *The Root*, March 1, 2010, http://www.theroot.com/views/root-interview-lynn-nottage-ruined-beauty.

63. "Enough, the Project to End Genocide and Crimes against Humanity," accessed February 3, 2013, http://www.enoughproject.org/about.

64. Chloe Christman, "'Ruined' Play Brings Glimpse of Congo to D.C.," *Enough*, last modified May 2, 2011, http://www.enoughproject.org/blogs/ruined-play-brings-glimpse-congo-dc.

65. "Raise Hope for Congo, an Enough Campaign," *Enough Campaign*, accessed July 31, 2012, http://www.raisehopeforcongo.org/content/initiatives/violence-against-women.

66. "Convention on the Elimination of All Forms of Discrimination against Women," *Division for the Advancement of Women: Department of Economic and Social Affairs*, accessed July 31, 2012, http://www.un.org/womenwatch/daw/cedaw/.

67. "Message from the NGO Committee on the Status of Women," *Global Network of Women Peacebuilders*, February 10, 2010, http://www.gnwp.org/message-from-the-ngo-committee-on-the-status-of-women.

68. Laura Edmondson, "Marketing Trauma and the Theatre of War in Northern Uganda," *Theatre Journal* 57, no. 3 (2005): 455.

69. Ibid., 452.

70. Ibid., 452, 458.

71. Ibid., 453, 456–57.

72. Murphy, "History of Omission."

73. Ibid.

74. Ibid.

75. Brian Crow, "African Brecht," *Research in African Literatures* 40, no. 2 (Spring 2009): 190.

76. Ibid., 192–93.

77. See Rebecca Ashworth and Nalini Mohabir's discussion of the ethical ramifications for audiences seeing *Ruined* who depend on the electronic gadgets using coltan. Rebecca Ashworth and Nalini Mohabir, "*Ruined*: From Spectacle to Action," *ex plus ultra: The Postgraduate Ejournal of the WUN International Network in Colonial and Postcolonial Studies*, no. 2 (2010): 12–13.

The Art of Making Community
Lia Perjovschi's CAA/C̶A̶A̶ (Contemporary Art Archive/ Center for Art Analysis) and the Knowledge Museum

CORINA L. APOSTOL

Introduction

In the context of post-1989 Eastern Europe, "self-historicization" has emerged as a powerful artistic strategy.[1] Self-historicization can be conceptualized as an artistic means to repossess the historical past that was censored or discarded before 1989, while putting forth a reexamined artistic subjectivity. This cultural strategy, particularly, characterizes nonconformist artists from the 1970s and 1980s, who feel an urgent need to reclaim the experience of the recent past and actualize its repressed signifiers in the present. Their approaches span from documentation to self-organization and alternative forms of education. These artistic endeavors are responding to the current negligible support and disregard for modern and contemporary art as well as for critical practices developed in the region.[2]

Self-historicizations can take the concrete forms of artists' archives, organizing informal sharing networks or even establishing unofficial art organizations and publications. On the one hand, these forms help compensate for the scarcity of institutional frameworks and critical discourse platforms around the practices of the artistic avant-gardes and neo-avant-gardes in the region and deficiencies in the art/educational systems in general.[3] Also, through self-historicization, artists are able to reclaim severed ties between cultural communities in the former Eastern bloc, faced with the dismantling of Soviet socialism after the fall of the Berlin Wall. By foregrounding the need for documentation, translation, and historical critical practices in the present, these artists preserve a vital piece of their cultural legacy for contemporary and future artists, curators, critics, and young intellectuals.

For example, some seminal initiatives emerging in the former Eastern bloc that resist the loss of cultural memory include Hungarian artist Tamás St. Auby's "Portable Intelligence Increase Museum" (2001), an interactive computer-based exhibition that exposes gaps in official accounts of Hungarian art of the 1960s and '70s that the artist documented. Uzbek artist Vyacheslav Akhunov has created miniature reproductions (in matchboxes) of all his works in "1 m2" (1978–2007). Hungarian artist György Galántai's "Artpool Research Center" in Budapest consists of contemporary international avant-garde media and Mail Art from the Soviet period. Polish artist Zofia Kulik's "KwieKulik" Archive in Warsaw documents Polish unofficial or nonconformist artists'[4] works in the period between 1978 and 1989. Last but not least, Russian artist Vadim Zaharov has assembled a collection on the Moscow Conceptualist group of unofficial Soviet-era artists, who have been active for the past forty years.[5]

In this chapter I focus on aspects of self-historicization, including artists' archives and models for future institutions in the vision of the Romanian artist Lia Perjovschi, who has been continually active in the local art scene since the early 1980s and on the international scene since the early 1990s. The artistic practices analyzed in my case study emerged in the aftermath of the Ceauşescu regime in Romania, and the conflicts and political upheavals left unresolved in the wake of the December 1989 Romanian Revolution and the Minderiads of the 1990s.[6]

Responding to the social chaos and political confusion, Lia Perjovschi's artistic and educational models are unconventional institutional and artistic platforms operating at the nexus of art theory, history, politics, science, and philosophy, which examine the construction of the archives of history, collective memory, and human knowledge. I suggest that the artist's conceptual works emerged from the need to create a space for knowledge and resistance in order to understand Romania's own recent past. Before the social and political transformations of the 1989 Revolution, Romanian citizens had little access to outside information. In the wake of transformations that gripped the country throughout the 1990s, during the so-called period of transition to capitalism and democracy, neosocialist and liberal political governments succeeded one another at a rapid pace. Driven to understand, discuss, and share knowledge with her audiences, Lia Perjovschi used her projects to span a heterogeneous realm of information, responding to social problems and needs. Her artistic oeuvre addresses the isolation felt by intellectuals during the dictatorship in Romania, as well as the present-day condition of trying to make sense of the information boom in society.

At the core of Perjovschi's practice is her desire to engage her community of viewers and compel them to think critically after experiencing her aesthetic and theoretical projects.[7] The artist's particular commitment stems from the historical conditions in which she grew up. In particular, the idea of "community" was first discredited by the repressive living conditions before 1989 and continued to invite scorn throughout the chaotic 1990s. During this time, the persistence of authoritarian political behavior and general mistrust plagued the nascent civil body in Romania, despite the country's opening to the international community. Indeed, from my experience interviewing visual artists, dancers, curators, and activists, the term *community* continues to be a polarizing one in the local cultural scene. Bereft of historical models of genuine solidarity and engagement, which are beginning to be rediscovered, contemporary cultural figures associate the term with the demonized memory of "communism" rather than with empowerment. This logic collapses the Soviet economic and political philosophy together with the lived experience of the communist dictatorship and the apparatus of state oppression. Further, the local artistic milieu continues to be fragmented, in part due to this multigenerational trauma, which, as art historians such as Kristine Stiles have argued, remains unexamined and unhealed.[8]

This traumatic affect is palpable in the case of the Secret Police (or "Securitate") Archives, which continue to be only partially declassified to the general public. Based on minute data gathering and privileged access, and geared toward institutionalized oppression, the "Securitate" Archives mark the disjuncture between official histories and suppressed narratives that continue to plague emerging democracy in Romania. During the chaos of the Revolution, the Secret Police attempted to discard these archives, but only managed to partially destroy some files. Throughout the 1990s the Romanian authorities refused to open these files to the public in order to maintain control over the interpretation of this negative chapter of recent history. The National Salvation Front, a new political union at the helm of the country, which included former members of the Ceaușescu regime, used some of these files as political leverage and blackmail against the opposition. Since 2008, the CNSAS (National Council for the Study of the "Securitate" Archives) has begun to allow access to the archives on an individual basis, while gradually publicizing lists of informers and collaborators. The "Securitate" Archives are symptomatic of both the suppression of recent history and its traumatic aftereffects in Romania, denying healing and reconstruction of civil society in the postsocialist era.

It is significant, thus, to compare Lia Perjovschi's aesthetic models and initiatives, which the artist gathered under the frame of an archive, an open studio, an activist base, and later an interactive museum plan, with the tightly controlled mesh that holds together Romania's recent history, informing its collective identity. Emerging from a deeply traumatic period of obedience to the dictator and to an ideology combining nationalism and social control, for many Romanians, collective identity continued to be fragmented throughout the 1990s, as it could not recover the signifiers of its past and subject them to public scrutiny. If the "Securitate" Archives are metaphors for the web of silenced voices that continued to be denied the meaning of their recent past, by contrast, Lia Perjovschi's archival and museum models stand as recuperative tools for opening history, enabling viewers to become subjects and not just objects of their past.

Methodology

My methodology is historical, informed primarily by trauma studies and social history, through which I examine the ideology and history of the Ceaușescu dictatorship and its impact on Romanian society over the past twenty years. Articulation of these cross-theoretical contours is not fully systematized, as the period and region covered in my case study are in the beginning stages of investigation within the fields of art history and Slavic studies (the two most prominent fields that have produced scholarship pertinent to my research). Adding to these methodologies, area studies may prove a productive lens through which to investigate these debates, as it emphasizes cultural regional specificity as well as the use of theoretical tools from the humanities and social sciences.

Since published material on artistic practices during the socialist period and the two decades following is somewhat scarce and for the most part unavailable in English, I emphasize the urgency of interviewing artists and cultural activists, who are priceless repositories of lived experiences and alternative histories that have yet to be fully fleshed out. Indeed, my chapter could not have been written had it not been for the generosity of Lia Perjovschi and her partner, Dan Perjovschi, who answered my questions and provided me with copies of their self-published works. The material I discuss here comes directly from the artists, in addition to documentation from international institutions that have exhibited their works.

As a cultural insider writing on this region but also aware of outsider views of Eastern Europe, my approach to analyzing the material draws on secondary sources published by scholars from the West who have had research experience in Romania, and balancing them with publications produced by those on the ground. I believe that juxtaposing these perspectives with the voices of the artists themselves offers a more comprehensive view of the period, the region, and its community(ies), placing their construction and transformation at the intersection of approaches from inside and beyond national borders.

The Contemporary Art Archive/Center for Art Analysis

Lia Perjovschi began her artistic practice with performances in her Bucharest apartment in the 1980s, which were witnessed and photographed by Dan Perjovschi. For example, "Annulment" (1989), staged in Perjovschi's apartment, was directed as a critique of current social and political conditions. Her action symbolically connoted the lack of communication and isolation that the dictatorship imposed on Romanian citizens. It is not accidental that this action was staged in their private residence, for artists of that period often carried out their work in their homes, usually for a very limited number of people whom they trusted. These extreme conditions reflected the total closure and control of public space in Ceaușescu's Romania, when even such hermetic performances were dangerous. Communication was difficult outside the borders of these communities, except for sporadic Mail Art circles, in which the Perjovschis took part.[9] These discrete and informal exchanges between artists working unofficially in the former Eastern bloc were an attempt to engender an alternative public sphere that was sustained through informality and trust to eschew the repressive power of the authorities.[10]

After the Revolution, several socio-cultural-political organizations emerged to facilitate the formation of a civil society, that is, a network of non-governmental organizations and institutions that represented the aspirations of citizens for a new political path for Romania.[11] In these collectives, scholars from the humanities and social sciences played an important role.[12] Due to the distinctive nationalist and purportedly socialist dictatorship in Romania and the absence of a free market economy, the struggle between the oppressive state and society was historically constituted through cultural-political alliances rather than economic-political ones. It is this legacy that shaped political interactions immediately following the collapse of socialism, during which Romania had not yet embarked on the path to dramatic economic and political transformation.

Along with attempts at opening up these isolated artistic endeavors to one another, cultural communities sought to connect with groups that were emerging from similarly repressive systems, and with artists in Western Europe and the United States—areas previously out of reach. The "Zone Performance Festival," organized in Timisoara in the 1990s by Ileana Pintilie, was a seminal initiative that offered Romanian artists the possibility of engaging with international audiences and artists, many of them for the first time.[13] It was under these auspices that in 1993, Lia Perjovschi performed "I Fight for My Right to Be Different." Over several hours the artist treated a full-size stuffed doll dressed in Perjovschi's own clothes to alternating displays of affection

FIGURE 1. "CAA Kit," Van Abbe Museum, 2010.

and violence, at times lunging her doll-double at members of the audience who remained passive throughout the performance. This figurative motion constituted a metaphorical pendulum between power, abuse, and submissive conformity, symptomatic of a community that had yet to come to terms with the recent past and the civil liberties and responsibilities that came with the emerging democracy.[14] While grounded in her experience of the intermittent repression and relaxation of the Romanian dictatorship, Perjovschi's oeuvre shifted from using her body as the main signifier for concepts and emotions to facilitating the critical reception of those ideas through educational-aesthetic models.[15] As Dan Perjovschi poignantly described this process, Lia moved from making "art with her body . . . to the research of the body of international art."[16]

Using her own "Contemporary Art Archive" (1997–present) as a tool for critical inquiry, directed at opening the imagination of the viewer, Perjovschi has consistently encouraged local and international exchanges between artists, students, and scholars from all fields, seeking to restore sociocultural connections that had been destroyed during the pre-1989 segregation. At the same time, her archive includes original artworks, conceptualized as aesthetic models for missing or alternative institutions, and as forms of reactivating suppressed or missing histories, while always maintaining a critical attitude toward all forms of abuse and repression by state power. These take the form of newspapers revealingly entitled "ZOOM-diaPOZITIV," "sens," "globe 1990-today," "short guide-art in public space (ro): some independent positions," and "waiting room"; timelines—such as "Subjective Art History from Modernism to present day. Art and its context" (1997–2004); and diagrams—or "Mind Maps" (1999–2006). Over the past twenty years, the value of her practice has been recognized internationally for its ability to subvert authority, emancipating the individual to generate his or her own system of formulating questions, finding answers, and acting in society.

Describing herself as a "Detective in Art, a Text Jockey, reading, copying, cutting and remixing texts and images," Perjovschi has stressed repeatedly the desire to recuperate for her community what her generation was denied before 1989.[17] In a 2007 interview with Kristine Stiles, Perjovschi explained that the archive, as she now conceives of it, is a repository of documents and space for critical thinking and exchange that was created in 1985.[18] That year, Lia and Dan Perjovschi opened their apartment in Oradea for informal gatherings with local writers, actors, anthropologists, artists, and curators. Although Dan Perjovschi was a graduate of the Academy of Arts in Iaşi and Lia Perjovschi studied at the Bucharest Academy, both artists confessed to me that they felt unprepared and constrained by their formal education. The Perjovschis conceived of this "opening" as a way to create a space for critical thinking and open exchanges during the difficult Ceauşescu dictatorship, when everyday life was extremely precarious and (self-) censorship was prevalent in all aspects of public and private life.[19] It was an act of affirmation of the power of sharing and teaching, laying the basis for an unofficial network that, as the artist describes it, was "a survival strategy." In 1990, immediately after the 1989 Revolution, the Perjovschis were offered a studio in the Scarlat/Robescu building in Bucharest, under the auspices of the now free Union of Artists, with the help of the artist Geta Brătescu.[20] They began transforming this Bucharest studio into an archive for books, magazines, and ephemera on international art and culture, as well as a repository for their works (drawings, photographs of performances, installations, art objects, and videos). This archive would become Lia Perjovschi's project, "Contemporary Art Archive/Center for Art Analysis" (abbreviated by the artist CAA/CAA) in 1997, imagined as a tool for critical inquiry, used to spur local and international interaction between artists, students, and scholars from diverse fields (art history, history, political science, anthropology, and philosophy). The CAA/CAA project is an aesthetic model for an alternative, interdisciplinary institution, filling a gap in art education in the country, a form of reactivating and recuperating suppressed or missing histories as a result of the pre-1989 segregation. During its two decades of existence in the art studio building across from the Art University, Perjovschi's project managed to inspire and educate young artists, curators, philosophers, and art historians. By transmitting seminal knowledge, concepts, and working methods, it engendered a more meaningful intellectual and affective exchange than the University nearby. As a resistance strategy and an alternative space for knowledge, it has been celebrated internationally in an era of globalization and political confusion.

Receiving increasing recognition from the artistic community, Lia Perjovschi began to travel extensively throughout Europe, North America, Latin America, and parts of Asia. She was not content with simply observing and reflecting upon those contexts in her works. Together with Dan Perjovschi, she hosted meetings between foreign artists, journalists, theorists, and specialists from all fields and local cultural communities. For Lia Perjovschi, what in 1997 she would call the "CAA (Contemporary Art Archive)" became an aesthetic model for collecting and organizing information, classifying, and developing critical-thinking tools. Driven by her broad quest for knowledge, she approached these goals from her own experience, coming from Romania where such necessary resources and strategies were simply nonexistent.

Further, Perjovschi challenged audiences to establish their own parameters for analyzing, categorizing, and absorbing the material that she collected. This emancipatory gesture stands at the opposite end of the mentality of fear and repression dominating the context from which her practice emerged. Using the archive as a basis, as well as the experience of international peers, the activities at CAA became focused on analyzing strategies in the Romanian art scene and beyond, supporting innovative programs, developing critical methodologies, and offering a basis for art activism.

In 2003, the CAA began operating under the title "CAA/~~CAA~~ (Contemporary Art Archive/Center For Art Analysis)." The change in the space's taxonomy marked a shift from the traditional understanding of the archive as a platform for collecting and presenting material, to what its actual function became over time—that is, a space for communication, empowerment, reflection, and activism around the social and political relevance of art in context. From group discussions, lectures, presentations, workshops, and exhibitions, Lia Perjovschi channeled educational impetus with sociopolitical engagement—a defining characteristic of leading a self-critical existence. Visitors to the CAA/~~CAA~~ also received Perjovschi's self-published documents, in themselves critical tools that commented on local and international initiatives in the art field. Her art grew from the isolated milieu of 1980s Romania to embrace different kinds of knowledge (from social sciences and technology to the humanities) as well as to respond to and be informed by exhibiting and teaching in countries including the United States, parts of Latin America, European countries (both West and East), and South Korea. In these contexts, Perjovschi engaged local communities through staging installations, giving lectures, teaching courses on contemporary art, and acting as an "artistic diplomat" engendering links between the cultural communities in Romania and abroad.

Since becoming a self-professed nomad artist, Lia Perjovschi has streamlined the documentation and practices of CAA/~~CAA~~ into what she calls a "CAA Kit." Traveling globally with her own Duchampian "Boîte-en-valise," she has invited international audiences to become detectives in art themselves—that is, to analyze, judge, learn, and act for the future.[21] Perjovschi's kit comprises "Detective Materials," "Timelines," and "Mind Maps," material carefully selected from her archive and centered around a certain theme or responding to particular historical events, depending on where it is exhibited. Also in this kit are posters documenting the activities at CAA in Bucharest, grounding this model in a commitment to create a culturally engaged community.[22] I will focus here on a few examples to emphasize their role in allowing the public to figure out their own models of analysis and organization of information that corresponds to each person's needs and experiences.

For contemporary Romanian art, institutional networks based on transparency are definitely an urgent need and one that the powers of the state have handled without consulting either the artistic community or the public who benefit from its productions. Denouncing the problematic establishment of the first National Museum of Contemporary Art in Bucharest (or MNAC when abbreviated in Romanian), inside the House of the People[23] in 2004, Lia produced "Detective Draft—The Museum of Contemporary Art in Bucharest," together with Dan Perjovschi.[24] This artistic publication investigated the context in which the Museum was established. It laid out for the general public the raging debates over the use of the space, which artists were invited to exhibit and which were ignored, all of which revealed the nontransparent appointment of its artistic directors. As the artists poignantly remarked:

> Between the city and the building empty fields stretch for about a mile. That is exactly the distance between the leaders and the citizens.... Absolutely no one was consulted: this is Romania where the process should be more transparent. The prime minister (an art collector) is quoted as saying about the location: "either here or nowhere." ... The museum was established putting all the state [museum] spaces together (6 venues) under the same umbrella. This was the year, 2004, when things were supposed to go the other way, toward decentralizing state power.[25]

Local and international scholars and artists were prompted to respond to the situation. Strongly criticizing the subordination of art to state politics, the publication decried the compromised democratic ideals this signaled in a period in which the sociopolitical climate was expected to move along the path of loosening the centralization of state power. Finally, in the artist's statement, she called for witnesses, the general public, to react to this historical injustice, providing them with facts and examples on how to act. Lia Perjovschi's intervention remains a model for exercising one's moral and ethical conscience through artistic practice that challenges the viewer into thinking politically and stepping outside of passivity. What the artist implicitly emphasized is that, in order to act, one must be thoroughly informed, must know the terms of the debate to adopt a position.

Lia Perjovschi recognized the need of artists at all stages in their creative lives to be in dialogue with the international community, by understanding the construction of art history in a global context, including politics, economics, and science. She responded to this need in her own art and writing. In a collection of texts and images brought together under the title "Subjective Art History from Modernism to Present Day. Art and Its Context" (1997–2004), Perjovschi organized information on local cultural developments and international art historiographies.[26] Critically deconstructing the traditional, academic art history from survey textbooks, she changed the focus of the discipline toward thinking about the cultural construction of texts and images about art in different contexts, and artistic practices related to seminal social and political events.

In her collection Perjovschi included not only artists and their works, but also magazine clippings, film stills, events in the popular media, snapshots of exhibition spaces, and various social and cultural institutions—entities that streamline the dissemination and reception of art. Organized into art historical terms, a timeline consisting of dates (ranging from 1826 to 2004), and images framed by both identifying information and the artist's comments and ending with quotes about art and a bibliography, Perjovschi gave art historians themselves a lesson on teaching art.

In a project related to her "Timelines," Perjovschi used diagrams, or what she referred to as "Mind Maps" (1999–2006), to explore and explode concepts constructed from information appearing in different spheres of cultural, social, and political life.[27] As she explained: "These works helped me to understand the development of history and then to see how my art also developed in different historical contexts."[28] "Mind Maps" are drawings consisting of handwritten concepts researched by the artist, presented as a network of interconnections and convergences. Each map is organized around a core concept positioned at the center of the composition. Building on the core that addresses themes such as "Ideology," "Communism," "Artist," "Sub-culture," "Space and Time," or simply "?," Perjovschi charted relationships and comments culled from different media (books, newspapers, artworks, popular culture). She then constructed each diagram by writing down associations and comments that visually revolve like galaxies around the center.

Perjovschi's "Mind Maps" are partly illegible, executed as shorthand mementoes or traces of research. However frustrating this strategy may prove for viewers and critics, the maps function as more than evidence of the artist's extensive knowledge or a simple exercise in deconstruction. Rather, they operate as idiosyncratic structures of language that deny audiences the complete understanding of these works. Similar to her "Timelines," the maps are meant to activate one's desire to know, to explore beyond mere contemplation by constructing one's own knowledge models with an awareness of the semiotic heritage of concepts.

The Knowledge Museum, A Blueprint for the Future

A new project called "The Knowledge Museum" encapsulates these various models, framing them into a more comprehensive, unconventional structure. In 2009, Lia Perjovschi started working on and exhibiting "Plans for a Knowledge Museum"—a museum-like installation based on the "Research Files" accumulated at CAA—which the artist hopes to build one day. Characterized by an interdisciplinary approach, this future artist-run museum is dedicated to moving away from the exhibition as spectacle or form of entertainment, and toward a learning process of working with an open-structured archival construction. Perjovschi envisioned a museum with seven departments: The Body, Art, Culture, The Earth, Knowledge and Education, The Universe, and Science, reflecting her own interdisciplinary approach to the organization of information.

The installation of "Plans for a Knowledge Museum" comprises drawings, objects, charts, photos, and color prints. Perjovschi conceives of her museum as a mental map, offering a lens into the processes of selection that inform the artist's view of cultural practices and their consequences in society, and inviting audiences to participate in a similar process of self-reflection. The project reveals Perjovschi's methods of associating objects and concepts and the building of her understanding of the world through experience doubled by research. This material is laid out for viewers to investigate and use. Enacting notions of self-archiving and openness, "The Knowledge Museum" is a blueprint for the decentralization of art institutions. This line of critique connects the artist to aforementioned experimental projects such as Hungarian

FIGURE 2. "Lia Perjovschi Knowledge Museum & Dan Perjovschi Time Specific,"
Contemporary Art Space of Castelló, 2010.

artist Tamás St. Auby's "Portable Intelligence Increase Museum" (2001),
Uzbek artist Vyacheslav Akhunov's miniature reproductions of his works in
the installation "1 m2" (1978–2007), Hungarian artist György Galántai's "Artpool Research Center" in Budapest (1992–present), or the installations of the
British collective "Art & Language," beginning with the late 1960s.

In a 2011 interview with Russian art historian Ekaterina Lazareva, Perjovschi remarked that her archival practices, out of which "The Knowledge
Museum" emerged, are focused on research instruments instead of being concerned with local art histories.[29] Building on this observation, I argue that Perjovschi's projects are an implicit critique of the Academy and the Museum, at
the same time that she adapts the language of institutional platforms in order
to decentralize their inherent tiered structures.[30] In the Romanian context, her
critique is a powerful statement against the practices of the National Museum
of Contemporary Art (MNAC), made by encouraging openness, debate, and
exchange as opposed to authoritarian practices under which this institution
was conceived and still conducts its affairs in society. To be sure, Perjovschi's
"Knowledge Museum" is based on the artist's conceptual models, but it is the

viewer that completes the project by being put in the position of creating one's own algorithm of interpretation in the search for meaning.

In her art, Lia Perjovschi grapples with approaches to bringing together theory and practice, while asking audiences to do the same. Her projects resist easy interpretation. They require an investment of time, careful consideration, and undivided attention. In a way, the interdisciplinary models that form "The Plans for a Knowledge Museum" demand a certain endurance to not just look, but to think and to act. The artist's practice is grounded in trust, yet she remains skeptical and uncompromising in a period of uncertainty and precariousness in Romania and around the world. Lia Perjovschi puts her faith in engaged viewers, showing them the way her mind organizes information, giving them the tools necessary to do more than criticize—to create.

Through her projects, the artist provides her audience with a wealth of information, accumulated over twenty years, based on extensive experience and exchanges with artists and scholars around the world. She also leaves unanswered questions, engendering the desire to know more, to ask for more. Her publications are filled with question marks and exclamations, while her installations present everyday objects in plastic bags as evidence for the viewer to open; one can then take the information and apply it to societal struggles. Perjovschi never gives her works a definite, self-sufficient meaning, but suggests further questions and unpacks concepts and situations. It is precisely this rigorous approach to developing intellectual resources, joined with the moral and ethical dimension of her work, that makes Lia Perjovschi a vital figure in the Romanian contemporary art scene as well as a mentor to generations of young artists, curators, and theoreticians around the world. As the artist herself noted: "In general, I am for engagement (with responsibility) for a better society for all. In art in particular, I am for state institutions to have, at the very least, a minimum budget for contemporary art and professional criteria in a global context. Education (with empathy and modesty) is the key word."[31]

Both Lia and Dan Perjovschi continue to act together as powerful advocates for substantial change in the postsocialist period. Between 1997 and 2010, the "Contemporary Art Archive" and the artists' studio in Bucharest provided a forum for debate for local and international audiences, freeing the Romanian community from isolation and stagnation. Unfortunately, official state institutions, such as the Art Academy (now the National Art University Bucharest), do not recognize the importance of Perjovschi's archive as a cultural heritage landmark of international significance. In August 2010 the artist—together with twenty-two other cultural producers working in the studios of the Art Academy—were sent a notice of evacuation under the pretext of the building's state of decay. The Perjovschis moved the "Contemporary Art Archive" to their native Sibiu, where it is now housed in a newly built studio. However, before leaving the capital, they invited several artists and scholars—including the author—to visit the empty studio and reflect on its rich history and its current precarious condition.[32]

As Lia Perjovschi then observed, while the "Contemporary Art Archive" would be temporarily closed for consulting, the "Center for Art Analysis" would remain open, as it never needed a physical space in which to exist. Lia's remark, in conjunction with the disappearance of the Perjovschi studio in Bucharest, sheds light on an indelible scar in the urban social fabric. One of the city's most valuable legacies had been all but erased: the theoretical basis of the Archive, and the presence of the artist herself, which contributed to a thriving network of civic-oriented individuals, a local critical community. In a period of indiscriminate change, social amnesia, and political confusion, the fate of Perjovschi's Archive constitutes a warning signal, calling for collective action against the destruction of cultural heritage in contemporary art in Central Europe.

This case study of Lia Perjovschi's theoretical and aesthetic models invites a critique of the disciplines of history and art history. Namely, the artist's unconventional renditions of time and events intrinsically question the notion of the certainty of historical facts and the linear progression of time applied in the scholarship. As aesthetic models for broader debates about the shape of history and its creators, CAA/CAA and the Knowledge Museum focus on key historical figures and representations of them in the art and politics of the time. Further, as the products of self-historicization—or, as Lia Perjovschi herself puts it, "Subjective Art Histories"—they bring to the fore the complexity of visual images' meaning and distribution, putting forth innovative ways of seeing in relation to time and memory.

Thus, the artist's practice uses self-historicization while also exceeding it, by suggesting an alternative system of radical criticism of knowledge production and encouraging the viewer to take an active public position in different fields of social activism. The use value of her work has been recognized and developed by generations of artists in Romania, and it continues to hold international relevance, as Lia is invited to organize workshops, teach-ins, and installations around the world, in concert with other international artists from outside her native region.[33]

Introducing a complexity of layers, Perjovschi's works simultaneously capture and emphasize the instability of history, activating the viewer in his or her capacity to act as a critical citizen. Thus, the artist puts forth the challenge of imagining different ways of understanding and constructing not only art history, but collective history. Taking apart its practices and theoretical models, the artist invites the public into the game of putting them back together again, and figuring out which side they are on in the process.

In conclusion, insofar as Lia Perjovschi's mutable artistic projects take the shape of educational platforms (Center for Art Analysis/Contemporary Art Archive) and institutions (The Knowledge Museum), they represent a form of resistance to conservative local structures and their immutable rules, from the University of Arts to the National Contemporary Art Museum. Concepts and formats such as the archive, research, informal education, and interdisciplinarity have been defined by the artist as subjects, working methods, and concerns that make possible a more authentic form of communication and genuine knowledge exchange, both intellectual and affective. While the CAA/ CAA existed in the center of Bucharest, right next door to the Art Academy, it managed to bring together and motivate a host of intellectuals from different backgrounds, including students and young artists. The fact that the Perjovschis lost their studio in August 2010 perhaps made their situation no worse than that of other artists who have similarly been expelled from the Scarlat/ Robescu artist studios building. However, the fact that the powers that be have taken over this space, glossing over its recent history, is symptomatic for a still amnesic local community. Since then, Lia Perjovschi has moved her Archive and Center for Art Analysis and Knowledge to Sibiu, where she continues to welcome international audiences in a space for transmitting knowledge and developing concepts, a place for history and collective memory. Telling complex stories of history, philosophy, politics, art, and everyday life through intricate yet appealing art installations, Perjovschi's art continues to affect her audiences and relate to topical political and social issues.

Notes

1. "Eastern European Art" is a much debated term in the art historical community and beyond. Some scholars consider Eastern Europe the group of countries that lie to the east of France, Germany, and Italy, referring to this region as "The Other Europe." Other terms for this region are Central Europe and the Balkans. Whether or not to include Russia in the definition of Eastern Europe is also still up for debate, even though more recent surveys do. On the debate concerning the terminology of Eastern Europe, see Janelle Rohr, *Eastern Europe: Opposing Viewpoints* (San Diego: Greenhaven, 1990).

2. This term was introduced by curator Zdenka Badovinac in conjunction with the exhibition she organized, "Interrupted Histories," at the Moderna galerija in Ljubljana, which dealt with the artistic-archiving strategies in the former Eastern bloc. However, in my essay I expand on the notion of "self-historicization" to refer not only to archives but also models for future institutions and experimental practices, using Lia Perjovschi's work as a case study. See also Zdenka Badovinac, "Interrupted Histories," in *Prekinjene zgodovine / Interrupted Histories*, ed. Zdenka Badovinac et al. (Ljubljana: Museum of Modern Art, 2006), unpaginated.

3. The avant-garde in art refers to artists active during the period of cultural blossoming between 1910 and 1950 in Romania. The neo-avant-garde refers to artists active in unofficial cultural circles from the 1960s until the end of the 1980s.

4. Unofficial or nonconformist artists refers to those artists who produced art in Eastern Europe and Russia after the death of Joseph Stalin in 1953 and up until the dissolution of the Soviet Union in 1991, outside of the canon of Socialist Realism.

5. For a more comprehensive study of archival artist projects in the former Eastern bloc, see Sven Spieker, *The Big Archive: Art from Bureaucracy* (Cambridge, MA: MIT Press, 2008).

6. During the period of Soviet Communism, Romania was under the influence of the Soviet Union, which appointed the country's top political leaders. This situation changed with the ascendancy to the presidency of Nicolae Ceauşescu, who pursued a politics of nonalignment with the Soviet Union, forming alliances with Western countries. The situation in Romania, an authoritarian regime unto its own, thus differed significantly from that in the other countries in the Soviet bloc. After the 1989 Revolution, the Mineriads were a series of violent actions of miners from the Valea Jiului region against protesters in Bucharest. The miners were called on to squash protests against the National Salvation Front, the ruling political party, and its leader Ion Iliescu, the president of Romania in 1990.

7. See Vlad Morariu, "Intervention Through Opposition: Spatiul Public Bucuresti | Public Art Bucharest 2007," *IDEA Arts + Society*, no. 28 (Cluj: Fundatia IDEA, 2007), 65–68.

8. See Kristine Stiles, "Shaved Heads and Marked Bodies," Strategie II: Peuples Mediterranées [Paris] 64–65 (July–December 1993): 95–117.

9. The Perjovschis in conversation with the author, August 13, 2010, Perjovschi Studio, Bucharest.

10. See Alla Rosenfeld and Norton T. Dodge, eds., *Nonconformist Art: The Soviet Experience 1956–1986* (New York: Thames & Hudson, 1995).

11. For example, "The Group for Social Dialogue," "The Civic Alliance," and "The Student League," all founded immediately after the Revolution, which continue to be active in cities across Romania today. For an analysis of the emergence of civil society in postauthoritarian regimes in Eastern Europe, see Jan Kubik and Grzegorz Ekiert, *Rebellious Civil Society: Popular Protest and Democratic Consolidation in Poland, 1989–1993* (Ann Arbor: University of Michigan Press, 2001).

12. Dan Perjovschi in an email to the author (May 11, 2011) explained that the Group for Social Dialogue was composed mainly of intellectuals living in Bucharest, in fields such as literature, history, and philosophy, many of them in "various degrees of dissidence with the communist regime." Dan Perjovschi became a member in 1996 as he was working at *22 Magazine*, the magazine edited by the Group for Social Dialogue. *22 Magazine* was an opposition magazine against neocommunist power; in Perjovschi's view, "actually it was very right to compensate the communist past and now it is more to the center."

13. Initiated and organized by the Romanian art historian Ileana Pintilie, "The Zone Festival" (which consisted of performances, symposia, and workshops) started out as a manifestation for artists from the former Eastern bloc (Romania, Bulgaria, Poland, Hungary, Slovakia, Serbia, Russia, East Germany) but soon grew to include artists and scholars from Ireland, Scotland, the United Kingdom, France, Norway, and the United States. For ten years it functioned as a regular artistic platform, even though developed in a country with extremely fragile and marginalized sociocultural networks. "The Zone Festival" was discontinued after 2003 because of insufficient financing. See http://www.zonafestival.ro/en/index.htm, accessed December 13, 2011.

14. For a comprehensive description of Lia Perjovschi's performances during the 1980s and early 1990s, see Andrei Codrescu, "The Arts of the Perjovschis," in *States of Mind: Lia and Dan Perjovschi*, ed. Kristine Stiles (Durham, NC: Nasher Museum of Art at Duke University, 2007), 115–30.

15. Here I make the distinction between communism as an ideology imposed from above by the Soviet Union, and the situation with different political opportunities built under the regime of Nicolae Ceauşescu, who followed a policy of breaking with the Soviet Union and establishing an independent nation under communism.

16. Dan Perjovschi, "Alone for the Others: Lia Perjovschi," in *Again for Tomorrow,* exhibition catalogue (London: Royal College of Art, 2006), 119.

17. Ibid., xiv.

18. Kristine Stiles, "Passages 1992–2007: Interview with Lia Perjovschi," in *States of Mind,* 176.

19. Interview with Dan and Lia Perjovschi by the author, August 2010.

20. During our interview at the Perjovschi studio in Sibiu in December 2013, Lia explained how Bratescu generously bequeathed them the studio she had been assigned by the Artists Union in 1990, as she already had a studio in Bucharest.

21. Marcel Duchamp's *Boîte-en-valise* is a portable miniature monograph, including approximately sixty- nine reproductions of the artist's work, created in different editions between 1935 and 1970.

22. Lia Perjovschi, *Research File. CAA Activities,* 1990–2000, black & white photocopy, 10 pp.

23. The House of the People became the seat of the Romanian Parliament in 1994. The building, which was begun in 1984, was completed in 1997.

24. Lia Perjovschi, *Detective Draft,* published in the context of "On Difference #1 Local Contexts—Hybrid Spaces," May 20 to July 31, 2005, Wurttemberghirscher Kunstverein, Germany (Bucharest and Stuttgart: CAA/CAA and Wurttemberghirscher Kunstverein, 2005).

25. Dan and Lia Perjovschi, quoted in *States of Mind,* 83–84.

26. Lia Perjovschi, *Research File. My Subjective Art History,* 1997–2004, computer printout, 35 pp.

27. Lia Perjovschi, *Mind Maps (Diagrams),* 1999–2006, sixty ink drawings on paper.

28. Kristine Stiles, "Passages 1992–2007: Interview with Lia Perjovschi," in *States of Mind,* 178.

29. "Lia Perjovschi in Dialogue with Ekaterina Lazareva," *CriticAtac,* May 12, 2011, accessed December 13, 2011, http://www.criticatac.ro/7112/%E2%80%9Esunt-convinsa-ca-astazi-nu-mai-este-suficient-sa-fii-critic-este-important-sa-propui-ceva-in-schimb-altfel-nu-dai-dovada-decat-d-e-aroganta-%E2%80%9D/.

30. Lia Perjovschi, *Knowledge Museum,* 2007, drawings, objects, charts, photos, and color prints.

31. See Olga Ștefan, "Interview with Dan and Lia Perjovschi," Art Margins Online, July 2012, accessed October 20, 2012, http://www.artmargins.com/index.php/interviews/670-interview-with-dan-and-lia-perjovschi-sibiubucharest.

32. This meeting was attended by the author at the former Perjovschi studio in Bucharest on August 13, 2010.

33. For a complete list of Lia Perjovschi's solo and group exhibitions, see Angelika Nollert, *Solo for Lia Perjovschi: Knowledge Museum Kit* (Nurnberg: Verlag Fur Moderne Kunst, 2012).

Street Art contra Police Abuse
Exposing Police Power in Post-Soviet Russia[1]

PATRICK CALLEN

As a medium, art carries with it a great deal of symbolic force and authority. Artists reflect upon and re-create the world around them, placing it in front of the public to elicit a personal response. What response does art elicit when it leaves its traditional habitats—museums, libraries, theatres—and stretches beyond the traditional conventions of artistic practice? What happens when art applies new methods that challenge political institutions? This study of the art collectives Chto delat' (What is to be done?), Voina (War), and Pussy Riot explores their effort to challenge the new post-Soviet authoritarianism and the police abuse of free speech by bringing free speech to Russia's urban streets, churches, metro stations, and stores.

Using as a background contemporary performance art, particularly the work of the Soviet era Moscow Conceptualist Dmitri Prigov (1940–2007), I examine the role of censorship and police abuse as tools for controlling the Soviet and post-Soviet public. Prigov's famous poem, "Apotheosis of the Policeman" (*Apofeoz militsanera*, 1982), has become iconic for the performance art movement in Russia. I am especially interested in the policeman as a symbol of the repressive state in Soviet and post-Soviet conditions. In later performance art, a pattern of artistic representations and challenges of police abuse emerges. I examine the artistic and political platforms of these collectives, as their theories and practice help us to understand how activists have commented on the conditions of urban life under Putin and Medvedev.

Artist activists work in solidarity with protest movements, bringing their expertise in various art forms to provide a cultural perspective to moments of political unrest and change. Through performative art, these activists encourage citizens to respond to their work not only as a piece of art, but also as sociopolitical thought. The art is imbued with a protest message, and it is up to the spectator to decide whether the message will influence their everyday social and political behavior. This falls in line with Henri Lefebvre's idea that everyday life can be lived as a political artwork. Citizens and politicians generate various locutions of power and representation that enter into dialogue with or struggle against one another.[2] The most successful protest movement is diverse, a unified body of citizens occupying spaces public and official, as both a form of protest and of place-making, one that exposes monuments associated with the state and other police-controlled "public" spaces as stages for demonstration to support and defend human and civil rights. As Lefebvre expresses it in his work, *The Urban Revolution*:

> Revolutionary events generally take place in the street. Doesn't this show that the disorder of the street engenders another kind of order? The urban space of the street is a place for talk, given over as much to the exchange of words and signs as it is to the exchange of things. A place where speech becomes writing. A place where speech can become "savage" and, by escaping rules and institutions, inscribe itself on the walls.[3]

Lefebvre, whose works treat the development of the urban environment as a space for citizens to challenge the bureaucratization and commodification of culture and society, envisions a utopian space that allows citizens to test authority. Protest becomes paramount in everyday life, the discursive means to new ends, "the only viable moral choice as well as a civic duty."[4]

The system of governance constructed in post-Soviet Russia, that of the "power vertical," is a depersonalized system created to place all control in the hands of one person who is completely uninterested in the opinion of the masses.[5] The decline of socialism and the emergence of the so-called market economy and "managed democracy," and their effect on business, ordinary citizens, and culture, are the most important events of Russia's transition. The concern of authorities to continue managing many, if not all, spheres of life in the Russian Federation is also at the heart of this study of these collectives' creative treatments of power. Voina, Chto delat', and Pussy Riot were the most active and public practitioners of radical street art in post-Soviet Russia, and their goal, in the words of Pussy Rioter Nadezhda Tolokonnikova, is to "rouse the part of society that has remained politically apathetic and has preferred not to work actively for civil rights, but rather to stay comfortably at home."[6]

Today's Russian institutions leave little room for participatory democracy to develop in the Russian Federation. When the public makes inroads into the Russian political system, however, the elites call upon their enforcers—policemen, the Federal Security Service (FSB), and other security organs—to restrain public action. Censorship, police brutality, and politically motivated incarcerations and trials are the most frequent tools of Russian authority to

control the public.[7] The present Russian political system has stirred the artists in Voina, Chto delat', and Pussy Riot to act as both artists and political
activists, to use art to expose and inspire action against abuses of power as
representatives of the Russian public.

Artistic Identity and Community after the Cold War

The aesthetic and sociopolitical projects of post-Soviet Russian art collectives challenge police rule, exposing the gap between authority and ordinary
citizens. The artist activist designs projects that raise the consciousness of
fellow citizens and uses art to inscribe their discontent, literally and metaphorically, on the walls.[8] These projects are the result of collective initiatives
spearheaded by "art soviets," similar to those found in revolutionary Russia in
the early twentieth century; indeed, Dmitri Vilensky of Chto delat' describes
the goal as "trigger[ing] a prototypical social model of participatory democracy, translating an open system for the generation of new forms of solidarity
into the realm of contemporary cultural work."[9] The artist is involved in the
urgent task of developing a new artistic language that addresses the realities
of society, politics, and economics after the fall of the Soviet Union. Artists
such as Banksy of the United Kingdom, the collectives Chto delat' and Voina
of Russia, and musicians like Russia's Noize MC and Yuri Shevchuk, Belarus's
Lyapis Trubetskoi, and American rap and hip-hop artists largely focus their
artistic efforts on exposing social, political, economic, or cultural inequalities
or injustices to the broad public.[10]

Examining the perspectives shared by artists through their work highlights
the various elements that have shaped definitions of identity and community
after the end of the Soviet Union. The artists mentioned above share a collective disdain for abuses of political power prevalent in the world today.[11]
Artists like Banksy, Chto delat', Pussy Riot, and Voina formulate platforms
steeped in a political language of art to expose the unconstitutional conduct
of the dominant political structures, thereby making ordinary citizens aware
of the loss of their liberties to political and economic elites. Street art offers a
way to escape these conditions, to realize the effects of this process and make
it laughable: "[Street art] shows how so much of power is just theatre, using
a certain symbol, design or way of communicating. By laughing at the spectacle we undermine its power and make room for a bit of original thought."[12]
Through parody and laughter, political institutions will be transformed from
the ground up, creating new sociopolitical conditions that citizens can identify with and that reflect their interests and aspirations.

Laughter, satire, and parody are crucial to contemporary Russian artists' larger artistic platform. While a relationship between these collectives is not evident, it is possible, I argue, to compare the artistic platforms of Voina and Chto delat' in a manner that shows how the tradition of a leftist art front, begun before the Bolshevik revolution, continues in Russia today. Chto delat' and Voina also share similar theories, methods, and traditions that allow for a single, composite definition of post-Soviet Russian artistic identity that includes seven goals and objectives:

1. the artist as facilitator of a new epoch based on creative emancipation founded in "leftist" political theory such as communism and libertarian Decembrism;[13]
2. creation of genuinely expressive art that elicits an unaffected emotional response, revealing the disparity between Russian "democracy" claimed by its rulers and the country's actual semiauthoritarian system of governance;
3. development of a new language that addresses post-Soviet sociopolitical conditions and is translatable to artistic practice;
4. revival of artistic practices that challenge repressive governmental institutions and resist art's view that the "enemies are the passive public, cops, and the regime" [Vragi—obyvateli, menty, vlast'];[14]
5. destruction of conformist, artificial, and consumer-oriented art and art markets;
6. formation of a genuine left front of the arts [levyi front iskusstv] like Russian avant-garde art of the early twentieth century;
7. local and global "war" against ultra-right reactions and obscurantism.

The manifestoes of both art collectives reveal the similarities between the groups, a kinship of sorts based on unifying artistic practice and thought, which offers insight into their aspirations to end the suppression of civil rights and the oppression of Russian citizens.

Political Transformation and Censorship after the End of the Soviet Union

The 1990s were a turbulent period in Russia and the world. Feeling vulnerable to growing threats from abroad and facing mounting discontent at home, political regimes, from authoritarians in the Middle East and former Soviet Union to Western democracies, reneged on constitutional principles, particularly civil freedoms of expression and assembly. According to Pussy Rioter Nadezhda Tolokonnikova, a system such as this "is afraid of the truth, afraid of the sincerity and directness that we bring."[15] While certain forms of censorship may benefit the public, censorship in the media or surveillance on the Internet or via security cameras, however, can impinge on civil liberties. These approaches to censorship and repression are a common tool for governments today to prevent sociopolitical activism and discourage the media from reporting or supporting oppositional perspectives that are critical of the government.

In his study of dissent in post-Communist Russia, Graeme B. Robertson notes that the tendency among post-Soviet authorities to use "preventive detention and harassment to preempt protest actions" is largely a Soviet-style tradition of repression from Leonid Brezhnev's tenure as general secretary.[16] Brezhnevian deterrence only serves to protect a regime's legitimacy for so long, however, and then authorities employ more punitive measures when they fear dissent will spread. These make up Robertson's definition of a "hybrid regime," which stands on democratic principles but maintains the elite's monopoly over power institutions, including protest, by any means necessary. The regime's ability to manage dissent and channel it into likewise managed political competition undermines the basic principles of democracy; rather than representing the conscious will of the people, protest becomes a tool of the state, which allows the public to express discontent without letting it slip out of control.[17]

Prigov's Parody of Police Power

When the government and its security forces are unable to manage its citizens, artist activists capitalize on the moment, seizing the opportunity to publicly display their discontent. Parody of authority has a long tradition in Russian cultural history,[18] but to understand the roots of post-Soviet artistic practice one need only turn back to the late Soviet period and Prigov's satirical treatment of Soviet authority and censorship in the "Apotheosis of the Policeman." Prigov was far more than a poet; he was a public action artist who enacted the figures portrayed in his poetry. Such enactments gave greater prescience and a more scathing bite to his satire on Soviet power.

Control and surveillance were among the primary tasks of what Prigov calls the Soviet-era "Policeman" [*Militsaner*]. Prigov's Policeman is a symbol of the ever-present government, creating spaces of order, "like an icon," which disrupts social, political, or artistic individuality and freethinking.[19] The Policeman's "beat" manifests a mobile and localized space of surveillance that is at once a site of protection and deterrence; the former against external threats and the latter against any impulses of Soviet citizens to question or criticize authority.

In one poem Prigov treats the question of order versus individual free-doms through the meeting of the Policeman and a terrorist. The Policeman says, "You are a disharmonious terrorist with the soul of an anarchist, and, in this world, I am correctness [*pravil'nost'*]." The terrorist responds, "But I love free will, which is no local freedom. Go away! Don't hang around by the becolumned entryway [*ne stoi u stolbovogo vkhoda*], you don't look to be armed. I'll kill you!" The Policeman replies: "You cannot kill me / You could smite my flesh and tear my uniform and skin. / My image [*obraz*, the image of Soviet power; also "obraz" as the usual word for "icon"] is more powerful than your passion."[20] The terrorist may be able to kill this Policeman, but the spirit of Soviet authority, which the Policeman embodies, cannot be vanquished.[21] Soviet power is total, widespread, and monolithic.

There is a thread of socialization that weaves through Prigov's poems, presenting the Policeman as the Soviet authority's archetype for the new Soviet person.[22] The Policeman is an enduring presence, like a monument, exuding the power and authority of Soviet rule. The protective presence of the Policeman in everyday Soviet life changed the fundamental structures of Soviet society. Citizens were considered safe and harmony was guaranteed only insofar as they submitted to Soviet socialist "legality," that is, Soviet cit-izens were expected to relinquish their identities, their freedoms to act on their own volition. The Soviet Policeman's presence created an environment that suppressed these radical, individual acts. Prigov's Policeman, satirically, finds great joy in conforming to the strictures of Soviet rule. The Policeman is proud of paying his debts or duties (*dolg*) to society as a representative of Soviet power. In this instance, however, the Policeman's duty is not to protect and serve but to protect and *control*, to enforce Soviet ideology and cultural history while artists and intellectuals are censored, sent to the labor camps (the Gulag), or erased from history.

Chto delat' and "The Urban Revolution"

Today's Russian artist activists continue to face harsh and often violent responses from the state's security forces. Post-Soviet art collectives often use performance art on a grand scale, taking to the streets or occupying symbolic spaces for mass displays of protest. The emphasis on public per-formance art is a testament to Prigov, an idol and source of inspiration for post-Soviet art activism and more critical sociopolitical dialogues in the future.[23] They have committed a great deal of time to producing a new artistic language—using traditional and novel artistic mediums—to engage the public in dialogue, forcing them to think about their current condition and the ways change can happen.

Chto delat' approaches the task from localized collective organizations of "art soviets" that "[take] on the function of a counter-power that plans, localizes and executes projects collectively."²⁴ Chto delat' is interested in making the transition from theory to praxis by inscribing socially relevant art on the walls and streets of Russia's urban spaces, specifically Moscow and St. Petersburg. The collective focuses on two initiatives of the translatability and actualization of leftist theory through artistic practices under post-Soviet conditions, and the recapturing and actualization of lost elements of "floating signifiers" of the Soviet past "before they are subsumed by the present mode of production."²⁵ By translating sociopolitical theory into artistic practice, Chto delat' hopes to foster a fundamental redefinition and reorientation of Russian identity. As artist and Chto delat' spokesman Dmitry Vilensky argues, "We don't need life as a work of art, or the work of art as life. We need a total reassessment of what art can give us and how it becomes part of our everyday life."²⁶ Chto delat' attempts to raise public awareness of issues that threaten to derail Russia's development through artistic projects and the publication of its eponymous online newspaper.

The crucial problem is how to engage the Russian audience and influence critical thinking about social and political issues. Art critic and Chto delat' member David Riff provides a solution to this problem, in which ordinary citizens come to realize that they "[live] in an age of the total internalization of the production line."²⁷ People are becoming increasingly attached to the Internet and Smartphones, which allow them to remain in constant contact with friends, family, their jobs, current events, shifts in commerce, and so on. These gadgets keep us informed and in contact with everything and everyone at all times, but social and political dialogues are often dismissed for trending fashions, music and movie stars, and funny pictures of cats.²⁸ Riff contends that these technological tools could be implemented with minimal effort to reclaim the lives of the public, and reenter into social and political dialogues as "productivists, factographers, muralists, biographers of things, and worker-correspondents."²⁹

Chto delat' contends that if a new sociopolitical dialogue does not emerge, and citizens do not unite in recapturing ownership of their cities, the Russian nation as a whole "threatens to become a half-shabby, semi-shiny, consumerist hell [*potrebitel'skii ad*], and heavily policed [*zhestko kontrolireumyi organami bezopasnosti*], a non-place with high-cultural pretensions, thousands of shopping malls, and millions of cars stuck in traffic."[30] Post-Soviet Russians, at least those nonaffluent citizens, are instructed by Chto delat' to think more critically about their current sociopolitical contexts. If these Russians do not fight for their right to voice their concerns, how will they fight the repressive measures taken by authorities against artistic creation?

The political demonstrations (December 2011–May 2012) set off by the contested parliamentary and presidential elections in Russia provide some early evidence that Russian citizens are becoming more critical of the regime. Chto delat' and Voina were among the demonstrators, and both collectives used their online presence to bring awareness of the necessity and potential of political and aesthetic representation. In the March 2012 issue of Chto delat''s online newspaper, *In Defense of Representation*, Dmitry Vilensky declares that the recent popular uprisings that swept the globe "clearly [show] that neither Putin nor Mubarak and Ben Ali, neither the bankers on Wall Street nor the IMF, neither the media elite nor the political parties, neither the deputies nor the artists and intellectuals—none of them—represents 'us,' nor can they or should they represent 'us.'"[31] Vilensky attacks the ambiguity of Russia's rule of law (or what little semblance of justice exists), commenting that even the Russian Constitution paradoxically defines the principle of sovereignty: "Article 3 of the Constitution of the Russian Federation: 'The people shall exercise their power directly, and *also through the bodies of state power and local self-government.'*"[32]

Chto delat' demands the transformation of political representation for ordinary citizens in Russia, citing last winter's demonstrations in their *songspiel* "Russian Woods," written by Olga Egorova ("Tsaplya") and Dmitry Vilensky. The work confronts the phenomenon of the use of mythic images and rhetoric among protesters and government officials throughout the course of the political demonstrations: "We found that this phenomenon is not by chance and really reflects the level of a political culture in the country. And we wanted to try to analyze it in the form of a fairy tale story that would be able to not only reflect the totality of socio-political structure of our society, but also think about the possibilities of its transformation."[33]

Chto delat' speaks out against the exercise of soft political authoritarianism in Russia, as it is destroying the possibility for the reintegration of sociopolitical dialogue into the city through art. While the artistic projects of Chto delat' do not garner the same media coverage as those of Voina or Pussy Riot, their political and aesthetic doctrines may prove more useful in raising consciousness among ordinary Russians than the radical, nearly anarchistic, artistic conduct of Voina.

Voina's War against Abuses of Power

The corruption of the police force in Russia has served as the impetus for numerous artistic actions by Voina. Former president Medvedev attempted to rebrand Russia's police, falling in line with the regime's stability efforts, and ordered that, as public intellectual Masha Gessen puts it, the "*militsiya*, or militia, be renamed *politsiya*, or police. As though that would magically render the police less corrupt and brutal, less likely to rape, pillage, and terrorize, and more likely to protect. As though it would magically make them human."[34] The Policeman is a frequent target for Voina. The Policeman, who once represented an enforcer, a brooding figure unaffected by ordinary citizens' cultural or social grievances, is cast, in post-Soviet contexts, as dishonest and corrupt, and frequently exploits his position of power.[35] Before Prigov's death in 2007, a genuine artistic relationship existed between the poet and Voina, one that used politically inspired, socially conscious satire to understand and criticize Russian power under post-Soviet conditions. Voina dedicated their actions to Prigov, finding in his satirical treatment of Soviet authority in "Apotheosis of the Policeman" a model for confronting authority.

In May 2010 the group protested the misuse of blue signal flashers by police and bureaucrats, accusing these groups of abusing their authority and breaking road traffic safety regulations. In the action, entitled "Screwed Lenya is our President!" (Lenia Ebnutyi—Nash Prezident), one of the members donned a blue bucket on his head, signifying the blue signal flashers atop police and bureaucratic vehicles, and crossed a dangerous section of Moscow's Tverskaia Boulevard.[36] Another action entitled "Palace Revolution" ("Dvortsovyi Perevorot"), staged by Voina against police corruption, saw the overturning of police cars throughout St. Petersburg in May 2010.[37] Oleg Vorotnikov, one of the leaders of Voina, proclaimed, "We located the pivot point and overturned the entire cop world. . . . We showed what is necessary to lead the reforms of the Ministry of Garbage Affairs (*My nashli tochku opory i perevernuli ves' musorskii mir. . . . My pokazali, kak nado provodit' reform ministerstva musorskikh del*).[38] Voina's message was clear, as Moscow-based journalist Danila Rozanov writes: there is "a more radical alternative to the police reform recently put forward by the Interior Ministry."[39]

Voina has received a great deal of media coverage since their June 14, 2010 "action," entitled "Dick in Captivity of the FSB" ("KHUI v PLENU u FSB)," described as an assertion of power of the "unconquerable Russian phallus" (*nepobedimogo russkogo fallosa*).[40] These actions, while radically different from Prigov's less confrontational Policeman poems, fulfill a similar

purpose—confronting state ideology in its trumped-up, grandiose nonreal-
ity, and promoting social dialogue through street art. Early in Voina's history
these actions were met with little attention from the authorities. More recently,
however, Voina has become increasingly ruthless, critical, and less respectful
of state authority. Voina protested recent abuses of police power in Russia by
setting fire to a police truck on New Year's Eve, "devoting their 'fire gift' to
Russian political prisoners."[41] Direct confrontations between Voina and Russian authorities in recent years and months have led to the frequent arrest of
the collective's members, especially Oleg Vorotnikov and Leonid Nikolaev.[42]
The authorities' actions taken against Voina led to the understanding of the
current state of Russian politics as fundamentally opposed to radical, politically critical, and socially relevant art.

The diversity and breadth of media coverage paid to these art collectives
and their current relations with the government necessitates further exploration of their projects. Voina in particular achieved worldwide acclaim
and support from the art community for its actions, evidenced by numerous awards and participation in art exhibits.[43] The group's influence was so
far-reaching, in fact, that it inspired a worldwide solidarity movement entitled "VOINA Wanted," which supports socially and politically relevant art
and artists, as well as Russia's political prisoners, who have been persecuted
for their actions.[44]

Pussy Riot: Rights contra Rites

The feminist punk rock collective Pussy Riot is perhaps the best-known
target of the Russian government and police forces. Like Voina, this collective
thrived on staging impromptu, unregistered public performances in unautho-
rized locations throughout Moscow.[45] The collective's structure and identity is
similar to that of Voina, because a number of Pussy Riot's members previously
made up the Moscow wing of Voina.[46] The collective was founded in September 2011 after Putin announced his decision to seek a third presidential term.
Pussy Riot member "Serafima" proclaimed that "at that point, we realized that
this country needs a militant, punk-feminist, street band that will rip through
Moscow's streets and squares, mobilize public energy against the evil crooks of
the Putinist junta and enrich the Russian cultural and political opposition."[47]
Like their fellow artists of Chto delat' and Voina, Pussy Riot exploits the revolutionary potential of urban spaces and the heavily guarded monuments to
Russia's past, in hopes of fundamentally transforming the relations of power
in Russia through grand displays of musical protest.[48]

Clad in their signature colorful dresses, tights, and balaclavas, Pussy Riot made headlines worldwide for their February 21, 2012, performance of their "punk prayer," "Mother of God, Chase Putin Out!" (*Bogoroditsa, Putina progoni*) in Moscow's Cathedral of Christ the Savior.[49] The choice of venue was deliberate: "Putin was next to God," and Patriarch Kirill had given Putin's election campaign his blessing, confirming suspicions that the Church and the State were reliable allies. Pussy Riot's works speak out against the culture industry and spectacle of governance, which, in the words of philosophers Max Horkheimer and Theodor Adorno, "perpetually cheats its consumers of what it perpetually promises."[50] Pussy Riot would make its stand against State-Church corruption from within, as they had intended at Lobnoye Mesto on Red Square.[51]

Pussy Riot's performance was promptly shut down by church officials— most likely the result of a leak from one of their collaborators. Member "Kat" (Ekaterina Samutsevich) was removed by a security guard before the group made it to the platform at the front of the cathedral. The unedited video recording was poor, but unmasked Kat could easily be identified by authorities. The edited video was synched with the audio and published on YouTube and a number of other social media sites by 7:00 p.m. that same evening with a description: "During Morning Prayer today, I realized what we need to ask of the Mother of God and how to do it so that something might finally change in our spiritually bereft land. . . . Since peaceful demonstrations give no immediate result despite being hundreds of thousands strong, we will address Mother of God herself before Easter and ask her to get rid of Putin as soon as possible."[52]

Pussy Riot's message was spread worldwide via these media, and support of the collective's efforts grew within the international community.[53] The performance was symbolic on a number of levels. Reminiscent of Voina's "Cop in a Priest's Cassock," the "Mother of God, Chase Putin Out" exposes the transformation of the Russian Orthodox Church into an organ of the Russian Federation's security services:

> Черная ряса, золотые погоны
> Все прихожане ползут на поклоны
> Призрак свободы на небесах
> Гей-прайд отправлен в Сибирь в кандалах
> Глава КГБ, их главный святой
> Ведет протестующих в СИЗО под конвой
> Чтобы Святейшего не оскорбить
> Женщинам нужно рожать и любить

Патриарх Гундяй верит в Путина
Лучше бы в Бога, сука, верил
Пояс девы не заменит митингов—
На протестах с нами Приснодева Мария!

— — —

Black robes, gold epaulettes,
All parishioners crawl on their knees
The illusion of freedom's gone to the heavens,
Gay Pride sent to Siberia in chains
Head of the KGB, their sacred boss,
Guides the protesters to the convoy of prison vans
So you don't upset His Holiness,
Women should stick to making love and babies.
Patriarch Gundyai [Kirill Gundyaev] believes in Putin
Better if you believed in God, you son of a bitch [*suka*]!
The Virgin's Girdle can't replace the protests—
Join with us in protest ever-virgin Mary![54]

Pussy Riot insists that their protest was strictly political, and criticisms lob-
bied against the Church are not made on the basis of religion, but rather
because of its role in Putin's system of governance.[55] Repression of Russian
citizens' rights continues, driven by homophobia and the perpetuation
of antiquated gender roles of the "traditional patriarchal family, in which
women play a secondary, subordinate role."[56] Pussy Riot explains that "we, as
feminists, are on the altar because women are traditionally not allowed there.
The Mother of God, for example, would not have been able to stand at the
altar."[57] In an interview conducted after her release from prison, Samutsevich
reiterated the power of art and of political artists, and explained the purpose
of Pussy Riot's work:

> [The "Punk Prayer"] was a work of contemporary art, a type of political ges-
> ture. We believe that *art must be political*, must address the problems of the
> country, social issues, and that's essentially what our work was about . . . you
> see that television is openly turning people into zombies, openly provides dis-
> information about what is going on in the world. You can see that the news
> shows are just making things up, that what they say has no connection with
> reality. And if you see all this, you understand that something is wrong and
> you begin thinking actively.[58]

The collective urges its listeners to fight for the civil liberties of all Russian citizens, rather than complacently leading their lives by the rites of Putinism.

Three members of the collective, Nadezhda Tolokonnikova, Maria Alyokhina, and Ekaterina Samutsevich, were arrested in early March 2012 for "hooliganism motivated by religious hatred."[59] Claims of "moral damage" to innocent parishioners and witness opinions made up most lines of questioning.[60] Tolokonnikova, Alyokhina, and Samutsevich were held without bail in a pre-trial detention facility and given little time to familiarize themselves with the case and their defense attorneys' strategies. The first day of hearings established a tone and pattern that recalled Soviet political trials "repeated as farce": the judge as bureaucrat, speeding the trial along at all costs so as to issue a preordained verdict, and the defense attorneys working tirelessly within the confines of a meaningful and respected body of law to establish innocence while distancing themselves from their clients and using the court as a stage of their own for political declarations.[61]

> The three young women were being represented by three lawyers who were more political activists than classic attorneys: they seemed to have given up before the trial had even begun. Instead of lawyering, they tweeted. Instead of trying to force the court, which wouldn't allow a single defense witness, back into the strictures of legal procedure, they went for theatrics.[62]

The Pussy Rioters would interject from the confines of their unventilated Plexiglas cube, but they were quickly silenced by the judge. The court had made its decision, but chose to lead them on, as the group's defense lawyer Mark Feigin summarized, "to lick the judge's boots, to humiliate themselves, to cry, to give the state the opportunity to rip them to shreds. Nothing has changed since the Soviet period: a defendant can hope for forgiveness, for humanity, only once he is destroyed."[63]

The three Pussy Rioters handled their closing statements as if they were their last piece of opposition art. They were biting, referential, and emotionally charged—like symphonic variations on a punk theme—and their sincerity reverberated through the courtroom as they declared that they were "not afraid of lies and fictions and of poorly coded deception in the verdict of this so-called court, because all you can do is take away my so-called freedom, the only sort that exists in the Russian Federation."[64] In her closing statements Samutsevich remarked that "Christ the Savior Cathedral has begun to be openly used as a flashy backdrop for the politics of the security forces, which are the main source of political power in Russia."[65] She asked why Putin felt it necessary to exploit the Orthodox Church when he and his circle of confidants could have employed their corporate strength, their "menacing police system," and the "obedient judicial system" to carry out their plans to dominate the Russian public. Samutsevich raised doubts about his effectiveness as president. In her opinion, Russian citizens should not have been so easily persuaded to give Putin a third chance due to the numerous failings of his government:[66]

> It was then that [Putin] felt the need for more persuasive, transcendent guar-
> antees of his long tenure at the pinnacle of power. It was then that it became
> necessary to make use of the aesthetic of the Orthodox religion, which is his-
> torically associated with the heyday of Imperial Russia, where power came not
> from earthly manifestations such as democratic elections and civil society, but
> from God Himself.[67]

Samutsevich's reply was dependent upon the various relations of power supporting the system of governance in the Russian Federation today. Pussy Riot's
performance and their closing statements exposed the gaps in the Russian
system, one that has failed to create an ideology that masks police control, one
of corporate strength backed by a strong and ominous police force operating
with the blessing of the Orthodox Church.

The verdict was handed down on August 17, 2012: "In sum, and in light of
the danger to society caused by the offense committed, as well as the circumstances of the crime and its goals and motives, the court believes that justice
can be served and the defendants can be reformed only if they are sentenced
to time behind bars and are ordered to actually serve this time."[68] A sentence of
two years was decreed. The Pussy Rioters appealed their sentence in October
2012. Samutsevich fired her lawyer, Violeta Volkova, and took a new defense
attorney, Irina Khrunova. During the appellate hearing, Khrunova stated that
the actions of the "punk prayer" did not constitute a crime, but "she added,
Kat had not even taken part in the actions the court had deemed criminal:
'She did not jump, pray, or sing.'"[69]

Khrunova was right. Samutsevich had been removed by church security
guards before she could reach the altar. The result of this summation, however,
proved to be a double-edged sword. Samutsevich's sentence was suspended
after she pleaded partially guilty to the charges of hooliganism, but Khrunova's
statement implied that a crime had been committed, and that Tolokonnikova
and Alyokhina were guilty of it. Julia Ioffe of *The New Republic* concludes
that while Khrunova did her job by freeing her client, "she also broke up the
group's unity and blocked off the one path to redemption that the group actually had: *ignoring the court's proceedings and denying its legitimacy.*"[70]

With a dose of hindsight, one might argue that denying the legitimacy of the Moscow High Court should have been the defense team's strategy all along. It is more likely, however, that punishment or incarceration was inevitable for the three Pussy Riot members. The Russian system has changed very little since the 1980s; therefore, punitive punishment, whether a probationary sentence or two years served in penal colonies IK-14 in the Republic of Mordovia, and IK-28 in Berezniki, Perm Krai,[71] is a simple way for the state to divide and conquer the opposition and, more importantly, to deter other would-be activists from following suit. On December 23, 2013, the State Duma granted Tolokonnikova and Alyokhina amnesty. They called the move a hoax and a public relations stunt, but no one seemed to care; Putin and Russia received the positive international attention they hoped for while putting the finishing touches on 2014 Winter Olympics host city Sochi.

Everything had changed by the time Tolokonnikova and Alyokhina were released from their respective penal colonies. The government had passed laws banning protests and "nontraditional" sexual relations, and it continues to curb press freedoms. The opposition movement has concurrently lost its vigor and is dominated by apathy.[72] Tolokonnikova and Alyokhina have hung up their balaclavas—except for a brief demonstration at the 2014 Winter Games[73]—and are now leading a prisoner rights nongovernmental organization, *Zona Prava* (Zone of Rights, Law Zone) and its online journalism project *MediaZona*.[74] Based on their experiences in prison, they are seeking real legislative change that will improve conditions and protect the rights of those incarcerated in Russia's prison camps. Their campaign has experienced its share of backlash from its beginnings in Pussy Riot. Tolokonnikova and Alyokhina were attacked in Nizhny Novgorod on March 5, 2014, by six *titushki* (provocateurs paid and supported by the police or pro-government forces) with medical paint after their trip to prison colony IK-2 the same day. The attack was likely sanctioned by the *Glavnoe upravlenie po protivodeistviiu ekstremizmu MVD* (Main Department for Combating Extremism of the Ministry of Internal Affairs, or "Center 'E,'" as it is sometimes known).[75] Perhaps nothing has changed after all.

Conclusion

Art and protest are kindred acts of self-expression. Through systematic practices the artist and the protester challenge their spectators in an attempt to persuade them to reconsider the rules and institutions that govern their lives. This is an asymmetrical relationship, however, as the amount of energy put into a work of art or a protest movement is often unrequited by its audiences. Performative art and protest movements continue to arise globally despite the absence of positive public reception. At risk of losing control, power institutions are quick to dispatch their security forces to quell dissent, silence protesters, and establish order under the pretense of law, sometimes by means of violence. The government disguises these measures in the language of national security: quelling perspectives that are critical of the government and suppressing those actions and actors that are viewed as harbingers of sociopolitical destabilization. These threats have led to the repatriation of military-style policing methods and security structures to urban centers, which have become "key [sites] in the militarization of security and law enforcement."[76]

The art and actions of Chto delat', Voina, and Pussy Riot challenged Russian citizens to join them in their public criticism and transformation of the Russian political system. The success of Russia's opposition movement, however, is contingent on the public's responsiveness to their cause: if the public is responsive to these artistic sociopolitical projects, then opportunities to transform the system could materialize; if the public is swayed by the system, however, then, no matter how vocal and widespread the movement may seem, the menacing security forces and governmental structures will continue to oppress, defeat, and incarcerate Russia's discontents.

Notes

1. It would have been impossible to write this chapter without the support of several individuals and organizations that provided their expertise and assistance. Prof. Edith W. Clowes challenged me to take up this topic and provided guidance throughout the research and writing of the earliest versions of this chapter. Prof. Clowes and Prof. Shelly Jarrett Bromberg were both exceptionally patient and worked with me by e-mail to finish this work. Comments by anonymous reviewers helped greatly to improve this chapter. I gratefully acknowledge that the research and writing of this publication was partially funded and completed with US Army Research Office support through the KU Ft. Leavenworth FMSO-CREES Research Assistantship Program. I am grateful to Mr. Ray Finch at FMSO for his expertise on the present media environment in Russia and its effects on state-citizen discourse.

2. Henri Lefebvre, *The Urban Revolution* (Minneapolis: University of Minnesota Press, 2003), 152–59.

3. Ibid., 19.

4. Masha Gessen, *Words Will Break Cement: The Passion of Pussy Riot* (New York: Riverhead, 2014), 288.

5. Maria Alyokhina, Nadezhda Tolokonnikova, and Yekaterina Samutsevich, "Pussy Riot Closing Statements," *n+1 Magazine*, Aug. 13, 2012, accessed Oct. 10, 2012, http://nplusonemag.com/pussy-riot-closing-statements.

6. Matthias Schepp, "Interview with Pussy Riot Leader: 'I Love Russia, But I Hate Putin,'" trans. Ella Ornstein, *Der Spiegel*, Sept. 3, 2012, accessed Oct. 10, 2012, http://www.spiegel.de/international/world/spiegel-interview-with-pussy-riot-activist-nadezhda-tolokonnikova-a-853546-2.html.

7. The transformation of postsocialist policing is examined at length in "Reflections on Policing in Post-Communist Europe," Elisabeth Sieca-Kozlowski et al., eds., *The Journal of Power Institutions in Post-Soviet Societies*, no. 2 (2005), http://pipss.revues.org/271. For a general study of post-9/11 policing methods and political violence, see *Violent Geographies: Fear, Terror, and Political Violence*, ed. Derek Gregory and Allan Pred (New York: Routledge, 2007).

8. The art and actions of Chto delat', Voina, Pussy Riot, and other post-Soviet artists are intended to reach ordinary Russian citizens, with the intent of triggering broader revolutionary dialogues between the public and the government. See Gregory Feifer, "Pussy Riot and Russia's Radical Artistic Tradition," *Global Post*, Aug. 17, 2012, accessed Oct. 10, 2012, http://www.globalpost.com/dispatches/globalpost-blogs/chatter/pussy-riot-russia-Putin-sentence; Alexander Rahr, "Pussy Riot, bor'ba tsivilizatsii i revolutsiia" [Pussy Riot, Clash of Civilizations and Revolution], *Izvestiia*, Aug. 8, 2012, accessed Oct. 10, 2012, http://izvestia.ru/news/532463#ixzz232uSjxLr.

9. David Riff and Dmitry Vilensky, "About group: Chto delat?,"*Chto Delat Online Journal*, accessed June 24, 2011, http://chtodelat.org/index.php?option=com_content&view=article&id=192%3Achto-delat&catid=91%3Afront&Itemid=331&lang=en.

10. See Jeffrey O. G. Ogbar, *Hip-Hop Revolution: The Culture and Politics of Rap* (Lawrence: University Press of Kansas, 2007); Adam Krims, *Rap Music and the Poetics of Identity* (New York: Cambridge University Press, 2000); Brian Whitmore, "Rock Against the Vertical," *Radio Free Europe/Radio Liberty*, March 9, 2010, accessed June 24, 2011, http:/rferl.org/content/Rock_Against_The_Vertical/1979019.html.

11. Gregory Sholette, *Dark Matter: Art and Politics in the Age of Enterprise Culture* (New York: Pluto, 2011).

12. Gary Shove and Patrick Potter, eds., *Banksy: You Are an Acceptable Level of Threat* (Berkeley: Carpet Bombing Culture, 2012).

13. Both collectives consider themselves leftist with regard to political theory, but they differ in practice. Chto delat' is interested in the practical emancipatory potential of leftist thinking, whereas Voina ascribes to radical leftist and anarchist demonstrations against the authorities. See Chto delat', "A Declaration on Politics, Knowledge, and Art," *Chto Delat Online Journal*, accessed Oct. 12, 2012, http://chtodelat.org/index.php?option=com_content&view=article&id=766%3Aa-declaration-on-politics-knowledge-and-art&catid=212%3Adeclaration&Itemid=357&lang=en; Voina, "Kto takaia Voina?" [Who is Voina?], accessed April 24, 2011, http://www.free-voina.org/about; Voina, "Tseli i zadachi gruppy VOINA v period 2008–2010," [Goals and Objectives of Voina, 2008–2010], accessed April 24, 2011, http://www.free-voina.org/about.

14. Voina, "O Voine" [About Voina], accessed April 24, 2011, http:/www.free-voina.org/about.

15. Gessen, *Words Will Break Cement*, 199.

16. Graeme B. Robertson, "Managing Society: Protest, Civil Society, and Regime in Putin's Russia," *Slavic Review* 68, no. 3 (Fall 2009): 537.

17. Ibid., 573. See also Graeme B. Robertson, *The Politics of Protest in Hybrid Regimes: Managing Dissent in Post-Communist Russia* (New York: Cambridge University Press, 2011); Sarah Oates, "The Neo-Soviet Model of the Media," *Europe-Asia Studies* 59, no. 8 (Dec. 2007): 1279–97.

18. For an examination of the history of satire, parody, and Russian laughing culture, see Karen L. Ryan-Hayes, *Contemporary Russian Satire: A Genre Study* (Cambridge: Cambridge University Press, 1995); Janet G. Tucker, ed., *Against the Grain: Parody, Satire, and Intertextuality in Russian Literature* (Bloomington, IN: Slavica, 2002); Lesley Milne, ed., *Reflective Laughter: Aspects of Humour in Russian Culture* (London: Anthem, 2004).

19. D. A. Prigov, "Organi vlasti: iz klassicheskogo Prigova," in *Napisannoe s 1975 po 1989*, accessed Oct. 10, 2012, http://modernpoetry.ru/main/dmitriy-aleksandrovich-prigov-napisannoe-s-1975-po-1989.

20. My translation. Original Russian text of the poem: Militsaner vot terrorista vstretil,/i govorit emu: Ty terrorist/ disgarmonichnyi dukhom anarkist/a ia est' pravil'nost' na etom svete.//A terrorist: No voliu ia liubliu/Ona tebe—ne mestnaia svoboda/Uidi, ne stoi u stolbovogo vkhoda/Ne posmotriu

chto voruzhen—ub'iu!.//Militsaner zhe otvechal kak vlast'/Imushchii: Ty ubit' menia ne mozhesh'/Plot' porazish', porvesh' mundir i kozhu/No obraz moi moshchnei, chem tvoia strast'. See ibid.

21. Prigov casts the Policeman as a divine, godlike figure throughout "Apotheosis of the Police-man." For a number of readings and interpretations of the Soviet Policeman's religiosity, see Evgeny Dobrenko, "Socialist Realism, a Postscriptum: Dmitrii Prigov and the Aesthetic Limits of Sots-Art," in *Endquote: Sots-Art Literature and Soviet Grand Style*, ed. Marina Balina, Nancy Condee, and Evgeny Dobrenko (Evanston, IL: Northwestern University Press, 2000), 77–106; Philip Metres, "The End(s) of Russian Poetry: An Interview with Dmitry Prigov," July 18, 2007, accessed April 26, 2011, http://behindthelinespoetry.blogspot.com/2007/07/ends-of-russian-poetry-interview-with.html; Groys, *The Total Art of Stalinism*, 95–99.

22. For a photo of Prigov in character as the Policeman, see Yelena Fedotova, "Dmitri Prigov: 'Great Russian Poet', Postmodern Artist, Incarcerated 'Madman,'" *Open Democracy*, July 8, 2011, accessed October 12, 2012, http://www.opendemocracy.net/od-russia/yelena-fedotova/dmitri-prigov-%E2%80%9Cgreat-russian-poet%E2%80%9D-postmodern-artist-incarcerated-%E2%80%9Cmadman%E2%80%9D.

23. Voina, "Kto takaia Voina?" [Who are Voina?], accessed April 24, 2011, http://free-voina.org/about.

24. Chto delat, "Chto delat?" [What Is to Be Done?], *Chto Delat Online Journal*, accessed April 16, 2011, http://chtodelat.org/index.php?option=com_content&view=article&id=192%3Achto-delat&catid=91%3Afront&Itemid=331&lang=en.

25. Ibid.

26. Alexei Penzin and Dmitri Vilensky, "O pol'ze iskusstva" [What Is the Use of Art?], *O pol'ze iskusstva*, issue 01-25 (March 2009), accessed April 7, 2011, http://chtodelat.org/index.php?option=com_content&view=article&id=557&3Aalexei-penzin-dmitri-vilensky&catid=204%3A01-25-what-is-the-use-of-art&itemid=400&lang=ru.

27. David Riff, "When Art Once Again Becomes Useful," in "What Is the Use of Art?," supplement, *Chto Delat Online Journal*, issue 01-25 (March 2009), accessed April 7, 2011, http://chtodelat.org/images/pdfs/24_use-value.pdf.

28. See Morozov, LOLcats chapter; Andrew Keen, *Digital Vertigo: How Today's Online Social Revolution Is Dividing, Diminishing and Disorienting Us* (New York: St. Martin's, 2012).

29. Riff, "When Art Once Again Becomes Useful."

30. Ibid.

31. Dmitry Vilensky, "In Defense of Representation," *In Defense of Representation*, issue 34, March 2012, accessed May 20, 2012, http://issuu.com/streetuniver/docs/representation_full_engl.

32. Ibid.

33. For Egovora and Vilensky's commentary, see http://chtodelat.org/index.php?option=com_content&view=article&id=1029&Itemid=478&lang=en. For a video of the performance, see http://vimeo.com/40309012.

34. Gessen, *Words Will Break Cement*, 58.

35. Alex Plutser-Sarno, "Cop in a *Priest's* Cassock," *The VOINA Art-Group ("War"). Actions 2007-2012*, July 3, 2008, accessed June 24, 2011, http://plucer.livejournal.com/266853.html; video at http://www.viddler.com/explore/Lord/videos/1/. See also Metres, "The End(s) of Russian Poetry: An Interview with Dmitry Prigov."

36. Voina, "Aktsii Voiny: 'Lenia Yobnutyi—Nash Prezident'" [Actions of Voina: "Screwed Lenya—Our President!"], May 22, 2010, accessed April 24, 2011, http//free-voina.org/actions. A video of the action can be viewed at http://www.youtube.com/watch?v=w0XdKh91k20&feature=player_detailpage.

37. Video at http://www.youtube.com//watch?v=Ue_Wd2AjKAI&feature=player_detailpage.

38. Alex Plutser-Sarno, "Svobodnaia pressa: 'Voina oprokinula militsiiu na kryshu!'" [Press Freedom: 'Voina Turned the Police onto Their Roof!'], accessed May 30, 2012, http://plucer.livejournal.com/333577.html. Vorotnikov's statement is a clever play on words. The Ministry of Internal Affairs is known as *Ministerstvo vnutrennikh del*, but Vorotnikov refers to them with the adjectival form of "garbage" (Ministerstvo *musorskikh* del). *Musor* is also close to the term *hussar* (*gusar*), the

light cavalrymen of Hungarian origin. In this sense, *musar* can be thought of by the English terms *cop* or, more derogatory, *pig*. My thanks to Prof. Irina Six for elucidating the finer points of Soviet/Russian slang.

39. Danila Rozanov, "Voina: Artists at War," *Open Democracy*, February 18, 2011, accessed April 17, 2011, http://www.opendemocracy.net/od-russia/danila-rozanov/voina-artists-at-war.

40. Voina, "Aktsii Voiny: 'KHUI v PLENU u FSB'" [Actions of Voina "Dick in Captivity of the FSB"], June 14, 2010, accessed April 24, 2011, http://free-voina.org/actions.

41. Anna Nemtsova, "Russian Protesters Use Art as Act of War," *The Daily Beast*, Jan. 6, 2012, accessed May 20, 2012, http://www.thedailybeast.com/articles/2012/01/06/russian-protesters-use-art-as-act-of-war.html. Voina also documented their performance and posted pictures, videos, and commentary about the action on LiveJournal. See plucer.livejournal.com/531761.html#cutid1.

42. Voina, "Arest Voiny" [Voina's Arrest], accessed April 23, 2011, http://free-voina.org/arrest.

43. Tom Parfitt, "Voina, Art Group Backed by Banksy, Wins Russian Prize for Erection," *The Guardian*, accessed June 6, 2011, http://www.guardian.co.uk/world/2011/apr/08/voina-banksy-penis-prize.

44. Dmitrii Volchek, "'Voina' na Karlovom mostu" ["Voina" on the Charles Bridge], *Radio Svoboda*, accessed Dec. 4, 2011, http://www.svobodanews.ru/content/feature/24380544.html.

45. Any public march, meeting, or demonstration must be registered beforehand; otherwise the organizers face hefty fines or jail time according to Article 20.2, "Violation of the established order of organizing or holding a meeting, rally, demonstration, march, or picketing," of the Federal Law No. 65-FZ. "Amendments to the Code of the Russian Federation on Administrative Offences and the Federal Law 'On meetings, rallies, demonstrations, marches, and picketing,'" approved on June 8, 2012. For the full text of the law, see http://graph.document.kremlin.ru/page.aspx?1615079. For a brief summary of the law, see "Putin podpisal zakon o mitingakh [Putin signs law on meetings], *Rossiiskaia gazeta*, June 9, 2012, accessed Oct. 14, 2012, http://www.rg.ru/2012/06/08/mitingi.html.

46. Tom Peter, "Photographer's Blog: Witness to Pussy Riot's Activist Beginnings," Reuters, Aug. 16, 2012, accessed Oct. 10, 2012, http://www.reuters.com/article/2012/08/16/us-blog-pussy-riots-idUSBRE87F0PW20120816.

47. Max Read, "The Know-Nothing's Guide to Pussy Riot, the Realest Punks Alive," *Gawker.com*, Aug. 2, 2012, accessed Oct. 10, 2012, http://gawker.com/5930925/the-know+nothings-guide-to-pussy-riot-the-realest-punks-alive; Henry Langston, "Meeting Pussy Riot," *Vice.com*, Feb. 2012, accessed Oct. 10, 2012, http://www.vice.com/read/A-Russian-Pussy-Riot.

48. Gessen, *Words Will Break Cement*, 103–107.

49. Pussy Riot documented the performance on their Livejournal. See http://pussy-riot.livejournal.com/12442.html (in Russian). A video of the performance can be viewed at http://www.youtube.com/watch?v=GCasuaAczKY.

50. Max Horkheimer and Theodor W. Adorno, *Dialectic of Enlightenment: Philosophical Fragments*, ed. Gunzelin Schmid Noerr, trans. Edmund Jephcott (Stanford, CA: Stanford University Press, 2002), 111.

51. Site of the group's January 20, 2012, performance, "Putin Has Pissed Himself" (*Putin zassal*). Of course, performing "within the walls" of the Kremlin is nearly impossible. Two hundred yards away would have to suffice. See Gessen, *Words Will Break Cement*, 103–107, 115. Video of "Putin Has Pissed Himself" available at https://www.youtube.com/watch?v=9OKPeMWXdmo.

52. Gessen, *Words Will Break Cement*, 121.

53. Numerous artists, musicians, and political figures have shown their support for Pussy Riot throughout their trial and detention, including Björk, Madonna, Stephen Fry, Faith No More, The Beastie Boys, and Red Hot Chili Peppers. One hundred twenty-one members of the German Bundestag sent a letter to the Russian ambassador to Germany, Vladimir Grinin, in support of Pussy Riot during their pretrial detention. See http://en.rian.ru/russia/2012/0808/175059708.html.

54. My (literal) translation of selections from the song. For a more poetic interpretation of the "punk prayer," see Carol Rumens, "Pussy Riot's Punk Prayer Is Pure Protest Poetry," *The Guardian*, Aug. 20, 2012, accessed Oct. 12, 2012, http://www.guardian.co.uk/books/2012/aug/20/pussy-riot-punk-prayer-lyrics.

55. Pussy Riot attacks Patriarch Kirill Gundyayev for being a "famous chekist" due to his ties to the Soviet KGB and the strengthening of church-state relations. For the lyrics and a discussion of the performance, see Pussy Riot, "Pank-moleben 'Bogoroditsa Putina progoni' v Khrame Khrista Spasitelia."

56. Ibid.

57. Ibid.

58. Emphasis added. "Freed Pussy Riot Member Says 'Art Must Be Political,'" *Radio Free Europe/Radio Liberty*, Oct. 12, 2012, accessed Oct. 12, 2012, http://www.rferl.org/content/interview-freed-pussy-riot-members-says-art-must-be-political/24737623.html.

59. "Police Open Criminal Probe into 'Punk Prayer' at Christ the Savior Catheral," *RIA Novosti*, February 26, 2012, accessed Oct. 14, 2012, http://en.rian.ru/russia/20120226/171537723.html.

60. Gessen, *Words Will Break Cement*, 176.

61. Ibid., 168–70.

62. Julia Ioffe, "Is Pussy Riot Breaking Up?" *The New Republic*, Oct. 10, 2012, accessed Aug. 29, 2014, http://www.newrepublic.com/blog/plank/108422/pussy-riot-breaking.

63. Gessen, *Words Will Break Cement*, 193–94.

64. Quoted in Gessen, 216.

65. Quoted in "Pussy Riot Closing Statements."

66. Samutsevich cites the submarine Kursk incident and the bombing of civilians as explicit examples of Putin's failures as president.

67. "Pussy Riot Closing Statements."

68. Gessen, *Words Will Break Cement*, 221–22.

69. Ibid., 242–43.

70. Emphasis added. Ioffe, "Is Pussy Riot Breaking Up?"

71. The locations of the respective women's penal colonies in which Tolokonnikova and Alyokhina served twenty-one months of their two-year sentences.

72. Lindsay Zoladz, "Interviews: Pussy Riot's Nadya Tolokonnikova and Masha Alyokhina," *Pitchfork*, April 10, 2014, accessed Aug. 29, 2014, http://pitchfork.com/features/interviews/9374-nadya-tolokonnikova-and-masha-alyokhina-of-pussy-riot/.

73. "*Putin nauchit tebia liubit' Rodinu*" [Putin Will Teach You to Love the Motherland]. The video can be viewed online at https://www.youtube.com/watch?v=gjI0KYl9gWs.

74. See http://www.zona.media/ (in Russian).

75. Tolokonnikova and Alyokhina's statements as well as video of the attack can be viewed at http://www.zonaprava.info/blog/2014/3/6/napadenie.

76. Derek Gregory, "Police/military/city," Geographical Imaginations, Sept. 26, 2012, accessed Sept. 28, 2012, http://geographicalimaginations.com/2012/09/26/policemilitarycity/. For a comprehensive study of military security structures in everyday urban spaces, see Stephen Graham, *Cities Under Siege: The New Military Urbanism* (London: Verso, 2010).

PART IV

Legacies of Empire and Shifting North-South Communities

Brief Introduction

For at least fifty years researchers have asked why democratic reform of authoritarian regimes often fails, citing among the major reasons for weak reform the powerful "socioeconomic, institutional, and cultural legacies of authoritarianism."[1] To authoritarianism the authors in this part of *Area Studies in the Global Age* are compelled to add colonialism and its legacy of socially segregationist and economically exploitative attitudes and behaviors on the part of the more powerful postcolonial partner with regard to the less economically and politically developed partner. In terms of place, these legacies frequently are situated in power relations between a powerful northern partner (former colonizer) and an exploited, more dependent, and less-educated southern partner (former colonized community).

The three chapters that comprise the legacies section of *Area Studies in the Global Age* address a number of issues in three parts of the world—east Africa, Central Asia, and South America and the Caribbean. One chapter treats the legacy of colonialism at the local, urban level; the second deals with the legacy of earlier hegemony at the level of intergovernmental relations; and the third chapter treats the imperial legacy at the national level. Sarah Smiley's chapter on neighborhood divisions in Dar es Salaam, Tanzania, uses mental maps sketched by residents of various parts of the city to show the imprint of a residual, psychologically embedded segregation at the neighborhood level, a legacy of colonial divisions. Smiley investigates the interaction between community, identity, and place for three groups of Dar es Salaam residents: mainly European and American expatriates or migrant professionals, more settled Tanzanians of Asian descent, and Tanzanians of African descent. Her data draw from archival research on colonial city planning; 416 surveys, interviews, participant observation; and 151 mental mapping exercises conducted among the city's residents.

In his chapter on US-Latin American relations since 2000, Walt Vanderbush
considers post-2000 Caribbean and South American efforts to create an economic community independent of the United States, designed to confront
perceived US arrogance about its leadership role and its perceived assumptions about the economic passivity and dependency of countries to its south.
This chapter examines US–Latin American relations through the lens of two
contrasting plans for the Americas. The first is an exclusively Latin American
plan spearheaded by a former Venezuelan president, the late Hugo Chávez,
and enacted by a number of Latin American nations. This plan excludes the
United States and Canada. The second is the US-led plan for a community
of all the countries of the hemisphere, excluding Cuba, to move toward a
hemispheric economic community reaching from Alaska in the far north
to Argentina in the far south. For his treatment, Vanderbush uses the form
of a traditional "case study," concentrating on Brazil, Cuba, and Venezuela.
His methodology relies on an "analytical historical" approach and rhetorical
analysis that draws material from the open press and published speeches by
government leaders.

Reuel Hanks's chapter on the emergence of national narrative in Uzbekistan, a post-Soviet Central Asian country, brings to the table a different sort
of problem from those treated in part I ("Reclaiming the National Narrative"), now at the level of state leadership. Hanks deals with one example
of the competition among several newly created states to claim the same
historical-mythical material, each for its own narrative of national identity.
In 1991 five Central Asian countries sprang from the Soviet republics that
Soviet dictator Joseph Stalin carved out of the old Turkestan—Kazakhstan,
Kyrgyzstan, Tajikistan, Turkmenistan, and Uzbekistan. In the two decades
since independence, all of these states have sought to establish their legitimacy through the elevation of alleged "national heroes" to mythic status.
In Uzbekistan, the foremost figure in the national pantheon is Amir Timur,
known more commonly in Western scholarship as Tamerlane. Basing his
study on the concept of the "ethnie," the community that, in brief summary,
shares a common myth, ancestry, and connection to territory, he argues that
these peoples, whose territory was so recently turned into countries, comprise a form of "ethnie." Of particular interest here is the conceptualization of
place as "homeland," which, as Hanks shows, is complicated by the Stalin-era
division of Turkestan. Whatever identity may have existed before the 1920s
was vague; the division of this territory created the motivation among each
of its various populations to find an identifying narrative of self. Contrary
to older, more familiar formations of national identity, this experience was
motivated by Soviet nationalities policy and territorialization of particular

groups in Turkestan. Hanks shows the process of building an Uzbek identity through strongly ideologized, Soviet-era "archaeological," "historical," and "ethnographic" research. In the early twenty-first century the result of this so obviously constructed history-myth and identity has been to buttress the cult of personality of Uzbekistan's dictator, Islom Karimov.

Each of these chapters adds an important dimension to understanding how liminal experiences structure realia of postcolonial community, place, and identity. This quality is true of the legacy of colonial segregation in urban neighborhood divisions as well as the unification of countries tied by language and colonial heritage against the hemispheric superpower. Likewise, the frequently encountered construction of national identity by academics commanded through the offices of the colonizing power and then through continued direction by the dictator of the new state lays bare a liminal quality as communities challenge these forced boundaries with alternative, unofficial identities. Ultimately, as with other contributions in *Area Studies in the Global Age,* these chapters highlight liminal experience as emerging communities articulate a particular place-oriented identity, while also acknowledging the enduring impact of earlier governing orders and ideologies.

Notes

1. Valerie Bunce, "Comparative Democratization: Big and Bounded Generalizations," *Comparative Political Studies* 33 (2000): 709.

Community, Identity, and Space in Dar es Salaam, Tanzania

Introduction

Geographers recognize that places have multiple meanings. What one person views as a safe place may be a place of fear to another, and what one person views as comfortable may be uncomfortable to another.[1] Dar es Salaam, Tanzania, is no exception. The various communities who live in this diverse and cosmopolitan city perceive and understand its spaces in vastly different ways. Thus, Dar es Salaam is many things to many people. It is a European town whose skyscrapers and fast-food restaurants would be at home in any British city. It is an Indian town filled with smells of curries and women dressed in saris. It is an African town with the sights, sounds, and energy of informal trading and vibrant street life. In many ways, Dar es Salaam is three segregated cities in one, and it is this complexity that provides an interesting setting for research on community and identity in a socially and spatially segregated city.

This chapter explores the relationship between community, identity, and space for three groups within Dar es Salaam: foreign expatriates, Asians, and Africans. I use the term *expatriate* to refer to a person living outside his or her home country.[2] Geographers use many other terms to refer to these people, including transnational professionals, transnational migrants, privileged migrants, and mobile professionals.[3] The city's Asian community is more accurately called "Tanzanians of Asian Descent" since its people are Tanzanian citizens and most can trace their families' presence in Dar es Salaam back for several generations. The majority are of South Asian descent, particularly from India. By Africans, I refer to black Africans born in Tanzania. These Africans constitute the majority of Dar es Salaam's estimated four million inhabitants.[4] My use of the term community follows Cohen, who suggests that a community refers to a group of people who have something in common with each other, and that this commonality also distinguishes them from other communities.[5] He especially highlights the boundaries of these communities since they encapsulate community identity. Rew and Campbell argue that identity cannot exist in isolation. Rather, identity—whether racial, ethnic, or religious—takes meaning from "the other."[6] German and British colonial policies in Dar es Salaam resulted in the compartmentalization of the city into same/other, us/them, colonizer/colonized spaces. The creation of these bounded and segregated spaces provided expatriates, Asians, and Africans with their distinct identities.

In postcolonial Dar es Salaam these divisions persist, both spatially and socially, even without formal legal policies of segregation. These divides can be attributed in part to the differing socioeconomic status of Dar es Salaam's residents.[7] The coastal areas favored by colonial-era Europeans have exceptionally high rents, making them accessible to many expatriates but inaccessible to most of the city's Africans. The more affordable neighborhoods continue to be those areas created by the colonial government to house the African population far from the European residential areas. As a white American in Dar es Salaam, my place is supposed to be the Msasani Peninsula,[8] an area inhabited by other expatriates. I am out of place anywhere else in the city. (Figure 1 shows the location of Msasani and other selected places in Dar es Salaam.) Thus, I argue, Dar es Salaam is a place where expatriates, Asians, and Africans occupy spatially distinct parts of the city.[9] Spatial segregation certainly has real and tangible impacts on society and everyday life. A clear example of these impacts concerns amenities, because where people live largely determines their service provision. Not all areas of the city receive reliable electricity provision or piped water delivery, and predominantly African areas tend to experience the most frequent power cuts and fewest hours of water service.[10] These patterns of spatial and social segregation were developed and are maintained by ideas of identity and difference.

The following sections demonstrate the imprint of social and spatial segregation that is still visible in the ways that different communities use the city. In this examination of population and place in Dar es Salaam, I first outline my multiple method qualitative approach to this project. Qualitative methods are particularly suited to this project since, as Dwyer and Limb put it, they help researchers "explore some of the complexities of everyday life in order to gain a deeper insight into the processes shaping our social worlds."[11] By combining archival research with surveys, interviews, participant observation, and mental mapping exercises, I attempt to understand life in Dar es Salaam from the perspectives of multiple communities. After this discussion of methodology, I review the history of these three groups and their spatial and social segregation. Finally, I discuss their everyday life patterns and the place of expatriates, Asians, and Africans in contemporary Dar es Salaam. These everyday life

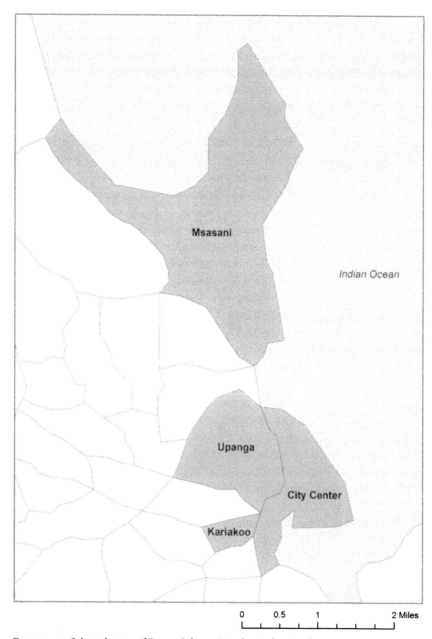

FIGURE 1. Selected areas of Dar es Salaam. Map by Andrea Szell.

activities are essential in understanding identity within the city. As Kong and Yeoh demonstrate, people give meaning to places through their daily lives and experiences, thus helping to define some spaces in Dar es Salaam as expatriate, European, or American and other spaces as Asian or African.[12]

Methodology

My first step in understanding expatriate, Asian, and African life in Dar es Salaam was to conduct archival research. Research at the Tanzania National Archives, and later the British National Archives, helped me understand the evolution of social and spatial segregation in the city. Working at the Tanzanian archives was not without challenges. Lost files, electricity outages, and vague finding aids all contributed to a difficult research environment.[13] Yet ultimately this archival research provided the foundation for this project by helping me understand how and why Dar es Salaam developed as a segregated space and how varying practices of housing construction and the provision of services such as water, sanitation, and electricity contributed to social segregation.

The archival research helped me to structure my qualitative surveys. I collected basic demographic data along with information on the locations of everyday life activities, including workplace, shopping, and entertainment. The survey also included a request that respondents draw a mental map of Dar es Salaam. Ultimately, I surveyed fifty expatriates, forty Asians, and 326 Africans, with forty expatriates, twenty Asians, and ninety-one Africans also drawing mental maps. These figures reflect the population composition of the city, as the vast majority of Dar es Salaam's residents are African. I also conducted follow-up semistructured interviews with a subset of my respondents. A semistructured interview uses preselected questions but allows the interviewer the flexibility to ask additional questions based on the interview's progression. I asked respondents to explain their everyday life patterns and why they chose certain locations for these activities. All of this qualitative research was complemented by my own participant observations in the city. For example, I attended a meeting of the Diplomatic Spouses Group and I socialized with members of the Corona Society, a philanthropic group whose membership is restricted to women living overseas. I observed Asian life, regularly going to an Asian social club and visiting mosques and temples. Since Dar es Salaam is a predominantly African city, I constantly observed African life while moving around the city, buying goods, listening to live music, and socializing at restaurants and clubs.

I identified my respondents in multiple ways. Bradshaw and Stratford propose several types of sampling techniques including "extreme," "typical," "maximum variation," "snowball," "opportunistic," and "convenience," and I consciously used all of these.[14] For example, I remained flexible and allowed unexpected opportunities to improve my research, such as an invitation to tour and eat dinner at a Sikh temple (opportunistic case). I also used my position as an American with access to my embassy to meet other expatriates who eventually became part of my research sample (convenience case). Because survey respondents were selected in these ways, my sample is not random, but the variety of techniques allows for a diverse sample that represents the complexity of Dar es Salaam.

As an American woman, I had a fairly easy time conducting the expatriate portion of this research. I was able to meet potential respondents at the US Embassy, and I was welcomed to social meetings of the Corona Society and the Diplomatic Spouses Group. In fact, the majority of my expatriate respondents came from my connections at those three places, and given the membership of these social groups, most of these respondents were women. My experiences in researching Dar es Salaam's Asian community, however, proved challenging. Some people refused to complete my survey. Since I assumed that my identity as an outsider and a woman contributed to these refusals, I turned to intermediaries to gain access to community members. These intermediaries introduced me to others in their community, explaining my research and vouching for my character. My use of these intermediaries was very successful with Goans and Hindus. In fact, a Hindu woman even presented me with a handwritten note to introduce me to others in the community. Intermediaries were less successful with Bohora and Ismaili Muslims. A Bohora man approached others on my behalf, but they refused to complete my survey. Although the survey was anonymous, they found a question about their Internet access too personal. The director of the Ismaili development agency (the Aga Khan Foundation) offered to assist with distributing my survey to members of his mosque. Again, those he approached suggested the questions were too intrusive and objected to their mosque becoming involved in outside research. It is difficult to confirm the reason for this reluctance, whether it was the nature of the survey questions themselves or my own outsider identity and gender.

My use of an African research assistant helped me gain access to that community, as did my language abilities; the fact that I was able to ask survey questions in Kiswahili surprised many respondents and often made them more willing to participate. My assistant did help with more advanced translations, but more importantly his deep knowledge of the city took me to remote areas I may not have found on my own. Still, this portion of my research was not without difficulties. When visiting a market in southern Dar es Salaam, we approached an old man who quite vocally refused to answer my questions. He angrily exclaimed that he had told other white researchers about his problems, and he was still waiting for solutions. Thus, he saw little benefit in talking to me. His outburst unnerved me since I did not view this research as harmful or without merit. My research assistant attempted to defuse the situation, and although the man eventually calmed down, he adamantly refused to participate in my survey. Fortunately this reluctance was the exception, not the rule, and I eventually found others in the market willing to talk to me.

Historical Background

Dar es Salaam developed as a segregated city during the colonial era (1887–1961). It was part of German East Africa, but after Germany lost its colonies in the aftermath of World War I, it became part of Britain's Tanganyika Territory. Although the territory's legal standing differed under German and British rule—a true German colony versus a British mandate—both administrations implemented the same segregationist policies.[15] Tanganyika did not experience legalized segregation (as in the case of South Africa) or segregation for the protection of European health (as in the case of Senegal or Sierra Leone).[16] Rather, both administrations implemented a series of building ordinances that effectively segregated the city without ever explicitly mentioning race. In fact, the British building ordinances were essentially a translation of those used by their German predecessors.

These ordinances established three zones in Dar es Salaam that each permitted a different style of construction.[17] Zone 1 allowed for European style residential buildings constructed of sturdy materials, Zone 2 allowed for residential or commercial buildings constructed of sturdy materials, and Zone 3 allowed for African style residential buildings of any material.[18] No law prevented an Asian from living in a European style building or a European from living in an African style building. In fact Tanganyika's chief secretary stated in 1932 that "it has not been the intention of Government to prevent Natives from building elsewhere than in Zone 3."[19] Even in the absence of any laws officially establishing racial segregation, the requirements for specific building materials effectively segregated the city by race. The governor of Tanganyika Territory even suggested that "though an Asiatic may buy a plot in the European residential quarter, we can require him to build on it a house of a type which would not suit his methods of life."[20] Ultimately, these zones acquired colloquial Swahili names to refer to the race of their inhabitants: Zone 1 became known as *Uzunguni* (the place of Europeans), Zone 2 as *Uhindini* (the place of Indians), and Zone 3 as *Uswahilini* (the place of Africans).[21]

The main European suburb was on the Msasani Peninsula, and it was provided with amenities such as stores and electricity to make it convenient and comfortable for its residents.[22] Significant numbers of Asians lived in the City Center, but the British also developed an Asian suburb in Upanga. It was envisioned not as a way to benefit that community, but rather to offer an Asian alternative to living in Msasani and therefore to maintain segregation.[23] Owing to its proximity to Dar es Salaam's City Center, Upanga did receive better services, such as sanitation, than African areas, but this was more a function of geography than of concern for Asian welfare. Europeans did benefit from the Asian community's control of the city's commercial sector, which meant that Asians rather than Europeans had the most day-to-day interaction with the African population.[24] Yet despite these perceived benefits, colonial rhetoric toward Asians focused on the dirt, filth, and squalor of their living areas, even calling them a "disgrace" to Dar es Salaam.[25] Owing to the city's large African population, much of its land area contained African housing, and these homes rarely received services such as water, sanitation, or electricity. These residential areas were generally located far from Msasani and the City Center, and Asian areas served as buffer zones between European and African neighborhoods.

Yet, more than establishing spatial segregation, these building ordinances also led to social segregation because there was very little interaction between these three communities. As Nagar indicates, "The physical distance between an Asian shopkeeper living near the Clock Tower and an African vendor living on Uhuru Street in Kariakoo may be a few blocks, but socially, the two are worlds apart."[26] Thus, Dar es Salaam developed as three cities in one. Three groups lived in distinctly different spaces, and these spaces bore little resemblance to one another in terms of housing quality and service provision. These patterns of segregation persist in postcolonial Dar es Salaam, and the spatially defined expatriate, Asian, and African communities have clear ideas about identity based on their place within the city. And as long as these ideas about place exist, social and spatial segregation will persist.

Expatriate Identity and Community

This research builds on the ideas of colonial continuities discussed in Fechter and Walsh's edited volume *The New Expatriates: Postcolonial Approaches to Mobile Professionals*, and considers the fifty expatriates whom I surveyed to be the contemporary equivalent of Dar es Salaam's colonial European population.[27] They came from a wide range of backgrounds, but they did share some common characteristics. My respondents were overwhelmingly female, and despite strong efforts to recruit male respondents, only ten were male. This female skew is an inevitable outcome of my identifying many expatriates through the Corona Society and the Diplomatic Spouses Group, since their members are predominantly women. In addition, many expatriate families relocate for male jobs.[28] In Tanzania, immigration and residency rules make it difficult for spouses to find jobs, so these women generally had free time to fill out my survey and participate in interviews.

Although my respondents were originally from eighteen different countries, most were from the United States and Western European countries. I found no noticeable survey differences between white and nonwhite respondents or between those from developed and developing countries. In this way, the race and ethnicity of expatriates matters little, although the effects of gender cannot be completely ignored. Socially constructed identities often link women to the private home and men to public space.[29] These identities, however, are not static and are constantly being challenged. For example, one of my female respondents worked in a senior position at the International Monetary Fund (public space) and her husband was unemployed and thus spent more time at home (private space). Still, the respondent who used the most space within the city was a male graduate student at the University of Dar es Salaam. Not only did he live near the university rather than in Msasani, he spent a considerable amount of time in bars and restaurants located around the city. Yet being male does not guarantee a wide use of the city. An American man who worked at the US Embassy completed nearly all of his activities in Msasani. Other than going to work, he only left the peninsula to purchase seafood at the City Center's fish market. Thus, it is socioeconomic status that distinguishes these expatriates from other residents in Dar es Salaam, and the social segregation that results from this hierarchy of difference contributes to ideas of identity and community. The degree of difference between expatriates and Africans is very apparent for Foreign Service staff members at the US Embassy. They receive the same base salary that they would in the United States, several cost of living allowances, and free housing.[30]

Within the expatriate community in Dar es Salaam, there is a clear relationship between space and identity. Expatriates are strongly associated with the Msasani Peninsula, and their everyday life activities occur primarily in this part of the city. In fact, forty-nine of the fifty expatriates I surveyed completed some activity there, with some expatriates living nearly their entire lives in this small space. One British woman suggested that she never needed to leave the peninsula because the rest of the city had nothing she either needed or wanted.[31] In fact, since I conducted these surveys, a new fish market opened on the Msasani Peninsula, providing an alternative to the main fish market—the destination of most expatriates who travel to the City Center. In this way, Msasani is a complete city containing essential urban functions such as a thriving commercial sector, entertainment facilities, and private residences.

Part of this narrow spatial focus can be explained by Msasani's colonial origin as a European suburb. Yet history is only a partial explanation, since the British government also built European homes, albeit in smaller numbers, in other parts of Dar es Salaam. The location of amenities such as a bookstore that carries English-language books, the exclusive members-only Yacht Club, and Western-style supermarkets that stock many imported goods also makes this area desirable to expatriates. For those products not readily available on the peninsula, expatriates have found innovative ways to purchase them without leaving Msasani. One of these creative solutions is purchasing seafood from door-to-door salespeople. Some expatriates view the city's main fish market, located in the City Center, as crowded, overwhelming, and unsafe. To avoid the market they are therefore willing to pay higher prices for home delivery. A British woman confessed that she purchased unwanted and overpriced items from her salesman, but she continued to buy from him for the sake of convenience.[32] A South African woman suggested that expatriates "like to live among our own kind."[33] This desire to live among similar people—whether in terms of race or class—is not as formalized as it was in South Africa under apartheid, but it does suggest that a degree of choice or self-segregation is involved as expatriates concentrate their activities in Msasani.

Certainly expatriates do carry out some everyday life activities outside of Msasani. For example, the predominantly African neighborhood of Mwananyamala contains several restaurants popular with expatriates, but its food is priced beyond the means of many of the Africans living nearby. The limited presence of Africans in these commercial spaces further supports the idea that community and identity are exclusionary—you either belong or you don't. Cresswell explores these ideas of belonging, suggesting that place can be more than a location. It can also combine the spatial with social expectations based on variables such as class or race. These expectations dictate both what is appropriate or proper activity for a space as well as where certain people should or should not be.[34] Sibley also addresses these ideas in his book *Geographies of Exclusion*. He describes how those people considered to be undesirable, marginal, or "the other" are excluded from some urban spaces, while people who are normal, mainstream, and "the same" are included.[35]

Still, expatriates consciously decide to concentrate their activities in Msasani even though they have the economic ability to eat and shop nearly anywhere, and their transportation options (such as personal cars or cars with drivers) allow them to travel easily within the city. One explanation for this concentration is that they learn about the city from other expatriates and from publications designed to serve their community, including the Corona Society's *Newcomers Guide to Dar es Salaam*.[36] This book seeks to help new expatriates adjust to life in the city by providing a list of restaurants, shops, and other places of interest to city residents. The vast majority of these places are located in areas with significant expatriate populations. For example, of the seven locations listed for fruit and vegetable shopping, five are in Msasani and a sixth is in an adjacent neighborhood that also has a sizable expatriate population. The places listed in this guide are owned by Asians, expatriates, Africans, and even foreign companies, but they definitely cater to a more affluent population. In addition, the Diplomatic Spouses Group and the US Embassy conduct driving tours to familiarize new residents with "important" areas of the city—most of which are located in Msasani. The tours do pass quickly through the City Center, pointing out hotels, art galleries, foreign cultural centers, and the fish market, but bypass areas of importance to most Asians or Africans. These publications and tours have a clear and narrow spatial focus on Msasani. For the expatriates who wrote the book and lead the tours, this emphasis likely makes sense because they are promoting the places they already know, but it also serves to reinforce the limited extent of expatriate daily lives.

Asian Identity and Community

I surveyed forty Asians, all of whom were Tanzanian citizens and practitioners of different religions. Twenty-five of these respondents were male. Nagar has written extensively about Asians in Dar es Salaam and demonstrates that factors other than religion, including organizations, institutions, and societal processes, influence Asian identity.[37] Campbell notes that individuals have multiple identities that depend on a person's social and spatial setting.[38] Thus, someone in Dar es Salaam can be a Sikh in one space and a Tanzanian of Asian descent alongside Hindus and Muslims in another space. In spite of these "differences in their social backgrounds and experience,

Asians as a whole have largely remained socially, politically, and spatially isolated from their African neighbors since colonial times."[39] Likewise, Campbell
notes that Asians' lives are "increasingly rooted in their physically bounded
'community.'"[40] They have maintained this self-segregation by creating their
own hospitals, schools, and social clubs to limit interaction with Europeans
and Africans.[41] Nagar does document some Asian segregation by religion
within Dar es Salaam's City Center, but the small land area of these neighborhoods means that any separation can be measured in blocks rather than
the more substantial separation observed between Africans and Europeans.[42]
Dar es Salaam's development as a racially segregated and compartmentalized
city has served "to make the Asians inward looking and to organize schemes
of self-help to supplement deficiencies" in government services.[43] The British
government helped to reinforce this view of a single Asian identity through
the formation of a Central Indian Council that was intended to speak with
one voice for the entire community.[44]

Unlike expatriates, Dar es Salaam's Asian residents are not temporary
migrants. The first documented Asian arrived in Dar es Salaam in 1856 from
South Asia and was followed by many others from South Asia over the next
sixty years.[45] Although Dar es Salaam's Asian population increased steadily,
they occupied a complicated and contested place in the colonial social hierarchy. The Germans viewed Asians as an important part of the city's trading sector, but they also used building ordinances to maintain physical and
social separation between Europeans and Asians.[46] Officially, the government
encouraged Asian settlement, but contradictorily, it also levied strict taxes on
Asian businesses and limited them to specific commercial endeavors.[47] These
complications did not end under British rule. As Joseph (herself a Tanzanian
Asian) points out, by participating in the mercantile and business communities, Asians were perceived to have benefited from colonial segregation,
especially through their achievements of high levels of property ownership,
and they were "projected in the popular imagination as opportunistic, ruthless businessmen, ardent capitalists with no political allegiances to either the
Europeans or Africans."[48] In postindependence Tanzania, these benefits were
challenged as the government promoted African interests at the expense of
Asian and European ones. For example, the 1971 Building Acquisition Act
nationalized nearly three thousand buildings in Tanzania, the vast majority of
which were owned by Asians.[49] Some Asians did leave the country in response
to this act, but unlike in neighboring Uganda, this community was not forc-
ibly expelled. Since that time, many Asians have reentered the commercial
sector and are again property owners.

There is a clear relationship between space and Asian identity in Dar es Salaam. Asians are strongly associated with the City Center, and their every-day life activities occur primarily in this part of the city. In fact, all forty of the Asians I surveyed completed some activity there, and some Asians live the majority of their lives in this area. As an extreme example, one Hindu woman's activities were concentrated within just a few city blocks so that she could walk between home, work, her temple, stores, and her library. This limited movement is not exclusive to female Asians. In fact, two of my male respondents also did not leave the City Center for any activities nor had they even lived elsewhere in Dar es Salaam.

The City Center has a historical connection to Asians. Under colonial rule, this area contained residential and commercial buildings that were almost exclusively occupied by Asians. Today the City Center remains the site of government offices[50] but also retains a large and vibrant Asian-dominated commercial sector. This area also contains other benefits and amenities important to the Asian community. It is home to a range of shopping areas and offers proximity to places of religious worship, including churches, temples, and mosques. The area allows Asians to be around others in their community. As a Goan woman explained, by living in the City Center she is within walking distance of her church, her elderly relatives, her friends, and her workplace.[51] Another important amenity for this community is the abundance of community halls and social clubs in the City Center. These places generally date back to the British colonial era and began as exclusive members-only organizations. For example, Hindus founded the Badminton Institute and Patel Grounds, and Goans founded the Dar Institute (originally named the Goan Institute). Today these spaces still require membership, but it is no longer limited to members of those religions, and the clubs also allow nonmembers to enter for a small fee. This fee contributes to the notion that community and identity are exclusionary by creating a dichotomy of members and others.

Although the City Center is extremely important to Asian everyday life, the British government also established a separate Asian suburb in Upanga. Today Asians do carry out some everyday life activities in Upanga as well as other parts of Dar es Salaam, including Msasani. In this way, Dar es Salaam's Asians occupy a larger space than the city's expatriates, although the City Center still remains the heart of the Asians' community. Many members of this community rarely venture beyond this area since shopping, worship, workplace, and home are concentrated in a small geographical area. For many Asians, there is little need to leave this compact, familiar space, so that the

City Center functions as a complete city much like Msasani. The perceived lack of importance of the wider city serves to maintain patterns of segregation and the related ideas of difference, spatial belonging, and spatial exclusion.

African Identity and Community

I surveyed 326 Africans from across Dar es Salaam, and 128 of these respondents were women. As with the city's other communities, these respondents were diverse, but they were all black Tanzanian citizens. They included people born in Dar es Salaam as well as people who migrated there from other parts of the country. They had varied educational backgrounds, with some never having attended school and others holding graduate degrees. They included unemployed Tanzanians and those employed in a variety of jobs ranging from informal traders to government officials. They also represented a sizable number of the country's approximately 120 ethnic groups. Yet in spite of this diversity, they are a cohesive community. The unified nature of the Tanzanian population is often attributed to the use of Kiswahili as a common language, and Brennan suggests that Tanzania represents one of the continent's most successful examples of an "African racial political identity."[52]

Since its founding, Dar es Salaam has been an African city. Today the city's Africans live, work, shop, and recreate in all of its areas. This does not mean, however, that Africans in Msasani or the City Center use the same spaces as expatriates or Asians. Rather, these groups frequent quite different places and tend to have limited spatial interaction. For example, a popular expatriate recreational space in Msasani is the members-only Yacht Club, while Africans are much more likely to visit the free public Coco Beach. Expatriates generally avoid Coco Beach, which is considered by many embassies to be one of the most dangerous spots in the city.[53] Limited, or even nonexistent, social interactions among these groups have spillover effects by strengthening ideas of identity and difference rather than creating a sense of wider community.

In spite of this broad spatial use of the city, one area stands out as the most important to the African community: Kariakoo. Seventy-eight percent of my respondents complete at least some activity there, and no other area comes close to this level of use. The second-most-frequented area is Msasani, with 26 percent of respondents completing some activity there—almost exclusively at Coco Beach. Kariakoo's role in African life can be explained by its historical origins and its contemporary role in the commercial sector. It was Dar es Salaam's first designated African residential area, originally proposed by the German colonial government and developed by the British. Even in those early days it played a bigger role than just housing Africans; it also contained amenities such as a large market, a beer hall, and an eating hall. As the city's African population grew, other residential areas developed, but Kariakoo remained a central part of commercial and social life in Dar es Salaam. Today it continues to be an important commercial space and is even considered a secondary Central Business District after the City Center.[54] It houses the city's largest food market that sells both wholesale and retail foods. It tends to have the best selection of goods and the best prices of all the city's markets; in fact, goods sold elsewhere in the city are almost always purchased in Kariakoo.[55] It is also the primary shopping destination for other products, especially spare car parts. It is often said that if something is not available in Kariakoo, it is not available in Dar es Salaam.[56]

Kariakoo is an important space for the city's Africans, who make everyday life decisions based on the interplay between location and price. A convenient location near work, markets, friends, or a bus station is desirable since it can limit transportation costs. Some respondents were willing to pay slightly higher prices to shop at convenient markets or to live in well-situated neighborhoods. Yet other respondents indicated a willingness to spend a significant amount of time and money on buses in order to get the lowest prices on goods or housing. Because of its low prices and central location both near the City Center and along major bus routes, Kariakoo attracts a large portion of the city's African community and is an area of primary importance for this population. Perhaps even more important is that for other groups in Dar es Salaam, Kariakoo is an area that is avoided. Because Kariakoo, and all of the city's African areas more broadly, are seen as different and dangerous spaces, the us/them dichotomy is perpetuated. The longer these ideas of difference remain, the harder they are to change. Guidebooks warn visitors of the high levels of crime and pickpockets found there. Some of my expatriate and Asian respondents do go to Kariakoo, but many others are not comfortable there. Yet for the Africans that I surveyed, Kariakoo is an essential part of Dar es Salaam.

Conclusions

Expatriate, Asian, and African communities in Dar es Salaam are closely identified with distinct spaces in the city: Msasani for expatriates, the City Center for Asians, and Kariakoo for Africans. These patterns were established with segregationist building ordinances in the German and British colonial eras, and have persisted throughout the postindependence period. The 1967 Tanzanian census demonstrates the importance of these areas to each community.[57] In that year, the areas of the city with the largest European populations were near the harbor in the City Center and in Msasani. The only area with a significant Asian population was the commercial area of the City Center. Kariakoo was one of several areas of the city with a predominantly African population. Myers explores the impacts of these colonial legacies, noting that attempts to transcend them have failed in many African cities, not just Dar es Salaam.[58]

In addition to my surveys, interviews, and observations, I also asked my respondents to draw mental maps of Dar es Salaam. Mental maps are "cartographic representations of how people differ in their evaluation of places."[59] These maps are personal products and reflect political, social, cultural, and economic components.[60] Thus these maps reflect how people think about Dar es Salaam and contain the places that people know and use, and these maps influence spatial decision-making.[61] Nagar's mental mapping research with Asians in Dar es Salaam found that their maps "reflect an 'Asian-centric' view of Dar es Salaam where the perceived limits of the city coincide with the limits of Asian residential and business area."[62] The lack of non-Asian places on these maps "indicates the role that Asian communal places and residential areas indirectly play in intensifying racial segregation and stereotyping and in strengthening racial identities of both Asians and Africans."[63]

The mental maps I collected were as diverse as my research respondents, but did illustrate some general themes that support the relationship between space, community, and identity.[64] Most expatriate maps included Msasani, either by name or the shape of the peninsula. Figure 2, drawn by an American woman, shows only the Msasani Peninsula, her workplace, and the general direction of the airport. She notes that "my world is quite small—just a corner of Dar." She recognizes that her spatial knowledge of the city is very limited. In this way, her map resembles other expatriate mental maps that include few places seen on those drawn by Asians and Africans. Many Asian maps, though not the majority, included the City Center or Upanga. Figure 3, drawn by an Ithna'sheri man, focuses exclusively on the City Center, although an arrow indicates where Upanga is located. This map is more detailed than most drawn by expatriates as it includes street names and significant landmarks such as the State House. Yet it still encompasses a very limited part of Dar es Salaam. Compared to the maps of other communities, African maps tended to depict larger areas of Dar es Salaam and included streets and bus stops more frequently. Figure 4 was drawn by an African man who narrated the process. He noted the inclusion of areas of importance: the bus stand he regularly uses, the office where he purchases electricity, and the Kariakoo Market where he shops for goods, including clothing. This mental map also uses arrows to note the location of other large residential areas. These three mental map examples help illustrate the connections between space and identity in Dar es Salaam by depicting the areas of importance to these respondents. They indicate the persistence of segregation in the city through these limited spatial illustrations of Dar es Salaam. The city's segregation occurs both spatially and socially, impacting not only what parts of the city people experience but also whom they interact with. Regardless of whether one considers expatriates, Asians, or Africans, all of the city's residents are impacted in some way by this segregation.

These ideas of space and place were evident in an interview I conducted with a Canadian expatriate. Her parents are East African Asians who migrated to Canada but later relocated to Dar es Salaam and opened a successful

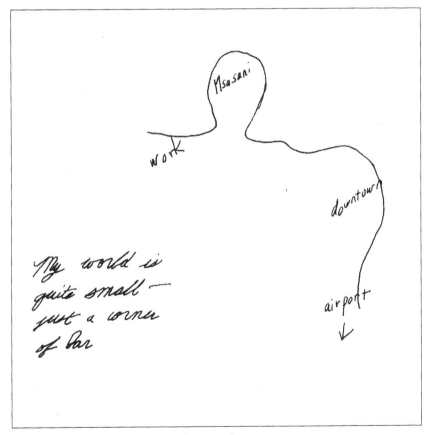

FIGURE 2. Expatriate mental map of Dar es Salaam.

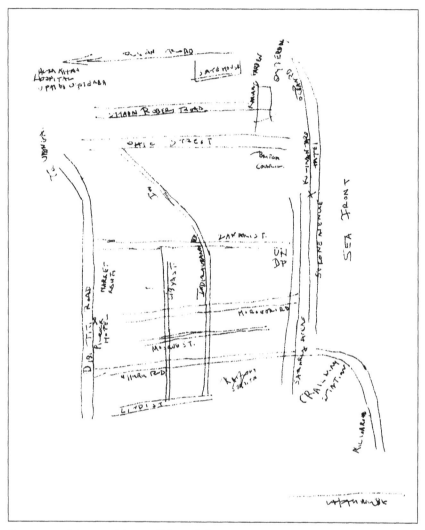

FIGURE 3. Asian mental map of Dar es Salaam.

supermarket in Msasani. When their daughter moved to Dar es Salaam, she first lived with her parents in Upanga. Although she looks Asian, she felt very uncomfortable and out of place in that neighborhood, so she eventually moved to a neighborhood with more expatriates. Her mental map focused exclusively on expatriate spaces within Dar es Salaam even though she obviously knows other parts of the city. She even commented on her map that "nothing else really matters" beyond what she included on her map. By suggesting that

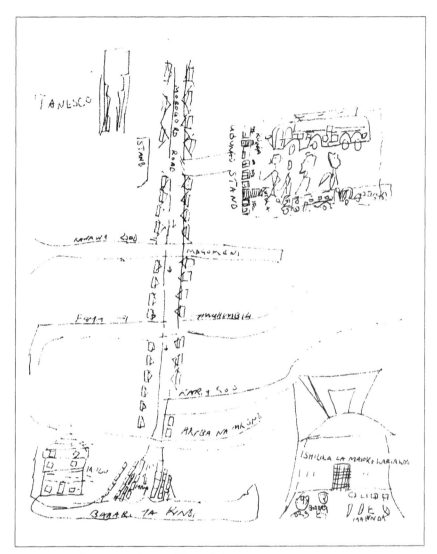

FIGURE 4. African mental map of Dar es Salaam.

Asian areas were insignificant or irrelevant, she appears to privilege her expatriate identity at the expense of her Asian identity.

As this example indicates, there is a complicated relationship between identity, community, and space in Dar es Salaam. Ideas of exclusion and belonging influence how residents use and perceive urban space and make everyday life decisions. In colonial Dar es Salaam, segregation occurred along racial lines. In contemporary Dar es Salaam, racial segregation persists but divisions also exist along socioeconomic lines. Thus, in today's city it is possible to find Asians living in Kariakoo, Africans living in Msasani, and expatriates living in Upanga. Yet as explained above, the presence of Africans in Msasani does not mean they use the same space as expatriates, nor does it change the fact that Kariakoo is exponentially more important to Africans than Msasani.

For these communities, their identity is shaped by space. Konings, van Dijk, and Foeken acknowledge that one aspect of African neighborhoods is that although they may be diverse, their residents have a "cohesive sense of identity."[65] I experienced these ideas of spatial belonging firsthand when I chose to live in a City Center apartment. My decision was not intended to challenge these spatial divides but was simply motivated by the convenience of the apartment's location. Yet when I told other expatriates about my new home, they were quite horrified at my decision to live "in the city," and my African friends laughed at me for living in the Asian area rather than in Msasani. I was out of place according to the identity that others assigned to me.

Identities—whether self-imposed or imposed by others—provide important insight into how people perceive of space and thus how they make decisions about everyday activities. Decisions may be based on fear—such as expatriates avoiding areas perceived to be dangerous. Decisions may be based on culture—such as Asians wanting to be within walking distance of religious spaces. Decisions may be based on economics—such as Africans choosing to travel farther to shop at a cheaper market. Regardless of what dictates these decisions, identity and community contribute to segregation as residents perceive different spaces within Dar es Salaam to be either comfortable or uncomfortable, either appropriate or inappropriate, and either containing "the same" or "the other." These ideas of belonging or exclusion are held by all residents, and understanding them is essential to understanding the factors that caused spatial and social segregation and the reasons why it continues to persist in contemporary Dar es Salaam.

Notes

    1. Carol Ekinsmyth and Pamela Shurmer-Smith, "Humanistic and Behavioral Geography," *Doing Cultural Geography*, ed. Pamela Shurmer-Smith (London: Sage, 2002), 19–27.

    2. Anne-Meike Fechter and Katie Walsh, "Examining 'Expatriate' Continuities: Postcolonial Approaches to Mobile Professionals," in *The New Expatriates: Postcolonial Approaches to Mobile Professionals*, ed. Anne-Meike Fechter and Katie Walsh (London: Routledge, 2012), 9–22. Fechter and Walsh acknowledge that the term *expatriate* is controversial since it often is used specifically for white migrants. Likewise, to some, this term implies a person's exile from his home country. In spite of any

controversy, I use "expatriate" for the same reason as Fechter and Walsh—it is widely used and is the term that these migrants use to describe themselves.

3. Fechter and Walsh, "Examining 'Expatriate' Continuities," 9–22; Anne Coles and Anne-Meike Fechter, "Introduction," in *Gender and Family among Transnational Professionals*, ed. Anne Coles and Anne-Meike Fechter (New York: Routledge, 2008), 1–20.

4. UN-HABITAT, *Citywide Action Plan for Upgrading Unplanned and Unserviced Settlements in Dar es Salaam* (Nairobi: UN-HABITAT, 2010).

5. Anthony Cohen, *The Symbolic Construction of Community* (Chichester: Ellis Horwood, 1985), 12.

6. Alan Rew and John Campbell, "The Political Economy of Identity and Affect," in *Identity and Affect: Experiences of Identity in a Globalising World*, ed. John Campbell and Alan Rew (London: Pluto, 1999), 1–36.

7. UN-HABITAT, *State of the World's Cities 2010/2011: Bridging the Urban Divide* (London: Earthscan, 2008).

8. In this chapter, I use the place names Msasani Peninsula, Msasani, and the peninsula interchangeably to refer to this space.

9. For more on this history of segregation, see Sarah Smiley, "The City of Three Colors: Segregation in Colonial Dar es Salaam, 1891–1961," *Historical Geography* 37 (2009): 178–96.

10. For more information on unequal water provision, see Sarah Smiley, "Complexities of Water Access in Dar es Salaam, Tanzania," *Applied Geography* 41 (2013): 132–38.

11. Claire Dwyer and Melanie Limb, "Introduction: Doing Qualitative Research in Geography," in *Qualitative Methodologies for Geographers: Issues and Debates*, ed. Melanie Limb and Claire Dwyer (London: Arnold, 2001), 1.

12. Lily Kong and Brenda Yeoh, "The Meanings and Making of Place: Exploring History, Community and Identity," in *Portraits of Places: History, Community and Identity in Singapore*, ed. Brenda Yeoh and Lily Kong (Singapore: Times Edition, 1995), 12–23.

13. Sarah Smiley, "Historical Geography Research at the Tanzania National Archives," *African Geographical Review* 25 (2006): 107–16.

14. Matt Bradshaw and Elaine Stratford, "Qualitative Research Design and Rigour," in *Qualitative Research Methods in Human Geography*, 3rd ed., ed. Iain Hay (New York: Oxford University Press, 2010), 69–80.

15. For an explanation of the similarities between the Mandate System and official colonies, see Susan Pedersen, "The Meaning of the Mandates System: An Argument," *Geschichte und Gesellschaft* 32 (2006), 560–82.

16. For a case study on segregation for health, see Myron Echenberg, *Black Death, White Medicine: Bubonic Plague and the Politics of Public Health in Colonial Senegal, 1914–1945* (Portsmouth, NH: Heinemann, 2002), and Stephen Frenkel and John Western, "Pretext or Prophylaxis? Racial Segregation and Malarial Mosquitos in a British Tropical Colony: Sierra Leone," *Annals of the Association of American Geographers* 78, no. 2 (1988), 211–28. For a case study on legalized segregation, see John Western, *Outcast Cape Town* (Minneapolis: University of Minnesota Press, 1981).

17. Tanzania National Archives G 7/18: Baupolizeiordnung für Dar es Salaam, 1906–1915 (Building Control Regulations for Dar es Salaam, 1906–1915); Tanzania National Archives G 7/198: Stadt und Baupläne, Dar es Salaam, 1891–1893 (City and Blueprints, Dar es Salaam, 1891–1893); Tanzania National Archives Laws of the Tanganyika Territory/1928/CAP. 29.

18. The British administration did modify the description of these zones. It changed the description of Zone 3 to include "buildings of any type, subject to the approval of the Authority," rather than including African or native style buildings. This shift was an attempt to make these zones seem to be about construction rather than racial segregation, but the government continued to refer to Zone 3 as the African area until independence. See Tanzania National Archives 11150, volume 2: Questions Connected to Township Regulations, Dar es Salaam.

19. Tanzania National Archives 11150, volume 2.

20. Tanzania National Archives AB 616: Segregation of Races.

21. James Brennan and Andrew Burton, "The Emerging Metropolis: A History of Dar es Salaam, Circa 1862–2000," in *Dar es Salaam: Histories from an Emerging African Metropolis*, ed. James Brennan, Andrew Burton, and Yusuf Lawi (Dar es Salaam: Mkuki na Nyota, 2007), 13–76.

22. Tanzania National Archives Acc. 189, 96I: Central Town Planning and Building Committee.

23. Tanzania National Archives 26160: New Layout of Upanga Area; Tanzania National Archives 13483, Volume 1: Town Planning Scheme for Dar es Salaam by Government Architect.

24. James Brennan, *Taifa: Making Nation and Race in Urban Tanzania* (Athens: Ohio University Press, 2012), 47–84.

25. Tanzania National Archives 13483, volume 1.

26. Richa Nagar, *Making and Breaking Boundaries: Identity Politics among South Asians in Postcolonial Dar es Salaam* (PhD diss., University of Minnesota, 1995), 192.

27. Fechter and Walsh, "Examining 'Expatriate' Continuities," 9–22

28. Coles and Fechter, "Introduction." The authors do note increasing numbers of expatriates moving for female jobs. Of my fifty expatriate respondents, several had moved to Dar es Salaam for female jobs, including at embassies and international organizations.

29. Doreen Massey, *Space, Place, and Gender* (Minneapolis: University of Minnesota Press, 1994), 177–184.

30. US State Department, "Summary of Allowances and Benefits," accessed Oct. 26, 2012, http://aoprals.state.gov/content.asp?content_id=134&menu_id=75.

31. Personal interview (Dar es Salaam, 2006).

32. Ibid.

33. Ibid.

34. . Tim Cresswell, *In Place/Out of Place: Geography, Ideology and Transgression* (Minneapolis: University of Minnesota Press, 1996), 97–145.

35. David Sibley, *Geographies of Exclusion* (London: Routledge, 1995), 14–31.

36. Corona Tanzania, *The Newcomer's Guide to Dar es Salaam*, 2nd ed. (Dar es Salaam: Corona Tanzania, 2004), 73.

37. Nagar, *Making and Breaking Boundaries*, 36. See also Richa Nagar, "The South Asian Diaspora in Tanzania: A History Retold," *Comparative Studies of South Asia, Africa and the Middle East* 16, no. 2 (1996): 62–80; Richa Nagar, "Communal Places and the Politics of Multiple Identities: The Case of Tanzanian Asians," *Ecumene* 4, no. 1 (1997): 3–26.

38. John Campbell, "Culture, Social Organization and Asian Identity: Difference in East Africa," in *Identity and Affect*, pages 169–198.

39. Nagar, "South Asian Diaspora in Tanzania," 62.

40. Campbell, "Culture, Social Organization, and Asian Identity," 179.

41. George Delf, *Asians in East Africa* (London: Oxford University Press, 1963), 54.

42. Nagar, *Making and Breaking Boundaries*, 122.

43. Yash Ghai, "Prospects for Asians in East Africa," *Racial and Communal Tensions in East Africa*, ed. The East African Institute of Social and Cultural Affairs (Nairobi: East African Publishing House, 1966), 9–26.

44. Campbell, "Culture, Social Organization and Asian Identity," 169–198.

45. Ibid.

46. John Iliffe, *Tanganyika under German Rule, 1905–1912* (Cambridge: Cambridge University Press, 1969), 82–117; Smiley, "The City of Three Colors," 178–196.

47. Campbell, "Culture, Social Organization and Asian Identity," 169–198.

48. May Joseph, *Nomadic Identities: The Performance of Citizenship* (Minneapolis: University of Minnesota Press, 1999), 85.

49. Nagar, *Making and Breaking Boundaries*, 87–91.

50. This area includes various ministries, the City Council, the country's High Court, and the State House.

51. Personal interview (Dar es Salaam, 2006).

52. Brennan, *Taifa*, 2.

53. Regional Security Office, *Safe in Dar* (Dar es Salaam: American Embassy, 2002).

54. Kenneth Lynch, "Urban Fruit and Vegetable Supply in Dar es Salaam," *Geographical Journal* 160, no. 3 (1994): 307–18.

55. Lynch, "Urban Fruit and Vegetable Supply."

56. *Dar Guide* (Dar es Salaam: East African Movies Limited, 2003, November issue).

57. United Republic of Tanzania, *1967 Population Census, Volume 1* (Dar es Salaam: Central Statistics Bureau, 1969).

58. Garth Myers, *African Cities: Alternative Visions of Urban Theory and Practice* (London: Zed, 2011).

59. Yi Fu Tuan, "Images and Mental Maps," *Annals of the Association of American Geographers* 65, no. 2 (1975): 206.

60. Peter Gould, *On Mental Maps* (Ann Arbor: University of Michigan Press, 1966).

61. Reginald Golledge, "Learning about Urban Environments," in *Making Sense of Time*, ed. Tommy Carlstein, Don Parkes, and Nigel Thrift (New York: John Wiley, 1978).

62. Nagar, *Making and Breaking Boundaries*, 189.

63. Ibid., 189–190.

64. For a more detailed discussion of mental maps in Dar es Salaam, see Sarah Smiley, "Mental Maps, Segregation, and Everyday Life in Dar es Salaam, Tanzania," *Journal of Cultural Geography* 30, no. 2 (2013), 215–44.

65. Piet Konings, Rijk van Dijk, and Dick Foeken, "The African Neighborhood: An Introduction," in *Crisis and Creativity: Exploring the Wealth of the African Neighborhood*, ed. Piet Konings and Dick Foeken (Leiden: Brill, 2006), 1.

The United States Confronts a New Latin American Community after the Cold War

WALT VANDERBUSH

The Community of Latin American and Caribbean States (CELAC) held its initial summit on December 2–3, 2011, in Caracas, Venezuela. The explicit goal of the grouping was to strengthen the relationships among countries of the Caribbean and Latin America separate from the influence of the United States (and Canada). Holding the first meeting in Venezuela seemed appropriate given the role played by Hugo Chávez, still that country's president at the time, in promoting the idea of a regional community that does not include the United States. Several months earlier, the Union of South American Nations (UNASUR), modeled in part on the European Union, had become fully operational; former Brazilian president Lula da Silva worked with Chávez and others to push for the continuing integration of South America made possible by UNASUR. The perceived need for these sorts of regional entities that do not involve US participation stands in direct contrast to the US idea following the end of the Cold War that all the countries of the hemisphere (except Cuba) shared interests and values that were moving them toward a hemispheric community extending from Alaska to Argentina. The geographical exclusion of the two countries furthest north, as well as an ideological resistance to free market orthodoxy by many in Latin America, suggested that competing perceptions of community remain a core concern when assessing the state of US-Latin American relations.

In this chapter, I argue that a number of Latin American countries have mounted a surprisingly successful challenge to the ambitions of the United States in the Western Hemisphere. Latin American leaders such as Chávez, Lula, the Castros, Bolivian president Evo Morales, Ecuador's Rafael Correa, and Argentina's Cristina Fernández called on countries in the region to construct a counterhegemonic community of nations to challenge the power of the United States. Less aggressive in his critique of the United States, President Lula da Silva in Brazil took a more pragmatic approach that complemented the more radical and ideological resistance to the United States by Venezuela,

Bolivia, and Cuba. Lula himself never wavered in his support of Chávez. In the lead-up to Chávez's final election, the ex-Brazilian president made his position clear: "A victory for Chávez is not just a victory for the people of Venezuela but also a victory for all the people of Latin America . . . this victory will strike another blow against imperialism."[1] As part of their resistance to US dominance, CELAC countries have created trade agreements, financial organizations, conflict-mediating institutions, and even security-focused alliances that purposefully exclude the United States. These sorts of initiatives are part of a strategy by Venezuela, Brazil, and others to rethink the region of Latin America and the Caribbean as a community that does not include the United States and Canada, much less one that is dependent on US leadership. In this chapter, I will explain the surprising success of the LAC (Latin America and the Caribbean) enactment of a different concept of community, and the impact of that development on US-Latin American relations.

For the first decade following the end of the Cold War, the United States continued to exert considerable influence in Latin American and the Caribbean. The 1994 Summit of the Americas produced a commitment by thirty-three of the thirty-four countries in Latin America to work toward a 2005 implementation of the Free Trade Area of the Americas (FTAA). At the time, with the exception of Cuba, the region's leaders were chosen through largely free and fair elections. And even if those elected leaders had criticized neoliberalism during their campaigns, once in office they pretty universally embraced the market policies favored by Washington. As Diana Tussie noted, "The US agenda of economic integration, neoliberal reform, democratic consolidation, and a campaign against corruption and drug trafficking enjoyed wide acceptance as late as 2001."[2] In the first decade of the twenty-first century, however, Washington became politically less influential, and Latin American autonomy from the United States increased. That shift was frequently explained as a function of US neglect in the wake of the 9/11 attack on its territory. In 2003, after resigning his post as Mexico's foreign minister, partly in frustration with Washington, Jorge Castañeda wrote an article describing the US lack of interest as a "forgotten relationship."[3] While US neglect played a role in the changes that have taken place in the twenty-first century, the argument here is that activism and resourcefulness displayed by various groups and leaders in Latin America played an even more important role in shifting the nature of US–Latin American relations in the new century.

Analysts of Latin American foreign policymaking after the end of the Cold War generally emphasized the limitations on countries in a region long dominated by the United States. Writing about a decade after the end of the Cold War, Robert Keohane argued that "Latin American countries are takers, instead of makers, of international policy. They have relatively little influence in international institutions. They will continue to participate in the international institutions, but mostly defensively."[4] Several years later, Diana Tussie made a similar argument about the Americas: "Latin America was the only region where American influence remained largely uncontested after the end of the Cold War."[5]

Conceptualizing Identity and Community

Foreign policymaking is rooted in conceptions of national identity and national interests. In some analyses, the idea of a shared identity is reduced to a discussion of national interests, but identity also includes ideas about a nation's position in the world that go beyond defining security, economic, and diplomatic interests. Guiding national myths such as Venezuela's Bolivarian socialism or the United States' "American exceptionalism" also become part of the national identity that explains foreign policy actions.[6] A component of American exceptionalism, for instance, is based on the caveat of the extraordinary "freedom" of our people, while the "others" are those who lack freedom (living under communism during the Cold War) or who "hate" freedom (terrorists or anachronistic socialists in the post–Cold War period). Donald Pease has argued that US "exceptionalism" is a "state fantasy" promoted through a discourse that secured citizen acquiescence to US foreign policy behavior during the Cold War, which seemed to violate principles such as national self-determination, whether in Latin America or elsewhere.[7]

The use of the term *community* in this chapter is seen in the various conceptions of a community of nations as promoted by different actors at different times. During the Cold War, the United States was explicit about the community to which it belonged and led—those countries actively opposed to communism. While any number of countries in Latin America and the Caribbean were considered, at times, to be straying outside the anticommunist community, Cuba provided the classic example of a country that was excluded from the US-defined and US-led community in the Americas during the Cold War. Since the end of the Cold War, the question of community has become more complicated and contested between the United States and Latin America. The United States in the post–Cold War period continued to promote the idea of a Western Hemispheric community of market democracies that followed the lead of the United States. In the twenty-first century, most of the LAC countries have developed an identity rooted in the idea of an increasing autonomy from the United States. That goal has led to the creation of a range of alliances and institutions that provide a framework for an LAC community able to distance itself from the United States in both domestic political economy issues and international relations.

Methodology

While there has been a significant increase over the last few decades in the numbers of international relations publications employing quantitative or formal modeling methodology, the case study method has held steady. This chapter uses a qualitative methodology, in the sense that it employs an analytical historical approach to US relations with Latin America. It verges on the case study method, but stops short of some criteria, such as making the principal aim of the work a definitive causal explanation. The cases of Venezuela, Cuba, and Brazil are selected in part because they are the countries that have offered the most powerful challenges to the United States in the early part of the twenty-first century. Their respective approaches to resistance, however, have taken on very different forms. First under Chávez and continuing with the current president, Maduro, Venezuela has never missed an opportunity to publicly excoriate the US government for its actions in Venezuela, all of Latin America, and the rest of the world. The Brazilian government, which has shared the Venezuelan leaders' interest in lessening the influence of the United States in South America, has maintained much friendlier public relations with Washington, even as they have effectively challenged both the Bush and Obama administrations on important issues. Cuba is also important to the chapter, in good part because Venezuelan president Chávez has helped to make the island nation a focal point of US–Latin American relations in the twenty-first century. Cuba also provides the best opportunity for the United States to demonstrate that its approach to the region has changed since the end of the Cold War. In fact, most of the changes in US policy toward Cuba have been in the direction of tightening the embargo. In the 1990s, trade was the target, with the Cuban Democracy Act and Helms-Burton. During the George W. Bush administration, educational travel unrelated to academic coursework was restricted for all US citizens, and family travel and remittances by Cuban-Americans were limited. President Obama did reverse the Bush changes; it is now easier for US citizens to travel for educational or religious purposes, and the 2004 limitations on Cuban-Americans have also been lifted.

Finally, there are other important countries in the region that have maintained different relationships with the United States during the new century. Mexico and Colombia have offered the most support to Washington among the larger Latin American countries; smaller countries in Central America and the Caribbean have maintained a nuanced approach toward the United States. Even those countries, however, are active participants in CELAC and other new agreements and institutions that challenge the US notion of community in the Americas. In the rest of the chapter, we focus on explaining the shift from a community heavily influenced by US interests in the first decade after the Cold War to one that in the twenty-first century has excluded the US voice from a number of summits and alliances.

Community and Identity in the Americas

At the risk of oversimplifying several decades of US–Latin American relations, it can be said that the story of the Cold War was one in which the United States claimed that there were "good guys" and "bad guys," and the US government always knew the difference. US violations of national self-determination in Guatemala, Chile, Nicaragua, or El Salvador were justified during the Cold War as being necessary to prevent Communist inroads in the Americas by the Soviet Union. When a country such as Cuba resisted efforts to eliminate communist influence on the island, the United States worked to isolate them in the Americas.

With the dissolution of the Cold War, many expected significant progress to be made in US–Latin American relations. During the first Bush administration (George H. W. Bush), the Sandinistas were voted out of office, other revolutionary groups in Central America put down their arms, and Cuba seemed an anachronism in a region that moved concurrently toward market capitalism and electoral democracy. On June 27, 1990, President Bush laid out his ideas for an Enterprise for the Americas Initiative (EAI) that would lead to a free trade zone reaching from "Anchorage to Tierra del Fuego." He argued, "Throughout the region, nations are turning away from the statist economic policies that stifle growth and are now looking to the power of the free market to help this hemisphere realize its untapped potential for progress."[8] Later in the same speech, Bush noted that "the challenge in this new era of the Americas, is to secure this shared dream and all its fruits for all the people of the Americas—North, Central, and South."[9] Cuba remained an exception, although Bush suggested that the "day is not far off" when it too would join the world's democracies. Cuba aside, the first post–Cold War US president clearly imagined a hemispheric community of "free government and free markets" in a new partnership.

When President Clinton attended the first Summit of the Americas in Miami in December 1994, optimism about US–Latin American relations remained high. In his opening remarks, Clinton declared, "History has given the peoples of the Americas a dazzling opportunity to build a community of nations committed to the values of liberty, progress and prosperity."[10] Clinton proposed expanding NAFTA to form a region-wide "partnership for prosperity," and a 2005 deadline was set for a Free Trade Area of the Americas (FTAA). At that point, there seemed to be neither ideological challenges in the region to the United States, nor anyone else outside the Americas capable of having any significant economic or military influence over the region.

When President George W. Bush took office in the beginning of 2001, most US analysts continued to agree that US–Latin American relations were "fundamentally sound," as Peter Hakim described them in *Foreign Affairs*.[11] President Bush noted during his campaign that he intended to "look south, not as an afterthought but as a fundamental commitment of my presidency."[12] Soon after taking office, while in Quebec City at a Summit of the Americas, he declared it to be "the century of the Americas" as he voiced strong support for the Free Trade Area of the Americas.[13] Four years later, in announcing President Bush's trip to the 2005 Summit of the Americas, the official White House statement noted: "This visit will allow the President to continue his dialogue with the Hemisphere's democratically-elected leaders, highlight our engagement in the region, and promote the consolidation of democracy and the expansion of economic opportunity and prosperity through open markets and free trade."[14] From the Reagan presidency through that of the second President Bush, little had changed in the US government's vision of leading Latin America toward a future of free market capitalism and political democracy.

With some variation in discourse, the current US administration has maintained similar goals in Latin America. President Obama spoke during his campaign in May 2008 in Miami about his vision for US–Latin American relations. The speech generally followed in the tradition of his predecessors in imagining a hemispheric community of like-minded countries, and his rhetoric emphasized the need for US leadership in the region. Titled "Renewing US Leadership in the Americas," the speech was critical of his immediate predecessor for having been "negligent toward our friends, ineffective with our adversaries, disinterested in the challenges that matter in peoples' lives, and incapable of advancing our interests in the region." That neglect did not allow us to "lead the hemisphere into the 21st century," but if Obama became president, he suggested, "we will choose to lead."[15]

In office, President Obama has continued to suggest that we inhabit a hemispheric community of shared values and interests and has punctuated his intention with a new meaning for being "American." In a spring 2011 speech in Santiago, Chile, he said: "But even more than interests, we're bound by shared values. In each other's journey, we see reflections of our own. . . . This is our common history. This is our common heritage. We are all Americans. Todos somos Americanos."[16] Using a Spanish phrase to suggest that the word *Americans* belongs not just to the people of the United States but to all of the Americas, Obama made a welcome rhetorical point. Still, the idea that the United States will lead a region of shared values and shared interests misses important divergences in both interests and values. From US interests reflected in its unpopular agricultural policies, to efforts to protect US manufacturing jobs from the impact of NAFTA, policies concerning Latin American immigration to the United States, and the even more universally opposed Cuba policy, there are a number of areas where many Latin Americans strongly disagree with the US government's approach to the region.

Lost among US presidents' rhetoric about shared values, ideas, and a hemispheric community of market democracies were developments on the ground in the region that challenged US power and influence. In President Clinton's second term, Hugo Chávez's rise to power in Venezuela added to the ongoing Cuban challenge to US ideas of a community of pro-US market democracies in the region. In 1992, Chávez had led an attempted coup against a Venezuelan government that was following economic policies mandated by the IMF and supported by the United States. Chávez served a couple of years in prison before being pardoned in 1994. Once released, Chávez made his first trip to Cuba in December, meeting with Fidel Castro. That visit took place the same month that the first Summit of the Americas was held about two hundred miles away in Florida. It would have been hard to imagine at the time that the Castro-Chávez meeting in Havana would mark the beginning of more successful regional integration efforts in the future than would the meeting in Miami of the heads of states from every country of the Americas except Cuba. Chávez was elected president of Venezuela with 56 percent of the vote and took office in February 1999.

At the start of George W. Bush's presidency, assumptions about US leadership in the region remained firmly in place: "Most American [Latin American] governments are happy to cooperate with Washington, and they expect it to take the initiative on many crucial matters."[17] Cuba remained problematic, and the situation in Venezuela was of some concern for the new administration, but those two countries were seen as exceptions. By the end of George W. Bush's second term in 2008, Latin American governments who were still content to simply cooperate with Washington had become the exceptions. In December 2008, Bush's last full month in office, Russian warships undertook joint maneuvers with the Venezuelan navy before visiting Cuba. Russian president Medvedev stopped by Cuba to pay his regards only a few days after

Chinese president Hu had finished up his visit to the island. President Lula of Brazil, who, that month, was hosting a region-wide summit notable for the absence of US representation, was also making plans to host Iranian president Ahmadinejad on an official state visit. By 2008, the Russian, Chinese, and even the Iranian presidents may have been as welcome in most Latin American capitals as the departing US president Bush.

Competition to define the Americas had intensified through the first decade of the twenty-first century, and the US vision of a hemispheric community of countries that shared US values and interests lost out to the reality of a region in which many opposed Washington's prescriptions for them. President Chávez played an important role in promoting unity among Latin Americans who opposed US hegemony. President Lula, who took office in Brazil in 2002, also assumed a newly assertive approach to his country's foreign policy in the Americas and the rest of the world. But that mobilization had many sources—the five hundred years of resistance movement that developed in response to the 1992 discovery of the Americas celebration; the Zapatistas in Mexico; indigenous mobilization in Ecuador and Bolivia; and the *piquetoros* (unemployed workers picketing or protesting) in Argentina. In even this partial list of the new "identity-based" movements of the late twentieth and early twenty-first centuries, one can see the potential challenge for the consolidation of a political-economic ideology favored by Washington. Those movements generally mobilized to oppose their own national governments, but those Latin American politicians targeted were seen as allied with multinational corporations, international financial institutions, and at least indirectly, the US government. While these "identity-based" movements are sometimes at odds with the official national stories of identity, as Nicola Miller puts it, "such movements mostly wanted to renegotiate, rather than reject, a role in the existing nation-states." As is the case across a range of sectors of Latin American society, that is because nationalism provides "a crucial defence against the encroachments of international capital and its avatars."[18]

While some suggest that these developments in Latin America were largely a result of the neglect of the region by a Bush administration focused on the Middle East, that argument understates both Latin American agency and the US foreign policy blunders in the region. The first major mistake by the United States was in Venezuela itself. By early 2002, the Chávez government was dealing with an economic downturn, based in good part on the decline in oil prices, and a political backlash, particularly from elite groups opposed to the government's reforms. Rather than allow events to play out on their own, some US officials looked for ways to help the opposition. Money from US organizations such as the National Endowment for Democracy (NED) and the United States Agency for International Development (USAID) went to opposition groups in Venezuela.[19] High-ranking US governmental officials, such as Otto Reich, met with the opposition in the weeks leading up to the April 2002 coup. Finally, when Chávez was removed from office in a political-military coup, the Bush administration spokesperson, Ari Fleischer, made it clear that the United States blamed Chávez. The Venezuelan president was said to have "provoked the crisis," and "now that Chávez has resigned the presidency," the United States planned to work with the "transitional civilian government" that had been installed.[20] Otto Reich summoned ambassadors from the region to his office on the day that businessman Pedro Carmona seized power to tell them that the United States would support the new government and to encourage them to do so as well.[21] In the end, governments across the region condemned the coup, with President Cardoso, Lula's predecessor in Brazil, among the most critical. Jorge Castañeda, Mexican foreign minister at the time, argued that Mexico and Chile countered an attempt by Washington to coordinate support for the post-coup government by a group that would include Spain, Colombia, El Salvador, and other Latin American governments seen as most likely to support the US position.[22] Chávez's return to power some forty-eight hours after he was removed marked a critical juncture in legitimizing the Bolivarian socialist movement and damaging the credibility of the US government's commitment to democracy and human rights in Latin America.

Newly empowered, Chávez moved forward on a variety of initiatives that challenged the power and ideology of the Bush administration. In part, he attacked the legitimacy of the US identity as a benevolent power with any claim to "exceptionalism" in its respect for human rights. For example, during the US air attacks in Afghanistan, Chávez argued that the killing of civilians by the US Air Force was no different from the killing of civilians by Al Qaeda.[23] But Chávez also challenged the idea that the United States was the only country capable of providing significant help to people in Latin America. When the price of oil began to rise again (in part because of US policy in the Middle East), Chávez began a program of providing discounted oil to a number of countries in the Caribbean and South America: Petrocaribe, for the alliance in the Caribbean, and Petrosur, for the South American countries, would receive preferential oil prices. An oil-for-doctors exchange with Cuba was expanded into the Bolivarian Alliance for the People of Our America (ALBA). While ALBA remains relatively small, the countries participating in the alliance are trying to develop complementary trade relationships, in which economic exchanges are based on promoting social equality and economic justice. That approach is in direct contrast to the North American Free Trade Agreement (NAFTA), whose supporters' measure of success is the large increase in cross-border investment and trade between the United States and Mexico since its 1994 implementation. Critics of NAFTA point to economic dislocation, growing inequality, and the general redistribution of power from communities and workers to corporate entities. That challenge to US-promoted trade agreements was matched in the area of communications with the development of Telesur, a television network of the South, based in Caracas and meant to provide an alternative media source to the programming based in the North for both those in Latin America and outside the region. In 2009, seven South American countries, headed by Argentina, Brazil, and Venezuela, announced the formation of the Bank of the South (BancoSur), which they hoped would offer an alternative to the IMF and World Bank. These initiatives posed a significant ideological challenge to the long-standing idea that Latin America needed US- and northern-led institutions both to develop economically and to save them in times of economic trouble.

Beginning in 2003, Brazilian president Lula da Silva actively pursued "a foreign policy strategy of global power diffusion."[24] That goal meant that there was potential common ground between Lula and his more radical colleague in Venezuela. Like Chávez, the Brazilian president sought a more united South America, stronger economic relations across the global south, and generally, a more multipolar world.[25] The Venezuelan president probably did not share Brazil's expectation that it was the natural leader of South America, but Chávez and Lula had more common interests than disputes. Both leaders sought greater autonomy from the United States and diversification of their international relations, including expansion of links across the global south, and they wanted new institutions to strengthen Latin American integration. To that end, the two South American presidents sought to promote enlargement of Mercosur, a common market of the south whose full members are Argentina, Brazil, Paraguay, Uruguay, and Venezuela, while blocking the FTAA, which they both saw as a vehicle for the United States to institutionalize its influence in South America.

In 2001, Chávez had been largely alone in his willingness to challenge the FTAA, questioning the idea that all members of the community needed to be "representative democracies" and suggesting that the 2005 deadline was too soon. By 2003 in Puebla, Chávez had been joined by Lula, who criticized the US unwillingness to negotiate on the antidumping and agricultural issues that were most important to Brazil. The Venezuelans provided an ideological critique supplemented by the more pragmatic approach taken by the Brazilians. By the 2005 meetings, the FTAA was on its last legs. The Bush administration had no chance in the face of opposition from Chávez, Lula, and the host country of Argentina.

As the FTAA dream was dying, South American integration was moving forward. In 2004, twelve South American nations agreed to establish the Community of South American Nations, which would change its name to the Union of South American Nations (UNASUR) in 2007. Importantly, the main focus of UNASUR was not trade, but security, political, environmental, and infrastructural cooperation and integration. UNASUR has shown the ability to respond to challenges by opposition groups to elected leaders in South America. A coup in Paraguay against President Fernando Lugo was answered quickly with a suspension of the country's membership and the withdrawal of most South American ambassadors from the country. UNASUR has also helped to facilitate better relations between Colombia and its neighbors, particularly with Venezuela. As Chodor and McCarthy-Jones argue, "UNASUR has created an important political space, through which South American countries are increasingly successful in sidelining the US in the articulation and management of the regional political agenda."[26]

Chávez was particularly interested in developing an organization that might challenge the Organization of American States (OAS), which he believed disproportionately responded to the interests of the United States. The Community of Latin American and Caribbean States (CELAC) was developed in 2010, and held its first summit in December 2011 to deal with both the outsized influence of the US in the OAS and the exclusion of Cuba from that institution. As CELAC has developed, the organization has taken on the role of representing the LAC community in biregional summits. The first EU-CELAC meeting was held in Chile in January 2013, and CELAC is expected to continue to serve as the counterpart to the Europeans in biregional summits and in the partnership between the two regions more generally. CELAC has also met with Indian and Chinese government entities. CELAC Summit II was held in Havana in January 2014. The symbolism of Cuba's hosting was clear, and the focus there on poverty, hunger, and inequality made it a historic summit for the region, according to Brazilian president Dilma Rousseff.[27]

When Barack Obama became president of the United States in 2008, there were expectations in Latin America that relations would improve. Even among the more critical leaders in Latin America, Venezuela's Chávez hoped to see a "real change," Bolivian president Morales felt that the "whole world will change," and in Argentina, President Cristina Fernández confirmed that she had "good expectations" about the new US president.[28] In early 2014, the common view is that although Obama has changed the discourse, the substance of the policy approach to the region has not changed. Basic commitments to a militarization of drug policy, the spread of neoliberal economic policies, and the maintenance of the Cuban embargo have continued. That famous handshake with Chávez at Obama's first 2009 Summit of the Americas in Trinidad and Tobago was followed only a couple of months later by a coup in Honduras. In part motivated by Honduran president Zelaya's decision to join the Bolivarian Alliance for the Peoples of Our America (ALBA), the political and military opposition seized him in his office and flew him out of the country. The initial response by the Obama administration suggested they had learned from the Bush administration's errors in Venezuela, but over time, the US position shifted. While Brazil allowed Zelaya to stay protected in their embassy in Tegucigalpa, the US government was making it clear that it would look favorably upon an election to choose a new president, even if it were held with the coup-government still in power. Once again, that position left the United States nearly isolated, while Chávez rhetorically attacked the Honduran government and the Brazilians more quietly made their opposition to the coup clear.

During the same period, the Obama administration signed an agreement with Colombia to give the United States access to seven bases in that country to replace a base in Manta, Ecuador. Both the United States and Colombia insisted that the agreement merely formalized already existing access, but none of Colombia's neighbors saw it that way. Brazil in particular complained that it had not been consulted by what it saw as new US military access in a country it bordered. The US position was further harmed when a Venezuelan-American lawyer, Eva Golinger, discovered that the Air Force documents justifying the expense in Colombia noted that the bases would provide the Pentagon with "an opportunity for conducting full spectrum operations throughout South America."[29] The document supported military operations because this "critical sub-region of our hemisphere" was experiencing "constant threat from narcotics-funded terrorist insurgencies, anti-US governments, endemic poverty and recurring natural disasters."[30]

The Obama administration's policy toward Cuba has not deviated significantly from that of its predecessor. The United Nations continues to condemn the US embargo on Cuba. The most recent vote in 2013 was 188 to 2, as only Israel joined the United States—a dismal vote for a US president who pledged to leave behind the unilateralism of his predecessor. Florida's Electoral College votes are frequently invoked to explain the embargo, and now that the embargo is codified into law, the US president cannot unilaterally lift it. In a policy decision that he does control, however, Obama left Cuba on the very short list of state sponsors of terrorism in 2014 along with Iran, Sudan, and Syria.

With countries such as Mexico, Colombia, and most of those in Central America, President Obama continued with aid to fight drug trafficking, while supporting existing and new trade agreements. In some parts of the Caribbean as well, it is clear that remittances, immigration (at least restrained deportation), aid for combating drug trafficking, interests in tourism, and US investment continue to provide reasons for maintaining good relations. But elsewhere, during Obama's second term in office, his administration has had some setbacks in relations with Latin America. The failure to recognize the election of Maduro in Venezuela was accompanied by support for the opposition's demand for a recount, and it left the US government pretty isolated. In explaining the US position in Venezuela, Secretary of State John Kerry's reference at an April 18, 2013, congressional hearing to Latin America's being "'our backyard' had the rare effect of antagonizing friends and foes in the region."[31] The US president has continued to take minority positions on developments in Venezuela, standing with only Canada and Panama in the OAS in opposing a resolution supporting the Maduro government in the wake of violent public protests in Venezuela against the government in early 2014. Both CELAC and UNASUR issued statements supporting the elected government and urging the opposition to negotiate peacefully. As a Heritage Foundation author noted in disapproval, "Instead, many Latin American countries—including historical US allies—have chosen to have the Venezuelan-allied sub-regional UNASUR mediate the conflict."[32]

Conclusion

Developments in US–Latin American relations since the end of the Cold War suggest that those who have challenged the US vision of community in the Americas have registered some successes. The Castro government in Cuba has survived, even in the face of an illness that has forced Fidel to leave the presidency, and Cuba has been fully accepted by the rest of the LAC. Venezuelan president Chávez lost his battle with cancer, but during his fourteen years in office he contributed to the development of institutions and alliances that continue beyond his death. Following Chávez's death, former Brazilian president Lula da Silva wrote an effusive op-ed in the *New York Times* eulogizing his Venezuelan colleague as instrumental to the creation of UNASUR, CELAC, and Bancosur: "The multilateral institutions Mr. Chávez helped create will also help ensure the consecration of South American unity. He will no longer be present at South American summit meetings, but his ideals, and the Venezuelan government, will continue to be represented."[33]

It is clear that the institutions and alliances that have been developing across the region are moving Latin America in the direction of a community that is not directed by the United States. In 2014, the United States remains an important player in the region, but Latin Americans have shown themselves to be "makers" of foreign policy and willing to challenge the United States. When a US spokesperson declared CELAC guilty of "betraying" democracy by supporting Cuba, Venezuelan president Maduro suggested that the "defeated" United States should swallow its declarations and understand that the region had adopted "a new model of integration."[34] For his part, Bolivian president Morales at the Havana meeting in 2014 declared again that CELAC is an instrument of liberation from the United States for the people of Latin America and the Caribbean.[35]

For more than two decades since the end of the Cold War, actors in Latin America and the United States have offered competing conceptions of community for the Americas. The United States has been slow to adapt to the Latin American–initiated changes. Post–Cold War US presidents have not moved beyond the idea of a US-led community of the Americas that universally embraces the ideas of market economies and political democracy as practiced in the United States. The diversification of political and economic relations sought by most Latin American countries, and the new political and economic architecture in the region, suggest a dramatic shift in US–Latin American relations in the twenty-first century. The United States clearly still matters, but its claims of regional leadership and expectations of deference are less credible than at any point since the end of the Cold War.

Epilogue

Since this chapter was written, Presidents Obama and Castro announced the normalization of relations between their countries, and embassies were opened in Havana and Washington. Brazilian President Rousseff and Venezuelan President Maduro have been weakened politically as their countries deal with economic setbacks. Even with these developments, the trend toward a Latin American and Caribbean community that does not defer to and continues to exclude the United States from important institutional developments continues in the region.

Notes

1. Mark Weisbrot, "Why the US demonises Venezuela's democracy," *The Guardian* (London), October 4, 2012.

2. Diana Tussie, "Hemispheric Relations: Budding Contest in the Dawn of a New Era," in *Inter-American Cooperation at a Crossroads*, ed. Gordon Mace, Andrew F. Cooper, and Timothy M. Shaw (New York: Palgrave MacMillan, 2011), 26.

3. Jorge Castañeda, "The Forgotten Relationship," *Foreign Affairs*, May/June 2003, 67–81.

4. Robert Keohane, "Between Vision and Reality: Variables in Latin American Foreign Policy," in *Latin America in the New International System*, ed. Joseph Tulchin and Ralph Espach (Boulder, CO: Lynne Rienner, 2001), 211.

5. Diana Tussie, "Latin America: Contrasting Motivations for Regional Projects," *Review of International Studies* 35 (2009): 177.

6. Simón Bolívar played a key role in the Latin American wars of independence in the early eighteenth century. The liberator then sought to unite independent nations in Latin America. Although Bolívar's attempts at union did not succeed, Chávez later declared his movement in Venezuela to be one of Bolivarianism, in tribute to the shared goals of Latin American sovereignty and unity, as well as the Venezuelan's commitment to social and economic justice. American exceptionalism is rooted in nineteenth-century interpretations of the unique mission of the United States as seen in the idea of Manifest Destiny and even Alexis de Tocqueville's book, *Democracy in America*, although the phrase itself was not used until the early twentieth century. In the contemporary era, the references to the exceptional character of the United States are part of the idea that US power and influence are indispensable to the greater good of the world as a whole.

7. Donald E. Pease, *The New American Exceptionalism* (Minneapolis: University of Minnesota Press, 2009).

8. George Bush, "Remarks Announcing the Enterprise for the Americas Initiative," June 27, 1990, online at Gerhard Peters and John T. Wooley, *The American Presidency Project*, accessed April 12, 2012, http://www.presidency.ucsb.edu/ws/?pid=18644.

9. Ibid.

10. Doyle McManus, "Clinton Links Free Trade, Jobs at Summit," *Los Angeles Times*, December 10, 1994, accessed April 10, 2012, http://articles.latimes.com/1994-12-10/news/mn-7304_1_free-trade-area.

11. Peter Hakim, "The Uneasy Americas," *Foreign Affairs* 80, no. 2 (March/April 2001): 46.

12. "Bush Looks South of the Border," CBS News, August 25, 2000, accessed March 22, 2012, http://www.cbsnews.com/stories/2000/08/25/politics/main227866.shtml.

13. George W. Bush, "Fact Sheet, President's Speech at the Summit of the Americas," April 21, 2001, press release, accessed March 22, 2012, http://georgewbush-whitehouse.archives.gov/news/releases/2001/04/20010423–1.html.

14. George W. Bush, "President to Attend Summit of the Americas and Travel to Brazil and Panama," October 5, 2005, accessed March 22, 2012, http://georgewbush-whitehouse.archives.gov/news/releases/2005/10/20051005.html.

15. Barack Obama, "Renewing US Leadership in the Americas," Miami, FL, *Chicago Sun-Times*, May 23, 2008, accessed February 13, 2012, http://blogs.suntimes.com/sweet/2008/05/obama_latin_america_speech_in.html.

16. President Obama's Santiago speech, "The Latin America That I See Today," March 21, 2011, accessed February 15, 2012, http://www.whitehouse.gov/blog/2011/03/22/president-obama-s-santiago-speech-latin-america-i-see-today.

17. Hakim, "The Uneasy Americas," 46.

18. Nicola Miller, "The Historiography of Nationalism and National Identity in Latin America," *Nations and Nationalism* 12, no. 2 (2006): 203.

19. Bart Jones, "US Funds Aid Chavez Opposition: National Endowment for Democracy at Center of Dispute in Venezuela," *National Catholic Reporter*, April 2, 2004, accessed March 20, 2012, http://natcath.org/NCR_Online/archives2/2004b/040204/040204a.htm.

20. George W. Bush: "Press Briefing by Ari Fleischer," April 12, 2002, online at Gerhard Peters and John T. Woolley, *The American Presidency Project*, accessed March 22, 2012, http://www.presidency.ucsb.edu/ws/?pid=62610.

21. Ed Vulliamy, "Venezuela Coup Linked to Bush Team," *The Observer* (London), April 21, 2002, accessed March 17, 2012, http://www.guardian.co.uk/world/2002/apr/21/usa.venezuela.

22. Juan Forero, "Documents Show C.I.A. Knew of a Coup Plot in Venezuela," *New York Times*, December 3, 2004, accessed May 25, 2014, http://www.nytimes.com/2004/12/03/international/americas/03venezuela.html?_r=0.

23. Daniel Flynn, "US 'Deeply Disappointed' by Venezuelan President Chavez's Speech on War," Reuters, October 30, 2001, accessed April 15, 2012, http://www.commondreams.org/headlines01/1030-07.htm.

24. Steen Fryba Christensen, "Brazil's Foreign Policy Priorities," *Third World Quarterly* 34, no. 2 (2013): 272.

25. Celso Amorim, "Brazilian Foreign Policy under President Lula (2003–2010): An Overview," *Revista Brasileira de Politica Internacional* (Brasilia) 53 (December 2010): 214–40.

26. Tom Chodor and Anthea McCarthy-Jones, "Post-Liberal Regionalism in Latin America and the Influence of Hugo Chavez," *Journal of Iberian and Latin American Research* 19, no. 2 (2013).

27. Patricia Grogg, "CELAC Summit Targets Inequality," Inter Press Service, January 30, 2014, accessed August 8, 2014, http://www.ipsnews.net/2014/01/celac-summit-targets-inequality/.

28. Andres Oppenheimer, "Commentary: Obama Already Getting Best of Anti-American Leaders," *Miami Herald*, January 22, 2009, accessed November 29, 2012, http://www.mcclatchydc.com/2009/01/23/60522/commentary-obama-already-getting.html.

29. Department of the Air Force, "Military Construction Program, Fiscal Year 2010 Budget Estimates," submitted to Congress, May 2009, pp. 214, 217, accessed April 16, 2012, http://www.centrodealerta.org/documentos_desclasificados/original_in_english_air_for.pdf.

30. Ibid.

31. Andres Oppenheimer, "What Obama Didn't Say about Latin America," *Miami Herald*, May 8, 2013.

32. Ana Quintana, "Crisis in Venezuela: UNASUR and US Foreign Policy," The Heritage Foundation, April 23, 2014, accessed May 18, 2014, http://www.heritage.org/research/reports/2014/04/crisis-in-venezuela-unasur-and-us-foreign-policy#_ftn4.

33. Lula da Silva, "Latin America After Chavez," *New York Times*, March 6, 2013, accessed May 25, 2014, http://www.nytimes.com/2013/03/07/opinion/latin-america-after-chavez.html.

34. Ewan Robertson, "Venezuela's Maduro Tells US to 'Swallow' Criticism of CELAC Summit," Venezuelanalysis, January 31, 2014, http://venezuelanalysis.com/news/10316.

35. "Evo Morales Highlights the Role of CELAC," *Granma* (Havana), January 26, 2014, http://en.escambray.cu/2014/evo-morales-highlights-role-of-celac/.

Ozbekchilik as an Ethno-Symbolist Construct
Articulating the *Ethnie* in Uzbekistan

REUEL R. HANKS

An Ethno-Symbolic Approach to Uzbek Identity

Identity at any level is never "established" in the sense of permanency—there is no such thing as a "stable," meaning immutable, identity. While some components of identity may be consistent over time, and their form and function may remain fairly constant, the concept of identity is frequently misrepresented as a static "endpoint" rather than as a fluid set of interacting influences that is temporally and spatially dynamic, as well as relational. Identity in the corporate sense is "incessantly negotiated through discourse."[1] This quality implies that the expression of identity in various manifestations is an evolutionary process, in turn suggesting that while there may be an inherent, "primordial" drive among groups of humans to recognize, organize, and legitimize themselves by differentiating their characteristics from those of other groups, symbols of identity are socially constructed. Even if one accepts a primordial origin of ethnic or national identity, based on what Clifford Geertz labeled "assumed givens,"[2] the physical expression and cultural content of these allegedly innate qualities is always conditioned by the social milieu in which they arise.

Second, identity may be expressed or demonstrated at any point along a continuum from personal to supranational, but regardless of its position on this scale, it represents a gestalt that is sui generis in each context. The sum of a collective identity is typically greater than its parts, making it difficult for scholars to arrive at any general theory that is broadly applicable. Traditionally, scholars attempting to understand national identity were divided into those who advocated the position that group identity, ultimately expressed at the national level, was anchored in natural, exclusivist tendencies of a primordial past; and those who held that national identity and its expression as nationalism is a social construction of the modern age—for most of the latter, this meant national identities as they are currently understood did not arise until at least the Age of Enlightenment.

The Ethno-Symbolism Model

Ethno-symbolism is a theoretical approach to identity formation that purports to represent a compromise between primordialism and modernism (or to use other common labels, perennialism and constructivism). Anthony Smith, as the leading proponent of ethno-symbolism, posits the emergence of an "ethnic core" in certain groups that may in turn emerge as an "ethnic community," or *ethnie*. The *ethnie* is defined as "a named and self-defined human community whose members possess both a myth of common ancestry, shared memories, one or more elements of common culture, including a link with a territory, and a measure of solidarity, at least among the upper strata."[3] For ethno-symbolists like Smith, John Armstrong, John Hutchinson, and Miroslav Hroch, *culture* then as an element of the content of national identity gains precedence over processes associated with modernization. The latter would include Karl Deutsch's concept of social mobilization in the construction of nationalism, Benedict Anderson's famous theory of "print capitalism," Ernest Gellner's formulations placing modern state institutions as the catalyst for national identity, and Eric Hobsbawm's related argument for industrial capitalism as the key instrument.[4] A theoretical approach that melds the primordial and modernist schools is perhaps appropriate, since their differences are not so stark as is frequently portrayed in the literature. As Henry Hale notes in a discussion of the theoretical approaches to ethnicity, "It indeed seems that even primordialists are constructivists."[5]

Ethno-symbolism accepts the premise that identity is socially constructed, but parts company with modernism on the central element(s) driving such construction. Hutchinson and Hroch, who along with Smith are generally considered among the most prominent supporters of the ethno-symbolist approach, argue that national identity formation may be accelerated or enhanced by modernization (Gellner) or the advent of print capitalism (Anderson) but also requires the substrate of collective, corporate memory over a significant duration.[6]

Smith's definition of the *ethnie* emphasizes the vital junction between identity and a spatial dimension. National identity is typically connected to the concept of a "homeland," either actual or mythological. *Territorialization* is the process whereby a bond is established between collective memory and the physical environment. In practice, this is achieved via a national narrative reinforced by symbology, linking a corporate identity to a specified landscape. Moreover, securing national identity requires temporal reinforcement (the so-called *longue durée*) of mutually accepted and shared memory, accomplished by quotidian encounters with the symbology of identity. Smith suggests that the appropriation of a "worthy" past, a "golden age," is vital to the recognition and continuity of national identities.

If there is some agreement between the modernist and ethno-symbolist views regarding the social construction of identity, the concept of the *longue durée* marks a sharp line of distinction between them. Modernists argue that national identity emerged during the late eighteenth century as a result of economic and political events. Gellner went so far as to write that "nothing before [the early eighteenth century] makes the slightest difference to the issues we face."[7] Borrowed from the French Annales school of social science, and most particularly from the work of Fernand Braudel, the *longue durée* concept in ethno-symbolism holds that nations and national identity are not the products of the modern nation-state system, set in motion at the Peace of Westphalia. On the contrary, from the ethno-symbolist position, the *longue durée* encompasses three processes that coordinate to solidify the identity of the *ethnie*: rediscovery, reappropriation, and continuity. This coordination transpires through a symbology of public culture, similar in many ways to what Michael Billig famously termed "banal nationalism."[8] The historian David Lowenthal has argued in his book *The Past Is a Foreign Country* that "remembering the past is crucial to our sense of identity . . . to know what we were confirms that we are. . . . We synthesize identity not simply by calling up a sequence of reminiscences, but by being enveloped . . . in a unifying web of retrospection."[9]

For the ethno-symbolist, the engagement of public culture is crucial for the development of *mythomoteurs*. This term was coined by John Armstrong, but is more explicitly used in the work of Anthony Smith, particularly in regard to the construction of national myth. Armstrong approaches the concept of the mythomoteur as an embodiment of group identity expressed through what he calls "myth-symbol complexes."[10] For Smith, the term represents "constitutive political myth."[11] For both, the mythomoteur is the fulcrum whereby the mythology of the state is transferred to the collective identity of the "nation." Myth, located in a past "golden age," is projected into the present through the veneration of historical heroes, tribulations that represent dramatic group sacrifice and tragedy, or other seminal events in the history (or alleged history, at any rate) of the group. National myth may be essential to territorialization of identity in what George Schopflin considers the "sacralization of territory." Cultural identity is bound up with a sacred space, "where the nation first discovered itself . . . or expressed itself in its finest form in and through that territory."[12]

The Transmutation of Uzbek Identity in an Ethno-Symbolic Context

Guntram Herb has argued in an interesting volume that "collective con-sciousness leads to homeland."[13] But this formulation, it seems, is suspect for Uzbekistan, and perhaps for most postcolonial states. In many instances in postcolonial Africa, Central Asia, and the Middle East, specific territories were assigned to alleged national identities that existed for the most part only in the rhetoric of national leaders. In fact, the converse appears to obtain just as frequently: framing national identity within a specific territorial context, i.e., a "homeland," leads to the emergence, over some stretch of time, to a shared identity. For Uzbekistan, the Soviet policy of *razmezhevanie* (literally, "divid-ing up") in Central Asia created a spatial context for broader identities (Uzbek, Tajik, Kazakh, Kyrgyz, and Turkmen) that were at best inchoate. In addition, the political boundaries thus introduced frequently failed to follow the eth-nic fractures in the region delineated by the Soviet authorities themselves. In the case of the Central Asian states, the process has clearly been "homeland leads to collective consciousness," although this is not the approach taken by state-promoted, nationalist ideology, either today or during the Soviet era.

Uzbekistan, like other new Eurasian states, in the past two decades had to abruptly reshape some of the parameters and nature of national identity while preserving, in Anthony Smith's terminology, a "usable past." This trans-mutation of identity was set in motion by the collapse of Soviet state authority and the accompanying nationalities philosophy. Ironically, it was also that very philosophy and the derivative set of policies that stimulated the coales-cence of a territorialized "Uzbek" identity. In Central Asia, Soviet nationalities policy centered on the alleged ethnogenesis of major *ethnies* in the region, and sought to reinforce the evolutionary process of national differentiation by assigning a geographical dimension. Each national group that met a numeri-cal threshold was territorialized through the creation of a specific "homeland," whose boundaries, at least in theory, were based on the preponderance of the eponymous group. Soviet policy was in fact a reification of the ethnic land-scape in the region, as the majority of the corporate identities promoted were not widely recognized by Central Asian peoples themselves.

Early Soviet policy held that these groupings, as well as all others based on the ethno-cultural principle, were ephemeral. Soviet commentators in the early 1920s could thus declare: "The nation is a historic, transitional category that does not represent anything primeval or eternal. Indeed, the process of the evo-lution of the nation essentially repeats the history of the development of social forms."[14] But this stance shifted abruptly by the end of the decade, and at the

Sixteenth Congress of the Communist Party in 1930, Stalin declared that as long as national distinctions remained among the USSR's peoples, "the ethno-territorial entities would have to be *preserved and reinforced* [emphasis added]."[15]

"Preservation and reinforcement" of ethno-identities that had only recently been recognized was crystallized by creating standardized literary languages for the new identities, although in the case of the Kazakhs this had already been accomplished in the latter half of the nineteenth century. Among the indigenous Central Asian peoples, literacy rates were below 10 percent when the USSR formed in 1922, and a standardized language was of little use in constructing national identity if few could use it, so universal public education was a cornerstone of the effort at "reinforcement." In the Uzbek SSR and elsewhere, this was largely successful on both counts, and by the 1950s the great majority in Uzbekistan not only were literate in standardized Uzbek, but a majority were conversant in Russian, the language of administration and technical higher education.

Building some of the elements of the cultural framework of an Uzbek identity was actualized by government directive. Increased literacy rates and the standardization of a literary form of Uzbek were readily accomplished by marshaling the coercive, organizational power of the Soviet state. Other cultural attributes were much more problematical. The ethnonym "Uzbek" itself was in fact rarely used either by outsiders in reference to most of the people settled in the space delineated as the Uzbek SSR, or by the inhabitants themselves. Even as late as the mid-1920s, Soviet historians and ethnographers doubted the viability of the term as an ethnic identifier, declaring that the label had so declined in use in the preceding era that it had been rendered to an "entirely meaningless status in the last few centuries."[16] The more general term "Sart," based not on ethnic identity but rather on urban residence along with linguistic duality, was apparently the most widely applied characterization of the settled population. Likewise, a commission formed by the All-Russia Academy of Sciences in 1925 (the year *after* the establishment of the Uzbek SSR), charged with investigating ethnic diversity in the country, reported that Uzbeks did not possess the same level of group identification as the major nomadic peoples of Central Asia. Moreover, the urban population (Sarts) had failed to "create a particular ethnic identification for itself,"[17] a finding that called into question the validity of the geographic division of the Central Asian region into homelands based upon purportedly precise and stark ethnic (in Soviet parlance, "national") groupings. The Sarts, it seems, were neither Uzbek nor Tajik, and in fact, according to the scholars on the commission were not even Sarts.

What, then, was the implication and meaning of *Ozbekchilik* [Uzbekness]? An "Uzbek" identity had been territorialized in 1924, but its legitimacy was immediately in doubt because of a paucity of historiography associated with the "Uzbek" people. There was no *longue durée* of ethnic antecedents in place, articulating a cultural history around which elites might consolidate. Ethnographers in the Uzbek SSR set about rectifying this conundrum in the decades after the delimitation of their ethnic homeland, a process that has continued into the era of independence. In the parlance of ethno-symbolism, this represents the process of rediscovery and reappropriation. Most Western scholars have typically assigned the emergence of a proto-Uzbek identity to the appearance of the Shaybanid dynasty.[18] However, from the early 1940s onward, scholars in Uzbekistan attempted to establish an ethnographic origin for the titular people that extended far into antiquity, a process that has continued and intensified in the wake of independence.

Two pillars of both Soviet and contemporary ethnography regarding the origins of the Uzbeks may be identified. The first of these is the alleged autochthonism of the Uzbeks in Central Asia. The second, intertwined with the first, is the teleological claim of the continuous expression of Uzbek identity in the region, a process that far predates the official territorialization of identity rendered in 1924. Some Western scholars, like the anthropologist Edward Allworth, have christened the initial arguments articulating these positions as "racialist" because they were philosophically grounded in notions of genetic exclusiveness.[19] As such, the Uzbeks were not only culturally and historically distinct from neighboring "nations," they were in fact physically unique and could be distinguished on the basis of facial features, stature, and other characteristics.

Through the middle decades of the twentieth century, Soviet-era historians "traced" the ethnographical lineage of the Uzbeks to a historical succession of Turkic groups, at each stage appropriating ever more ancient antecedents of ethnogenesis. In the 1940s the prevailing progenitors were the Karakhanids, but by the 1970s these Turkic overlords of the tenth century had been displaced by nomadic Turkic tribes who, it was (and is) claimed, occupied the territory of the Amu Darya and Syr Darya valleys from as early as the seventh century. For example, the Uzbek ethnographer Karim Shaniyazov in the 1970s postulated that the Karluks, a loose tribal grouping of nomadic Turks, who according to Chinese records migrated into the Fergana Valley in the seventh century, represented the initiation of Uzbek identity. Shaniyazov, who was enormously influential in ethnographic circles in the Uzbek SSR (in the 1980s, most of the scholars in Uzbekistan who specialized in the study of nationalities were his former students), a decade later added the Kipchaks, yet another Turkic tribal cluster, to the mixture.[20] Only in this instance, he differentiated between two waves of Kipchak migration into Central Asia, holding that the earlier arrivals in the tenth century were a component of Uzbek ethnogenesis, while the latter movement triggered the ethnogenesis of the Kazakhs and Kyrgyz in the fifteenth century. Thus the autochthonous claims of *Ozbekchilik* were validated via the "historical" record.

From the vantage point of ethno-symbolism, the drive by Soviet and contemporary scholars in Uzbekistan to precisely capture and pinpoint the essence of ethnogenesis represents a legitimization of the *longue durée*. The Uzbek people did not simply appear via the *fiat* of the Soviet state in 1924, nor had their ancestors been a component of an amorphous Turkic presence that provided a platform for cultural crystallization in the fifteenth century. Certainly "Uzbek" identity had emerged along lines that had little if any intersection with Persian elements. Accordingly, "Uzbeks" had occupied the ethnic homeland from time immemorial, a *longue durée* confirmed by the archeological, historical, and ethnographic research.

This effort has been advanced through state structures, including academic institutions, which are controlled by the regime and have their research agendas dictated by government entities. In 1998 in a published speech before the Oliy Majlis, President Karimov directly called for the Institute of History, a unit of the Uzbekistan Academy of Sciences, to "establish" the ancient origins of the country, declaring that the nascent state could not move forward without the foundation of "historical memory."[21] Any efforts to define the ethnic geography of Uzbekistan and the nature of *Ozbekchilik* outside of the official strictures are met with opprobrium by the regime and its academic supporters, as was the case with the *Ethnic Atlas of Uzbekistan*. The *Atlas* was sponsored by the Soros Foundation and written by Uzbek scholars, but its content was not vetted by the Karimov regime, and it was published outside of Uzbekistan. Immediately upon its appearance, a host of well-known Uzbek historians attacked its accuracy, mostly on the grounds that it misrepresented the facts of the ethnogenesis of the Uzbek people, and specifically made a false claim that Tajiks had been assimilated by force in the early Soviet period.[22]

Timurids as "Uzbek" Paragons

The Karimov administration seeks to monopolize the character and presentation of *Ozbekchilik*, manufacturing a mythic identity that correlates with state rhetoric and goals. Yet this process frequently wanders far afield from historical reality, and it remains unclear to what extent the fictionalization of the Uzbek identity myth may undermine that identity itself. *Ozbekchilik* is the core of the Uzbek *ethnie*, and who qualifies as an "Uzbek" is obviously therefore central to the identity. Incorporating figures whose linkages to that core are questionable and contradictory, as irrefutably illustrated by the historical record, may serve to delegitimize the process of identity formation. Especially problematical in this regard is the adoption into the *Ozbekchilik* mythomoteur of various national heroes from the Timurid era in Central Asia, such as Alishir Navoi, Babur, and Amir Timur himself.

Navoi was christened the "Father of Uzbek literature" by Soviet scholars because of his dedication to make Chagatay, the Turkic language of the Central Asian intelligentsia emerging from the Mongol era, into a literary language that would rival, if not supplant, Persian at the court of the Timurids. Soviet-era linguists in Uzbekistan decreed that Chagatay was in fact "Old Uzbek," the precursor tongue to the standardized modern form of Uzbek developed by Soviet authorities in the late 1920s. Scholars in independent Uzbekistan have reiterated this claim, holding that modern Uzbek is the "closest" of Central Asia's Turkic languages to "Old Turkish."[23] Edward Allworth has questioned this assertion, arguing that the alleged evolution "distorts" the historic process of linguistic evolution in Uzbekistan, creating a distinctive literary pedigree where none actually exists.[24] Regardless of the derivation of the modern Uzbek language, it is quite indisputable that Navoi did not regard himself as connected to the ethnonym "Uzbek" in any sense, and he and other Timurid writers differentiated the Uzbek tribes who spoke a Kipchak dialect, who had recently penetrated the southern steppe regions of Central Asia, from their own linguistic identity.

An ethno-symbolistic strategy of identity construction frequently employs the public arena as a canvas for inculcating the imagery of the national myth. Alexander Diener and Joshua Hagen have articulated how urban places are vital to constructing national narratives in the former Soviet Union, and other scholars have recently turned to investigating the role of architecture in this process.[25] In independent Uzbekistan, the Soviet-era incorporation of Navoi into the Uzbek mythomoteur has been intensified under the Karimov regime, projecting this figure into a collective space in which the public inescapably encounters the image of Navoi on a daily basis. The National Literature Museum is named after Navoi, and the State Park adjacent to the assembly hall of the Oliy Majlis (the national legislature) is named after the Timurid writer. The park features a large domed cupola with a ten-foot-tall statue of Navoi at its center, while the interior of the dome is inscribed with his verses. In addition, a major thoroughfare in Tashkent bears his name, as does one of the most decorative and busy metro stations in the city.

Despite his sanctification as a key "Uzbek" figure, Navoi's public veneration is secondary compared to that of Amir Timur himself.[26] Although he was vilified by Soviet historians during the 1920s and 1930s, later Soviet scholars

occasionally offered a somewhat friendlier evaluation of the Central Asian
warlord,[27] but Timur was not deified as mythic founder of Uzbekistan until
independence. Laura Adams, who has produced an exhaustive study of the
role of public spectacle in Uzbek identity, argues that Islom Karimov has uti-
lized the ubiquitous symbol of Timur to solidify and justify his own monopoly on political power.[28] Moreover, this strategy serves to link Karimov's
political fortunes to those of the Uzbek state itself, subliminally implying
that Karimov's public persona is a component of national identity. Accordingly, Timur, the greatest of "Uzbek" leaders, built a strong, successful state via
the wisdom of authoritarian policies and institutions, and the modern Uzbek
state may achieve a similar status using the same strategy, under the strong
leadership of Karimov.[29]

Timur's image is even more pervasive than that of Navoi in the urban space
of Uzbekistan. In Samarkand, Timur's imperial capital city (and also the home
town of Islom Karimov), an enormous recumbent statue of the conqueror
commands the intersection leading to his mausoleum, the Gur-i-Emir, and in
Tashkent a massive bronze representation dominates the city's central park, a
location that under the Soviet regime featured statues of Stalin and Marx. In
1999 the Karimov government financed the construction of a large museum
devoted exclusively to Timur, adjacent to the park. President Karimov has
provided glowing and historically sanitized versions of Timur's career on
numerous occasions, including a virtual paean articulated in 1996 in Paris,
in which he praised Timur's administrative skills and historical achievements.

The rehabilitation of Timur as mythomoteur extends to popular culture
as well. In the years following independence, Uzbek writers produced a spate
of novels portraying him as a sage, paternal figure who, although stern and
a product of his time, nevertheless embodied all the qualities a great leader
should exhibit. Two examples among many are *Velikii Timur* (Great Timur) by
Erkin Berezikov and *Amir Timur* by Bahodir Akhmedov. The official adula-
tion of Timur in Uzbek historiography is in arrant contrast to his image in the
national myths of neighboring Central Asian states, especially in Tajikistan,
where his Soviet-era evaluation has remained largely in place.

This canonization of Timurid figures is oddly combined with an almost
complete disregard of the Shaybanids, a Turkic nomadic confederation that
controlled virtually the entire steppe region between the Caspian Sea and the
Tien Shan in the fourteenth century. The Shaybanids are frequently referred
to by contemporary writers, both Persian and Timurid, as Uzbeks and were
using this ethnonym to self-identify themselves by the early 1500s. Beatrice
Manz believes that the Shaybanids are largely ignored in the national narrative promoted by the Karimov regime because of their nomadic origins
and historical connections to the Mongols,[30] but this argument is somewhat

undermined by the historical record: Timur himself never disowned his Mongol origins, and in fact viewed himself as the rightful inheritor and preserver of Mongol glory and empire. Timur's presentation as the central figure in the Uzbek mythomoteur, the "father" of the modern Uzbeks, at the expense of the Shaybanid heritage, highlights an essential contradiction of *Ozbekchilik*: the paternalistic origins of the modern Uzbeks are a nationalistic trope that fails to coordinate with the history of the ethnonym, instead coopting figures who, prior to the arrival of the Shaybanids, occupied the territory of the modern state but did not recognize or share in Uzbek identity.

Ozbekchilik and Cultural Resources

Since the early 1990s, the Uzbek regime has attempted to develop the symbolic capital required to construct a national ideology based on an ethno-symbolic framework. All national ideologies engage in this process to a certain degree, as it is necessary to separate the basis of identity from competitors while carving out a unique historical niche for identity to support the basis of *longue durée*, substantiate mythomoteurs, and inculcate national myth. In Central Asia this process is directed by the differing philosophical positions concerning the basis for national identity, dating to the *natsional'noe razmezhevanie* (national division) in the region, which still stands as the rationale underlying conflicting historical myths. The Karimov regime recognizes the necessity of imposing the conceptual strategies of the *longue durée*, mythomoteur, and a "golden age" inculcated through an inescapable public culture, although, of course, it may not address the process in these terms. The regime utilizes a legitimized violence that directs the population to a revised concept of national identity. This revision is achieved by controlling the educational and academic spheres of society, and by establishing an iconic, pervasive presence of the mythomoteur that is engaged on a daily basis.

Moreover, the achievement of independence for the "Uzbek" nation, within its associated sacralized borders, confirms the continuity of an ages-long drive that is historically inevitable. Adopting this framework has two advantages from the perspective of the Karimov administration. First, it authenticates the spatial parameters of *Ozbekchilik*, not a small matter in a state where the inhabitants of several large cities speak Tajik as their first language, and where the largest regional subunit, the Karakalpak Autonomous Region, represents an alternative, if not competing, ethnic consciousness. Secondly, it allows the regime to draw a direct line of descent via ethno-symbology to its historical antecedents (at least those claimed to be of ancient provenance), equating the glory of the past to the promise of the future. The articulation of an Uzbek historical legacy draws directly from Anthony Smith's concept of a "worthy past," and it forms the raison d'être of an emerging, modern Uzbek identity. The origination of *Ozbekchilik* in the conceptual fabric of ethno-symbolism presents an interesting, and to some extent unique, conundrum. Can a resilient national identity be constructed on a symbolic foundation if the symbols are historically suspect, and indeed, offer a counternarrative to actual ethnogenesis? All mythomoteurs inscribe elements of myth involving national heroes that can be proven to be apocryphal—George Washington's veracity was never proven by the destruction of a cherry tree, nor did King Canute actually attempt to hold back the tide. But what is the result if the *identity* of those heroes can be legitimately challenged? Smith may provide a partial answer:

> On the whole, those communities with rich ethno-histories possess "deep resources" on which to draw, and so can sustain themselves over long periods and maintain an extended struggle for recognition or parity. . . . Communities that lack these well-documented ethno-historical resources may well rise up in protest. . . . If they cannot create . . . an ethno-history and even a golden age of heroic resistance to be recalled and emulated in times of crisis, they will not have those "deep" cultural resources to fall back upon when internal conflicts and dissentions break out.[31]

The next several decades may well reveal how "deep" the ethno-symbolic resources of *Ozbekchilik* lie, and provide a metric of the efficacy of national identity construction in Central Asia.

Notes

1. Michael Lane Bruner, *Strategies of Remembrance. The Rhetorical Dimensions of National Identity Construction* (Columbia: University of South Carolina Press, 2002), 1.
2. Clifford Geertz, "Primordial Ties," in *Ethnicity*, ed. Anthony D. Smith (New York: Oxford University Press), 1996.
3. Anthony Smith, *Ethno-Symbolism and Nationalism: A Cultural Approach* (London and New York: Routledge, 2009), 27.
4. See Karl Deutsch, *Nationalism and Social Communication. An Inquiry into the Foundations of Nationality*, 2nd edition (Cambridge, MA: MIT Press, 1966); Ernest Gellner, *Nations and Nationalism* (Ithaca, NY and London: Cornell University Press, 1983); Benedict Anderson, *Imagined Communities: Reflections on the Origin and Spread of Nationalism* (London: Verso, 1983); Eric Hobsbawm, *Nations and Nationalism Since 1780* (Cambridge: Cambridge University Press, 1990).
5. Henry Hale, *The Foundations of Ethnic Politics* (New York: Cambridge University Press, 2008), 15.
6. John Hutchinson, *Modern Nationalism* (London: Fontana, 1994); Miroslav Hroch, "Real and Constructed: The Nature of the Nation," in *The State of the Nation: Ernest Gellner and the Theory of Nationalism*, ed. J. A. Hall (New York: Cambridge University Press, 1998).

7. Ernest Gellner, *Encounters with Nationalism* (Cambridge, MA and Oxford: Blackwell, 1994), 366.

8. Michael Billig, *Banal Nationalism* (London: Sage, 1995).

9. David Lowenthal, *The Past Is a Foreign Country* (Cambridge: Cambridge University Press, 1985), 197–98.

10. John Armstrong, *Nations Before Nationalism* (Chapel Hill: University of North Carolina Press, 1982), passim.

11. Anthony Smith, *Myths and Memories of the Nation* (Oxford: Oxford University Press, 1999), 18 and passim.

12. Geoffrey Hosking and George Schopflin, eds., *Myths and Nationhood* (New York: Routledge, 1997), 28–29.

13. Guntram Herb and David Kaplan, eds., *Nested Identities: Nationalism, Territory and Scale* (Lanham, MD: Rowman and Littlefield, 1999). 17.

14. Yuri Slezkine, "The USSR as a Communal Apartment, or How a Socialist State Promoted Ethnic Particularism," *Slavic Review* 53, no. 2 (Summer 1994): 437.

15. Ibid., 438.

16. Edward Allworth, *The Modern Uzbeks: From the Fourteenth Century to the Present: A Cultural History.* (Stanford, CA: Hoover Institution Press, 1990), 179.

17. Ibid.

18. John Schoeberlein-Engel, *Identity in Central Asia: Construction and Contention in the Conceptions of "Ozbek," "Muslim," "Samarquandi," and Other Groups.* PhD diss., Harvard University (1994), 61–64. The appellation of "Uzbek" was widely applied in the chronicles of Timurid and Persian historians when referring to the nomadic Turkic confederation led by Shaybani Khan, which evidently coalesced in the region between the Aral and Caspian Seas in the early 1500s.

19. Allworth, *The Modern Uzbeks*, passim.

20. Karim Shaniyazov, *K etnicheskoi istorii uzbekskogo naroda* (Tashkent: Fan, 1974).

21. Islom Karimov, *Tarixiy xotirasiz kelajak yo* (Tashkent: Sharq, 1998), 15.

22. Marlene Laruelle, "National Narrative, Ethnology, and Academia in Post-Soviet Uzbekistan," *Journal of Eurasian Studies* 1 (2010): 107–108.

23. Tahir Qahhar and William Dirks, "Uzbek Literature," *World Literature Today* 70, no. 3 (Summer 1996): 616.

24. Allworth, *The Modern Uzbeks*, 230. Allworth notes that Alexander Semenov and other well-known Soviet ethnographers and historians in the late 1930s began elevating Navoi to the status of "founder of Uzbek literature," once the process of creating a distinct "Uzbek" literary history was encouraged by the Soviet authorities.

25. Alexander C. Diener and Joshua Hagen, "From Socialist to Post-Socialist Cities: Narrating the Nation Through Urban Space," *Nationalities Papers: The Journal of Nationalism and Ethnicity* 41, no. 4; also see Antoine L. Lahoud, "The Role of Cultural (Architectural) Factors in Forging Identity," *National Identities* 10, no. 4, 389–98.

26. A short but insightful summary of the emergence of Timur as a national symbol may be found in Stephen Hegarty, "The Rehabilitation of Temur: Reconstructing National History in Contemporary Uzbekistan," *Central Asian Monitor,* no. 1 (1995). See also Charles Kurzman, "Uzbekistan: The Invention of Nationalism in an Invented Nation," *Critique: Critical Middle Eastern Studies* 8, no. 15 (1999): 82–84.

27. Alexander Iakubovskii's assessment of Timur published in the 1940s, and A. Novoseltsev's writings in the early 1970s, both were revisions of Timur that noted his "positive" qualities.

28. Laura Adams, *The Spectacular State: Culture and National Identity in Uzbekistan* (Durham, NC and London: Duke University Press, 2010).

29. Beatrice Manz notes that Timur has been elevated to the status of "father of the Uzbek nation," a term that on occasion is applied to Karimov himself. Beatrice Forbes Manz, "Tamerlane's Career and Its Uses," *Journal of World History* 13, no. 1, 21.

30. Ibid., 21–22.

31. Anthony D. Smith, *Myths and Memories*, 265.

Afterword

Creating a Community of Area Studies in a Changing World

AYŞE ZARAKOL

What you have read is an unusual volume. There cannot be many edited books that contain essays on countries as varied as Uzbekistan, Tanzania, Romania, the Dominican Republic, Taiwan, Russia, and South Africa, as well as regions separated by so much distance, such as Siberia, Latin America, and Eastern Europe. Yet it is not an accident that brings these chapters together. The authors all share a preoccupation with identity and want to explore its complicated relationship to space/territory, to time/memory, and to community and its many symbols. The authors in this volume also share a strong commitment to rethinking area studies as an enterprise. They want to move beyond the existing (but increasingly diminishing) state of area studies as islands unto themselves, and to start having conversations about how, for instance, studying Dominican identity side by side with an ethnography of Siberian voices can help us make better sense of the world. In this reconceptualization, area studies does not merely serve policymaking concerns, but in fact is *itself* a major avenue for theorizing about the world. This reconceptualization challenges the assumption—held by certain social-scientific approaches—that the scholarly contributions of area studies should be limited to the testing of theories generated by the "disciplines."[1] It also moves social science theorizing away from its Eurocentric origins and points to more robust ways of thinking about the world.

In this short afterword, inspired by the epistemological and methodological commitments in this volume, I want to speculate about the direction that social sciences need to take if they are going to stay relevant in times of change. I start by suggesting that we are about to enter a post-post–Cold War era in which "liminal" states will play a larger role in world politics. By liminal, I mean "borderline," as in not belonging to a clearly defined regional, geographical, or civilizational category. And by liminal states, I mean states that are caught between the West and the East and/or the South. Some obvious examples are Turkey, Russia, and Japan (more on this in a moment). This era we are about to enter will likely be the first non-Western era since at least the beginning of the nineteenth century. Given this transition, the first and foremost challenge will involve transcending the Eurocentric origins of many social science disciplines.

The West and the Rest?

Our ongoing transition to a "non-Western" era entails more than the rise of China (or the other BRICS) to superpower status. That is not happening as quickly or radically as some observers claim (though there is little doubt that a material shift away from the West is underway). The real shift we are experiencing is more profound than simply geographic variation in super and regional powers. It is actually an ontological shift, from the West to the liminal, from a world with a center to a world without a center. In the liminal age, large liminal states like Turkey, Russia, and Japan will be less bound by Western demands than in the previous era. Yet the liminal age is not just about such states. In fact, most states in the modern international system are liminal states in one way or another. This is why the coming age is a *liminal age* and not an Eastern age.

In everyday discussions, we often talk about a tension between the East and the West—but that is a false dichotomy. There is perhaps a West, but there is really no East, except as a catchall category defined in opposition to the West. In fact, there is no region in the world, barring some island and jungle territories, that has not been transformed through its interaction with the modern, Western, and now international states system. In contemporary politics, the focus is very much on how different we are from each other. But if one thinks instead of how much similarity exists between nation-states and then puts it in historical perspective, the homology is staggering. We often forget this. It is easy to overlook what a homogenizing force modernity has been when we glance at the world map and see it carved into nation-states, all emphasizing their particularity as justification for their right to exist. Yet in a sense, the nation-states are like the individuals in modern society—their desire to be distinct is what makes them so similar. There is no pure, no entirely distinct "East" left anywhere in the world—everyone has been Westernized, to varying degrees. Liminality is now a worldwide condition.

This should not be read to imply that the "East" is somehow inauthentic due to this experience of being Westernized (or that all difference has been eradicated). Deeming something as "inauthentic" implies a belief that it is possible to be truly authentic, a belief that there was a time before borrowing, during which the self was pure and untainted. In other words, to believe in authenticity one has to argue that actors have ontologically real essences. There are indeed people today in places like Syria or Afghanistan or Somalia (or even in pockets of Western society) who do believe they have protected themselves from the influence of modernity by rescuing the pure version of their religion or culture from the mists of history, and by stripping away the modern "inauthentic" impositions. What they do not realize is that the obsession with purity and history is all part of the modern mindset. The worry about authenticity is a particularly modern preoccupation. We worry about authenticity precisely because of the modern realization that identity is constructed and eminently constructible. In a world where identity construction is not imagined to be in the realm of the possible, there is no reason to police boundaries to distinguish the "genuine" ones apart from the "fakes."

Every individual is an amalgamation of numerous influences. This was probably the case for all of human history. What modernity changed was our awareness and recollection of these processes. Instead of changing glacially throughout many generations, or changing quickly during wartime but in societies that could not afford to dwell on such matters, identities in modern society came to be changed quickly, deliberately, and in ways that were remembered, creating existential anxieties about authenticity. Modernity in some ways has been about finding a solution to that problem by affixing fluid identities to seeming immutable collectivities like the nation. (Western) postmodernity has been about embracing the uncertainty, the mutability, the liminality of identity, a journey towards the admission that we are all impostors and the genuine item simultaneously. The backlash underwriting the various nativist and fundamentalist movements around the world is part of the same process.

Since that is the case, why even bother to distinguish between the West and the East, or the West and the liminal states? If all are Westernized to some degree, what is the difference between the West and the Rest? It is a historical (though not immutable) difference that comes from ownership of the current international system, of its rules and norms. Even today, "Westernness" still rides on a certain feeling of being the narrator of your own story, the hero of your own movie, being in the center of the world. This is a feeling that important things happen "here" and its corollary that if something happens "here," to "me," it must be important to everyone else. This is what being a "Westerner" has meant in our modern global system. The desire to feel this way is one of the things spread by Westernization, and the ability to take it for granted is "Westernness."

To some degree, it is human nature to feel that one's group is better in many ways than other groups out there and to exaggerate the importance of events that one personally experiences. This is a "normal" reaction. What is unique in the evolution of our modern international system is the globalization of this general human experience in a particular form as filtered through Western eyes. Because those of us in liminal countries have all been Westernized to some extent, we have implicitly accepted that the West stands for all those great things such as order and enlightenment and civility and standards and whatnot. We live in a world where events that happen in the West, from actual events with global consequence to nonevents such as celebrity gossip, get more coverage. Even those who hate the West have implicitly granted in their vitriol its significance as a "center" of global politics. There is not yet an exact "Eastern" corollary to the West (and has not been for a while). Because involvement in the modern international system has necessitated and facilitated the internalization of the modern Western ontology, liminals came to agree on a certain hierarchy of things. Defenses of the "East" are always formulated in the "you have x, which is great, but we have y" type of arguments—that "y" is usually some fuzzy value like warmth or spirit or courage. This is arguing from a position of having already ceded the assumptions of the argument.

Unlike the Westerner, the non-Westerner does not imagine that he is in the center of the world. This is not to say that he goes around in his daily life worrying about that. I am talking about a more general feeling of looking in from outside when it comes to world affairs, as also discussed by Turkish novelist Orhan Pamuk. The non-Westerner, the Easterner, the liminal person has a love-hate relationship with the West, as was well recognized by the Russian novelist Fyodor Dostoyevsky. Neither rejection nor embracement of Western values is enough to escape the imaginary gaze of the West continuously assessing how civilized or modern or developed or democratic one's country is. The Standard of Civilization has changed over time, but an internalized rubric of assessment, the condition of always having to measure oneself against the West, continues to persist. For now.

Evolution of the Modern International Order and What Lies Ahead

The above section generalizes about a period of two hundred years in East-West relations.[2] This has not been a static relationship and its normative standards have gradually improved over time toward more inclusivity. It is possible to divide the modern international system into three broad periods when it comes to its social hierarchies: the nineteenth century (especially the second half) with its Standard of Civilization; the Cold War period with its "standard of development,"[3] and the period we are about to enter now.

The first period was characterized by rigid notions about who stood where in the hierarchy of nations (and races), and it was inherent or nearly inherent characteristics such as religion, ethnicity, and race that determined one's fate in terms of sovereign recognition. This is probably the most "racist" period in human history and in the history of the modern states system. Heterophobia may have been common throughout history, but it was in the nineteenth century that racism was turned into a science, a legal code, and even a test of good manners. This is also the period when most non-Westerner elites absorbed the values of Western civilization and began a cycle of behaviors motivated by the desire to escape stigmatization and self-shame. The only way to improve your position vis-a-vis the West in this period was to quibble with the definition of what it meant to be European/Western—Russia successfully did this for a brief period, Japan tried to do it but still came up against racial standards. This era of overt racism lasted until World War II and the horrors of the Third Reich.

The second period was during the Cold War. In this period, standards of civilization came to be replaced by economic indicators of progress and development. This was an improvement over the previous period, in that "developing" countries, many of them former colonies, could theoretically "work hard," pull themselves up by their bootstraps, and join the club of advanced industrialized nations. Race or religion did not automatically exclude a group of people from achieving worth (often defined as the right to self-determination and recognition). This period was also interesting because there was a supposed alternative to the Western model in the Soviet model, but there was more agreement than disagreement between these two ideologies about the teleology of development.

The international norms of the second half of the twentieth century were more inclusive than the norms of the first half and of the nineteenth century. Yet very much like the workplace norm that is abstracted from the white male experience, the norms of development were abstracted from the Western experience (and an idealized one at that). To pursue development did not do much to get non-Western countries away from taking the West always as a referent. Of course, even within this second period we have come a long way. There is quite a difference between the modernization theories of the 1960s and how we conceptualize development today. Yet we have not fully entered the new era either. We continue to rely on old problematic binaries and dichotomies. Many commentators still see no problem in using the categories of *advanced* and *developing* to describe the complex institutional patterns of human collectivities.

However, we *are now* living through a profound shift. This shift started with the end of the Cold War but has not yet settled into its new form. It is possible to think of the period we are in as the equivalent of the interwar years. World War I was the end of an era, just as the Cold War was, and the end of World War II signaled the beginning of a new one. We have not yet had our equivalent of World War II.[4] But there is a shift underfoot, and that shift will usher in a new era where there is not just one standard to evaluate countries, but multiple yet not overlapping assessments. Currently we have many dichotomies like modern/traditional, democratic/authoritarian, honest/corrupt, stable/chaotic, clean/dirty, healthy/diseased, peaceful/warlike, orderly/terroristic, etc., but in everyday usage, and too often in academic usage, these dichotomies are treated like different faces of the same GOD of dichotomies—West and the Rest. It is assumed that if you are on the correct side of one binary, you are on the correct side for all.

This is going to change. When the transition is over, Eurocentrism will no longer be the dominant assumption of social science analysis. Part of this will be due to the economic and demographic troubles that have recently plagued Europe, as well as the political weathering of the American model since the end of the Cold War. The real change, however, is going to come from states like China, Brazil, Japan, Russia, and others who embrace their liminality as opposed to fighting it.

In the 1920s, the famous British historian Arnold Toynbee wrote a number of books about countries in what was then called the Near East, and he concluded that basically only two choices awaited the non-Western world in the face of a by-then inevitable Western hegemony: that of the Zealot or that of the Herodian. He said the question facing the non-West was: "Shall they accept the civilization of the West and attempt to adjust their own lives to it, or shall they reject it and attempt to cast it out as a devil which is seeking to possess their souls?" The experiences of the twentieth century have proven both choices pernicious. Neither blindly embracing the West as countries like Turkey have done nor rejecting it as countries like Iran have attempted to do brings salvation out of the existential bind that liminal countries find themselves in. The only way out of this bind (for the "non-West" as well as the "West") lies in refusing to make a choice. It lies in embracing the condition of ambiguity, incategorizability, a world without a definite center and a fixed universal rubric of worth. This requires accepting the condition of uncertainty and complexity as a fact of life.

Implications for Area Studies and the Social Sciences

As a way of conclusion, it should be underlined that these lessons apply to us as academics as well. We have to be cognizant of our role in perpetuating normative hierarchies in the international system.

For instance, in my home discipline of International Relations (IR), for much of the twentieth century concerns of "identity," not to mention nationalism, religion, culture, honor, etc., all were considered to belong to the "past" of human history, or those regions in the world still living in that past. Despite the various disagreements between them,[5] rationalist accounts in IR share certain unstated modernist assumptions.[6] To begin with, their conceptualization of the state as a rational, purposive agent comes directly out of the European/Western experience with modernity: "In the Western picture, humans have the capacity and responsibility to modify society and intervene in lawful nature."[7] Furthermore, there is a certain teleology, at least in liberalism (but implicitly also in realism), that holds rationality as defined to be the end of human development—the "end of history" so to speak. If certain "individuals" (or states) are not acting to assumptions of rationality, that is because their development is delayed, not because the assumptions themselves are problematic. Such irrationality may deem from the fact that the collective is too influential in these persons' lives, which is a sign of backwardness. By contrast, in the positivist understanding that dominated social science throughout the twentieth century, the "individual" exists in society, but does not need it and is not necessarily shaped by it. The individual's interests are formed a priori, rationally, before interaction with others. Rationalist, positivist approaches to IR simply extrapolated assumptions from such theories at the domestic level (e.g., utilitarianism) to state behavior.[8] The treatment of states as instantaneously (and endogenously) constituted for the moment of international interaction (and never considered to be shaped by that interaction) fits this utilitarian mold.

For these reasons, the indifference to "community" and "identity" in IR has gone hand in hand with a general disciplinary indifference to areas outside of the "West," except as testing grounds for theories derived from the European experience. The end of the Cold War challenged these disciplinary assumptions to some extent. The inability of rationalist/positivist/materialist theories to predict (or even explain) the end of the Cold War created an opening for approaches that argued that issues of history, identity, and community mattered in international relations.[9] Furthermore, both nationalism and religion moved back to the center of politics in the two decades after the Cold War. The materialist, rationalist, and individualist approaches in international relations were not prepared to explain those developments either. However, this does not mean that approaches concerned with "identity" have come to dominate IR in the post–Cold War era. The full impact of the transition discussed above has not yet been felt in our research practices.

For instance, despite my own research criticizing the "West vs. Rest" dichotomies, as discussed in the previous section, I still have to endorse these dichotomies whenever I interact with my disciplinary association(s). I have to check the box "developing countries section" in order to get my paper proposal considered for the annual meeting. Every time I check that box, I am conceding that certain countries are always in a condition of BECOMING, with the implication that perhaps this process is everlasting, while at the same time implicitly granting that certain other countries simply ARE, with the implication that they will always BE advanced. The Standard of Civilization and Modernization Theory may be out of fashion these days, but the academic divisions they have wrought are still with us. It is high time for the new approaches such as the one exemplified in this volume to correct these institutionalized biases.

The world is changing in a way that will make all of the aforementioned binary categories obsolete, and social sciences need to catch up or be rendered irrelevant. The global changes outlined in the previous section will impact our scholarship in three primary ways. First, the rise of non-Western powers will challenge the implicit teleology of rationalist models, i.e., that assumptions of universal rationality can be derived from the behavior of Western states and that identity does not matter at all in such behavior. Second, the rise of non-Western powers (and regions) will introduce more non-Western voices to the scholarly conversation (a trend already underway),[10] and such voices will be more likely to care about identity, culture, history, and community. Finally, there has been a long-term trend underway of waning trust in nineteenth-century positivist models of science.[11] Despite the fact that positivism has long been discredited even in the hard sciences, mainstream IR has hung on because of a misguided desire to demonstrate "scientific" bona fides. However, such anachronistic insistences on positivism are sure to give way once ethnocentric understandings of rationalism as well as established disciplinary hierarchies are toppled by global developments that are now underway.

Our disciplinary divisions as they currently exist are also problematic because the way we study things perpetuates insularity. As liminal countries start to embrace their liminality, they will increasingly cease to see the West as the only center of global politics. Asia, Africa, and Latin America will discover each other. These processes are already under way, as exemplified by various South-to-South cooperation efforts. This means that various area studies scholars will also need to start talking to each other at a much greater rate than they have before. If there is one thing that unites the so-called "developing" world, it is not language or religion or culture, but rather the common experience of being absorbed into the Western international system in terms not entirely of their own choosing. Once we realize that, it becomes apparent that opportunities for comparison are endless. This book is a first step in the right direction.

Notes

1. The distinction between "disciplines" and "area studies" comes out of American universities during the interwar years. "Disciplines" such as economics, political science, sociology, etc., "asked universal questions" from "fields which investigate the particular." See Andrea Teti, "Bridging the Gap: IR, Middle East Studies and the Disciplinary Politics of the Area Studies Controversy," *European Journal of International Relations* 13, no. 1 (2007), 123.

2. See also Barry Buzan and George Lawson, *The Global Transformation* (Cambridge: Cambridge University Press, 2015).

3. For more on this subject as well as other themes I touch upon here, please see my other works such as *After Defeat: How the East Learned to Live with the West* (New York: Cambridge University Press, 2011).

4. This cataclysmic event does not have to be a war.

5. For example, the possibility of cooperation under anarchy, absolute vs. relative gains, or the impact of international institutions on an uncertain environment.

6. See John G. Ruggie, "Territoriality and Beyond: Problematizing Modernity in International Relations," *International Organization* 47, no. 1 (1993): 139–74; see also Naeem Inayatullah and David L. Blaney, "The Dark Heart of Kindness: The Social Construction of Deflection," *International Studies Perspectives* 13, no. 2 (2012): 164–75.

7. John W. Meyer and R. L. Jepperson, "The 'Actors' of Modern Society: The Cultural Construction of Social Agency," *Sociological Theory* 18, no. 1 (2000): 102.

8. See, e.g., Alexander Wendt, *A Social Theory of International Politics* (Cambridge: Cambridge University Press, 1999).

9. Fred Halliday, "International Relations and Its Discontents," *International Affairs* 71, no. 4 (1995): 740–41.

10. See, e.g., Robbie Shilliam, ed., *International Relations and Non-Western Thought* (London: Routledge, 2011); Shogo Suzuki, Yongjin Zhang, and Joel Quirk, eds., *International Orders in the Early Modern World: Before the Rise of the West* (London: Routledge, 2014).

11. For an overview of the relevant philosophy of science debates, see Patrick T. Jackson, *The Conduct of Inquiry in International Relations: Philosophy of Science and Its Implications for the Study of World Politics* (New York: Routledge, 2011).

Annotated Bibliography

Ackah, William. "The Intersection of African Identities in the Twenty-First Century: Old and New Diasporas and the African Continent." In *Reframing Contemporary Africa: Politics, Economics, and Culture in the Global Era.* Edited by Peyi Soyinka-Airewele and Rita Kiki Edozie, 131–140. Washington, DC: CQ Press, 2010.
   Examines relationships between a new African diaspora based on postcolonial migrations and the old African diaspora formed by the process of enslavement. Considers flexibility regarding ideas of identity and community in African diasporan spaces. Discusses the intersection of African diasporic identities in the twenty-first century by asking, "What is Africa to me?"
Agnew, John, Katharyne Mitchell, and Gerard Toal, eds. *A Companion to Political Geography.* New York: Blackwell, 2003.
   This volume is designed to be an introduction to political geography. The contributors cover the major currents of thought within the discipline, and introduce several contested concepts that draw the attention of much contemporary scholarship. The book covers scale, territory, the state, and social movements, which are necessary for understanding geographical perspectives on identity and community. Contributors include some of geography's leading scholars on issues of territory and identity, including John Agnew, Anssi Paasi, and Joanne Sharp.
Allen, Joseph R. *Taipei: City of Displacements.* Seattle: University of Washington Press, 2012.
   This excellent study consists of interpretations of the history of Taipei as articulated through exhibits, parks, statues, maps, and other creations. Allen examines important themes concerning the city of Taipei in great detail and analyzes the rehabilitation of past moments in Taipei's history, a reconceptualization of Taipei as a multicultural space, and the construction of new narratives of Taiwan's, and Taipei's, history.
Anderson, Benedict. *Imagined Communities: Reflections on the Origins and Spread of Nationalism.* London and New York: Verso, 1983.
   In this seminal work, Anderson explores how nations and the communities within their boundaries create and imagine themselves, the other, and their place in the world. He is especially concerned with the role of post-Gutenberg printing and popular movements that began in the Americas but quickly spread throughout the world.
Bach, Jonathan. "They Come in as Peasants and Leave as Citizens." *Cultural Anthropology* 25 (2010): 421–48.
   The author takes an ethnographic and constructivist approach to studying urban villages in the southern city of Shenzhen, China. He suggests that the urban villages and villagers are part of the urban landscape and not simply part of the transition.
Badovinac, Zdenka, ed. *Body and the East: From the 1960s to the Present.* Cambridge, MA: MIT Press, 1999.
   The term body art includes a wide range of practices in which the artist's own body is the bearer of social, political, metaphorical, and philosophical content. The earliest "body art" was created in Eastern Europe in the early 1960s. This book includes essays on eighty artists from fourteen countries. The art survived not only despite the absence of any art market, but also despite its marginalization by political regimes. The artists turned their marginalization to an advantage, creating art out of the contingencies and necessities of survival. The art represented here reminds the reader of the psychological and intellectual freedoms that artistic expression affords under politically repressive conditions.
Bassin, Mark, and Catriona Kelly, eds. *Soviet and Post-Soviet Identities.* Cambridge: Cambridge University Press, 2012.
   Examines the institutions and discourses of national identity, mainly in the context of post-Soviet polities.

Beverley, John. *Latinamericanism after 9/11*. Durham, NC: Duke University Press, 2011.
Taking the "marea rosada" (pink tide) of key twenty-first-century Latin American countries and the demise of the neoliberal policies of the Washington Consensus as his points of departure, Beverley reassesses Latin America studies in the post-9/11 context. Building on the work of past and current Latin American intellectuals from Rodo to García Canclini, Beverley calls for a redefinition of US–Latin American relations from the political to the cultural level if Latin American studies is to survive.

Bhabha, Homi. *The Location of Culture*. London: Routledge, 1994.
This is a groundbreaking collection of Bhabha's work with a particular focus on some of his most important theories including cultural hybridity, cultural liminality and interstitial perspective. Bhabha poses these theories to counter the linearity of Western notions of time and space in general and historicism in particular.

Brown, Melissa J. *Is Taiwan Chinese? The Impact of Culture, Power, and Migration on Changing Identities*. Berkeley: University of California Press, 2004.
Using ethnographic and historical case studies, Brown's volume challenges notions that identity is shaped by blood lines or culture and argues instead that shared social experience is most important in the development of identity.

Brubaker, Rogers, and Frederick Cooper. "Beyond Identity." *Theory and Society* 29 (2000): 1–47.
Calls for a rethinking of "identity" as an analytical concept and suggests the use of other less ambiguous terms. Draws on examples from Africa, Eastern Europe, and the United States. Echoes a similar debate in African studies circles that emerged around the concept of "tribe" in the late twentieth century.

Clowes, Edith W. *Russia on the Edge: Imagined Geographies and Post-Soviet Identity*. Ithaca, NY: Cornell University Press, 2011.
Examines the importance of Russia's peripheries and borders for the renewal of Russian political and cultural life.

Corcuff, Stephane, ed. *Memories of the Future: National Identity Issues and the Search for a New Taiwan*. Armonk, NY: M. E. Sharpe, 2002.
This edited volume explores the messy process of Taiwan's formation of a national identity from a variety of perspectives and makes it clear that identity formation is indeed a process that is not linear, not predictable, and not easily controlled.

Crandall, Russell C. *The United States and Latin America after the Cold War*. New York: Cambridge University Press, 2008.
Crandall, a former advisor to G. W. Bush as well as Barack Obama, takes a decidedly conventional approach toward US-Latin American relations in this book, especially concerning the role of the United States as a democratizing influence in the region. In addition to chapters on early twenty-first century relations between the United States and Latin American leaders such as Hugo Chavez of Venezuela and Daniel Ortega of Nicaragua, his analysis includes coauthored discussions of Haiti and Mexico.

Dittmer, Jason. *Popular Culture, Geopolitics, and Identity*. Lanham, MD: Rowman and Littlefield, 2010.
Dittmer's book deals with many important issues of identity in geography, most interestingly within the realm of popular geopolitics. He has structured the book to explain his chosen topics by presenting clear definitions of theoretical concepts paired with well-established examples, along with fresh and contemporary ones. The book is filled with text boxes that provide a review of relevant literature.

Fechter, Anne-Meike, and Katie Walsh, eds. *The New Expatriates: Postcolonial Approaches to Mobile Professionals*. London: Routledge, 2012.
This volume first appeared as a special issue of the *Journal of Ethnic and Migration Studies*. The authors use ideas of postcolonialism to explore the ways that the past influences today's expatriate migrations. They consider expatriates around the world, including in Indonesia, China, and Namibia.

Groys, Boris. *The Total Art of Stalinism: Avant-Garde, Aesthetic Dictatorship, and Beyond*. London: Verso, 2011.
A captivating reassessment of Soviet art and politics in which Groys contends that the Soviet experiment, despite the dissolution of the Soviet Union, ushered in a new era of political thought and imagination. Dictators unwittingly pursued the goals first expressed by avant-garde poets and artists of creating a new world as one would an opera, using all forms of art, writ large, to realize ideological goals. Groys sharpens our perceptions of "public" institutions by exposing the artificiality of their representations. Though he paints equally dark portraits of the power struggles of artist and politician alike, he offers new avenues for understanding the public role of art in society.

Harrison, Mark. *Legitimacy, Meaning and Knowledge in the Making of Taiwanese Identity*. New York: Palgrave Macmillan, 2006.
Harrison's book provides a history of Taiwan while simultaneously examining the history of the study of Taiwan. He looks in particular at how narrative has been used to legitimize various conceptions of Taiwan's identity.

Hartlyn, Johnathan, Lars Schoultz, and Augusto Varas. *The United States and Latin America in the 1990s: Beyond the Cold War*. Chapel Hill: University of North Carolina Press, 1992.
This collection of essays by US and Latin American scholars is an early response to the post–Cold War era. Many of the chapters are both predictive of and cautious about the future of inter-American relations. Analyses address topics from the importance of the rise of the new Right in several Latin American countries to the impact of Latin American migration to the United States in the final decade of the twentieth century.

Herb, Guntram, and David H. Kaplan, eds. *Nested Identities: Nationalism, Territory, and Scale*. Lanham, MD: Rowman and Littlefield, 1999.
This book is designed to demonstrate important theoretical concepts through various empirical examples. Herb and Kaplan present important "conceptual issues," explaining national identity and territory and showing how geographic scale is vital to their understanding. The eleven chapters in this book examine various world regions where issues of nations and nationalism have been influential in the development of geographies at multiple scales.

Hirsch, Francine. *Empire of Nations: Ethnographic Knowledge and the Making of the Soviet Union*. Ithaca, NY: Cornell University Press, 2005.
Studies ethnography and census-taking during the first two decades of Soviet rule to understand the formation of nationalities.

Hobsbawm, Eric. *Nations and Nationalism since 1780: Programme, Myth, Reality*. Cambridge: Cambridge University Press, 1990.
Building on yet deviating from Benedict Anderson's concept of "imagined communities," Hobsbawm argues that nations are modern constructs intentionally created through shared experiences, histories and ideologies. The apparent homogeneity of these relationships, however, proves to be conflicted and complex. Hence, Hobsbawm argues, concepts of nation, nationalism and nationhood are illusive and transitory throughout Western thought.

Hoptman, Laura, and Tomas Pospiszyl, eds. *Primary Documents: A Sourcebook for Eastern and Central European Art since the 1950s*. Cambridge, MA: MIT Press, 2002.
The manifestoes, photo essays, proposals, scripts, and other writings assembled here comprise the first anthology of this material in any language. The source materials presented—almost all of them previously untranslated into English—are from Bulgaria, Croatia, the Czech Republic, Estonia, Hungary, Latvia, Macedonia, Poland, Romania, Russia, Serbia, Slovakia, and Slovenia. The book is introduced by Russian artist Ilya Kabakov. Each chapter is preceded by a brief introduction and is followed by a case study that chronicles an event or the creation or reception of an artwork, illustrating the issues raised in that chapter.

Hunt, Lynn. *Inventing Human Rights: A History*. New York: W. W. Norton, 2007.
Lynn Hunt traces the implications of eighteenth-century literary genres, such as the epistolary novel, that allowed European readers to imagine others—even those of a different class or

gender—as equals. This new capability to imagine strangers' inner lives, Hunt suggests, was a crucial element in the institutional and legal shifts in Europe at the end of the eighteenth century concomitant with and subsequent to Rousseau's use of the phrase "the rights of man" in *The Social Contract* (1762).

IRWIN, ed. *East Art Map: Contemporary Art and Eastern Europe*. London: AfterAll, 2006.
This book is an attempt to reconstruct the missing histories of contemporary art in Eastern Europe from an East European and artistic perspective. The editors invited art critics, curators, and artists to present up to ten crucial art projects produced in their respective countries over the past fifty years. The choice of the particular artworks, artists, and events, as well as their presentation, was left to the individual selectors. In addition, the editors asked experts from both East and West to provide longer texts offering cross-cultural perspectives on the art of both regions.

Joseph, Gilbert M., and Daniela Spenser, eds. *In from the Cold: Latin America's New Encounter with the Cold War*. Durham, NC: Duke University Press, 2008.
This essay collection focuses on the history of the Cold War in Latin America, with important contributions on Brazil, the Caribbean, and Mexico. This is a valuable contribution to Cold War studies in Latin America because of the intentional inclusion of primary sources from Latin American and Soviet archives, many of which have only recently been opened. The inclusion of these sources, along with frank discussions about the role of truth commissions in formerly Cold War–torn areas such as Guatemala and El Salvador, presents a much more nuanced picture of the use of Cold War rhetoric by both US and Latin American officials.

Keith, Michael, and Steve Pile, eds. *Place and the Politics of Identity*. New York: Routledge, 1993.
This book comprises chapters by some of geography's most important authors, including David Harvey, Doreen Massey, and Edward Soja. Each chapter covers a theme in which identity politics have been spatialized. Many of this book's topics, such as gender identity, class relations and social justice, urban identity, and racialization have continued to remain at the forefront of geographic scholarship, leading to the popularity of this volume.

Khalid, Addid. *Islam after Communism: Religion and Politics in Central Asia*. Berkeley and Los Angeles: University of California Press, 2007.
This monograph offers insightful analysis of transformations and continuities of Islam in Muslim societies as a result of Soviet policies. It overviews experiences with Islam in all Central Asian republics but focuses on Uzbekistan. An accessible presentation of the modern character of Islam in Central Asia is one of the valuable features of the book.

Konings, Piet, and Dick Foeken, eds. *Crisis and Creativity: Exploring the Wealth of the African Neighborhood*. Leiden: Brill, 2006.
This volume includes multidisciplinary approaches to the African neighborhood, with particular emphases on geographical and anthropological perspectives. Of particular note are a chapter by Eileen Moyer on places of importance to street youth in Dar es Salaam, and a chapter by Deborah Pellow on using mental maps to understand the identity of a migrant neighborhood in Accra, Ghana.

LaCapra, Dominick. *Writing History, Writing Trauma*. Baltimore: Johns Hopkins University Press, 2001.
Trauma and its often symptomatic aftermath pose acute problems for historical representation and understanding. LaCapra provides a broad-ranging, critical inquiry into the problem of trauma, notably with respect to major historical events. In a series of interlocking essays, he explores theoretical and literary-critical attempts to come to terms with trauma as well as the crucial role that posttraumatic testimonies—particularly Holocaust testimonies—have assumed in recent thought and writing. In doing so, he adapts psychoanalytic concepts to historical analysis and employs sociocultural and political critique to elucidate trauma and its aftereffects in culture and in people.

Lefebvre, Henri. *The Urban Revolution*, trans. Robert Bononno. Minneapolis: University of Minnesota Press, 2003.
Protest and revolution are often associated with urban spaces and the conditions of urbanity. The realities and possibilities of urban space in revolutionary thought and action are the

subject of this book by a French philosopher, originally published in 1970. Lefebvre expounds
upon his idea of "the right to the city," the right of citizens to change or remake themselves by
way of the city, which becomes a canvas for revolutionary sociopolitical thought. This process
is threatened, however, by various powers designed to observe, suppress, and socialize citizens.
Lefebvre challenges his readers to think more critically about their surroundings, to understand the methods of control and governance forced upon them by the state, and to express
their discontent in the streets or on the walls of the city.

Liu, Yuting, Shenjing He, Fulong Wu, and Chris Webster. "Urban Villages under China's Rapid Urbanization: Unregulated Assets and Transitional Neighborhoods." *Habitat International* 34 (2010):
135–44.
This article presents the general characteristics of urban villages using empirical data on eleven
urban villages from six large Chinese cities. One of the key findings is that ambiguous property
regulations in the urban village provide landless urban villagers an opportunity to earn a living
by providing low-cost residential space for migrants. For the municipal governments, this is an
informal way to accommodate rural migrants and urban villagers.

Louw, Maria E. *Everyday Islam in Post-Soviet Central Asia.* New York: Routledge, 2007.
This book offers a detailed account of the everyday practices of Islam in Uzbekistan, including
the local forms of Sufism and saint veneration, with some illustrations from other parts of
Central Asia. It challenges many sovietological, essentialist, and modern Western assumptions
about Islam.

Moyn, Samuel. *The Last Utopia: Human Rights in History.* Cambridge, MA: The Belknap Press of
Harvard University Press, 2010.
Samuel Moyn examines key historical moments in the history of human rights rhetoric, which
has complicated a contemporary teleology of human rights that has gained currency recently.
Moyn focuses on key moments in the history of human rights to show that definitions of
universal rights often articulated with states' interests, or had little bearing in international
affairs. Ultimately, Moyn argues against the notion of human rights as a normative paradigm
that has naturally gained momentum and influence over the centuries. Instead, he proposes an
understanding of human rights discourse as particular and contingent expressions of utopian
thought and practice.

Myers, Garth. *African Cities: Alternative Visions of Urban Theory and Practice.* London: Zed, 2011.
This book explores cities from across the African continent (including Dar es Salaam),
encouraging readers to see them not as problematic failures but as complex and vibrant
spaces. It highlights several important issues in these cities, including colonial legacies and
informality.

Pejic, Bojana, ed. *Gender Check—Femininity and Masculinity in the Art of Eastern Europe.* Köln: Wal-
ther König, 2009.
The catalogue has been published on the occasion of the exhibition of the same title. It contains
a major part of the exhibition's artworks as well as theoretical approaches and perspectives.
The art history research for this project, which examined the artistic output of these countries
since the 1960s, also serves as a basis for reevaluating internationally accepted and entrenched
ideas about gender issues in history, both in the context of art and in scholarly discourse.
Gender Check extends and supplements the scope of the discourse, and also presents it in a
new historical and topographical context that encompasses the dialogue between the "East"
and the "West" as a prerequisite for further research into and interpretations of the gender
issue on a global scale.

Ranger, Terence. "The Invention of Tradition in Colonial Africa." In *The Invention of Tradition,* ed. Eric
Hobsbawm and Terence Ranger. Cambridge: Cambridge University Press, 1983.
Ranger examines nineteenth-century European invented tradition in Africa as Europeans
sought control and power through colonialism. He argues that Europeans and Africans came
to view invented practices and symbols, such as those of monarchies, as quite "traditional" in
African societies even as Africans manipulated invented customs for their own needs.

Rasanayagam, Johan. *Islam in Post-Soviet Uzbekistan: The Morality of Experience.* New York: Cambridge University Press, 2010.
An anthropological study of Islam in Uzbekistan, this monograph also shows the ways in which the repressive political system can shape the moral contexts of people's lives, their understandings of what it means to be Muslims, and their religious practices.

Rigger, Shelley. *Why Taiwan Matters.* New York: Rowman and Littlefield, 2011.
This accessibly written book provides an excellent introduction to Taiwan's political, economic, and cultural history and explains to the novice why people should bother paying attention to this small island. Taiwan matters, she argues, because of its rapid economic growth, its role in the global high-tech economy, its strategic location, and its successful democratization.

Robertson, Graeme B. *The Politics of Protest in Hybrid Regimes: Managing Dissent in Post-Communist Russia.* New York: Cambridge University Press, 2011.
Robertson details the construction of the Russian "hybrid regime," which claims to have democratic foundations but maintains the elite's monopoly over all institutions, including protest. The inability of Russian citizens to channel discontent and put pressure on the government without elite involvement in social movements is pivotal. The regime's ability to manage dissent and channel it into likewise managed competition undermines true democratization; rather than representing the conscious will of the people, protest becomes a tool for the state to let society express discontent, but without letting it get out of control.

Ro'i, Yaacov. *Islam in the Soviet Union: From the Second World War to Gorbachev.* New York: Columbia University Press, 2000.
This monograph offers a detailed historical account of Islam under the postwar Soviet regime, using previously classified archival materials. By surveying the uneasy relationship between the Soviet government and religion, the book illuminates reasons for the survival of Islam despite the ostensibly antireligious Soviet policies.

Said, Edward. *Orientalism.* New York: Vintage, 1979.
Ground-breaking scholarship on how Western perceptions of the "East" created the romanticized and patronizing concept of "orientalism." Said traces the development of orientalism throughout Western history with a particular focus on colonial and post-colonial Western attitudes. Ultimately, *Orientalism* was a call to arms for scholars in a variety of fields to read more carefully the defining texts and contexts of non-Western cultures.

Slaughter, Joseph. *Human Rights, Inc.: The World Novel, Narrative Form, and International Law.* New York: Fordham University Press, 2007.
Slaughter examines the linkages between literary form and legal narratives for imagining the human. In particular, he traces the role of the bildungsroman, or coming-of-age novel, in helping readers make sense of the "commonsensical" notion that all individuals are imbued with rights and therefore hold obligations to others. Specifically, Slaughter traces the relationship of the bildungsroman and rights discourse from the Universal Declaration of Human Rights in 1948 until the present.

Spivak, Gayatri. "Righting Wrongs." *South Atlantic Quarterly* 103, no. 2/3 (2004): 523–81.
The author critiques a human rights paradigm that does not recognize the existence of a global "class apartheid" characterized by one class empowered to "right wrongs" and a subaltern class that is consistently wronged. This "unexamined universalism," Spivak claims, is the legacy of colonialism, a project justified by the notion of a "white man's burden." To counter the notion of those in control of institutions as agents of change and the subaltern as objects of the "responsibility" of another class, Spivak calls for the pedagogy of the subaltern.

Starrs, Paul, and Dydia DeLyser, eds. Special Issue on "Doing Fieldwork." *Geographical Review* 91, no. 1/2 (2001).
Contains fifty-six short essays by geographers at all stages of their careers, working with various methodologies and in locations around the world. These authors outline their own experiences in the field and offer reflections on their own successes and shortcomings.

Suny, Ronald G., and Terry Martin, eds. *A State of Nations: Empire and Nation-Making in the Age of Lenin and Stalin*. New York: Oxford University Press, 2001.
An overview of nationalism and nation-building in the Soviet period.

Swanson Goldberg, Elizabeth, and Alexandra Schultheis Moore, eds. *Theoretical Perspectives on Human Rights and Literature*. New York: Routledge, 2012.
This volume offers an important resource for scholars who seek to understand what the book's editors term a "[developing] Interdiscipline," a field of study attentive to the history, and the stakes, of the relationship between human rights and literature.

Vail, Leroy, ed. *The Creation of Tribalism in Southern Africa*. Oxford: James Currey, 1989.
Details how European officials and African intermediaries actively invented ethnic categories among various southern African peoples. These new "tribes" came to have deep and real meanings for African communities in the colonial and postcolonial periods.

Warikoo, K., ed. *Religion and Security in South and Central Asia*. New York: Routledge, 2011.
This collection provides an overview of traditional and moderate Islamic beliefs and practices in addition to the emergence of radical extremist and violent Islamic movements in South Asia and Central Asia. It offers local perspectives on religion, security, history, and geopolitics in these regions.

Wu, Fulong, ed. *China's Emerging Cities: The Making of New Urbanism*. London and New York: Routledge, 2007.
This volume explores the profound transformation in Chinese cities and the political, economic, and social consequences of urbanization in China. Building upon previous theoretical approaches, such as modernization theory, dependency theory, the development state theory, and the postsocialist transition theory, the authors develop a new "hybrid" theory that can help better understand the "urban revolution" in China. They grapple with the phenomenal urbanization in China through cities understood as an emerging institution, transition in economic and social spheres, the rebuilding of residential space, and the emerging practices in leisure, retail, and consumption.

Yeh, Wen-hsin, ed. *Mobile Horizons: Dynamics across the Taiwan Strait*. Berkeley: Institute of East Asian Studies, 2013.
This superb volume includes a set of very well-researched essays that consider an array of social, economic, and intellectual networks and connections between Taiwan and China. The essays in the volume reveal the complexity of Taiwan's relationship with China, a relationship that is at the heart of the identity question.

Zhang, Li. *Strangers in the City: Reconfigurations of Space, Power, and Social Networks within China's Floating Population*. Stanford, CA: Stanford University Press, 2001.
Through an ethnographic case study of the largest migrant community in Beijing, Zhang explores the privatization of space, power relations, and social networks within the mobile population. Her main contribution is her view that the migrant community challenges the assumptions of modernization theory that economic and social changes in China will inevitably lead to capitalism and democracy.

Contributors

Corina L. Apostol is a PhD candidate in the Department of Art History at Rutgers University. She holds a curatorial research fellowship at the Norton and Nancy Dodge Collection of Nonconformist Art from the Soviet Union. She is a co-founder of ArtLeaks and co-editor of the *ArtLeaks Gazette*.

Shelly Jarrett Bromberg is associate professor and chair of the Department of Spanish and Portuguese at Miami University of Ohio. She has published articles in *Latin American Literary Review*, *Antipodas*, and the *Connecticut Review*. Her research interests focus on how US interventions and/or occupations have impacted expressions of identity and experience in Hispanic Caribbean literatures and cultures.

Patrick Callen holds a master of arts in Russian, East European, and Eurasian Studies from the University of Kansas. His research interests include satire and parody in the music of Dmitri Shostakovich, postmodern Russian and Ukrainian literature, and socially engaged art in the former Soviet Union. He lives in Lawrence, Kansas.

Dan Chen is assistant professor of Political Science and Asian Studies at Elizabethtown College. She received her PhD in political science from the University of Kansas in 2014. Her research interests include the role of the mass media in China's authoritarian politics, Chinese public opinion, and authoritarian durability.

Edith W. Clowes is the Brown-Forman Professor in the Department of Slavic Languages and Literatures at the University of Virginia. Her research interests encompass literature, philosophy, religion, and utopian thought; and more recently, imagined geography and perceptions of space and place in Russian writing culture. Her first book, *The Revolution of Moral Consciousness: Nietzsche in Russian Literature, 1890–1914*, was published with NIU Press. Her most recent book is *Russia on the Edge: Imagined Geographies and Post-Soviet Identity*.

J. Megan Greene is associate professor of history at the University of Kansas. Her research focuses on the history of the Republic of China under the KMT both in China and on Taiwan. Her specific research interests include nation and state-building projects in the areas of science, the economy, academia, and ideology.

Reuel R. Hanks is professor of geography at Oklahoma State University and holds the Humphreys Endowed Chair of International Studies in the College of Arts and Sciences. Dr. Hanks was a Fulbright Scholar in Tashkent, Uzbekistan, and has published three books and more than thirty articles and book chapters on national identity, Islam, security issues, and political geography on Central Asia.

Adrienne M. Harris is associate professor of Russian at Baylor University. She publishes on Soviet collective memory of World War II, heroism, combatants' memoirs, war poetry, gender, and Czech film. She is currently drafting a monograph entitled *Martyr, Myth, and Memory: The Dynamic Image of Zoia Kosmodemianskaia, a Soviet Saint*.

Marike Janzen is assistant professor of humanities at the University of Kansas, where she also coordinates the Peace and Conflict Studies Program. Her research focuses on the intersections of world literature, literature of human rights, international solidarity, and authorship. She has published on Anna Seghers, Alejo Carpentier, literary performances of tolerance in the Berlin Republic, and teaching human rights literature. She is working on a book titled *Writing to Change the World: Anna Seghers, Authorship, and International Solidarity*, which takes Seghers as a starting point from which to describe a global practice of leftist authorship during the twentieth century.

John James Kennedy received his PhD at the University of California, Davis, in 2002. He is associate professor in the Department of Political Science at the University of Kansas (KU). He has consistently returned to China to conduct research on rural politics since 1994, and he is also co-founder of the Northwest Socioeconomic Development Research Center (NSDRC) at Shaanxi Normal University, Xian, China. His research is on local governance and social development; topics include local elections, tax reform, rural education, health care, and the cadre management system. He has published research articles in the *China Quarterly*, *Journal of Contemporary China*, *Asian Survey*, the *Journal of Chinese Political Science*, the *Journal of Peasant Studies*, *Asian Politics and Policy*, and *Journal of Diplomacy and International Relations*, and *Political Studies*.

Elizabeth MacGonagle is associate professor of history and African & African-American Studies at the University of Kansas and the director of the Kansas African Studies Center. She is the author of *Crafting Identity in Zimbabwe and Mozambique*, and other work on history and memory in Africa.

Mariya Y. Omelicheva is associate professor of political science at the University of Kansas. She holds a PhD (2007) from Purdue University and a JD (2000) from Moscow State Law Academy. She is the author of *Counterterrorism Policies in Central Asia and Democracy in Central Asia: Competing Perspectives and Alternative Strategies*, and multiple articles on Eurasian security and Russian foreign policy.

Sarah L. Smiley is associate professor of geography at Kent State University. Her research interests include culture, segregation, and development in Tanzania. Her current project examines how water access is defined and measured. Her work has been published in *Applied Geography*, *Social and Cultural Geography*, *Journal of Cultural Geography*, and *Historical Geography*.

Austen Thelen is assistant professor of geography at Imperial Valley College in Imperial, California. He specializes in political and economic geography, with specific research interests in place and identity studies, territoriality, and substate regionalization, particularly throughout Russia and the former Soviet Union. Having benefited from an area studies focus throughout his education at Michigan State University and the University of Kansas, Thelen aims to promote student engagement in interdisciplinary approaches to regional and global awareness in California's community colleges.

Walt Vanderbush is the director of Latin American, Latino/a and Caribbean Studies and associate professor of Global and Intercultural Studies at Miami University. He co-authored a book titled *The Cuban Embargo: Domestic Politics of American Foreign Policy*, and he has published articles and book chapters in the areas of US–Latin American Relations and Latin American Political Economy. His current research is on the Caribbean with a focus on regional resistance to external pressures.

Ayşe Zarakol is lecturer in international relations at the University of Cambridge, Department of Politics and International Studies, and a fellow at Emmanuel College. She is the author of *After Defeat: How the East Learned to Live with the West*. Her articles have appeared in a variety of international journals including, most recently, *International Studies Quarterly*, and *European Journal of International Relations*.

Index

literary texts, 165–166, 171–174, 176n36, 176n37; locating human rights work as "above politics," 162; relevance to area studies, 162–163, 174
Hunt, Lynne, 279–280

I

Identity, 16n1, 278; and authenticity, 67, 118, 269–270; and colonialism, 18–31; and community, 4, 5, 7–8, 9–10, 14–15, 18, 53–54, 67, 85–88, 109–110,115–116, 121–124, 126–127, 132, 137, 161, 165, 197, 215, 217, 218–236, 242–244, 268; and ethno-symbolism, 257–266; and language, 110, 129–130, 136, 260, 263; and memory, 48–49, 77, 79–81, 257, 263; and religion, 132, 140, 143–144, 146–147, 150, 155; as basis for political mobilization, 247; as gestalt, 256; as evolutionary process, 256, 259; as liminal, 140, 217, 270; as non-immutable, 3, 256, 270; as part of the past, 31, 258, 274; as socially constructed, 18–19, 21, 25, 30, 33n24, 109, 121, 123–124, 227–229, 256–258, 278; "being Western" vs. "being non-Western," 269–272, 273, 275, 282; collective, 34, 43, 47, 77, 121–122, 126, 128, 155, 180–181, 256; cultural, 65–66, 74, 80, 117, 147, 258, 260; debated between primordialists/essentialists and constructivists, 109, 256–257; formed in response to "the other," 9, 85, 123, 219, 227, 236, 256; institutional, 86, 88, 90–91, 101–102, 104–105; "place" identity, 86, 88, 92, 104, 121–124, 136–137, 225–227; relationship with space, 121–137, 225–227, 229, 232–236, 257, 268; social, 88–89, 91–93, 95, 98, 101–102, 104–105, 122
International Monetary Fund (IMF), 202, 225, 246, 249
Irkutsk (Russia), 116–117; contemporary writers in, 113–114
Islam, 280, 282–283; activism in Central Asia, 151–155; and Muslim identity, 144, 147, 155, 157n14; as coercive practice, 140, 147, 149; connected to national cultural renaissance in Central Asia, 147, 155; connected to ethnicity in Central Asia, 146–147, 157n13; debates in Central Asia over aspects of orthodoxy, 149–151, 155; Hanafi school, 145, 149–150; Hizb ut-Tahrir (Liberation Party) in Central Asia, 153–154; Islamic school, 149, 151–155, 156; jihad, 143, 150, 152, 153, 158n37; local identity-oriented forms thereof, 140,

144–148, 155; multi-faceted rebirth in Central Asian states, 140, 143–158; origins in Central Asian region, 144; politically-oriented forms thereof, 143, 151–155; Quran, 150, 155; regional variation in Central Asian rebirth, 146–147; Salafi school, 149–153, 155; Sharia law, 149; Shiite school, 145; study of basic principles in Central Asia, 148–149; Sufi school, 145, 150–151; Sunni majority in Central Asia, 145; theology-oriented forms thereof, 143, 148–151; treatment of pseudo-Muslim groups by Central Asian governments, 154–155, 156; Wahhabi school, 149, 156

J

Japan: as liminal state, 269, 272, 273
Joseph, Gilbert, 280

K

Kaplan, David, 279
Karimov, Islom: cult of personality, 217, 264; regime in Uzbekistan, 152, 262–265
Kazakhstan, 216; Hizb ut-Tahrir in, 154; Islamic revival in, 143, 146, 151; Kazakhs converted to Islam, 144; Muslim population in, 145; religious infrastructure in, 145–146, 148; Sufism in, 151
Keith, Michael, 280
Kelly, Catriona, 34, 277
Kennedy, John F.: and Fidel Castro, 69; measures taken to prevent revolutions in Dominican Republic, 69–70; role in Dominican Republic politics, 70–72
Khalid, Addid, 280
KMT. See Chinese Nationalist Party
Konings, Piet, 236, 280
Kosmodemyanskaya, Zoya: and brother Sasha, 47–48, 51n34; as center of debate about Soviet Union's legacy, 38, 39–41, 43, 49–50; as cult hero in Soviet Union and beyond, 34–35, 37, 39–40, 43, 47, 49; as both polarizing and unifying figure in post-Soviet Russia, 35, 39, 48–50; as hagiographic figure, 35, 37, 45–46; as komsomolka, 37, 45; as historical figure, 40–41; as martyr, 14, 39, 41, 43, 45–47; as Soviet saint, 39, 43, 45–48, 49; as Stalinist figure, 45, 46; commemoration of in Russia, 40–46, 48–50; death, 37; historical background, 45–46; impact of Sergei Strunnikov's postmortem photo of, 37–39, 45; in poem by Vladimir Lesovoi, 47–48;

Lightning Source UK Ltd.
Milton Keynes UK
UKHW011525140220
358721UK00013B/223